Capitalism, Socialism and the Environment

Dedicated to
Simon, Fabian, Tim and Sally

HUGH STRETTON

Capitalism, Socialism and the Environment

CAMBRIDGE UNIVERSITY PRESS

CAMBRIDGE

LONDON · NEW YORK · MELBOURNE

Published by the Syndics of the Cambridge University Press
The Pitt Building. Trumpington Street. Cambridge CB2 1RP
Bentley House. 200 Euston Road. London NW1 2DB
32 East 57th Street. New York. NY 10022. USA
296 Beaconsfield Parade. Middle Park. Melbourne 3206. Australia

ISBN 0 521 21057 7 hard covers
ISBN 0 521 29025 2 paperback

First published 1976
Reprinted 1977

Printed in Great Britain
at the University Press, Cambridge

Contents

Acknowledgments

I thank Paul Streeten and Michael Young for critical advice, Alex Ramsay for most of my education in what public business management can do and David Donnison for the help and hospitality which allowed this book to be written at the Centre for Environmental Studies, London.

Apart from any influence their writings may have had those four must by now have planned, directed or managed several billion dollars' worth of three or four countries' capital resources, mostly to the purpose (one way or another) of reducing inequalities. They are ambitious men at the top of severely competitive professions. They deploy talents as formidable as any to be found in private enterprise. They are much, much more useful to the world than most millionaires are. As far as I know each pays his taxes, takes home two or three times the average family income, has turned down opportunities to make more and would work as well for a good deal less if more equal societies required that. They use cheap cars, public transport, a motorbike; they help their wives about the house and spend time with their children. With plenty of other successful public enterprisers they should above all be thanked for showing what material incentives are *not* needed to get the very highest performance from the very ablest people – and what rubbish the lovers of inequality talk on that subject. H.S.

Argument

This book is about the distribution of environmental goods: the shares that go to rich and poor in the developed democracies of Europe, North America, Japan and Australasia. It relates environmental programs to other programs for the future of capitalism, and compares conservative, liberal and socialist approaches to environmental reform. It argues that conflicts about inflation, inequality and scarce resources are parts of one central problem of democratic distribution.

The democracies face three troubles at once. They are misusing or exhausting too many natural resources. They are inflating their social currencies by producing more bargaining power than goods. And they distribute influence and goods so badly that some vital bits of capitalist machinery are now running wild: inequalities of wealth and income are suddenly unstable and some of them are increasing in ways which won't be tolerated much longer by people who grow steadily more interested in the economic power of their equal democratic votes. Depending on your ideology you may see these troubles as a crisis of capitalism, a crisis of democracy, or a confrontation (at long last) between democratic distributions of power and capitalist distributions of goods. Multiple problems of justice and social cohesion are forcing each national society, whatever the color of its government, to take public control of its resources and (through price and income policies) its inequalities. The public control is inevitable. But its methods and purposes are wide open to choice. They may range from gentle to savage, to produce societies from very equal to very unequal. The most unequal are likely to be more unsociable and corrupt than any democracy is now. The most equal, if they are lucky and skilful, may be free, democratic and more equal than any capitalist or communist society is now.

Conflicts about inflation, inequality and environmental management are the obvious elements of the new disorder but they mask a more important sea-change in the capacities of democracy itself. If they realize it, people have a new freedom to choose between diverse social systems and futures. They can make their own histories, as Marx expected, though not exactly in the way or for the reasons that he had in mind.

This book does not contribute to the continuing scientific disagreements about the depletion and spoiling of the world's natural resources and the physical action needed to conserve, replace or do without them. Between Repentance Now and Growth Regardless it offers no opinion. Instead it explores the social principles which might apply at any likely level of environmental use. That makes it long, an offence for which I offer the following reasons.

In times when political problems change faster than political ideas and habits do, re-thinking needs to be specially thorough. Old relations between means and ends don't hold; action frustrates its own intentions; new purposes flounder for want of expertise. It is easy to describe the mess the world is in, and to preach large changes of heart. Short, saleable books which do that may be useful if they persuade people in good directions, but only if people know how to move in those directions. Brisk visions of doomsday (or a no-growth society, or an alternative culture, or socialism with a human face) can easily be consolations rather than cures – articles for sale, consumption and enjoyment rather than productive use – if they don't incorporate their aspirations competently into workable programs. The same is true of attempts to persuade the Left that its old values call for new lines of action. If people are to drop faithful programs that have 'never yet had a fair trial' they want good reasons, and convincing replacements.

So the first part of this book guesses at the range of workable futures which may be open to the democracies through the next generation or two. The second part debates the values of different directions of change. The third part sketches some principles of a social-democratic program as a way of working for the best of the alternatives.

Plain language should not need to define its terms but it may be helpful to explain some habits of expression. Except as traditional party labels I use 'Left' and 'Right' not for forms of government but for attitudes to equality: 'Right' means wanting present or greater inequalities, 'Left' means wanting to reduce them. (The capital letters are to avoid confusion in sentences like 'the Left was right and left the Right behind'). 'Equal' and 'unequal' can't be shortly defined and are discussed in Chapter 7. 'Environmentalist' stands all too vaguely, as in everyday usage, for a variety of movements and opinions. And I believe that people including social scientists should write 'good', 'bad', 'right' and 'wrong' when those are what they mean.

Introduction:
Environmental politics

People can't change the way they use resources without changing their relations with one another. For example there are dozens of ways to economize energy: some would stop the rich wasting it, others would freeze the poor to death. Forests or beaches or country landscapes can be conserved to be enjoyed by many, by few or by nobody. Rich and poor can be made to contribute very fairly or very unfairly to the costs of reducing pollution. Old city streets and neighborhoods can be conserved for the people who live in them, or they can be conserved by methods which drive those people out, bring richer people in and make speculative fortunes for a few richer still. How to conserve is usually a harder question than whether, or what, to conserve.

So however urgent it may be to wake people up to physical and ecological dangers, environmental reformers also need political philosophies. They need them for quite practical purposes. Besides being less or more effective in technical ways environmental reform will usually also have to be Right, Left or otherwise contentious in a social way. Until the citizens know exactly which way they may not vote for much of it. Rhetoric about universal benefits for everybody fools scarcely anybody these days.

At the same time there are reasons for expecting intensified conflicts about inequalities. Distributive justice is the heart of the new problems of inflation. Those, and rising environmental costs, are making distributive justice once again a central concern of the Left. It should certainly concern environmental reformers. Tactically their programs will succeed or fail by the gains and losses they offer not so much to 'humanity' as to powerful parties and classes of it. Historically, particular inequalities have had crucial effects on the form and timing of agrarian and industrial revolutions. Environmentalists want another economic revolution. What roles are inequalities expected to play in it?

It is rarely helpful to isolate environmental problems or to argue (as many environmentalists do) that they are so urgent that they should replace the traditional concerns of government. In fact they tangle

3

inextricably with the traditional concerns of government. The questions which environmentalists ask make sure of that. What resources should we use? What goods should we produce? Who should get them, who should pay for them, who should do without them? Those are the minimal environmental questions without which there can be no environmental policy; but as surely as Karl Marx ever did, they question the foundations of social organization. To be effective – to be put into operation – a program of environmental reform has to be part of a program of more general social change.

Nor does it usually help to think of conservation (as many of both its friends and its enemies do) as a program to replace economic growth.[1] Relations between growth and conservation are more complicated than that. Both are programs to provide for people in the future. Believers in growth stress the reproducible resources (capital, education, technique) which future people will need. Environmentalists stress the exhaustible resources (fuels and metals, natural species, unspoiled environments) which they will also need. Each kind of resource is likely to be very little use without the other. Factories and factory skills may be no use if there is no fuel – but saved oil may be no use if there are no petrochemical plants and skills. A great deal of energy could be saved if buildings had insulated, integrated energy systems – but to provide them would take more growth and capital formation, not less. Growth is not always in the interest of present people and conservation is not always in the interest of future people. And so on – simple across-the-board attitudes to either don't help. As in principle, so in detail: practical disagreements about environmental policy are rarely simple conflicts between growth and conservation. They are conflicts about what to use, what to produce and how to pay for it – conflicts between people competing in familiar ways for rival values or for shares of scarce goods.

People compete here and now. They can also compete over time. Morally speaking time may not make much difference to the merits of the case but politically it often determines who wins. Should limited fossil fuels serve rich people now, rich people later, poor people now, poor people later? Should scarce metals (or for that matter any scarce resources or productive capacity) supply luxuries to rich Americans and Europeans, comforts to poorer Americans and Europeans, life-saving necessities to much poorer Brazilians or Javanese – or what goods to the grandchildren of which of them? If a general principle is wanted it can only be some principle of equality; but a principle of equality will usually contradict any simple principle of either growth or conservation. Conservation is not worth having if it merely shifts hardships from rich to poor, or from later to now. Growth is not worth having if it merely speeds up the rate at which the rich can guzzle resources which the poor need both now and later. Most questions about whether or not to save or use resources (growth questions, conservationists' questions) are really about *who* should use the resources. They are like any other questions of distributive justice.

They are therefore fit for regular politics. Except on occasional special issues it won't usually be sensible to look for alliances of all conservationists against all believers in economic growth. In self-interested politics there will be alliances for one pattern of growth and conservation against other patterns of both – for conserving my neighborhood by polluting yours, saving my oil by burning yours. In high-minded politics people who want to conserve and develop good things and distribute them well should be in alliance against people who want to conserve and develop worse things and distribute them badly. And the traditional divisions and alignments of Right and Left become more appropriate than ever as three new circumstances – the new inflation, environmental costs and shortages, and a new trend to inequality – concentrate political attention on the relations between growth, conservation and equality.

2

Three things are prompting people to think about equality again, to worry about the wealth of the rich as well as a decent minimum for the poor.

First, that twentieth-century compromise – a decent minimum for the poor with unlimited inequalities for the rich – was tolerable chiefly because industrial capitalism itself seemed to be improving equalities for a century or so. But in most rich countries that trend seems to have been reversed about 1950.[2] Since then there have been some better distributions of housing and domestic equipment; some wages and salaries have continued to converge; but other trends provide that incomes as a whole, and the ownership of income-earning wealth, are now (in ways that matter to many people) growing less equal. As the mass of losers come to understand that they are falling behind in a systematic way, and think about the implications of that for the future, they may become less willing to tolerate the 'decent minimum' compromise.

Second, the new inflation is destructive and unpopular, but for reasons which will be argued later no country is likely to succeed in controlling it except in the context of a guaranteeable trend toward greater equality.

Third, the new environmental troubles will bring on some lopsided relations between growth and inequality. People who tolerate unequal sharing of ordinary goods feel differently about goods which they come to think of as absolutely limited and exhaustible. People also feel gains and losses with different intensity. While economic growth gives them gains each year they may not mind much if others' gains are greater – even disproportionately greater. But if they face cuts they often demand equal rations. If poor people once used a quarter of the coal and a tenth of the oil per head that the rich used, and now use perhaps half as much as the rich use, a downturn of supplies may well drive them to demand equal shares, which they would never have expected while growth continued. The division of gains which they accepted on the way up will not be the division of losses which they will want to accept on the way down. Besides particular goods like coal and oil, those feelings may apply to whole incomes if shortages of energy or other resources ever force a general fall in living standards. Passing (say) $2,000 annual income per head on the way up, a society may be very unequal; passing the same figure on the way down it is likely to be more equal, or more bloodstained, or both. Even if growth merely slows or stops without actual losses, equality may suddenly seem more important. If further social improvement has to depend on fairer sharing that will reconstruct the politics of people accustomed to inequality but also hopelessly addicted to social improvement.

Detailed relations between conservation and inequality vary with the environmental facts. Exhaustible resources are one sort of problem, reversible pollution is another, irreversible damage is another. Most of them are problems chiefly in relation to numbers of people (one sort of problem) and their unequal uses of resources (another). (Gross population numbers are not discussed in this book, because I have nothing to add to conventional wisdom on the subject. Most of what follows assumes that humane efforts to restrain numbers are for the good; limiting poor numbers is likely to reduce poor suffering and limiting rich reproduction is likely to reduce poor suffering even more. Limiting the numbers of poor who are allowed to get rich is more contentious, and *is* a subject of this book.)

If things are running out, who should have what shares of them, now and later, until they are gone? On this subject simple moralities are sometimes less moral than they seem. Using exhaustible resources later is not necessarily better than using them now. It depends who gets them at either date. Poverty and premature death are as bad for poor people now as for their grandchildren later: except for its uncertainties, time does not alter most principles of distributive justice. Nor does exhaustibility. If exhaustible goods ought to be distributed fairly, so should any other life-saving or comforting goods, whether they are scarce because they are running out or because of ordinary costs of production. If environmentalists are moralizing (rather than trying to corner their own supplies) they can't consistently want fair sharing of goods that may run out, but not of equally necessary goods that won't.

Equal rationing at controlled prices may wring more wellbeing from less material. It may buy time to develop substitutes. It may reserve scarce resources for essential uses, and prevent wasteful uses of them. But equal rationing at controlled prices is not what some oil sheiks and some environmentalists have in mind when they propose (for example) to slow down the rate at which the world burns up its oil. Rationing by price, or by quota proportionately to past use, usually means that the poor get less now so that the rich can enjoy more for longer. Over the whole time needed to exhaust the resource, that makes sure that more rich and less poor will get shares of the stuff. If it can't be equally rationed it might well be fairer to burn it up cheaply and quickly without restraint. Many environmental programs are careless of these effects. With good intentions they aim (say) to raise the selling price of pollutant products to reflect their true social costs. That often has the effect of distributing their benefits more unequally than before.

Other programs express genuinely unselfish desires to suffer more scarcity now in order to reserve resources for people not yet born. These have political as well as moral difficulties. Those unborn people are not here to fight or sue or vote for their shares. They can be represented only in the weak sense that present-day sympathizers can beg on their behalf. This can be compared with attempts to persuade rich countries to give international aid. The purpose is the same: to save total strangers from hardship and early death. A quarter of a century of passionate and expert effort has not persuaded any national population to give as much as 1% of its output for that. On the face of it, intergenerational aid looks even less likely than international aid. The people to be helped are more remote. They are so far off in an imperfectly predictable future that we cannot be very sure about their needs, or that aid will actually reach them or do them much good. Yet the quantity of sacrifice required is presumably greater – to make much difference to prospects of human survival an environmental revolution would have to forgo much more than 1% of

7

current consumption. Rich societies do not give that much to poor societies now. To forgo much more, for the uncertain benefit of unborn generations, would be revolutionary generosity.

If people do nevertheless become as generous as that, why should they give to unborn poor rather than to poor Indians and Javanese here and now? In truth most of these programs, though generous, have nothing to do with equality. They are inheritance programs, to bequeath resources from the rich now to their rich grandchildren. Believers in equality need not necessarily oppose them; if resources are conserved, reformed societies may one day distribute them more equally. But if rich-to-rich bequests are morally respectable, poor-to-rich transfers are not (though plenty of them happen in ordinary economic life). Rationing by price is usually reactionary. So can some gifts and bequests be, especially when the people who decide the gifts are not the givers. Rich elites sometimes decide aid programs which transfer wealth chiefly from the masses in rich countries to rich elites in poor countries; or they give technical aid which increases inequality within the poor countries. Aid from rich to poor nations does not always improve equalities, and aid between generations need not always improve them, or reduce suffering.

Practical as well as moral problems may trouble societies which try to help their grandchildren by staying poor themselves. To abstain from cutting forests or mining beaches as a policy of permanent conservation, so that those resources can be enjoyed in other ways, is one thing. To abstain so that later people can cut or mine them is another. Either may be easy enough to do if the capital and labor which might have extracted the saved materials are fully employed at other tasks instead. But if people need the saved resources (especially coal, oil, hydroelectricity, timber) so badly that the switch of productive capacity leaves them noticeably poorer, or if the capital and labor are not switched but left unemployed, then people will see themselves as simply under-producing – which is exactly the deliberate self-denial that many environmentalists have in mind. Such deliberate scarcity must inevitably change some of the basis of social competition for scarce goods – the daily politics of wages, taxes, profits, prices, pensions and welfare services. The more a society has of deliberately unused capacity, the more temptation it creates for itself. Whenever there is serious conflict for social shares there is available a peace-making, no-loser solution at the expense of remote third parties. The third parties need not even be thought of as people; the healing solutions can be presented blandly as raids on kitty, as 'drawing on the resource bank' or on 'the reserves which our own prudence and sacrifice

have provided for just this emergency'. Within its generation the temptation might often lead in the direction of social peace and justice. Any
society which resisted it – which kept resources in the bank while people
suffered or died for want of them – would be practising very novel
politics. They might well be vicious politics in societies as unequal as
most societies are now. Politically as well as morally, more equality
here and now is probably a condition of any better equalities between
generations.

The morals and politics are simpler when the purpose of conservation
is not to bank resources but to save them from degradation. If earth, air,
water or species are irreversibly spoiled nobody can use them – rich or
poor, now or later – so there may be genuinely common interests in
conserving them; though there may still be conflicts about distributing
the costs of doing it.

Action against reversible pollution can have various effects on equalities. Sometimes benefits can be distributed deliberately, to improve
particular activities or to clean up particular neighborhoods. Sometimes the benefits are general, as in purer food or drinking water.
Equalities may be affected by distributions of costs; but that need be
no different from the problem of distributing any other costs of production.

Environmentalists and their programs are even more diverse than the
problems they face. And they are not spread conveniently along a line
of intensity, with moderates and radicals and revolutionaries wanting less
or more of much the same things. Many of their differences are contradictory. The contradictions are partly technical, partly matters of value.
For example some reformers want to limit population by stopping
economic growth, others by accelerating growth. Some want to stop
science and investment; others think intensified research and investment
offer the best chance of arresting population growth and economizing or
substituting for scarce materials. Some want threatened resources to
become public property, others think they will be safer as private
property. As consolations for material austerity some want more privacy,
others more community; others think those are not alternatives but go
together and there should be more of both. Some want to restrict
consumption by restricting supply. Others want to restrict demand by
teaching people to desire less goods. Some hope to tame or change human
nature, others don't. Most of these programs would reconstruct inequalities, for better or worse. Some of them will be explored in later chapters

9

– they are too complicated for simple summary. Here it will be enough to notice some practical political relations between environmental movements and the Left.

3

There are equal and unequal ways of conserving resources. There are also equal and unequal ways of squandering them. So there is no inevitable general relationship between the Left and the environmental movement. Instead there is a tangle of common, overlapping and conflicting interests, and plenty of opportunity for negotiation.

There can be conflict about distributing the costs and benefits of conservation. The Left may want to make wilderness accessible to more and poorer people; environmentalists may want to preserve it from too much use by any people. The Left may want jobs located where environmentalists don't want them. The Left may want high-wage, capital-intensive production of cheap goods; where that squanders energy or pollutes, environmentalists may want lower-paid, labor-intensive production of dearer goods. Some of these conflicts are inescapable. The parties may still do better to compromise than to fight each other, because they both have more dangerous enemies. Their common enemies are the winners from both 'time' and 'class' maldistributions: those affluent producers and consumers who won't willingly give much away to the poor now, to anyone later, or to 'quality of life' at either date. They include some leaders of the greediest, most powerful, most improvident societies – leaders who know from choice or democratic necessity how to use reformer against reformer. Some of them already use environmentalist support against the spread of various mass housing and motoring benefits; at the same time they use mass support against environmental programs which threaten profitable production and employment. In that three-party game the two generous parties too often mistake the enemy, and both lose.

Such cross purposes deserve to be explored with care. Some conflicts of value between environmentalists and the Left are real but others are not, or needn't be. Some economists expect 'environmental class conflict' because, they say, the rich desire higher environmental standards than the poor do. This is half true at best. There may be differences of taste about trees or caravan camps but there is plenty of agreement about dangers and necessities – about safety, noise, clean air and water, sufficient food and shelter and energy. For those solid goods nobody has discovered much difference between rich and poor desires. Theorists

10

have merely reasoned about rich and poor capacities to pay. Even about those they have often been misled. They observe for example that in some noisy polluted cities the rich can afford houses and gardens in quiet districts with clean air, while the poor can't. In fact the rich have often put the dirty industries and the cheap crowded housing together into the poor districts, and kept both out of the rich districts, by investment and zoning policies at very little cost to the rich residents' incomes. In extreme cases those tactics can keep the land under rich houses cheaper than the land under poor houses so that the rich get most of the environmental benefit and the poor pay most of the cost of it. The conventional theory about class tastes is specially misleading where, as often happens, private land and public goods like parklands and school playgrounds and clean air are distributed more unequally than incomes. In all these cases what the poor suffer proves something about their political weakness. It proves nothing about their values and less than some experts suppose about their marginal utilities.[3]

There may be solider causes of conflict in the Left's defence of existing jobs and wages against dislocation by new environmental policies; and in some of the policies themselves. Some schemes for intergenerational aid are generous, others are reactionary. Some ways of protecting natural resources would incidentally protect class privileges. Many environmentalists are political innocents who do not see themselves as enemies of equality. But they do equate any spread of affluence with environmental degradation. They do want to restrict car ownership – in practice, to the rich. They do want to ration oil by price. They do defend rural land from development for cheap housing. They do want to make the polluter pay, which often has the effect of taxing consumers regressively. They do want to restrict access to some coasts and countrysides and wild places by making the access more expensive. They do insist on the stark impossibility of stretching world resources to supply even the poorest western standards to Indian or Chinese numbers. Most of the implied policies would freeze or increase inequalities. The proposers often have unselfish intentions. But it is not surprising if some of the Left come to believe that the old Right which keeps the rich rich now has an ally in this new Right which wants to keep the poor poor.

And those are among the best, the most generous of environmentalists. Worse also exist. The worst are simply rich and lifeboat-selfish. Aid should be cut, to help Indian and Javanese children to die before they breed. Democracy should be cut because 'there is no time left for politics'. The first chairman of Australia's Atomic Energy Commission

11

urged his country to develop atomic weapons to frighten off refugees who might try to reach it after ecological disasters elsewhere. Hopefully the environmentalist movement will take less and less notice of such callous projects, and leaders.

But if environmentalists and the Left are to work usefully together the Left also may need to revise some policies. If sharing between generations does become deliberate the Left should apply their values to it – also their brains, as the only thinkers likely to study seriously either the moral or the causal relations between time and class distributions. And it is time to revise the holy old schedule of things which socialists believe ought to be distributed equitably. Opportunity, for example, could move down the list. In unequal societies opportunities are never likely to be equal. The myth that they could be may well make the reality harder for losers to bear; and it diverts reformers from the work of reducing the inequalities absolutely. In the usual philistine meaning of a scratch start for every child in a race to get rich at each other's expense, equal opportunity seems an unimportant ideal for either a socialist or a conservationist society, and it applies oddly if at all between generations. But a different kind of opportunity – broadly, to have a good experience of life at any level of the going scale of incomes – should move up the list. For that purpose there need to be some additions to the conventional list of equalities. Some of the Left's own mistakes in urban planning and housing have done enough, even if there were no other evidence, to show that income and some traditional public services like health and education are not the only things that need thoughtful distribution. Many other free, public, environmental and locational goods need it too. Some of them are easier to distribute well than wealth and income are: space, privacy, community services, access to nature, access to good city centres; and perhaps also chances for individuality, self-respect, stable social networks (and chances to escape them). It would be good to blur some distinctions between work and leisure. Work could often be made more interesting. It could often be designed with more care for the social relations that go with it. And there could be many more opportunities for people to work for themselves, in creative and self-expressive ways, when they've finished their weekly stint for someone else. Finally if the uses of wealth and the directions of economic growth need to be revised the Left should not confine itself to a stubborn defence of wages and existing relativities. In any program of substantial economic change or self-restraint there are latent opportunities for large gains in equality, and the Left should exploit them.

In those ways it can be argued that each of the two movements, even if the other did not exist, needs to overhaul its ideas of distributive justice. Some Left ideas of distributive justice are obsolete; some environmentalists' ideas of it are careless and some seem to have no idea of it at all. But for all their shortcomings the two still divide between them much of whatever hope and reformist talent the world has got. Can they learn to cooperate more, instead of frustrating each other for the advantage of their common enemies? That may be as difficult as other apparently rational alliances have been, for example between workers of all countries, or blacks and poor whites. But any chances are worth exploring.

They are worth exploring especially because without them, rich countries may face serious social as well as environmental degradation. Changing uses of resources reconstruct old as well as new sources of conflict. Stabilized populations will have more old and less young people, and perhaps more generational conflicts. Most young people are comparatively affluent until they have children; many old people are poor, and may want to use their increasing electoral strength to force some redistributions. If production is cut by unexpected shortages or by drastic restraints on pollutant or high-energy industries, that will make for one range of social troubles; different troubles can be expected if underemployment is spread more evenly over the workforce. If energy-conserving policies turn the clock back to more labor-intensive methods of production, the troubles will be different from those to be expected if new sources of energy are tapped and conservationist effort goes into intensive waste absorption and technical substitution. Any of those directions of change will set citizen against citizen in one way or another, but the stresses are likely to be more severe if there are great inequalities of reward and lifestyle to fight for, and less if there are less. To build better equalities into programs of environmental reform, the only imaginable equalizers and peacemakers are the political parties of the Left. But they will need broader alliances than most of them have now. They will need more environmentalists, repentant rich, middle-class reformers and women of all classes to vote for them. They must try to attract that diverse support not so much by abandoning class politics as by diffusing egalitarian values into more and more areas of policy, offering equitable environmental action, equitable housing and urban policies and fairer distributions of physical resources as well as better distributions of wealth and income. It is with equitable policies on all those fronts that environmental policies must be designed to fit, if they hope to get enough support to be effective.

13

Simple impulses can improve the world in many ways but environmental policy-making offers too many chances – some of them quite enticing – for simple-minded warriors to shoot the wrong people, including one another. Environmental reform can easily languish for lack of support. Organized labor, consumers, taxpayers – voters generally – will recoil and block it if its high costs are unfairly distributed. And it can be attempted in ways so various, from reactionary to revolutionary, as to point to grossly different directions of social change.

For that last reason above all, movements for environmental reform are unlikely to get far by closing ranks and transcending party politics, as some eco-preachers recommend. They need to get into real politics rather than out of them; to talk about rich and poor, city and country, costs and distributions, prices and taxes, rather than about humanity at large. They need to show plainly how the new costs and benefits they propose should be distributed between neighborhoods, regions, classes. There will be more effective environmental reform when politicians stop asking who is for it or against it, and begin instead to count the numbers for urban or rural, capital-intensive or labor-intensive, nationalist or internationalist, equalizing or unequalizing, Left or Right environmental action.

The first five of the following chapters compare some of those alternative directions of change.

OPTIONS

1
The rich rob the poor

To compare alternative approaches to environmental reform in rich countries it is usual to begin by comparing alternative aims or utopias. But in real history programs adapt through many conflicts and compromises and people change their minds and mistake the likely effects of their own and other people's actions, so that events follow nobody's program exactly. Many presently-fashionable forecasts rely on estimates of physical resources and extrapolations of population, economic growth and current ways of doing things. Those calculations define some limits of possibility. Within them actual futures, perhaps including changes of mind and historical direction, will be worked out as any history is, by political processes. Those processes – rather than forecasts of resource limits, or ideal social destinations – are the business of the next chapters, which sketch three alternative futures of social and environmental change.

At best the sketches guess at a range of possibilities; real futures will mix compulsions and choices and cross purposes in much more complicated ways. The sketches can't even be good fiction because they have to be deliberately vague as to the expected quantities of environmental trouble. But they start from here and now and try to deal in real types of social interest and conflict and realistic mechanisms of historical change. None of them is a forecast of what is likeliest to happen. Each is rather a guess at the political conditions – the least unlikely political conditions – which would have to be met for its particular environmental and social program to succeed. This is one useful way to judge programs. If the history which seems to be required to fulfil a program is implausible, that may prompt second thoughts about the program.

The first history is so far to the Right that I do not believe that any society will succeed with it, or even try it. It is here nevertheless to spell out some practical implications of the most conservative (and widely held) environmental philosophies. The second is a little to the Right of the middle of the capitalist road, and all too probable. The third, through Chapters 3 to 5, is moderately Left and perhaps moderately unlikely but

it is my own guess at the politics of the possible: the best future that might
be practicable in some at least of the capitalist democracies and therefore
the one to work for. (How to work for it is then the business of the rest
of the book.) All three sketches are in another sense conservative – they
try to set men as they are into institutions as they might develop,
imagining some better behavior here and there, but not the transforma-
tions of human nature of which some reformers dream.

1

This first history begins with an incisive contemporary diagnosis.

Although it may strain some liberal hypocrisies, let us for once be
honest about the environmental problem. It consists of too many people
using and spoiling limited resources. We must therefore reduce the
number of people or the allowance of resources to each, or preferably
both. If we don't, nature will. Man has had a population explosion of
a type perfectly familiar to ecologists. It will be followed by a population
slump. Is it best to let that slump happen by natural disaster, or should
it be managed deliberately to reduce suffering and conserve resources for
a tolerable life for the survivors? Environmentalists believe that a
managed transition would be better than the mass killing by war and
famine and poisoning, followed by survival in a stripped and polluted
wasteland, which are the likely alternatives to it. For the duration of the
crisis the duty of government is to ration resources and cause human
numbers to breed down gently. Many people will try to resist or evade
these policies; therefore many people will have to be coerced. There need
be nothing terrible about that. All government is coercive to some degree,
and most historical government has lacked the explicit consent of the
governed. The governed had reason to be glad of it just the same,
because it protected them from worse disasters.

This rigorous approach is necessary because the problem is urgent, and
because no amount of voluntary environmental restraint can cope with
it. The fallacy of voluntary restraint is that it only needs every tenth or
even every hundredth citizen to be a sinner for sin to win by engrossing
whatever resources are spared by the virtuous nine or ninety-nine.
Moreover if wealth buys power, as it usually does, the sinners will soon
be the government. Sufficient restraint is not likely to come by democratic
coercion either, especially not if the democracy is at all local or partici-
patory. To make scarcity scarcer is a harsh thing. Decent men will not
willingly bring it on their own families or neighborhoods, even if they

16

see its logic as a general policy. If government has to answer to popular control, politicians will be driven to outbid each other in offering short-term prosperity to the voters. Any who don't compete will be beaten by those who do, and any who preach the environmental virtues will probably be discredited by clever mockery of their puritanism. 'He has a doomsday syndrome... He's guilt-ridden, can't spend or enjoy... He's an anal-retentive, wants to keep it all in the piggy-bank...' So democracy is improvident. But dictators may be no better – they also can run improvident policies, and if they do they are harder to expose or criticize.

There is no perfect solution to this problem.

The least imperfect solution is to get power into the hands of people who have reliable motives of their own for making sure that resources are conserved. Such motives need to be self-interested – it is absurd to trust in the altruism of ruling classes. But it has to be expected that a self-interested ruling class will consume more than its personal share of scarce resources, so if the purpose of installing the class is to conserve the resources, the class had better not be too numerous. It does however need to include everybody with any influence or talent – skilled people left outside the ruling class tend to be ungovernable nuisances.

If a class which includes all managers and professionals and other responsible skills is nevertheless to be small in number, the economic system needs to be a simple one. This agrees with the program of the most conservative environmentalists. The most conservative environmentalists are those who have no faith in further research and development. They fear that any increase of technical capacity is more likely to be used badly than well. It would be better to stop the growth of knowledge and turn back to simpler styles of life with simpler methods of production – methods which use less fuel, create less pollution, keep people closer to nature and one another, and allow more local self-sufficiency. Such simple friends of the earth may perhaps underestimate the values that would be lost in returning rich societies to the simple life, and the strength with which the attempt would be resisted. But it is true that the simple economy which they have in mind would need comparatively little specialist skill, and could be managed by a small ruling class.

Such a ruling class moreover should be naturally motivated to steer a middle course between the two main threats to its own security. As the class with most to lose from an environmental doomsday it should want to conserve resources. As long as it is powerful enough to bequeath its privileges to its children it should have an aristocratic interest in making the conservation permanent; because it is a sort of extended selfishness,

17

privileged family interest is the most reliable basis of concern for future generations. The other general threat to such a class is rebellion, whether in the form of revolution or in the form of intolerable levels of guerilla activity or sullen insubordination. So the class should know better than to drive or starve its subjects any harder than is absolutely necessary. Between the dangers of doomsday if consumption rises too high, and rebellion if it is held too low, the ruling class should be motivated to be good judges of the rates of depletion and conservation which will offer the best balance, and minimize suffering, in the long run.

Such a regime would be severe. It would not necessarily have to be hated – it might be trusted as were the dictatorships which the democracies more than once created for themselves in wartime, when for a time they also had nothing but duties and hardships to distribute to their citizens. (Democrats themselves are well aware that democratic machinery cannot perform that austere task.) But class rule for purposes of environmental discipline has to be more permanent than a wartime dictatorship, and more permanently insulated from feckless changes of popular feeling. That is why government needs to be motivated less by individual ambition for office and more by entrenched family and class interest. And of course by fear – fear of doomsday, and probably also mutual fear between rulers and ruled.

This scenario is inspired by feelings which in themselves are humane and respectable – the repentant, anti-materialist, nature-loving, nostalgic feelings of the more conservative ecologists. The social and environmental vision may be reactionary but it is gently, almost romantically so. Nevertheless it was the unromantic Thomas Hobbes, three centuries ago, who grasped its central political necessity, which is not gentle or romantic at all.

2

How might such impulses be put into practice?

We have to imagine that the alarmist eco-preaching continues, and proves to have been correct: there really are disasters from misuse of the environment. City life becomes intolerably noisy, smelly, dangerous and unsociable. Atomic wastes play up, power stations blow up. More and more people die from food poisoning, lung diseases, radiation sickness and violent crime. It becomes particularly expensive to depend on oil supplies – larger and larger fractions of people's incomes have to be spent on transporting themselves, heating and powering their houses and buying products of oil-fuelled industries; and there are mounting threats that the wars for the Arab oilfields may spread around the globe. Fear itself – of drugging and mugging and urban guerilla terror, of poison and cancer and global doomsday – has alarming effects: affluent cities, socialist as well as capitalist, have rising rates of mental as well as physical disease. Societies lurching from one shortage and disaster to the next can no longer provide their people with safety, tolerable expectations, or plausible ideals. People become so troubled by all this and so impatient of the half-measures offered by their democratic politicians or their cliques of colonels that in one way or another, by coup or plebiscite, suddenly or step by step, emergency regimes are installed. The richer communist countries arrive at much the same new resolves as a result of similar economic experiences, and the personal conversion of their leaders.

The new regimes do not begin as reactionary, class-ruled regimes. They begin with widespread goodwill. Many workers support them, having borne the brunt of the physical dangers and rising prices. Many environmental scientists and bureaucrats and publicists are glad to have decisive political masters at last. Many businessmen welcome the prospect of orderly rationing and pricing as the best way out of the rising industrial chaos. There is also a repentance widely felt by many people of all social classes – a revulsion from mechanism and materialism, a nostalgia for more natural and neighborly styles of life, and a genuine willingness to live on less.

It is this goodwill, mixed with panic, which brings majorities, actively or by passive acquiescence, to surrender authority irrevocably to the emergency governments. But when these new governments begin to justify themselves by effective environmental action, most of the goodwill evaporates very quickly. This happens chiefly for two reasons. First it was an innocent goodwill which had underestimated the real and painful costs of putting its generous intentions into practice. Second it was also innocent in having no clear notions of distributive justice, no acceptable principles for distributing sacrifices. So there are shocks when sacrifices are suddenly exacted from people who didn't expect them. The rich are shocked by some of their sacrifices, the poor are shocked by some of theirs, both are shocked by some strictly equal ones, and there is the usual quota of sacrifices which seem to have been distributed by accident, corruption, favoritism or sheer administrative muddle. The righteous indignation which took many people into the environmental reform movement now brings them smartly out of it. From shouting slogans against the polluters they would soon turn to shouting the slogans of liberalism – of constitutional rights, individual liberties, and the evils of arbitrary government – if they were still free to shout slogans at all. But by now they are not.

Many people had supposed that it would be enough to give up luxuries and vulgarities – the second car, the second house, the second bathroom. Englishmen thought it would do if Americans returned to English standards of living; Italians thought it would do if the English returned to Italian standards. The middle classes thought it would do if the journey to work returned to public transport. Moderates of all nationalities hoped for a sensible underpowered electric car for social and leisure-time uses. They looked forward to modest houses with open fires again. They looked forward to stable fashions so that clothes could be worn until they wore out, and hair could be washed and brushed without chemical rinses and sprayed-on glue. A surprising number who were too young ever to have met the crabbed, misshapen, wormy fruits of natural orchards, or lost money or gone hungry because of the rates of mouldy ratshitty loss from unprotected granaries, imagined that food grown without chemical and industrial aids would somehow grow fuller and rounder and smoother than the full, round, smooth provender that used to come plastic-wrapped from controlled-atmosphere storages to pre-revolutionary supermarkets.

Best of all, it had seemed postively enticing to get rid of the needless excesses of production by the simple method of letting everybody work less. People would then be freed to walk and talk and laze and make love, climb and camp and sail and ski, turn their own pottery and weave their own clothes and grow their own flowers and vegetables, all in environmentally wholesome and socially warm and personally self-expressive ways, through the extended weekends and long golden summers and frequent long-service leaves and early, long retirements which were to be won merely by doing without the electric toothbrush, the power mower and the kids' motorbikes, and the excessive packaging and advertising of washing powders and breakfast foods.

The truth is that, defined by the people who use them, the useless vulgarities of modern society may perhaps be 20% of its product in North America and are probably below 10 or 5% anywhere else. To be effective – to make real savings of energy and reductions of pollution, and to do it chiefly by reducing production rather than inventing any radically better methods of production – reform has to bite deep into real standards of living. Doing with less fossil fuel does not allow people to take longer holidays. It means they have to work harder and longer for less return – not just less vulgarities, but less food, less shelter, less warmth, less clothing, shorter life. Harnessing artificial energy to modern productive technology was what chiefly raised a quarter or so of the human race above the breadline and doubled its babies' expectations of life. Those are precisely the achievements that have to be rationed when the energy and technology are rationed.

The new governors are aware of this. They also believe that if fuel is scarce any gram of it will do more good in production than in consumption. Incentive allowances of consumable goods to the ruling class count as productive; but with that exception the rationing and pricing of fuel are biased to favor industrial over domestic uses. The hardest hit are domestic power and heating, and private motoring. Which of those two losses hurts most depends on local facts of climate and inherited urban forms and standards.

The loss of the private car is quite surprisingly painful in the temperate countries. Intellectuals have generally underestimated its contribution to real social goods; and doing without it now is much worse than doing without it used to be. This is because the cities have changed their shapes and systems in the meantime. Office workers and executives may still be able to reach city centres by radial public transport routes, but increasing multitudes of industrial and service workers live in suburbs a long way from good services, and have to make cross-radial journeys to other suburbs to work. When the rich cities in the temperate zones sprawled out into shapes and densities impossible to serve well by any pattern of public transport, they turned cars from luxuries into necessities for a lot of their citizens, *especially* their blue-collared citizens. Cars took people to work, brought their shopping home from bigger but more distant supermarkets, kept their families together at weekends. Cars also brought home handymen's staples: soil, stone, timber, turf and shrubs, wire netting and roofing iron, old tyres and bookshelves and second-hand refrigerators. In fact cars allowed so much unrecorded goods delivery, family transport and productive do-it-yourself activity – real production of economic goods, as well as personal recreation – that when the cars were taken away the social product fell much further than ever appeared in the national accounts.

Cars had helped many people to develop hobbies and skills. They had pulled cheap boats, caravans, picnic and camping gear. Whatever might have been accessible in the old days to affluent people who could afford hotel bills or country cottages or boats at private moorings, it was only when the blue- and white-collared masses of the cities got their cars that most of them and their children got regular access to the freedoms and

21

pleasures and skills of the sea and the countryside. In all history there was never a riding-horse per average family, much less a horse-drawn vehicle. A car per family was arguably the longest single stride in modern times towards real equality – towards similar and shared experience regardless of income, towards a common lifestyle regardless of class, towards access regardless of class to a marvellous diversity of pleasures of landscape and seascape, and the skills that go with those. Private cars may not have opened many such opportunities to the crowded workers of London or New York – who sometimes had other consolations – but cars liberated the larger numbers who had their own back yards in hundreds of smaller, duller cities, with less congested roads and shorter routes out of town.

Now in the environmental revolution the ordinary family loses its car within a generation of getting it. The loss is the more bitter because it is not shared. The rich still drive. So the car stays in sight, not this time as the cheeriest promise of capitalism but as a symbol of privilege abused and trust betrayed.

In colder climates, chilblains and thick old greatcoats are what chiefly symbolize betrayal. The colder cities were more compact than the temperate ones. They had always used more fuel for heating and less for private transport. They heaped their work and housing closer together so their public transport works better. But they are cold, and the effects of fuel rationing range (with the climate) from bleak to brutal. Domestic heat is rationed by a price which rules all but a life-saving minimum of it out of most working-class households. The central heating is turned off in schools, and off or down nearly to zero in most mass housing. Very few modern buildings have fireplaces even for those who can steal fuel. So most housing is cold, and public housing is coldest. There are some sad crimes in those cold old tower flats. Men usually kill their families first and then themselves; women more often jump with their children in their arms. The governors are less worried about those wilful resignations, or the shivering old and sick, than about the political behavior of able-bodied workers who must brood resentfully at home under a heap of blankets in front of the censored television, or go out and exchange rebellious feelings in the warmth of public bars. When Russian workers froze through the winter of 1918, or English workers had too little coal in the rationing of 1940 or too much snow in the long freeze of 1947, at least they were promised peace, prosperity and social justice if they held out. There are no hopes like that for the victims of environmental reform, the scores of millions who now face cold winters all the way to death.

22

There is also a mixture of licensing and price-rationing of energy for industry. Some essential manufactures and services still get most of the oil, gas, or centrally generated electric power that they need. More trades use coal directly, but that also is rationed – and of course patrolled everywhere by guard dogs, with the cold millions eyeing it covetously through the high wire fences that now have to surround all fuel yards. Some textiles, pottery and food-processing have returned to hand-and-foot energy. Most big building and earth-moving have simply ceased. House-building was always less mechanized so it goes on much as usual on the site; but its costs are doubled by the effects of fuel restrictions and prices on factory-made components, and by fuel and other environmental restraints on the extraction, processing and transport of quarry-rock, cement, bricks, ceramics, plastics and timber products. Throughout most of industry harder work, lower wages and dearer products are the rule – and besides those permanent austerities there is plenty of transitional dislocation and unemployment.

And those are the successes – the resources saved, the rivers cleaned, the forests climbing back up the hillsides, the atomic power stations dismantled, the coal and gas banked in the ground for other centuries. There are also failures. The worst failures are with farming. There is some return to open-range animal feeding, and to hand-weeding instead of herbicides. Or simply, to more weeds and less edibles. Insecticides and hormones are withheld from vegetable gardeners, whose tomatoes some-times taste better as a result but always look worse and cost more. But with the basic production of grains and meat and dairy products the new policies simply fail. Farmers are the hardest of all workers to coerce. If they are not allowed the chemical and mechanical tools of their trade – especially fuel and tractor parts – they do not retreat half a century to draught horses and harder work. They retreat much further, to farm for their own subsistence and to hell with the hungry cities. Once they identify cities and governments rather than weeds and pests and weather as the enemy it becomes technically impossible to feed the cities without their consent. The price of consent includes reasonable access to fertilizers, insecticides, industrial methods of packing, refrigerating and transporting perishables – and power on the farm wherever and whenever it's needed. The authorities have to decide whether to try to bring the peasants to heel by the methods the Russians used in the 1930s. Prudently they decide not to – apart from anything else the necessary military policing would use more fuel than the farms do. A few early attempts by zealous regional administrators to return to organic farming and local self-sufficiency came near to starving whole cities. They stopped abruptly when even the security forces felt hungry and began to fraternize.

On the whole the masses seem to have decided that hunger is worse than cold. Certainly hunger is what brings them nearest to rebellion. This may be because there are no substitutes for food. People short of heat can wrap up their old folk and cuddle their children close, but they can't huddle away hunger. Most people can also see that the fossil fuel restrictions are rational – more oil or coal now *does* mean less later – but food is not that sort of exhaustible resource. Most rich countries have the means to produce an overabundance of it. It merely burns oil if the farmers are allowed the fuel they want, and it has poison risks if they are allowed all the chemicals they ask for. The governors who will not go hungry in any circumstances would like to enforce fuel economy and very pure food, however that might restrict output and mass rations. The masses who have to live on the rations feel entitled to choose their own levels of eating and risk. So do the farmers. Between them, the masses and the farmers win. Food is thus the outstanding subject of compromise, on which the new regimes concede most to producers' and consumers' short-term demands. The farmers are allowed to spray almost anything, and burn fuel as if they belonged to the ruling class. Directly and through roundabout food and soil-and-water chains the poisonous content of human food continues to rise, and so do illness and death from that cause. The authorities finance some expensive organic farming to supply their own tables. Otherwise they adjust the regulations to permit what they can't prevent, and they begin to falsify some of the medical statistics.

3

So what is the new quality of life like, as a whole, for ordinary people? It is not at all like the conservative dream of a return to wholesome community values and home-baked bread. The rich snap up the few country cottages, and there are no resources for building more. Ordinary people go on living in the cities. They have to, that is where the houses are. But there is less to spend on maintaining them, and the cities soon begin to look as if the 1931 depression was back again. Shabby figures populate a depressed townscape, both growing steadily seamier since plastic clothing and plastic paint were banned. It is true that some things are better than they were in 1931. Medicine is better. Sex is closer to being a trouble-free pleasure. Alcohol and cannabis are plentiful. People and goods – anything heavy – may be dearer to move, but sight-and-sound communications are universal; radio and television get high priorities for the comparatively little power they use. There are nevertheless depressing resemblances to 1931. There is drab overcrowded public transport. Goods come home from the shops in baskets and prams and pushers, wrapped in old newspaper and brown paper. In flat cities thousands ride bikes, in other cities they trudge. At work there are fewer conveyors, no forklifts, no long-distance point-to-point road haulage. Products are packed small again, and manhandled by millions of low-paid man-hours from store to bench, from floor to trolley to truck to railcar, from wharf to pallet to hold.

At home there is some return to the three-generation household but only because of poverty and housing shortage. Building costs have doubled, so what there is of new housing is cramped and expensive. For most couples rooming and sharing and postponing children, and bickering with mother-in-law and with one another, go on long after marriage. It is here in the furniture and equipment of the house and of women's daily lives that the costs of environmental reform are harshest. Beds and people are clothed in wool and and cotton again. But those excellent materials are now a lot of trouble to wash by hand with common soap in warm water, then rinse in cold. They have to be wrung by hand or put through hand-turned wringers and mangles. Most households can afford power to cook and refrigerate food. They run the family one after the other through a tub of cooling bathwater twice a week, then put laundry through it after that. Sensible families put both through at once – the kids agitate the laundry like peasants used to trample grapes. Meanwhile clothing and furniture and kitchen utensils are themselves manufactured with half the former supplies of power, so they mostly cost twice what they did, and households can afford about half what they had in the old days. There are many total losses. Outside the ruling class there is no family car, there are no motor bikes, no power mowers, no dishwashers or washing machines or indoor driers; not much room heating and no cooling. There are no home-use detergents, very few permitted uses of plastics, no garden poisons or home insecticides. So there are a lot of flies and mosquitoes, and weedy gardens that brown off in dry seasons.

There is deep tension about children. For some people the company and love of children is the last good thing, the one indestructible good thing. But to more and more it seems selfish to rear them into a world likely to offer them so little. Birth rates fall quickly and in due course population follows them down. This is the one major reform that comes more easily than was expected. Besides contraception and abortion there

25

are tax and welfare and cash-for-sterility programs to depress the birth rate, but it really declines as it did in the 1930s for reasons of pervasive personal depression and loss of faith in the future for children.

Unemployment also looks a little like the unemployment of 1931, though there is less of it in any permanent way. People in jobs work listlessly for long hours. People without jobs work listlessly for shorter hours, often at much the same municipal earth-moving projects as in 1931. Bureaucrats seem to spend as much time frustrating each other as regulating the citizens. As more environmentally-sensitive industries have to be taken into public management, rationing and pollution control become more difficult and confusing in the public sector than in private industry. Many of the controllers' conflicts are between one state office and another. Arrogance bounces off arrogance and nobody can predict what sudden shortage will strike next. Out in the streets life is weary, ordinary, bleak. There are queues. Sometimes it is like Manchester or Detroit in 1931 but sometimes it seems more like Moscow in 1931 – or 1918.

But although it looks like 1931 it does not really feel like 1931. There is one dreadful, black-bordered difference: these hardships, this time, are for ever. No Recovery or Normalcy or Victory or Peacetime waits around the corner. There are no rewards for being good; merely a lot of new punishments for law-breakers trying to be comfortable. The drab cold has set in, like old age, for whatever time is left.

It is true of course that most of the historical generations of men have experienced life chiefly as a long hardship, without much fresh paint or winter fuel or hope of material improvement, and they have borne it somehow – cheerfully, often enough. People are irrepressible – they make love, fun, friends, music and make-believe in the most unpromising circumstances. Such things keep life from being wholly intolerable under the new regimes or the regimes would not survive. But in one way it was better for the poor in the old days than it is for the masses now. The generations since the environmental revolution are spoiled by the folk-memory of that short glorious century when it was different: when it was for each generation better, richer, warmer, growing more, knowing more, discovering and inventing, doing and making more, travelling far, living longer. When men have once tasted that wonderful apple of growth and lived through that springtime, nothing can be as good again. For those who now shuffle in queues to the local shortage-shop, and huddle into bed early with their shivering children – or with none – perhaps nothing can really be any good again.

But it is not like that for everybody. For one family in five the good things are still there. A somewhat insecure, somewhat shifty, somewhat arrogant ruling class continues to enjoy ample housing, warmth, servants, children, cars, privileged jobs and incomes, separate education and superior culture. Through the schools and the media they preach an environmental philosophy of austerity and anti-materialism. At home they justify their own comfortable culture as the point of the whole environmental enterprise – the 'survival of civilization' which makes all sacrifices worth while.

How did this happen? How were such people corrupted? They began as a prudent ruling group, genuinely anti-materialist, genuinely repentant. Many of them were chosen for high office because of their personal zeal and talent in the environmentalist cause. What changed them?

Briefly, some imperatives of social control did.

The first generation of governors might have been willing to live austerely and share the common sacrifices, like Platonic guardians. But it was a different matter to ask the rank and file for that sort of holy self-denial. Tens of thousands of clerks and checkers and inspectors – low-paid public servants, brought up to desire a home and family and car and a good future for their kiddies, and scattered now through dusty little offices in every city and suburb and town, often out of reach of any very close supervision by superiors – these had suddenly to impose confusing new restrictions on hundreds of thousands of shop assistants, petrol vendors, warehousemen and transport workers, who in turn had to impose the nuisances on a grumbling public. These hundreds of thousands were the people who had to enforce the environmental revolution where it mattered, and where it hurt. As the restraints bit into their own standards of living it was inhuman to expect such humdrum arms of government – and eyes and ears of government – to go on faithfully tightening up controls which were steadily eroding their own comforts and necessaries, and their children's life-chances.

Classical signs of sullen non-cooperation began to appear. Some people fell for technically-hopeful philosophies which suggested insidiously that the hardships were not *really* necessary – or anyway not *yet*. Some tried to use go-slow and work-to-rule tactics to bargain for privileges for themselves as public servants. Others developed too much compassion for the public. They wrote uncalled-for memoranda about the effects of the new policies on sick children or cold old ladies. Their monitoring grew careless, or worse. They connived with people they were supposed to be policing. More and more of them began to cheat. They took bribes to under-report waste emissions, pollution levels, decibel counts. They stole, forged and sold ration books, and began to turn official blind eyes first to one another's private supplies and evasions, then to everybody's. Black markets flourished. Despite a good many falsified statistics it became less and less possible to obscure the widening gap between policy and performance. Depletions continued, but it was hard to see where the resources went because shops could no longer meet their customers' ration entitlements. Oil spills still fouled the beaches, poisons still ran in the rivers. The new regimes seemed to have achieved the worst of both worlds – all the hardship and grumbling resentment which were the costs of the new policies, without much of the effective conservation which was supposed to make the costs worthwhile. Environmental control began to look as unenforceable, and as corrupting, as any historical attempts to prohibit alcohol or fornication.

Thus the first generation of honorable, self-denying, personally austere governors faced failure – failure in the shape of the very compromises and half-measures and slipshod performance and paralysis of will that had brought down their democratic predecessors.

To the radical originators of the movement – the environmental Robespierres and Lenins – the slow revelation of the reasons for failure was painful. But in the end they shed their sentimental illusions, developed some realistic contempt for the slovenly, corruptible humanity they had to govern, and saw the root cause of the trouble clearly enough. It was one thing to rely on the missionary zeal of a few leaders. But if all the members and minions of the ruling class had to share in the hardships of deliberate scarcity then inevitably, sooner or later, they would succumb to the perpetual temptation to water it down or call it off. Why in any case should they be expected to govern without the time-honored rewards of governors? In cold fact, they would enforce the great experiment permanently only if their personal and class interests pointed that way. So they had better be re-educated to regard the threatened environmental resources as their own, as family property to be defended from the greed of other people. They could then be personally exempted from the hardships. But they must know – really *know*, in their minds and hearts and guts – that their own and their children's children's supplies depended on their enforcing the environmental disciplines on the rest of society. They could have for themselves only what they could prevent other people from getting – the traditional condition of ruling classes before steam and democracy set in.

While ideologists were arguing along these lines something more potent happened – a practical man did a practical thing. A rationing administrator carpeted one of his subordinates, a local rationing officer who was suspected of forging and selling licences for domestic fuel. Under pressure the officer confessed to forging several hundred licences. Then he offered to identify and help to convict their several hundred buyers in return for immunity and a continuing fuel licence for himself. The administrator reflected for a minute or two about his own career prospect, and the good that a few hundred exemplary prosecutions might do for it. He accepted the offer. The local officer thereupon had his cosiest winter since the revolution, while his town had its coldest and most law-abiding, with a full jail. On the strength of that success the local officer was told that his personal licence would continue for as long as he ran his town strictly according to the book. He agreed, but he had to come back before long to ask for similar personal licences for the rank and file in his office because they were his eyes and ears and he needed their active coopera-tion. By this time the central government was watching the experiment, and it now intervened to ask whether the energy-cost of such extra licences could be saved out of the town's allocation, i.e. shaved off the public fuel rations. It could be, and it was.

Within a couple of years that special fuel licence, with hundreds of thousands like it, had become the dynamic of the environmental revolu-tion. Above-ration entitlements were graded and adapted to rank, or to payment by results, and extended to all tenured public servants during good behavior, then to approved lists of managers, professionals and other key personnel throughout the private as well as the public sectors. Along with the licences went an educational campaign to remind licensees that the good things would keep coming only as long as the good things were still there – only as long as conservationist policies were strictly conceived and enforced. A licence-holder convicted of any environ-mental breach lost his licences and reverted to standard subsistence rations; and anyone helping to detect and convict such an offender became entitled to a cut from the cancelled licences.

Thus the revolution began to work when the people who had to enforce it got an interest in enforcing it. It was a tense, difficult kind of government and it was vital that they do it well: it needed subtle policy-making, able management, persuasive justification. To ensure the quality of these skilled services there had to be graded incentives in the

2-2

tough competition for jobs within the ruling class – but also a broad solidarity within it. Those two requirements of competition and solidarity could be reconciled by giving the class as a whole graded rewards, but substantially higher rewards than their subjects. Higher consumption by the ruling class is not necessarily a betrayal of the revolution. It is environmentally acceptable as long as it motivates more-than-equivalent savings elsewhere. With experience, it does. The ruling class is toughened by internal competition, and further toughened by a growing dislike and contempt for the increasingly sullen and petty-corruptible subject class. Widespread and penetrating networks of information and control are now built on the central principle that there is only so much, and the biggest shares of it go to those with the power and ingenuity to cause the biggest reductions in other people's shares without provoking suicidal revolts. It is a sort of reverse piece-rates system – people are rewarded *pro rata* to the production they prevent.

The basic instrument of control has been improved since its primitive beginnings. Fuel officers want to be rewarded with other goods besides fuel, housing officers want other goods besides housing, and innumerable people whose jobs do not give them such direct control of particular products must nevertheless be motivated in the same way. The *ad hoc* special licences have been replaced by an all-purpose ration currency which can buy above-ration quantities of any rationed goods. So members of the ruling class now have dual incomes: regular scales of money, and variable *ex gratia* allowances of ration currency. Some government economists would prefer a single currency – obviously a free market would then distribute the scarcer goods to the higher incomes, and that should provide differential incentives. But the governors prefer to keep direct control of everybody's basic rations, if only to avoid needless strife between the classes. It would be bad if either class could bid for the other's staples. The rich should not be allowed to outbid the poor for their rationed necessities of life. At the same time a great many unrestricted goods are produced to keep the poor happy – low-energy entertainments, hand-made furnishings and clothes and toys, various personal services, and plenty of lollies, alcohol, tobacco and hallucinators. (The last few may harm their users but producing them does very little harm to anyone else.) It is essential that the masses be given purchasing power adjustable to the supply of these unrestricted goods, but it has to be a form of purchasing power which cannot be used to increase their market demands on the restricted goods which supply vital incentives to the ruling class. The rationing arrangements and the dual currency achieve this.

Important decisions had to be taken as to which goods should be restricted, and at what values of ration currency. Most material goods and services could be classified by their use of scarce materials or their spillover of pollution. Other goods were more difficult, especially the shared facilities whose over-use had inspired the idea of 'the tragedy of the commons'. As the classical method of reducing the use of commons, the governors were at first inclined to sell the relevant land or water back into private or club ownership. But this soon annoyed too many influential people. A ruling class wants access to all its favorite mountains and woods and coastlines, and it wants them well managed at public expense. Ways had to be found of excluding unwanted users without excluding the ruling classes themselves. Surprisingly, the methods finally adopted have been – in part, and after a fashion – egalitarian. It happened that those who originally led this very conservative revolution included a few friends of the earth who were driven chiefly by love of the wilderness. After the revolution these romantics were too unworldly to be trusted with anything else, so they were appointed to manage the national parks. They are aristocrats, but strictly of the spirit. They remember that if Scott of the Antarctic was a gentleman, Amundsen was not. A colonial farmer and a native porter conquered Everest. People of every social class used to hunt the American woods in season – and poach them out of season. There are such natural aristocrats in all social classes, and it is for the natural aristocrats that many wild places are now reserved by the simple method of making them hard to reach. They are a very long way from roads or railway stations. It is necessary to walk, climb, swim, sleep out. There are no trail-bikes, no four-wheel-drives, no helicopters. Of course there had to be exceptions. It was not possible to keep all the wild places out of reach of the more banal reactionaries who increasingly constitute the ruling class. Some conventional attractions – mechanized snow slopes, pine-scented alpine lakes, idyllic tropical islands – are kept accessible by road, rail or air, to those with the necessary licences, cars or cash.

So in the end there are three general kinds of resort. The natural aristocrats have the true wilderness to themselves, to climb the peaks, walk the trails, canoe the rivers, photograph the wild life and camp out of reach of mechanical noises or services. Then the bulk of the ruling class have areas modified by roads and power and resort hotels but protected as appropriate by toll-gates, high prices, sharkproof fences or the exclusion of public transport. Here they do their Palm Beach sunning and boozing and fornicating, their shooting and fishing, skiing and skating, trail-bike and dune-buggy driving, skin-diving and water-skiing, and even some simulated camping with trailer tents, battery lights and bottled gas. Finally, in and around the cities, the masses can ride buses or bikes to picnic in hard-wearing public parks studded with inspectors, litter bins, lunch kiosks and public lavatories. They can visit a few Coney Islands and Blackpools, paddle from suburban beaches, and save up for more ambitious coach tours to view certain natural wonders and panoramas from defined viewing areas. Thus there is something for everybody – just as there was in that golden age of the early twentieth century when a few discriminating people could walk with rucksacks or drive by private car deep into an unspoiled countryside, while the rest had a good old booze-up and community sing on occasional excursions by Sunday train or bank-holiday charabanc or paddle-steamer.

Like the parks and countryside, the cities also have their zoning arrangements. Most of these are of the conventional kind – rich suburbs are zoned for rich residents, poor suburbs are zoned for homogeneous degradation by industry and public housing; and so on. Segregation is a sensible principle whenever it is desired to give radically unequal treatment to different classes of people. It has a long history in city planning and government, and in the management of subject races. In the 1960s some environmental economists re-named segregation 'separate facilities' and one of them even claimed to have invented it. But it was left to the new regimes to adapt the principle to their distinctive problems of surplus population.

These particular population problems were unexpected. Unemployment should in theory have been entirely cured by the shortage of energy. But however widely the industrial societies returned to manual energy, they were still troubled by surplus people – not just by a general pressure of numbers on resources, but by specific blocs and strata of unskilled or inappropriately skilled people, structurally surplus to any likely requirements of the economic system. Ways had to be found for these unfortunates to live out their lifetimes, preferably contributing as much as possible to their own upkeep but as few children as possible to the perpetuation of their dysfunctional kind. They threatened to become a permanent, sad and perhaps dangerous presence in the big cities, rotting and breeding and surviving there on petty theft and public relief.

At the same time, independently, within the central government the general notion of decentralization was being passed around from desk to desk in a slightly embarrassed manner. It had been pressed hard in environmentalist propaganda before the establishment of the emergency regimes. But in practice it was making no progress – nobody knew quite

how to decentralize in circumstances of static population, doubled building costs and no economic growth; and not many administrators wanted to go administering in distant country towns.

Then one day somebody earned himself a lifetime of double rations by connecting the problem of decentralization with the problem of the welfare population. The link arose from correcting an old misunderstanding of the significance of South Africa's Bantustans. Those native homelands had always been debated as right or wrong answers to a *racial* problem. Why not see them as answers to a *surplus* or *welfare* problem? Even South Africa does not send all blacks to the homelands, only unwanted blacks for whom the white economy has no use. Once there they are out of the whites' way, cheap to maintain, and they have only each other to prey on so they can be left to handle most of their own law and order.

On that basis the new regimes developed what their residents call Siberian Bantustans or Dakota Poorhouses, while the authorities after various nervous changes of nomenclature now call them New Life Settlements. Suitable country districts, usually of marginal farmland, are cleared and proclaimed as New Life Settlements, and most forms of public relief then cease to be available anywhere else. Residence in a Settlement becomes the normal condition of permanent welfare support.

The policy is not as cruel as it sounds, or as it may one day have to become. Much of the old environmentalist enthusiasm for the simple life close to the soil finds its fullest expression in the Settlements. The family is respected. It always can and often does go into the Settlement together, where it may begin by building its own family shack with its own labor and the natural materials to hand. After that there is work of one sort or another for most of the inmates. They cannot of course be paid economic wages for such sub-economic work, and the Settlements cannot be given vast quantities of first-class land, which they would anyway mismanage. But they do have the means of contributing a good deal to their own support. They raise some pigs and poultry, and some fruit and vegetables. Requirements of professional qualifications are suspended to allow them to supply most of their own teaching and nursing and other personal services. They do their own building and public works. Considerable numbers could thus live off the land and survive after a fashion if they had to. So far, they do not have to – welfare allowances continue, and are spent on importing some food and electric power and other necessaries into the Settlements. The scale of this external aid is not lavish but it is no worse than it often was in the displaced persons' camps of Europe or Palestine, with which it seems fair to compare this new provision for a similarly unwanted population. No mass medication or forced birth control is applied.

Like the Bantustans, the New Life Settlements are quietly being fenced so that their boundaries could be policed if necessary. It would be possible to seal them and require them to live off their own resources. Natural factors rather than any direct unpleasantness could thus be brought into play to effect any necessary run-down of unwanted numbers.

5

In these and other ways the successors to the rich consumer societies have moved back towards aristocratic patterns of inequality. There are comparatively high rewards for small minorities of rulers and their necessary entourage of technicians and enforcers. There are not many social theorists under the new regimes, and they are not encouraged to stray to Left or Right, but 'soft' and 'hard' tendencies are tolerated. In print the soft theorists sum up the distributional system as 'a sufficiency for all, graded to motivate the social function of each, within the overall discipline of ecological survival'. Over whiskies at sundown the hard party sum up the arrangements for motivating the masses as a square meal at bedtime and a clear view of the gallows at all times. Both parties brush off any self-righteous criticism from the few remaining foreign liberals. They insist that their societies use inequalities as all societies have done. Their unequal rations perform functions of incentive and social control that are performed anywhere else by unequal incomes. If policing and coercion have to be rather severe through the transitional phase, that also has been normal whenever historical transitions have had to intensify scarcities or inequalities. The new regimes are no tougher than the British were through their last round of enclosures, or the Russians through their first collectivization.

They are nevertheless severe. They have to be. Many millions of households have had to give up their precious cars and gadgets. Millions of over-educated men have had to descend to lower-grade labor at half the real incomes they once expected. Millions who dreamed of imaginative futures for their children must now see them brought up to monotonous work as a subject race of poor-whites. Worst of all, the transitional generation had to live through the painful sorting-out in which each member of the old, vaguely-defined middle classes had to be distributed either to the clear-cut new ruling class, or to the new mass. That sorting-out was the point of no return. It left the winners quite clear about the feelings of the losers, and aware that they themselves could never now survive any return to democracy.

But what else could the governors have done? Fair sharing of the hardships of deliberate scarcity had been tried. It had failed. To let the old middle and skilled classes – half or more of the population – return to their old indulgent standards of living would have fatally frustrated the frugal purposes of the revolution. The limited ruling class was an inescapable necessity of the no-growth, simple-life type of revolution which the conservatives had chosen. So inescapably, such a limited ruling class had to be sorted out from the rest. In the process, a great many average-aggressive heads of households were forced to accept second-class citizenship – some because they happened to be in high-energy or pollutant lines of work which were simply closed down; some because they had liberal or leftish records; some because they lacked well-placed friends or relations at vital moments; some because they wouldn't demean themselves in the murderous scramble for the lifeboat. Meanwhile the lucky fifth of the population who happened to be indispensable technicians or public servants, or politically acceptable, or quick with their footwork at critical moments – or rich – landed above the line, where their descendants now strut, rewarding themselves with unfair shares of the common resources, the self-appointed bearers of Civilization As We Know It.

So the sanctions do have to be severe. In their milder moments the subjects do sometimes call their new masters the South African Whites, and some of the masters do boast of their achievements in distinctly South African tones of voice. After all, the South African subject class has long been the best-fed, best-paid subject class in Africa. Similarly it is where the new environmental regimes have maintained the toughest discipline that they have done most to stabilize their natural resource systems and to weather the environmental crises which carried them to power in the first place.

But the policing does have to be severe. It has to include censorship of 'anti-environmentalist incitement' and 'eco-suicidal sedition', which is how the authorities define any criticism of their class privileges or their rationing and policing arrangements. It has to include undercover surveillance to pick off potentially rebellious leaders before they have time to build any networks. It has to include plenty of administrative punishment – the whole point of the ration-currency is that it is a privilege not a right, to be taken away at will by anyone's superiors. There is also administrative house-arrest, imprisonment, and confinement to the New Life Settlements – there has to be, or the social discipline based on the New Life Settlements could never be effectively maintained.

Sometimes the problems of persuasion and belief seem even more difficult than the problems of coercion. For example, the governors know that the general austerity is a preferable alternative to doomsday, and it is not impossible to persuade most journalists and schoolteachers of that. But the governors also know that the necessary environmental disciplines could never be maintained without the special motivation of the ruling class. It is much harder to persuade journalists and teachers of *that* – especially as between them they make up the numerous bottom rank – the lowest-paid rank – of the ruling class. The teachers' disaffection shows in various ways. Sometimes it is positive – they inculcate critical and disaffected attitudes into the children whom they teach. More often it is negative – they fail to teach positive explanation and support for the class structure and the vital functions it performs. Some of the governors think it prudent to leave the teachers alone if they go no further than that – if they form no undercover organizations and circulate no seditious papers. Nevertheless such low-keyed disaffection does make more occasions for coercion and police work in the end, because it is in such disgruntled atmospheres that active opposition and conspiracy flourish. There is consequently some pushing and pulling between the soft and hard factions in government. For a year or two the teachers are left alone. Then a few of them go too far and tougher policies take over for a while. A few score are jailed and a few hundred are purged from the profession, which means from the ruling class. Intellectuals ejected from the ruling class are so automatically dangerous that they are automatically ordered to the more remote New Life Settlements, and jailed if they don't go there. Eventually the soft faction persuades the governors that the pressure is doing more harm than good to the loyalty of the schools, and the pressure eases. It is a subtle problem. The regime would be happy to see less education all round, and to kick the teachers out of the last of their ruling-class privileges. But on the other hand schoolteaching is a fine cheap non-pollutant occupation for keeping otherwise dangerous people marginally privileged and at least half contented. Voluntary loyalty is *always* best, if you can get it.

And so it goes on. The regime should be given its due. It maintains the discipline which is the condition for environmental self-restraint and survival for the whole society. And for the sake of its own peace and security it does genuinely try to maintain the discipline with as little violence as possible, and as much peaceful persuasion and voluntary support as possible. It is this genuine concern to gentle the autocracy, to economize force and even fear, to preserve wide areas of upper-class freedom, and to establish a hereditary ruling class of about a fifth of the whole population, which gives the enterprise its South African flavor and its special debt to South African experience. Nevertheless, as in South Africa, one of the most unexpected and disappointing features of the whole experiment has been the extent of its inroads into the personal liberties of the ruling classes themselves. There is still a wide, if uncertain, freedom of speech. But rebellious youngsters and other dissident individuals who persist in abusing their liberties do eventually encounter the full severities of a police state. Even loyal conformists are irked by the routine quantities of delay, suspicion and red tape which are unavoidable in the administration of such all-inclusive economic and social controls.

So the price is high. But so is the achievement – a successful environmental stabilization, achieved in a safe conservative way without gambling on unpredictable technological futures. Within the rich white world this historic change of direction has been achieved without mass death from environmental disasters, or mass murder provoked by the fear of it, or mass extermination of the Nazi kind.

6

Some Anglo-Eskimo scholars – the last enclave with an uncensored English-language press – have drawn attention to what they see as the nearest historical parallel to the achievement, namely the general reconstruction of English life and landscape which took place in the century between about 1740 and 1840.

Through most of that time (the Anglo-Eskimos say) political power belonged to a small class of town and country proprietors. They used it by legal, military, commercial and other means to change the ownership and management of about half of the arable land in England – and from a Red Indian point of view a fair proportion of the land in North and Caribbean America. These transfers, together with the new techniques applied to the consolidated acres, were used to establish radically new scales of domestic and international inequality. Subsistence levels for the masses held steady or even fell; for a century the lion's share of all improvement was creamed off by the proprietors through rent, wage, industrial, tax and military policies of unparalleled profitability. Through much of central England one whole agrarian eco-system was replaced by another. In little more than a generation the new proprietors and their tenants built what is now remembered nostalgically as the 'immemorial' English country landscape of hedged and ditched fields, naturally ferti-lized rotational farming, protected waters and forests, lonely coasts and highlands, and the stable eco-systems of permanently stocked partridge woods, fox coverts, deer parks, grouse moors and trout and salmon streams.

In the course of the change, many common rights to arable land and pasture, fuel, fish and game were converted to private property by Act of Parliament or other legal process. Of course such transfers of wealth and rights, with new extremes of hardship and inequality, required severe enforcement. At home the death penalty was extended to three times as many offences as formerly. Record numbers crowded the prison hulks and penal colonies. Labor discipline was harsh, at home and overseas. For every white life in England in that century there was an early black death in the separate facility across the Atlantic. But the most beautiful landscape in English history was ready for the romantic poets. Unhappily a good deal of it was soon spoiled again; but it might all have been there still if the steam engine had not started other changes.

The makers of the new environmental revolution and the new environ-mental landscape have taken better care of that latter sort of danger. They permit very little research or technical change, and they keep what there is of it under watchful political direction. Contraceptive research continues and simple methods have been developed for early abortion and for determining the sex of children at conception. These are the main items in the reformed societies' international aid programs. Poor societies are helped to contracept, to abort, and (less successfully) to implement social preferences for male children. A 'three to one' campaign made some progress in one or two territories where the white professionals in the aid services played tricks with the contraceptive and sex-determinant pills. The programs were doubly effective while they lasted. As the imbalance developed within the native peasantry and proletariat the female minorities were brothelized (as expected) but also enslaved and overworked to keep up the farming and domestic services traditionally expected of women in poor societies, so they developed abnormal rates of miscarriage, exhaustion and early death. In all cases the males rebelled before long, and the recoil often hit the contraceptive as well as the sex-determinant services.

Meanwhile no aid is given to increase conventional production, consumption or length of life. News of African and Asian famine is received gravely in the reformed white world – but as good news nonetheless. In the interest of humanity, the rich have learned to welcome the death of the poor.

2
Business as usual

Instead of that fanciful scenario, what really happened was much less dramatic. The democracies continued to follow commonsense American leadership. They improved their scientific, technical and administrative approaches to environmental problems, and found gentler ways of increasing their inequalities.

1

Environmental stresses varied from year to year and from country to country according to national luck and resources. But however the problems varied, the democracies dealt with them routinely. They developed their existing machinery for rural and urban conservation, national parks, clean air and water, pure food, public health, and so on. Whenever they found those well-tried methods insufficient they made pragmatic innovations of the kinds recommended by their environmental economists and administrators.

Inequalities increased. That was not because environmental politicians introduced reactionary philosophies – being democratic politicians they assured the world as blandly as ever that their policies had scarcely any costs and benefited everybody. But although there was no systematic philosophy of distribution there was a systematic effect: inequalities increased. They did not increase to a South African scale. The democracies were not as bad as the frostbitten oligarchies of the previous chapter. For one thing they were not as frugal. Perhaps self-government is always self-indulgent, as the oligarchs alleged. Democracies do seem to behave, like many of their investors and economists, as 5 percenters – they discount futures at 5% per year and rarely worry more than twenty years ahead. That is far enough to iron out short fluctuations – after the famous one in the 1970s there have been no more *temporary* fuel crises – but of course it is not far enough ahead to guarantee the perpetual stability that some conservationists dream of. Democratic administrators can't prove that there will never be a global doomsday. But they do invest heavily in research and technical development. Whether or not that averts any doomsday it makes life more comfortable meanwhile. Whenever a technical change ameliorates an environmental problem, to that degree the need for abstinence is less.

So the hardships are less. For democratic reasons they are also a little better distributed. Traditions of welfare have survived, the votes of the poor still carry some weight, labor unions have held on to some entrenched positions. There were also for a while some traditions of common cause and shared sacrifice. They lived on as sentimental memories of national crises rather than as peacetime principles of commercial or political behavior, so it was only in times of crisis that they had much effect – which accounts for an ironical rhythm in the relations between inequalities and environmental troubles. There were periods when new troubles were mild enough to be met without actual loss – the year's new corrective measures absorbed only part of the year's increase of productivity. Such light costs were spread as imperceptibly as possible, usually through inflation and price movements, to fall chiefly onto the mass of householders and consumers. Thus the years of least trouble saw least increase of hardship, but most increase of inequality. At the opposite extreme were times of crisis when there was negative economic growth, with sudden unemployment and acute shortages of particular resources. Those more dramatic hardships had to be distributed with a greater show of fairness. There were emergency doles and transfers, emergency rations. Some rich accepted symbolic losses, sometimes real, usually temporary. So in bad years there was more suffering but slightly less inequity.

The democracies were thus gentler in the way they increase inequalities – but they did increase them. They did it negatively by their responses to shortages, involuntarily by their mechanisms of inflation, and positively by the way they distributed the costs and consequences of environmental reform.

2

Some early problems with energy illustrated the negatives well enough. There were permanent oil price increases and temporary refining shortages in the 1970s. National responses varied. Sweden distributed free fuel to any poorer householders who still depended on oil-fired heat, and rationed gasoline at prices high enough to discourage its use and pay for the free heat too. Britain rationed oil products, controlled prices for a couple of years, had to subsidize them, and policed black marketing with

41

fair success. The United States avoided national rationing or price control, but encouraged people to economize. Airlines rationalized bookings and shared some flights. A lot of firms diverted commercial gasoline to supply their employees. Defence gasoline filled more than a few civilian tanks, police consumption of gasoline mysteriously trebled. But the racketeering was not thought to be doing any serious harm. There were emergency arrangements to heat most hospitals and schools. Most cold states and cities went on heating their public housing without abnormal increases of rents. Office temperatures moved a few degrees nearer to outside temperatures; streets were darker at night. And all the screens and speakers in the land beat out the message to save fuel, or energy generally, or the planet once more – people were exhorted to turn it off, do it in the dark, rinse it by hand, share a shower, ride instead of drive, walk instead of ride, pray at home this Sunday. Responses went beyond strict relevance to the price of gasoline. Supermarkets choked under another general return of containers. Some of the fuel saved elsewhere was used to transport New England plumbers to attend to cisterns that had been overfilled with bricks, often in the dark.

On balance the American rich got more than their share of whatever was short. But at least they paid high prices for it, or their firms did, though of course it was mostly paid to other rich, who collected the same prices from the American poor also. The British rich got exactly their share, with poor taxpayers helping to subsidize it. Working-class motorists did better in Britain than elsewhere, but there were less of them there than elsewhere. The very poor probably did best in Sweden, except a few who tried to distil something drinkable from the free boiler fuel.

There were longer-lasting effects on general energy and conservation policies, and these effects also were very mixed. Norway moved to reduce its dependence on staple exports of shipping, timber and hydro-electrics: Norwegian North Sea oil should fuel Norwegian ships and industries, and beyond that it should finance such an international capital portfolio that the country need never sell another tree or refine another ton of aluminium. In Scandinavia the conservationists had won. In the United States they knew they had lost, and surrendered without a fight to the Alaska pipeline and a dozen new nuclear and petro-chemical installations that they had been successfully resisting for years.

A more significant effect of the crisis was the massive switch of investment into research and development for alternative energy sources. Returns to this investment have been famously uneven. There are now

New Zealand cities with nearly-free geothermal energy for everything except motoring; while in other countries on other geology, geothermal stations generate some of the dearest electricity in the world. About half the English who ran cars in 1975 don't have them now, and many of the other half trundle around close to home and avoiding hills, battery-driven. Their loss may nevertheless be less painful than some alternatives to it. Australian working-class incomes are now more than twice British, but a large part of the difference goes to pay for the oil the Australians still use because their cities were never shaped or equipped to do without it. There are similar contrasts between solar programs. In what seemed once to promise a brilliant reconciliation between the conservationist movement and the defence and airspace industries, immense amounts of American effort were written off in attempts to develop safe orbital sun traps. The European governments who trampled over so many conservationists and peasants and exotic nesting grounds to clear the fearful expanses of their ground solar stations have really served their poorer citizens better, and they may also have saved other land and seascapes from other devastations.

The cost of energy, the economizing of it, and what you can enjoy without it – the local relations of those three are what determine most people's fortunes. In the least-favored national and local circumstances, low incomes are thought to be losing as much as a third of their 1975 values to direct and indirect effects of the movement of energy prices since that date. No rich anywhere have lost that proportion of spendable income to the same cause. Effects vary with location, climate, urban forms and spending patterns. But for the masses everywhere, more has depended on basic economic developments and on the luck of local resources than on crisis-management and other band-aid policies. Nothing saves the masses in the long run from the effects of rising costs for their necessaries. Even to save their relativities – to spread losses fairly over rich and poor incomes – would usually require permanent rationing and price control. With many commodities that could only be enforced by nationalization and public ownership. And that whole radical package might only be worth its costs in countries self-sufficient in the materials and processes concerned.

But there are very few places left in which radicals could imaginably make effective use of the machinery of government. Most American government, and a good deal of French, is for practical purposes privately owned. There is so *much* unofficial money about these days, such overwhelming offers you can't refuse. Countries which still have honest politicians and public servants tend to be conservative in other ways too. Frightened majorities of their voters look backwards, and cling wherever they can to the symbols and substance of past stabilities. They don't want government to add wilfully to the quantity of change, which is already unnerving. Social-democratic parties stick to the middle of the road or languish out of office. Rougher radicals make money rather than progress – assassination can be profitable but it cannot govern.

In business – overlapping more than ever into crime and government – there are more and bigger collapses than there used to be, but also wilder personal fortunes. The fortunes don't buy much art these days. The sheiks and their successors bring new subtleties of law and order to the desert, while their sons and lovers and compradores bring new devices of pleasure and personal security to the tourist coasts of the western world. Most of their money snowballs lawfully under respectable management from Zurich and Wall Street, but enough of it is laundered elsewhere to buy whatever law, immunity or terrorist service they need.

3

Bad as the effects of shortages were, positive environmental reforms did just as much to increase inequalities.

That was not because new environmental goods were distributed unfairly (though they often were). Who benefited by them was a matter of political choice and investment policy. New parks were built into poor as well as rich districts. Local clean-ups benefited poor as well as rich localities. Cleaner food, water and air often benefited everybody. The choice of programs varied with time and place, from progressive to reactionary, but at least it was deliberate and open to democratic influence.

It was in distributing the costs rather than the benefits of reform that the democracies were systematically reactionary. When the conventional wisdom of the environmental professions was combined with conventional remedies for inflation and the conventional principles of democratic administration, the increase of inequality was automatic.

A very few environmental reforms, such as better urban planning and some technical economizing of energy, were costless or even profitable. But most reforms had costs. There were capital costs of conservation and public works, costs of administrative and monitoring services, capital and current costs of producing goods and services by less pollutant processes or with more expensive materials. The public costs came from taxes and user-charges. The private costs were occasionally subsidized from taxation but they normally went onto retail prices. Local taxes were regressive, national taxes were not much better and a great many of the higher prices were for food, transport, services, consumer durables and other necessaries. So the cost of environmental reform began by going onto everyman's cost of living, usually at flat rates with regressive effects. Most of the strong bargainers in society – owners, professional and salaried people, some self-employed and the stronger sectors of organized labor – then protected their real incomes by pushing their pay ahead of the rising costs of living, while weaker bargainers couldn't and didn't. Thus the regular mechanism of inflation made sure that the final distribution of costs was not even 'flat', i.e. the same for rich and poor. A high proportion of all the costs of environmental reform came out of the consumption of the weak bargainers – the poorer half (or so) of most national populations.

That further unequalizing of material shares was bad enough. Its effect on real welfare and real suffering was worse, for a number of reasons most of which applied to any cost increases, environmental or otherwise. First (to simplify some complicated welfare philosophies) the poor usually needed their whole incomes more desperately than the rich did. The satisfactions which different people derive from their incomes cannot be compared with scientific precision but there is not much doubt that marginal changes to low incomes tend to help or hurt people more than marginal changes to high incomes do. (If you doubt it, as most orthodox economists professed to do through the third quarter of the twentieth century, imagine families with respectively $1,000, $100 and $50 a week. Try subtracting 50% from each. Try subtracting $50 from each.)

Second, rich and poor had different freedom to save or spend. Poor saving (when the poor could save at all) tended to be necessitous, or directly related to consumption: debt repayment, savings-bank accounts for clothing, equipment, holidays and emergencies, insurance for old age. The rich could afford to be more flexible. So when the poor lost income they lost goods. If the rich lost income they could choose to consume less, to save less, or to spend capital. For people on middle incomes saving less might mean consuming less one day, perhaps in retirement. For the solidly rich, saving less at one time merely meant saving less later too – a slower accumulation of capital with no necessary effect on consumption at any date. So when everybody 'equally' lost a dollar, the poor often had only one course of action, people with middle incomes could choose between two and the solidly rich could choose between three or four.

Short of rationing or drastic capital levies, governments couldn't touch the material living standards of the rich. So sacrifices of consumption were never distributed equitably.

Third, when public environmental action caused private losses most rich losers passed their losses on, or collected compensation. But for most poor losers the losses were inescapable. Rich 'losers' were manufacturers or traders who passed higher costs on to the selling prices of their products; or they were proprietors and the effect of public action on their properties could be proved, measured and compensated. The poorer losers were the innumerable consumers of regulated, taxed or higher-priced goods and services, or they were direct or indirect sufferers from spreading ripples of industrial dislocation and unemployment. Even if governments wanted to help them it was not usually possible to identify them all or to draw any politically acceptable line between those who deserved compensation and those who didn't. For example if a pollutant factory was shut down in a small town, should compensation stop with its labor? Or with shopkeepers who lost business, or residents whose houses lost value, or families who must uproot and move from what must now be a dying town? With the best will in the world (a phrase whose frequency of use was usually proportional to the suffering going uncompensated) such people must usually carry their own losses. When the losses were spread through higher prices compensation was out of the question – it would have defeated the purpose of reforms whose whole point was to restrain environmentally-undesirable consumption.

These effects were reinforced by entrenched legal and ideological discriminations between rich and poor losses.

It had long been accepted that governments could confiscate income or restrict consumption. Income and sales taxes, production quotas and price supports, controlled inflation and other official manipulations of private income and purchasing power were as American as apple pie. Governments were not supposed to cause direct unemployment if they could help it, but if they did, the victims rarely had an enforceable case for compensation and it was anyway orthodox to believe that *full* compensation for unemployment would destroy incentives to work. (This morality of course depended on the class of the worker. Wage earners would be demoralized by unearned income so unemployment compensations or doles must always be less than wages and must cease if the people went back to work. But if executives, managers or members of parliament had their jobs extinguished it was right to compensate them heavily, by capital sums or permanent pensions.)

By contrast it was thought absolutely wrong for the state to cause capital losses. Modest capital or inheritance taxes might be tolerable but to make any general levy of capital or to shut down particular factories or injure particular investments without compensation would amount to revolutionary confiscation. It would be an offence against democratic rights and liberties as well as against property; many countries had entrenched constitutional protections against it. So if government endangered *earned* incomes by closing a factory, wage earners might get a few weeks' pay then a few months' unemployment dole; salaried staff might get a few months' or years' pay; but the owners' *unearned* incomes had to be continued in full, in perpetuity, by full capital compensation. There could be argument about such differential morality but there was no doubt about its effects: the poor paid and suffered most of the costs of reform.

The economists of the time generally shrugged off these effects. 'Rising environmental costs are like any other rising costs. Of course they have to go onto prices, as any costs do. If society doesn't like the resulting distribution of real incomes it can correct it by independent political action through taxes and welfare policies.' That was all very well, but compared with normal industrial and commercial cost increases, environmental costs often had some special and additional bias. First, many of them were caused by state action so that richer 'sufferers' were compensated as they would never have been for ordinary business hazards. Second, most normal increases to costs of production arose in practice from rising labor costs. Consumers suffered but labor gained, so there might not be much class loss. But there tended to be very little of that wage element in environmental cost increases. Environmental costs rose for other reasons. (Buy more machinery to process waste or suppress smoke; build the power station at a less efficient location; use more fuel and transport to bring aggregate from more distant quarries; use less energy and more manual labor; and so on.) The changes might employ more hands but they didn't raise anybody's wages; they raised prices without much in-built class compensation.

When compensation problems did arise they were so troublesome that governments developed an experienced order of preference among alternative approaches to reform and the distribution of its costs. It was a 'least trouble' order of preference. The most-preferred methods were those which would distribute costs unobtrusively through marginal movements of prices, employment or general inflation. Next came methods which used tax money (or inflationary budgeting) to finance comparatively few capital compensations – such big compensations were usually simple to assess and administer, and to fight through the courts if need be. (In corrupt states that big-money method went to the top of the preferred list because it allowed the biggest personal gains to industrialists and public officials alike.) The least favored methods were those which called for large numbers of re-training and relocation arrangements, or many small individually-assessed compensation payments to employees, residents or small businesses. Those had high administrative costs and were a trying nuisance to administrators, while politicians usually lost more support than they gained if there were too many cases of disputed individual entitlement – the bureaucrats were always clumsy with a few of them, and a very few aggrieved or evicted households could generate indignation on a great many front pages.

On the central issue the economists were nevertheless right. *Some* environmental reform could be designed to distribute its benefits and costs with deliberate fairness, but most of it was not of that kind. For genuinely technical reasons its costs would distribute themselves with automatic unfairness. Therefore it needed to be accompanied by other, independent action to redress the inequalities it caused. It rarely was so redressed. The reasons for that failure were chiefly political.

4

Environmental reform offered some natural tactical advantages to the Right.

Right and Left would often agree that a particular industry must be made to reduce some pollution or recycle some wastes. Unless that could be done by using otherwise unemployed resources it reduced national output. How should the corresponding sacrifice of consumption be distributed? For various reasons Right and Left usually agreed to begin by making the manufacturers clean up their operations at their own expense. The manufacturers put the costs onto their selling prices. If the products were the sort that most people bought, the end costs of the reform were thus spread regressively. To restore the original relativities would have required some independent adjustment of taxes, welfare or subsidies. But tampering with those national distributions was no part of the parties' limited cooperation to abate some smoke or recycle some metals. So at that point, the Right would simply lose interest. Pollution had been visibly reduced, inequality had been quietly, almost invisibly increased and the Left had joined in voting for both. What could be better?

Similar tactics worked over a wide field. When costs of reform had to come from taxation the Right voted to keep the taxation local, indirect or otherwise regressive. They defended the distinctions between compensatable proprietors and less compensatable consumers and wage-earners. As between proprietors, they perpetuated the old practice of compensating industrial and commercial owners (for 'profits forgone') more liberally than owner-occupiers of houses. Tenants were rarely compensated at all. As between banning, regulating, taxing, pricing, purchasing or confiscating environmentally troublesome activities, they worked in each case for whichever method cost the rich least.

Time after time the Left lost to the asymmetry illustrated above: the nature of the problems was such that the Left usually needed two independent reforms, one environmental and the other distributional, while the Right needed only the first one. So the Left could win only where they governed by undivided majority. Wherever it was hard to get majorities for change and environmental action depended on some support from both sides or from many factions – wherever there were international agreements, federal systems, divided powers, unstable majorities or coalitions with factions wheeling and dealing without much party discipline – the Right did almost as well as when it governed alone. One or more of those conditions held most of the time in most rich democracies so the Right rarely did badly.

Meanwhile the Left was often weakened by internal splits and disagreements. It had traditional disunities, for example between communists and social-democrats or between old unionists and new technocrats. Environmental issues added new causes for dissension. Some fraction of the old Left or the labor unions could usually be found to defend almost any environmental abuse – to defend automobile, airspace, defence or petro-chemical workers from loss of work, to defend quarrying or timber-getting or power-generating or chemical-processing industries from threatened cut-backs or shut-downs – and also to defend the needy of their own generation from high-minded proposals to leave the gas in the ground or the fish in the sea for somebody else's grandchildren.

Those stubborn rearguards of simple materialism seemed myopic to other branches of the Left – the New Left, the environmental Left. Left environmentalists did not believe that they stood to the Right of their traditional brethren – in putting redistribution before economic growth they could often claim to stand to the Left of them. Some were quite offensive about it. They noticed what strange bedfellows seemed suddenly to be protecting pollutant and luxury industries. Auto workers supported auto makers who went on making over-powered cars. Petro-

49

chemical workers supported the building of new oil terminals and refineries. There was across-the-board support in Bristol and Seattle for the supersonic transport of the very rich. And so on. All those happened to be high-wage trades. Had the Labor Aristocracy sold out?

Stung, the old Left began to observe that other people had funny friends too. What was 'Left' about deserting the wage interests of the working class to go wooing swinging voters on gimmicky issues like ecology (money for animals instead of people) and quality of life (money for trees instead of people)? What were the leaders of *any* Left doing on conference platforms with the millionaires of the environmental movement who wanted to take away the worker's gasoline, car, washing machine, home heat, industrial aids and other material fruits of a century of struggle?

While each half of the Left thus exhausted its energies shouting 'Right' 'sold out' or 'outdated' at the other, the real Right got on quietly with the up-to-date business of the Right – government coped with another shortage by 'letting the market adjust', put peak-hour tolls on more public roads, spent tax money to clean up more private rivers, dismantled 'oppressive' rationing, shifted another tax from incomes to commodities, traded more arms for more oil in the Middle East.

5

In these reactionary activities the leaders of the Right generally managed to appear as pragmatic middle-of-the-road liberals simply facing environmental facts and accepting the best technical advice. Plenty of the best technical advice was thoroughly reactionary. Some of it was politically committed but most of it came with apparent innocence from three professions whose members often believed themselves to be, in a professional way, politically neutral: public servants, the publicists of the environmental movement, and environmental and cost–benefit economists.

The public servants were most criticized by the Left but often deserved it least. They certainly had a pervasive influence over the choice and administration of public policies, and that quiet sort of influence had always been important. It normally took time, great gathering of forces and some public drama to win significant political victories for the poorer half of a democratic society. From time to time such a big effort did establish a big principle – of franchise, civil rights, progressive taxation – but a lot then depended on how the principle was administered or eroded in detail. Environmental administrators had similar opportunities. Their tastes did sometimes prompt them to spend too much on protecting wilderness parks, umbrageous suburbs, salmon fisheries or oyster beds, and too little on the landscape and services around slum schools or public housing. They didn't show much creative ingenuity in diverting burdens of cost away from the comparatively poor, or extracting taxes from the comparatively rich. Many of them nevertheless worked with more social conscience than their political masters. Some were outright dissenters, able critics of their own services, in-service spies on behalf of consumer-protection or other agitators. And the more conservative administrators' sins were usually negative – like everyone else 'with the best will in the world' they too often surrendered too easily to the technical difficulties of the environmental and economic problems themselves.

Some of the evangelists of the environmental movement were much more virulent. The worst were simple-minded doomsday men and eco-preachers who insisted that distribution didn't matter. If they had *reversed* the conventional belief that production mattered more than distribution they might have laid foundations for valuable alliances with the Left. But instead of reversing it they revised it: *stopping* production mattered more than distribution. The new message was nastier than the old – on a low income, taking more than your share of costs and cuts felt rather worse than getting less than your share of growth. The new principle was often helped along by a polemical trick. The trick was to treat all arguments about distributing environmental costs as if they were arguments against environmental action. Reformers who wanted to make the rich pay for reform were shrilly misrepresented as enemies of reform, feckless advocates of doomsday. 'The eco-crisis cannot wait on party politics – stop pollution NOW'.

The same message came more soberly, and to many people in government more persuasively, from many environmental economists. They wanted to let market prices distribute costs and shortages, and they wanted to affect business behavior by taxing rather than rationing or regulating. Such indirect methods nearly always had unequalizing effects. So did the use of cost–benefit analyses which took no account of distributions. In theory cost–benefit analyses could be designed to weight decisions in favor of any desired principles of distribution. In practice, weighting them for any except existing distributions had the effect of exposing the analysts' values very clearly. Some thought that damaged the scientific pretences of their work. Some thought it would provoke a lot of argument and prevent environmental action. So most analysts left the problems of distribution out of their calculations and encouraged politicians to do the same. If governments wanted to redistribute income they could do that afterwards by other methods, independently of their environmental policies which were already quite complicated enough. The difficulties were often genuine; but it was also true that separating the environmental from the distributional policies gave the Right all the tactical advantages described earlier.

The Left compromised or despaired or lived as ever on hope. There might yet be historical change, creative innovation, or new attempts at old-fashioned socialism. But very few of those hopes were realized in the affluent democracies in the last quarter of the twentieth century.

6

To sum up what happened instead and set it into historical perspective the first thing to do is to separate what changed from what did not.

What did not change was the material culture. As the twenty-first century opens, most daily life is much as it has been for three generations past. Except for a few jetsetters the range of lifestyles which the democracies offer, and the everyday quality of each style in the range, are much the same in 2001 as they were in 1975 or 1950 – or 1925, in most respects. Different proportions of the people are enjoying each of the available styles, that's all. The rich countries did not invent new ways of life in the twentieth century as they had done so copiously in the nineteenth. Twentieth-century people were frequently told that they were experiencing unprecedented rates of change; but in most of what mattered to most of them they were not. They were working at the production problems and the lateral diffusion and consolidation of a material culture put together long before by the generations of Watt and Stephenson, Pasteur and Lister, Otis and Edison, Benz and the Wrights and Marconi.

Consider an example of that material culture:

In the lucky countries which have enough fossil, hydroelectric or solar energy, a family gets up in the morning from comfortable beds in separate bedrooms in a house served by electric light and power, hot and cold water, sewerage, powered cooker and refrigerator, vacuum cleaner and washing machine. A phone call brings technicians to service the machinery when necessary; collectors take rubbish from the door. The house is in touch with the world by mail, books, magazines, newspapers with worldwide instantaneous communications. Electronic receivers bring some of the world's best entertainment (and enlightenment) into the house. For personal maintenance there are hairdressers and spectaclemakers, doctors and dentists and ambulance and hospital services; and strict social control of the qualifications of most of those experts.

To get to work and school the family may use anything from very little to a hundred miles or more of powered transport each day. The options include car, cab, bus, train, tram, motor or pedal cycle; or walking on sidewalks that are mostly paved, lit at night and policed with fair security. At school the children learn their own language and sometimes others; some literature; mathematics; natural and social sciences; some arts; and whether for work or pleasure, various skills and crafts. They may also publish their own papers, act, play music, go on excursions. They use boots and bats and other gear of strictly traditional design to play a strictly traditional repertoire of games. Adult recreations don't change much either. People play or watch indoor and outdoor ball games, gamble on some of them, race dogs and horses and each other. They play in the sea or the snow, they fish and shoot. They practise many arts and crafts. Those who can afford it eat out in restaurants decorated in nostalgic styles; they dance, hear music, watch plays on stage or screen, ask each other home, throw parties. They ride or drive to the beach, to picnic in the country, to visit friends and kin. Most of those pastimes and the gear they use change very little from generation to generation.

In the cities, powered transport moves people and goods about a dense maze of structures and activities. Workers work seven or eight hours a day five or six days a week, eleven months a year, and retire at sixty or sixty-five. After that the less successful have a room or two with necessaries and electronic entertainment, if not much else in a material way. The more successful may keep their family houses and vehicles through retirement, and travel a bit. The young can often travel too if they want to, working their way from coast to coast or saving for cheap tickets round the world.

The point of this familiar recital is its extreme familiarity. It describes the material circumstances in which middle-class people born under President McKinley or Queen Victoria married and began their careers and families in the 1920s; and line by line it fits most of the circumstances of their grandchildren's and great grandchildren's lives too. I am an old man now. My father was born in the nineteenth century, my sons and grandsons are working on into the twenty-first; our lifestyles, work and concerns are surprisingly alike. In the previous century there was indeed a revolution – next to none of the facts of 1920 were there in 1800. Most of the material kit, the household routines and schooling and games and leisure activities, many of the civil rights and social controls and most of the political parties and machinery of modern government were invented in the nineteenth century. The twentieth simply concentrated on mass-producing them.

So what has changed?

First, special effects: methods of war, trips to the moon, faster intercontinental travel. These don't affect most people's daily lives much, except vicariously, stocking their imaginations differently.

Second, methods of production change radically even though the products don't. Coal used to fire the electricity, then oil and uranium did, now sunshine and purpose-drilled volcanoes do some of it; but grandfather and grandson switch on the power in similar houses for similar purposes, and the 8.12 to the city hasn't varied its function or timetable in a hundred years. From grandfather's first Hupmobile through vehicles of changing efficiency and environmental menace to the electric runabouts of 2001, cars have done the same services for the families who owned them. Twentieth-century discoveries may have big effects on daily life one day – through genetic engineering, direct access to the brain, techniques of social surveillance, control of weather – but not yet. Since the kit for the twentieth-century lifestyle was put together eighty or a hundred years ago technical innovation has not changed it much. People have simply concentrated on producing it more efficiently, or profitably, or safely.

Third – as the most important social fact of the century – better production allowed distributions to change. In 1900 a few of the rich had a good deal of the new services and domestic equipment. By 1925 most middle-class business and professional families had all of it. By 1950 white-collared workers and skilled tradesmen had it or were getting it fast. By 1975 most laborers' families had most of it. The dates need advancing for some countries and retarding for others – the Japanese were fifty years behind the Americans just as in either country the laborers were fifty years behind the rich. But in lavish or modest form, most of them got most of the kit in the end. That was why it felt like a century of change: it was a century of changeover.

One way to look in retrospect at those distributions is to gross them up and see them as a single share-out of the century's increase of output. In that perspective, how was the biggest bonanza in human history distributed?

In one crude classification there were four possible ways to distribute it. One: supply the basic kit to more people. That would improve internal equality in the rich countries. Two: try to supply the kit, or the means of making it, to poor countries whose people still lacked it. That might redress some international inequalities which arose from the west's productivity. Three: produce special effects. Space travel was the most spectacular but weapons were the most important. Four: supply increasingly mechanized luxuries to people who already had the basic kit. That increases internal and international inequalities. It also forces more of a fifth use of resources: corrective action against troubles created chiefly by the fourth use. A big slimming industry chases a big overeating industry. More resources go to protecting bigger private hoards from more business-like thieves and vandals. New costs follow from subjecting the service populations of big cities to too much commuting or crowding; and there are other public and private costs of coping with congestion and with over-complicated systems and system-breakdowns in those cities. The burdens of these defensive and corrective costs are variously distributed, but rarely to reduce inequalities. Other people pay most of the costs of securing the rich in their unnecessary possessions, and maintaining their head offices high over their favorite cities, in easy reach of everything and everybody they may wish to use.

When too much of the increase of output went to the last two-and-a-half of those uses, famous social evils followed. There is no need to detail them – they are still with us and instead of ending them we savor them, describing them to each other incessantly in buoyant industries of song and story and social science. A brisk reminder will do. First, such enticing and punishing inequalities encourage avarice in everyone, often as a social and family duty. Second, it is nevertheless doubtful if wealth above and beyond the first house and car adds much to most people's felicity; the same resources could do more for larger numbers of people who are still short of their first outfit – short of house or car, health or security, education or holidays. Third, the process of increasing the inequalities has sometimes made class relations worse. Fourth – less lamented but much more damaging to happiness – the same process degrades relations *within* classes, which is where most close and important human relations exist. It may even have done so for the rich. Readers can consult their own impressions about that – or the many artistic exposures of rat-races, executive anxieties, corruption in high places; alcoholic poolside culture; affluent matrimony seen through the eyes of its complaining children, the marriages often worse than the divorces. I suspect that those are minority effects – that most rich lives are as wholesome or unwholesome as any others – and anyway rich sufferers can, as the saying goes, covet all the way to some Caribbean tax-haven. Through the second half of the century it was to personal and social relations within poorer classes that increasing inequalities did most damage. Many of the poor still lacked necessaries. Many on middle incomes were driven to greater anxiety about success and failure. As both watched the voluptuous values and law-avoiding immunities of those who got ahead, the contrasts put increasing strains on the self-respect and the competitive methods and morals of many; and some turned on one another, as the only targets within reach. In the poorest classes desertion and bastardy probably caused most misery; then violence and theft, likewise committed mostly by poor on other poor. And there were other increases of harshness, cynicism, alienation, lumpish misery. The grosser the inequality the harder it seemed to be for modern workers and poor at the bottom of the pyramid to see their own as a solid or backbone class, self-respecting, either with a satisfying culture of its own or fairly sharing in a classless culture of the whole society. More – workers and non-workers, housewives and aged poor – saw themselves or their parents, husbands or children simply as losers, victims, failures. When they saw themselves as that they very often liked each other less and treated each other worse.

Inequalities tend to have their most savage effects not on relations between classes, but on relations within them. In affluent democracies at most dates through the last half-century the worst of those internal class relations could usually be found where working classes already divided by race or religion were suffering also from low employment, cramped housing, wage lags, or other effects of widening class inequalities. Those conditions were widespread within the American working class. The troubles were not usually the effects of absolute poverty though they occasionally caused it, nor were they effects in any direct way of economic differences between the races. Until the Scandinavians overtook it the American working class was the richest in the world but its worst relations were between blacks, or between blacks and the whites nearest to them in income. The hatreds didn't arise from gross economic differences between the haters. They were much more clearly related to increasing class inequalities from which all the haters suffered together.

The inequalities were often worse than simple figures indicated. In overcrowded cities with property prices rising against other prices, rents could soak up high money wages while living space was still distributed with extreme inequality, as for example between suburbia and Harlem or the Chicago ghettoes. Whatever their money prices, land and other private and public urban space are a fundamental item of real wealth; and lack of living and schooling and recreational space may be specially destructive to human relations. American racial and ghetto troubles are sometimes contrasted with the comparative lack of such troubles in New Zealand where (as in some quiet uncrowded towns in the United States) every measurable indicator of social pathology is less in the equivalent classes, whether between black and white, white and white, or black and black. Through most of the century the American sufferers were richer. American street cleaners and bus drivers and factory hands often took home more pay than New Zealand teachers, engineers, bank officers; American welfare allowances were above many New Zealand wages. The sources of social peace in New Zealand are complex and open to argument, and may have a good deal to do with small numbers, clear responsibilities and direct face-to-face relations between governors and governed. But New Zealanders also have the world's most nearly equal shares of private urban land and houseroom, and their other inequalities of wealth and income are among the lowest and unlike most others they are not visibly increasing. New Zealand workers may find life undramatic but they suffer less from any other social cause. They also get bonuses, including honest government and police. Failures with those continue to be well-publicized effects of American inequalities, and underrated causes of them.[4]

7

The democracies suffered these troubles in different ways and degrees, depending on their situations, traditions and resources.

When the heavy environmental costs and energy shortages began in the 1970s differences of national situation became very important. To survive best a country needed plenty of land, lightly populated, still able to absorb reasonable flows of wastes. It needed its own supplies of energy and enough other raw materials to avoid being a net importer of them. It needed a diversified economy without too much compulsory dependence on foreign trade. Countries with any of those advantages tended to have most of them: the USA, Canada, the USSR, France, Australia. By contrast it was unlucky to be densely populated and already pollution-saturated; to have living standards dependent on skill in processing rather than on rich natural resources; to do much of the processing in pollutant types of industry; and to depend on a large exchange of manufactures for imported fuel and raw material. Countries with any of those disadvantages tended to have most of them: the UK, Japan.

Four examples will illustrate how environmental reforms and rising inequalities were linked in different circumstances of national luck and politics.

America was lucky in its land and resources though less so in some of its institutions. Broadly, environmental and resource problems were attacked on three fronts. Early in the 1970s it was estimated that an effective attack on pollution in the United States might cost between a quarter and a third of each year's economic growth. That effort was made through the last quarter of the century, with uneven effect – most of the visible wastes were cleaned up, most of the radioactive ones were not. Second, attempts to economize petroleum and to maintain a united front of oil-buying nations were not successful. American oil producers were as keen on the new prices as any Arab; and through the wars for the Middle Eastern fields, each new regime tended to be greedier than the last. In any case, as war and depletion reduced the flow, Americans were bound to push the price to the level at which they could get what they needed of the world supply. Third, there was massive investment in developing other energy sources though none of them was a satisfactory substitute for oil for petrochemicals or long-distance motoring.

There were three general kinds of distributional effect. Energy prices, and other price increases which arose from cleaner manufacturing, distributed most of the new costs regressively. There was also some bad distribution of benefits. And the business itself often worked – as many old city-planning and federal housing programs used to do – to pour plenty of public money into private pockets. Fortunes were made in environmental improvement rackets just as they had once been made in urban redevelopment rackets.

Through all these massive efforts clean air was probably the only commodity that got more equal distribution. There were no solutions to the ghetto problems. Poor Americans did not get fairer shares of urban services or living space. On the contrary, more of the capital accumulating in the hands of a quarter or a third of the population was used to buy its owners more private space – sometimes capitalized and powered like a small factory, sometimes gardened on strict environmental principles. That left less accessible urban land for the rest, so dwindling proportions of urban Americans had any at all.

That was one way to be poor. There were others. American rates of inflation were restrained by old-fashioned methods at severe social cost. Among the 18% of households living on public doles by the 1980s, 10%

were chronically unemployed. The doles were less comfortable than welfare used to be, for a number of reasons. The first was the policy of giving the poor 'money instead of paternalism'. It was much easier for the rich to get money back from the poor than it would have been to extract much profit from direct provisions of housing, medicine, dentistry, home help or social advice and support. Capitalist enterprise did get a good deal of negative income tax back, especially when adult males got it by one means or another from the women and children most of it was meant for. But by the 1980s less of it was meant for mothers and children. There had always been opposition to handouts for 'welfare bastards'. Those backwoods feelings got unexpected allies and a winning margin of support when in the course of the campaign for zero population growth the eco-preachers and environmental economists succeeded in persuading enough voters to believe that payments to *care for* children were really incentives to *produce* children.[5] Most tax and welfare entitlements for children were abolished or reduced. The tax changes made childless people richer and families poorer, which increased inequalities. The welfare changes drove more deserted mothers out to work, which increased worse things than inequality. National welfare payments fell noticeably. They fell further when price and income controllers battling with inflationary industrial troubles got most public doles and services withheld, sometimes for a full financial year, from the families of anyone who struck or whose representatives even threatened it.

But the worst effects didn't come from government. They came in the natural course of the new rat-race – the universal competition to win rather than lose by inflation. In that rat-race everyman did what he could. The rich added some gimmicks to their ordinary business advantages. Executives bartered their services for inflation-proof share entitlements and perquisites. Fringe benefits which had been negligible in 1945 were estimated to be a third of average executive rewards in 1965 and two thirds by 1985; some of the richest executives were by then on visible salaries of a dollar a year. More and more salaries, loan agreements and consumer-credit contracts were written in 'real' price-indexed terms. Various other inflation-proof currencies were invented, usually for insiders only. In an innocent attempt to damp property prices, reformers persuaded governments to issue 'paper land', i.e. inflation-proof bonds. They were meant to divert big money away from land so they were offered in big denominations only; thereafter the rich lent to governments on better terms than the poor could. (Curiously, the British had pioneered the principle for the opposite purpose of pushing money *into* the land market. To drive small savers' money from the banks to the building societies the British government in 1973 ordered the banks to pay lower interest on small deposits than on big ones. Full market interest was thus reserved for the richest 10 or 20% of lenders.)

Humbler Americans, following their leaders, were spurred to develop humbler rackets. No anti-strike or anti-welfare measures could stop auto workers and other labor aristocrats from keeping ahead of the indexes. Transport and essential-service workers had varying fortunes. Resistance to wage blackmail by black porters, jail warders, male nurses and the like was very tough. School teachers were judged to be dispensable, and won nothing by locking the children out of the schools through occasional strikes. But self-help and coercive bargaining were infectious and in the innovative, adaptable American atmosphere bargaining was more flexible than in other countries. Margins that couldn't be got from employers could often be got from other sources. Employers couldn't always prevent the help from robbing the customers. Service workers insisted on regular gratuities. Garbage left the gate or stayed there or had a fresh load heaped on top of it according to the householder's rate of cooperation. More and more public permissions or services came with percentages of private tax; environmental licensing and monitoring were not always exceptions. Police took more graft. Any serious protection of property came to depend on four-cornered arrangements at high rates between insurers, police, private security services and the local burglars. As the inflation progressed, suppliers and shopkeepers and the assistants on the cash registers all found that they could fiddle their margins with greater freedom. With prices leapfrogging all the time the customers got confused and lost their old capacity to tell a fair price from a fiddle. A lot of them were easier to fool. The easiest tended to be the poorest, shopping for cash. Some resort to barter didn't change that. Like the rich, plenty of ordinary joes were developing private currencies proof against government and other hazards.

These ways of life didn't improve human relations, but even as they cheated one another people basically forgave one another. They were all scrambling up the same down escalator. American life had always been competitive; inflation merely quickened the pace and the penalties. Standing still meant slipping back so the only way to keep up was to get ahead. Any poor breadwinner who failed to optimize whatever official or unofficial opportunities his job happened to offer was a failure like any other failure.

There have been more than enough characterizations of the harsher facts of American life – the anxious mobility, the pervasive distrust, the warm handshake and the empty heart – and there is no point in adding another. Through the fourth quarter of the twentieth century the society intensified its competitive avarice and its unloving cruelty to losers. Corruption spread, muggings multiplied, witnesses melted away, compassion dwindled. The national product continued to grow as measured by the sort of economist the schools continued to produce, but rising proportions of the product were defensive and corrective, adding nothing positive to anybody's welfare. There was increasing truth in Henry Cabot Lodge's old vision of the bigger cities as areas of ungovernable disorder criss-crossed by sanitized corridors policed for use by commuters and tourists. Between the street Arabs and the Wall Street Arabs, respectable folk picked their way with uncertain safety. There had to be regular levels of robbery by addicts, to pay the pushers what *they* had to pay the police. There were soon as many private firearms as people – about ten times the number possessed by the defence and police forces of the Union and all its states and cities. Not counting tax theft, about 15% of the national income was criminally earned. Of forty million people dependent in one way or another on public doles more than ten million were unloved or unprotected children of broken or non-existent households. More than a million of them went missing every year. They had – or felt they had – no one worth telling where they were going. Most of them wandered off safely enough to other corruptions and disillusions, to wars with other cops and deals with other pushers. Nobody knew how many came to real harm, or were used for unlawful purposes of business or pleasure.

At the same time hard-working, modest, friendly, talented, sensitive, honorable and agonized Americans still flourished in large numbers. The decent poor protected their families as best they could and the decent rich spun cocoons of gentility around them in many wholesome households and arcadian neighborhoods and ivied colleges. Those insulated rich were the luckiest of the winners – but their means of keeping ahead were really no gentler than anyone else's, if sometimes more indirect. It was an unloving society in which some were corrupt, many were scared or resigned, the best were baffled, and they all helped themselves as best they could, which was very unequally. The rest of the world worried chiefly about the uses such people and politicians might make of their appalling weaponry.

The French had almost every kind of luck except oil, which they got chiefly by bartering some of the arms that were used to fight the various

3-2

CIA–KGB wars among the Arabs. Otherwise they were well placed with plenty of food and very little import–export dependence.

Pollution had been quite severe. Costs of coping with it were spread through prices, with some aids and subsidies for farmers. But if all French were lucky, rich French were luckiest. Ineffective taxation of their incomes was traditional; now in the Common Market they wrung more advantages from a more eclectic federalism than even American or Australian rich had dreamed possible. They were big profiteers from the massive European revival of migratory labor – not since Irish navvies dug the English canals or the imperial Junkers kept their Slav seasonal labor moving had employer-nations accepted so little responsibility for the upbringing, education, housing, family life, old age, welfare, or civil rights of such masses of mobile poor. Meanwhile the redistributive policies which were supposed to equalize incomes through Europe's regions were quietly killed by what should have been the donor countries – French wealth was not for the Irish or Italian poor.

The quasi-federal economic arrangements of the Market had the usual federal effect of extinguishing a good deal of sovereignty altogether and proofing capitalist ownership against what remained of it. Any attempt at large-scale expropriation, capital taxation or radical regulation of trans-national corporations could be blocked by any one of a dozen national vetoes. Most means of subsidizing distressed consumers' standards of living were prohibited, while wage restraints were not. Socialism may always have been impractical in western Europe but now it was illegal too, and so was any effective increase of equality. The French, German and British rich used weak international federalism against any radical initiatives within member-states much as Metternich had used it against liberal initiatives before 1848.

With those protections for proprietors and good tax and income arrangements for the salaried rich and well-to-do, France distributed environmental costs and shortages to her urban working and lower middle classes in a normal nineteenth-century manner. The victims complained, and sometimes rioted in the spring months. Marxism, Maoism and various post-existentialist frolics of the spirit continued to flourish, chiefly as literary movements. However aggrieved, the French working class in its silo housing and its two-cylinder cars was still richer than most working classes, and exceptionally well fed and inebriated. A good deal of its dirty work was done by women or by migrant workers from out-of-town camps and shanty-towns.

The French and American developments were logical products of Right government. The British and German histories were – for the Left – odder and sadder. The richer Germans spent most of the 1970s and 1980s under nominally Left government. The poorer British alternated their parties in office, chronically dissatisfied with both. So in each case the increase of inequality owed as much to the Left as to the Right – to confused failures of nerve in the British case and to overconfident technical blundering in the German.

The United Kingdom had only two scraps of luck. It had quite good sources of energy, and it had achieved mass private motoring so late that it had not reconstructed its old cities and public transport systems beyond restoration. Between 1975 and 2000 it suffered the affluent world's largest absolute decline of real income per head. (Japan suffered a worse percentage decline from a lower peak.) But a good deal of that loss was absorbed in car-owners giving up their cars after the briefest experience of them, in a country well equipped to do without them. Calm, intelligent, good-natured administration rescued a good deal from the painful transition to poorer standards. The transport reconstructions were skilful. A lot of detailed conservation was done lovingly and well. The welfare services were good at coping with acute poverty. But they did not shift any significant quantity of income from the richer to the poorer half of the population or protect the poorer half from taking most of the national loss of consumption.

That loss was not usually perceived as new or 'environmental'. It was merely another variation on some facts of life with which the English were already long and wearily familiar: the imperial decline, the exchange gap, the inflationary spiral. For twenty years the political parties had taken turns at much the same middle-of-the-road approach to those chronic problems. By the 1970s the country's productivity had lagged behind its European competitors', annual inflation was moving from 12 towards 20%, the property boom was enraging one half of the nation and a desperate, defensive labor militancy was enraging the other half. Both halves lost some of their old faith in the middle of the road. Each party dragged its leaders some distance away from the Centre. But neither proved to be very good at the business of radical government. The Right shifted wealth from the poor to the rich at a great rate[6] but couldn't balance the foreign exchanges, discipline labor, control inflation or get re-elected. The Left ran deflationary economic policies which reduced employment and standards of living, improved trading balances by rationing and import control, but couldn't control inflation or get re-elected. Altogether the Left showed more radical feeling than skill. They nationalized land and a good deal of industry, but they paid full capital compensation to its owners. That made very little difference to the price of land. It brought more strike-and-lockout confrontations between state employers and labor. It did very little to restrain wages and prices and even less to reduce inequalities. British private capital was the most unequally owned and often the most unproductively invested in the democratic world but there was still no leadership capable of attracting a majority for confiscating, redistributing or levying it.

The rich did suffer some losses. There was some general decline of profits. Owners did the best they could about that – there were still some gains to be wrung from property, usury and tax dexterity. There were weak governments abroad, and ways of weakening the one at home if its respect for property ever wavered. Chairmen would declare in statements for release from their registered head offices offshore that when the British worker came down from the clouds ready to make cars or tyres or drugs or ceramics for Spanish wages, then Britain would again attract British investment as Spain was doing – provided there was reliable compliance with the Brussels tax limits, and rules against expropriation.

The upper middle classes survived well enough. They hung on to their cars, country cottages, holidays abroad and immigrant servants at home. There was some decline in share income and in self-employed professional earnings but the class did well in executive pay and in the public sector – public and academic salaries and professional and managerial rates in public industries were almost alone in holding their real values while most other wages, piece-rates, pensions, welfare and unemployment allowances lagged behind prices to distribute the downturn in consumption in a quietly unfair way.

While the well-to-do hung on to the standards of 1970 various institutions eased the descent of most other people to the mass living standards of about 1948. The parties took turns in office but in a more general sense there was stable government, good morale, and plenty of a safe old style of British grumbling. There was also a long tradition of emigration. North America and Australasia would now accept skilled or well-endowed migrants only: but if emigration did nothing for the very poor it was nevertheless a political and social safety valve because so many recalcitrant people departed, leaving the remainder easier to govern. Petulant rentiers went to Mediterranean or Caribbean islands. Militant shop-stewards and reactionary doctors went to Australia. Racist clerks and shopkeepers went to Rhodesia. Of those who stayed a few in Glasgow, Liverpool or Wolverhampton were sometimes violent, more often against poor blacks than against rich proprietors. Most were not. The English were better than anyone else at suffering without savaging one another. But no foreigner – Right or Left, capitalist or worker – could understand why they misused that gentle talent to put up with rich like theirs.

The English rich thus did well by being as immovably reactionary as any Portuguese. By contrast their German equivalents, though almost as few and quite as selfish, were more adaptable when history really seemed to demand it. They could make deliberate Teutonic reappraisals and set off in novel, even theoretical directions. By 1985 most big German enterprise was co-owned with its labor. Most labor had enforceable rights to share in improving profits and productivity. The labor movement itself ran third or fourth among German corporate investors, and hedged its own radicalism with a growing portfolio of overseas real estate.

None of that necessarily made for a kinder or juster society. Most productivity arose from capital intensity and it was not particularly equitable to adjust wages to it industry by industry. When strong labor won its place in the establishment there were other losers, including migrants, women and many unprotected consumers. But most of the organized male working class was prosperous as never before. It should have been happy as never before, and might have been but for some disastrous mistakes of Left government. The German history of this quarter-century is a history of good democratic intentions distorted by technical incompetence in public and technical services.

Alone among the big democracies West Germany was governed continuously by a party of the Left through most of the 1970s and 1980s. As they affected proprietors and the salaried rich, the policies of the Social Democratic Party were moderate. Since the German rich were able to exploit federal divisions of sovereignty at internal as well as European levels they survived Left government well enough. But the working classes did less well because their wage, welfare and share-owning gains were offset by the effects of two kinds of environmental policy. Controlling pollution was expensive in Germany and raised costs of living accordingly. At the same time the Social Democratic governments made a bold attempt to improve both the environments and the equalities of the cities. They set out to shift the balance of advantage from rich motorists to poor residents, to improve local services and centres and to reduce the impact of oil prices on lower incomes by encouraging their cities to develop strong pedestrian preferences and massive improvements to public transport systems. These were admirable aims but they went awry in the course of translation into detailed city-planning and housing policies. It is important to understand just how they went wrong – and how wrong they went.

As if to console its citizens for the separation of Berlin the Federal Republic inherited unrivalled opportunities for civilized and egalitarian city life. There was an efficient nationwide network of small and medium-sized cities of considerable diversity, each with a past and a personality. Most of the cities combined the advantages of small size with remarkably few of its usual disadvantages. Excellent intercommunications knit them into efficient networks of economic activity – there was no greedy central metropolis to monopolize all the more interesting investment, skill and head-office power at the expense of the rest. Hamburg could specialize in commerce, Frankfurt in banking, Bonn in government, Munich in the arts. Many of the cities had once been sovereign, and inherited fine civic and cultural traditions and facilities. Just as they shared in business networks, so they did in cultural networks. There was no greedy Paris or London to attract all the high culture away from them. Their electoral boundaries gave most of them Left administrations. The urban growth of 1950–2000 could therefore occur in the most natural, efficient and popular way. With moderate and manageable reconstructions and additions to scores of cities in the network, everybody could share in – without overloading – the attractions and services of old-established cities of character.

In these fortunate circumstances social-democratic policy and orthodox planning theory had common ground. To save the countryside from urban sprawl, to defend the old cities from degradation by automobile and to keep their good things accessible to poor as well as rich, their growth should be shaped to keep all their residents in reach of good local centres and efficient public transport systems. That did not merely call for investments in public transport; it required careful relationships between the locations of industry, business, shopping, recreation and housing. There can be various workable patterns of those relationships. Each pattern will include, among other things, requirements about residential density.

Choosing a system – a set of relationships for a particular city – is partly technical: some kinds of urban layout and system are better than others at reconciling high standards of workplace, housing, communica-

66

tion and urban quality. But with the best technique in the world the critical questions are still questions of value. How much residential quality is worth how much travelling time? How much motoring freedom is worth how much loss of central-city urbanity? What costs are worth incurring for how much diversity and choice of housing forms? What is the best balance between private space and space for communal activity? And so on. These are political questions but because they are complicated and interdependent they rarely get direct democratic answers at election time. Politicians and public servants decide them piecemeal, with effects which depend partly on the skills but chiefly on the values and political prudence of the men concerned. On this occasion, too many of the men concerned were technocrats – systems analysts, systems engineers, computer men, new-style social scientists interested only in the quantifiable facts of life that their mechanized methods (and minds) could process with proper precision.

When the German Social Democrats took office, first in cities and provinces and then in national government, they told their public servants to put systems-analysis and systems-engineering to work in the interests of the masses. But only one of those interests was strictly quantifiable and mathematically manageable: the interest in good cheap public transport. From then on, decision-making was designed to optimize that value only. The effect on transport systems was brilliant; for small and medium-sized cities Germany soon had the best in the world. But to concentrate traffic for them some tough residential policies were enforced. The higher the residential density if rightly located (the computer said) the higher the potential cost-efficiency and time-efficiency of rapid-transit systems. How high could densities go? There were political constraints. Point-blocks of flats rising twenty or more floors had become unpopular. But some other housing forms, just as insensitive and almost as dense – long, lumpish wall-blocks eight or ten floors high – were already common in municipal housing when the Social Democrats took over central government, and the party itself had been responsible for them in many Social Democratic cities. Municipal housing was however too small a proportion of the whole stock. National housing and mortgage-lending policies were therefore revised to generalize the lift-served housing forms to all but the richest of new urban housing, private as well as municipal.

Planning times are long; the full physical and social effects were slow to appear. The party continued to hold power on the strength of its good wage and welfare and foreign policies, so the housing policies also held for fifteen years, by which time (with the blocks built at earlier dates) more than a third of national population, including half the urban population and two thirds of all working-class families, were in modern rectangular apartment blocks between six and twelve floors high, surrounded by varying quantities of rule-ridden public grass. The Right were quick to notice the similarity to policies in force in Russia since the 1930s as Hamburg, Frankfurt, the Ruhr cities and even Munich reproduced the physical envelopes of working-class life in Moscow or Omsk.

The whole enterprise was both politically and technically mistaken. Even with full understanding of the transport and environmental consequences, democratic majorities (if the issue had been put squarely to them) would have opted for more varied housing forms, mostly nearer the ground, with some private land for most households. The balance between private and public space, and between housing quality and transport efficiency, had been set where a properly-informed democracy would certainly not have set it.

But the democracy could never have been properly informed by *those* experts. Their technical misjudgments were worse than their political ones. Though journeys to work and city centres might go by public transport, the constraints of working-class life in lift-served apartments made for more private motoring for other purposes; and when petroleum got too dear the masses were tethered to homes with a sad – and dangerous – lack of private space, resource and flexibility. The planners had expected the local public spaces and resources would compensate for that. In that also they were mistaken. It is when families have versatile private space and resources at home that they also make appropriate use of local community resources and meeting places. When on the other hand they have too few or cramped resources at home, so that they can't make or build anything there, or dig holes or grow anything or alter anything, or develop the finer workshop skills or play the rougher family games, then they are driven to use communal resources inappropriately, crowding or misusing or vandalizing them until many activities have to be banned from public places; so that *neither* the private *nor* the communal needs of family and social life are sufficiently provided for. Competent systems-analysts would have known the limits beyond which private and communal resources are not substitutable but are complementary components of a system in which neither works properly without a due balance of the other.

Those were minor mistakes. But the experts also managed to mistake some fundamental relations between transport accounting and social accounting, and between transport densities, housing densities and housing forms. Neither in theory, nor in the practice of scores of efficient western cities, was it true that good public transport depended on those particular housing forms. A wide variety of forms, including mixtures to meet diverse tastes, and private gardens and workshops and playroom for plenty of poor as well as rich, could allow tolerably efficient transport densities and any desired restraint of private motoring at peak hours and to city centres. It would always have been wrong to sacrifice the quality of forty or fifty weekly hours of home and social life to the few weekly hours of adult travel, at a time when most working-class families wanted to use their rising affluence to enrich, above all, the hours of private life and leisure. But it was technically wrong to suppose that most of the sacrifices were ever necessary. The transport efficiencies did not require those housing forms; those housing forms were not even an unmixed aid to transport efficiency. The alternatives to mass family life in lift-served flats did not *have* to include unlimited suburban sprawl, unduly expensive services, choked city centres, or compulsory dependence on private cars. In perceiving Omsk and Los Angeles as their only options the technocrats of state and party were simply incompetent at precisely the urban systems-analysis they were supposed to be expert at.

When the backlash eventually came it was thorough, putting the Left out of office for decades. The social ill-effects were as lasting as the political. Those massive commitments of bad housing had to continue in use for a very long time before enough of them could be made over for offices or storage, or types of residents who didn't mind their shortcomings. Foreign visitors stereotyped them as comic examples of 'German efficiency'. But at home, at election after election through decade after decade, Christian Democratic candidates of 'the party that treats humans as people, not statistics' used the lumpish, everywhere-visible 'socialist silos' to reinforce a much more deadly stereotype of *socialist* theory-arrogance, *socialist* monotony, *socialist* uniformity, *socialist* regimentation, *socialist* contempt for the environment of family life.

8

A simpler summary of effects, for comparison with the conclusion of the previous scenario, might be this.

Since what are now the affluent democracies began their great economic acceleration in the eighteenth century there have been four phases in the history of their inequalities. Through the first century of agrarian change

69

and industrial beginnings, to about 1850, the masses generally got less than their shares of increasing national outputs. Especially in the United Kingdom, subsistence standards improved comparatively little while most of the gains of the new productivity were creamed, whether for reinvestment or for consumption, by an expanding class of proprietors.

A second phase with massive industrialization and the transformation of society to its modern form ran for a century to about 1950 and its gains were better distributed. 'Proportionate' shares can be variously interpreted but by almost any standard the masses did relatively better than before or since. All real wages improved. A great increase and spread of skills saw a great increase in the number and spread of middle incomes. Some of the new goods were more important than the new incomes. Mass literacy, health, housing, transport and domestic equipment allowed more and more daily experience and life-style to be common to all classes; and there was a general diffusion of political goods to match the economic ones. Differences of wealth and income and life-experience were still great but they were diminishing. Thus from technical and political causes there was a century of progress towards greater equality.

That progress ceased in the third phase, through the third quarter of the twentieth century. By most methods of measuring inequality it began to increase again. For a time the poor had some compensations for that. Full employment was more reliable than it used to be. Real wages continued to rise. Many people were able to complete the basic twentieth-century kit of household goods and physical mobility. Nevertheless, however slowly at first, the rich were gaining again as in the eighteenth century.

The fourth phase came in the fourth quarter of the twentieth century with the onset of serious environmental and resource problems and runaway inflation. Both were dealt with by methods which quickened the third-quarter trend toward greater inequality. There were no masterly new decisions about distribution, except perhaps by the very rich as they built their new federal, international and offshore immunities. But as a general consequence of a great many detailed policies the masses paid most of the new environmental costs. They suffered most painfully from shortages and shortage-prices of energy. The real value of their wages, savings and pensions came under continuous attack in continuous battles with inflation. So did their peace of mind. Battles with inflation were really battles for shares at the expense of one another. They eroded solidarities of trade, neighborhood, class and nationality, forcing competitive behavior on everyone in a rat-race not even to get ahead but merely to keep up. It was this universal, inescapable, anxious competition, rather than any fancy advances in co-ownership, which fully and finally incorporated the workers into the cut-throat system and spirit of capitalism.

The new relation between class incomes was a variation of an old eighteenth-century relationship. Before 1800 or 1850 poor standards of living had been pegged while the rich took most of the gains of rising productivity. After 1975 it was the rich who held their material levels of living while the masses absorbed the losses – the various environmental shortages, dislocations and costs of conservation and reform.

How could poor majorities have acted to reverse that last relation?

3

Trouble

Three chapters now record a history in which equalities improved, and environmental reform was more efficient: its benefits did more good and its costs caused less pain because both were better distributed.

This chapter reviews the troubles that made people think again about capitalist democracy. Chapter 4 describes what they thought. Chapter 5 describes what they did.

1

Some early signs of a change of course were neglected because they contradicted very settled and scientific expectations. Readers old enough to remember the 1960s will recall some of those expectations. Middle-class writers said that 'quality of life' was a middle-class concept. The working classes were not expected to favor much of it. Nor were the rich expected to encourage much of it as corporate owners and managers, whatever frills they might be willing to pay for as suburban householders and consumers. Closer cooperation between business and government was assumed, by the Left and often by the businessmen, to mean more neo-capitalist use of public power for private profit. These somewhat ideological forecasts were confirmed by the many social scientists of the day who predicted chiefly by extrapolating. They extrapolated conventional economic growth; general replacement of public transport by private motoring, and of city centres by car stacks and office towers; increasing prefabrication and standardization of mass housing; and a continuation of narrowly materialist conceptions of welfare and self-interest. When they found that inequalities of wealth were increasing again, they extrapolated that trend too. So from Right, Left and Research Institute the forecasts converged: environmental reform would come chiefly from the Right; it would be quite profitable to private enterprise; its costs would come out of mass standards of living. That was how it was getting under way in the United States, which led the world in most lines of environmental research and reform. After the usual time-lag other democracies would follow in similar directions.

Those expectations made it easy not to attach much weight to minor exceptions in minor countries. In Norway the environmental movement was led politically from the Left. It was a Labor government that dealt so prudently with North Sea oil, and acted to conserve the remaining forests and waterfalls from exploitation. In Australia the first upsets came, with even less affluent help, from the grassroots. A few hundred people of mixed race had been inbreeding and scratching a living on a sandy peninsula that nobody else wanted, when state authorities decided to run a coastal highway through their settlement. The people didn't want it but they couldn't stop it – until several hundred miles away, a stevedores' union offered to close the port of Newcastle if the settlers were disturbed. In the same city coal miners blocked the building of a new offshore coal loader – they earned their livings mining the coal but they also fished and surfed from the beach it would foul. Other unions blocked other attempts to load coal off other beaches. Then a building laborers' union moved into the conservation business. It protected historic buildings, a good deal of Sydney's past and a lot of old inner-city housing from demolition, and broadacres of forest and coastal land from suburban development, more effectively than public authorities could protect them, and regardless of whether public authorities *wanted* to protect them. Within a very few years its green bans had prevented several hundred million dollars' worth of development which would all have employed the union's members.

These were cases of militant labor acting, for environmental reasons, to block wage-paying economic growth. They also brought together what in any other circumstances would have been startling alliances between labor unions, Left parties, affluent defenders of rich neighborhoods, rough-house defenders of poor neighborhoods, and all the poets and professionals and serious-minded scientists of the environmental movements. Most of the rich democracies had similar signals, as unexpected as the Norwegian and Australian ones. They were misread partly because they contradicted expectations, but paradoxically also because there seemed to be nothing new about them. The new activists were using traditional modes of public action, and it was easy not to notice what novel alliances were being born.

The dialectic of old and new appeared earliest at local levels. From the 1960s most of the affluent world saw a mushroom growth of informal local organizations and action programs. They often began as last-ditch defences against motor traffic and bureaucratic urban surgery. People turned out to stop evictions and demolitions, new highways, commercial redevelopments. They blocked roads to stop juggernaut industrial traffic. They fought new quarries, dams, airports, container docks, trucking terminals, oil moorings, refineries, power stations. They also did constructive things. They started shopfront services to help neighbors with their private and public rights. They staffed school grounds and vacant lots and disused railway cuttings to occupy children out of school. In school hours they led the children out into the city and countryside for practical exercises in conservation. They encouraged public authorities to pedestrianize town centres. They beat local planning schemes by designing better ones. They ran 'human face' candidates at local elections. Some who set out to scare City Hall found they had captured it; sometimes they used its powers imaginatively.

There was nothing new in the forms of action – in citizens' reform leagues, petitions, protest meetings, local alliances across class or party lines to lobby central governments for local benefits. The new energies were effective partly because such hallowed modes of action were there to be used. But it was new to enlist quite such a spread of age and income – teachers and flocks of school children turned out with amateur and professional politicians, affluent residents, elderly conservationists and young nature-lovers in sandals and beads. It was new for local associations to outclass the public authorities in the quality of their lawyers, planners, publicists, natural and social scientists. It was new to be agitating so often against, rather than for, local economic growth and public works. It was new for respectable citizens to join in road-blocking breaches of the peace. It was new for radicals to want to conserve so much of existing local life and fabric.

Of course nonsense also proliferated. Participation was the new panacea and absurd miracles were expected of it. Often it achieved nothing, sometimes it tore neighborhoods apart. But people learned, and especially they learned to pick horses for courses. It became part of the developing art of community organization to know how to separate common interests fit for community action from conflicts better resolved by more distant institutions; and when to bypass the institutions and get the numbers into the street to demonstrate or obstruct. There were other discriminations. People learned to tolerate works which offered net environmental gains: bypass roads, sewage treatment works, new routes for public transport. They learned to distinguish works which could be stopped from others which could only be unloaded onto other neighborhoods. If not always generous about the latter, they did learn that brawls between neighborhoods were rarely fruitful. Soon local groups were forming federations to share professional services and mutual support. They learned to distinguish campaigns which deserved fraternal support from other campaigns which didn't. Attempts to unload traffic or municipal incinerators onto neighbors were among those which didn't. Nor, before long, did efforts to protect rich wards from rate-sharing or public housing or ethnic immigration. Selfishness persisted but at least some of it was muted – speaking publicly against low-income housing came to be classed with speaking publicly against Jews or peace or contraception. Through time and experience there was a steady increase in the power and sophistication of local action.

The same was true of the new generation of national and international environmental movements which went to war for everything from arctic whales to rural ramblers' rights-of-way. They developed monitoring services, industrial espionage, expert scrutiny of tons of the published and unpublished print of industry and government. They played clean or dirty according to temperament and opportunity. They publicized politicians' corporate links, conflicts of interest, and voting records on environmental issues. They dogged to the end of his days any public official who left government to work for a pollutant private enterprise. Their publicists used space and time in the most penetrating media to associate revealing analyses of corporate profits with insidious fears of doomsday. They wrote simple environmentalist philosophies into every school curriculum, with scarcely a nod to other points of view. They audited auditors, they inspected public inspectors, they forced law-enforcers to enforce laws. Like the local organizations, they became skilful, hard to fool and dangerous to tread on. It was a long time before many of them took much direct interest in questions of justice or equality; but from the beginning their work overlapped into the fields of consumer protection and community action, and they came to share democratic aims and methods with both. Whatever a few of them might say about 'bypassing politics' they soon learned that most practical achievement depended on mobilizing more, not less, popular democratic power.

The most important effects of all these efforts were educational. Local action did not produce major social changes but in indirect ways it opened the way for them. Old bastions of wealth and power no longer looked impregnable. If local action could succeed in blocking the multi-million-dollar projects of national governments and multi-national corporations, it became plausible to think of forcing more positive transformations. People who had been reluctant or resigned conservatives, merely because the established arrangements looked unbeatable, began to vote for other possibilities. Many grew less doctrinaire, either way, about the comparative demerits of public and private enterprise. More and more of the pollutant industries obviously had to be brought under closer public control. Notions of public ownership which had once been tainted by association with the red menace became respectable by association with the green rebellion.

There was also new scope and respect for some hairy styles of leadership. The aims of grassroots campaigns were often conservative enough but their methods called for activist leaders. The leaders were often sobered veterans of student and anti-war campaigns, who enjoyed direct action and knew how to go about it. Their old radical interests led them to add equitable requirements to many environmental campaigns. The details mattered less than the increasing association, in a general way, of once-hostile people and values. Respectable conservative names appeared on the platforms and deputations and letterheads while radical organizers planned the tactics, got out the numbers and researched and wrote the publications. In the rhetoric of these movements connections were constantly made between practical local issues, global environmental philosophies, and increasingly the fair sharing of burdens and benefits.

The targets of some of the campaigns were industrial corporations or public utilities. Those leviathans often survived the first confrontations. They cleared their routes or sites, built their works, took their profits. They were often right, the works were often necessary. But more and more of their victories were Pyrrhic victories. Their public figures had to put up with expert abuse and wide unpopularity, while the conservationists got most of the television time, and wrote the best-sellers. Defeat left the losers spoiling for the next battle, and more and more of the winners swearing 'never again'. Such wars and delays were expensive, financially and politically. Consultation and diplomacy, however irksome, might be quicker in the long run. Avoiding contentious projects altogether was increasingly attractive. Among the bureaucrats and politicians themselves there were misgivings, personal conversions, deft changes of stance. No achievements of the local activists were in the end as important as the responsive changes of aim and style in the big organizations. Criteria of success changed, criteria for promotion changed. Only ironically, after some particularly disastrous public backlash, was anyone now called 'a forceful administrator'. Ambitious men wanted to be known as communicators, listeners, grassroots men. 'Investing is participating' they would say; 'planning is a community learning process'; and 'what looks bad to *any* American is bad for General Motors'. Their grandfathers had worked one revolution in corporate relations with labor. Their fathers had worked another, in sophisticating the style of internal executive competition. The sons now extended the same tenderness – with similar proportions of substance and hypocrisy – to corporate relations with local residents, landscapes, flora and fauna.

There were even some egalitarian effects. Investors and utility planners learned to offer all sorts of improvements and compensations to the communities they had to disturb. Often the most effective compensations were the widest-spread, partly because they would touch more local voters, partly because 'caring for people' would look good to wider audiences if confrontations did occur. So power stations piped cheap heat to residents for miles around. Spoiled land was developed for popular recreations. Commercial forests laid out their access roads in romantic curves and contours and opened them to ramblers, with expensively rough-hewn overnight cabins, and electric cookers to reduce fire risks. The London Docks Redevelopment Authority eventually had to dispose of some of the world's first glut of surplus youth centres. Once upon a time, railroad executives had a duty to their owners to get the best financial return they could for any disused railbeds or siding land. Now they would not dare to put such land into the property market. Any railbeds and stations and sidings that are not returning to public transport uses are lacing the big cities through with rustic walks and cycle paths from one adventure playground to the next. The poor might once have had to pay for such blessings indirectly through public transport fares. But nowadays taxes subsidize public transport, and it is even harder to raise fares than to sell off public land.

2

For historical purposes all this shuffling of public issues and values, with so much cross-bench and cross-class cooperation, needs to be interpreted with care. Environmental enthusiasms did not signify a moral regeneration of human nature. People still competed; class interests did not melt away. Much of the new corporate sensitivity and diplomacy, the elaborate participant planning and environmental consultation, merely replaced a hard sell by a soft sell; and the softening-costs went onto the prices of the products. Most of the unequalizing effects of environmental reform described in the previous chapter were at work. Nevertheless some of the public values were genuinely changing and some of the Left's early cynicism was mistaken.

Good examples could be found in changing attitudes to urban bulldozing. In the reconstructions of the big cities between 1945 and 1970 the bulldozer was the most visible instrument of social change, and its constructive symbols were the public housing tower and the multi-level motorway interchange. People did sometimes exaggerate the importance of those big works in the big cities. Larger quantities of roads and housing continued to be built in conventional old forms in the smaller cities and towns where larger numbers continued to live. But the visible brutalities of the biggest cities got most publicity and sociological attention; and where they led, lesser places were expected to follow in due course. The poor were the worst sufferers from both the towers and the motorways; and the unrecorded human costs of uprooting and stacking or dispersing them were often worse than the money costs.

From the beginning there were critics of these policies. The critics could be ignored – and were, for ten or twenty years – as long as the sufferers were poor. But the urban surgeons eventually grew overconfident and threatened richer neighborhoods. Long afterwards it was said of the English-speaking cities that their environmental revolution did not date from the startling books of Rachel Carson or Paul Ehrlich, or from the troubles with the new housing towers, or from the revelations of corruption in the redevelopment works, or even from the new gasoline prices: it dated from a New York proposal to bulldoze Jane Jacobs' neighborhood, and a London proposal to drive motorways through Hampstead and Kensington.

Cynics noticed the sudden social conscience of the rich when their own precincts were threatened. But they were wrong to doubt the change of heart. Men of influence had at last been brought to understand what it would be like to have their houses taken, their neighborhoods smashed, their local acquaintance dispersed, their children forced from school to school. Abruptly they believed what victims and critics had been trying to tell them for decades: much of the physical and social fabric being destroyed was worth conserving; most of the new motorways did more to congest than clear the cities; the silo style of working-class housing didn't make the cities any denser or more efficient, and it brought high costs in money, suffering and disorder. So the rich banned the bulldozers, much as their forefathers had eventually banned slavery or child labor. The revulsion was genuine, and thorough. It developed its own rigidities, sometimes preventing quite wholesome projects simply because they were big, or high. Commissions of inquiry reached far into the past to uncover the corruption that had accompanied many clearances, disposals of cleared land, and expensive novelties in high-rise construction. In the better-governed countries a few malefactors went to jail, a few national and local politicians retired from public life. Many honest policy-makers repented. Honest or not, everybody knew that a phase had ended. The poor were now protected from one more hazard, partly by new rights and allies, but mostly by a new orthodoxy: a permanent change in some values and assumptions of the governing classes.

There were other developments of that general kind. They happened especially in areas of policy in which options were still open because the political parties did not have too many rigid beliefs or class commitments. Urban planning and housing; transport systems; action against pollution; nature conservation, energy conservation, and social and architectural conservation in the cities – all these allowed experiment, disagreement within parties, cooperation across party lines, and scope for the growing popular interest in participant politics, and quality of life.

All this had effects on the range of political possibilities. Besides Left and Right parties and ethnic and regional and special-interest blocs there could now be general environmental alignments, and campaigns for particular lines of town or country conservation; and the new alignments were sometimes strong enough to split or reunite the old. The fragmentation of traditional patterns of opinion and loyalty did not of itself make for large changes of system, but it produced a situation in which good leadership might organize critical shifts of numbers.

Prospects for equality were affected in three general ways:

First there were detailed effects of the kinds noticed already. Most costs of reducing industrial pollution were distributed to reduce poorer rather than richer consumption. On the other hand some improvements to neighborhoods and urban services tended to improve equalities. Between the two there was no general reduction of inequality.

But second, that early phase of urban and environmental action was an easy one in the rich countries. Until the oil prices began to bite, those countries had suffered no serious shortages or dislocations. Reform could be painless, eclectic, voluntary. It did take massive investment to turn the pollution indexes downwards, but it was still a modest proportion of new investment each year. Nobody really *felt* the costs that enabled those famous fish to swim up the Thames again, under such novel blue skies. It cost a lot of inspectors' wages, and wasted fishing, to get the mercury out of the canned food, but that didn't get onto everyman's list of the causes of inflation. Most environmental action was a pleasure. It was not thought of as an approach to 'deliberate scarcity'. It looked and felt more like a welcome shift of values. People traded old goods for new ones. They accepted slower-rising private incomes and enjoyed better public services. They accepted the discomforts of public transport to get to more convivial city centres. They paid more for brown bread and brown sugar, and developed a taste for them. When action groups forced City Hall to block and plant a lot of their local streets their rates went up – but they felt more neighborly. Even the increase of inequality was gentle. Most poor incomes still rose, however slowly. And although the equalizing effects of the new environmental policies were more than offset by their other effects, the equalizing effects were often more noticeable. New local safeties and services, shopfront aids to poorer citizens, clean rivers and beaches, centres full of people and street-life instead of cars – these were the fairly-shared achievements of adventures in community action, and David-and-Goliath victories over bureaucrats and environmental despoilers. So the easy first decade allowed environmentalist values to be entrenched in popular feelings and institutions, and associated with values of fair sharing and direct democracy.

But, third, although there might be new opportunities to organize better equalities, there was no automatic tendency in that direction. The multiplication and cross-cutting of issues, the fragmentation of old alignments, the large number of local initiatives, the technical difficulty of distributing many of the new costs equitably – all these tended to push European and Australasian politics in American directions. They made it harder for the Left to build its traditional popular front on the traditional issues of wages and working conditions, taxes and welfare. The United Kingdom offered an excellent illustration. Through the 1960s and early 1970s its most-canvassed political issues were: economic growth and full employment; inflation and costs of living; education and technological change; urban smog, congestion, motorways, housing, rents, property prices; entry into Europe; and the social and environmental impact of the proposed Maplin airport, Concorde aircraft, and Channel tunnel. On scarcely any of those issues did the nation divide on class or party lines. Most of the processes in question were helping to increase inequalities. But most people, most of the time, thought they were facing difficult and confusing technical decisions rather than simple Right-or-Left, us-or-them issues.

As long as the mounting environmental problems were canvassed without much reference to their distributive implications it was hard to base politics on class at all. But that did not mean there was classless government. The fragmentation of forces and the complexity of issues allowed a pervasive, unopposed influence to the affluent class which included most owners, administrators, managers and professional skills. (That class did also include reformers, but some of them were more interested in efficiency than equality, and they were anyway outnumbered.) In what somebody dubbed 'the new pluralism' the pervasive class interest at work in complicated, diffuse and detailed decision-making was likelier than ever to prevail over any scattered self-defences of the unorganized poor and their sympathizers. Complexity worked for the rich, because there seemed to be no commanding positions from which anyone could prevent them from working for themselves, from innumerable positions of influence, on innumerable separate fronts.

That trend changed only when enough of the rich split, enough of the poor organized, and enough of the complexities were forcibly simplified.

3

Many causes converged to upset old beliefs and solidarities of the rich, and to reconstruct some of their relations with one another and with government. They brought some of their troubles on themselves. Others were forced on them by indignant democratic action. Others were systematic problems of capitalism which grew acute enough, under environmental stress, to compel systematic changes. For summary purposes they can be listed as lawless scandals, lawful scandals, conflicts of legitimate interest, and technical difficulties of national economic and environmental management.

The lawless scandals included both traditional corporate and governmental corruption, and the novel exploitation of international and offshore immunities. Traditional corruption flourished where it always had – in most institutions levels of corruption or honesty are strongly self-perpetuating. But this social inheritance was modified by the conditions noticed earlier – size, complexity, and trends to greater or less equality. By the 1970s the four or five richest nations in Europe were also the smallest, the most equal, and the most honest. Some growing understanding of that syndrome may have affected opinion in the bigger countries, whose scandals increased in step with their complexities and inequalities. In north-west Europe the increase was not great – most business and government was law-abiding – but the exceptions were vividly reported and people grew less tolerant of them. If shareholders couldn't police their boards reliably; if auditors and stock exchanges couldn't; if government couldn't, partly because some of its members were corruptible by the people they were supposed to police, then the self-government of the rich was breaking down, and perhaps it was time to abolish some of their temptations altogether.

But relations between scandal and reform varied critically with circumstances. North Europeans and Australasians generally assumed that they had reserves of honest performance. Whenever necessary, slipshod institutions could be reformed to work honestly, by changes of system or personnel. It was not always thought necessary to reform them – besides conservative entrenchment there were often misgivings about personal rights and bureaucratic inefficiencies. But honesty was always a possible policy.

Americans had different misgivings. They had a different inheritance of corruption. Percentages varied from field to field – from very little in banking and the US Treasury, through an average 100% of salary in state and local police forces, to massive dimensions in some political machines and labor unions, the clandestine public services, the purchase of Congressmen, and from time to time the Presidency. In some fields it took continuous effort to keep the level of corruption stable; in others, stricter public control (or attempts at it) might merely enlarge the scope for extortion, or shift its benefits from small men behind counters to bigger men at head offices. City planning had shown how 'a whole new province for law and order' could create a whole new shake-down industry; giving planning permissions to developers might be honest in Stockholm or Frankfurt but in many of the United States it was like printing money for friends. Old abuses continued alongside new ones. Industry and government continued to generate flows of 'political money'. Some each of big business and big labor had links with big crime, so labor laws protected worse things than the workers' and employers' rights they were meant to protect. Corporations cooperated with clandestine agencies of government to corrupt – or assassinate and replace – puppet regimes abroad. Army generals, intelligence agents and police officers joined in the drug and vice trades. Under a corrupt President, Vice-President and Attorney General the White House used common criminals for uncommonly criminal purposes. Corruption may have been no bigger than it had been in the Gilded Age or under Prohibition, but bigger men than ever were into it.

Optimists hoped for countervailing effects. American villains certainly faced the strictest codes, the freest press and the ablest investigators in the world; but villainy on a similar scale kept the equilibrium stable. Almost all Americans underrated its effects on their collective social options. All parties tended to see honest government as a consumer good, morally desirable or needlessly puritanical according to taste, but rarely important beyond that. Americans were not afraid to confide power and resources to immense public agencies, the biggest in the non-communist world. But whatever else those potent instruments could do, nobody supposed they could do much to reduce domestic inequalities, or routine percentages of graft; and the two limitations were interdependent. Practical redistributive reforms usually aim to shift very small margins of income year by year; small percentages of graft can therefore offset them. Despite the scale and daring of American experimentation, a great many social and economic reconstructions which were open to political choice in Europe, Japan and Australasia were not practical options at all in the USA. In Europe, scandal tended to encourage radical reconstructions; in America it tended on balance to discourage them, by reminding people of the incapacities of corruptible government – even slightly corruptible government. On both sides of the ocean scandals probably had marginal effects in raising tempers and lowering respect for established institutions.

They had more direct effects when they did direct damage. In all countries, manufacturers of food, drugs, vehicles and synthetics sold occasional batches of dangerous goods. Developers and engineers built a few dangerous structures. Oil and chemical firms got planning permissions for installations which then did not behave as promised, and polluted air or sea or rivers. There was some dangerous dumping and escape of poisonous wastes. Most of these incidents might have passed as routine mishaps of technical progress, if some of the responsible executives had not been such wanton liars. Most were not, of course; but those who were were virtuosi. They lied about past, present and future; about their costs, techniques, waste outputs, products and intentions. They lied to labor, shareholders, conservationist agencies, parliamentary and congressional committees. They lied in suave four-color public-interest advertisements; the handsomer ones lied live, worldwide, by Telstar. They induced sad numbers of their chief engineers and chemists to lie with them, and expensive consultants to lie for them. They were unkind – or sometimes too kind – to their critics. Technical officers doing their duty in public services were silenced by political pressure. Politicians were tempted by secret contributions to private or party funds. Bureaucrats were bought over into corporate service. Public relations firms were hired to defame independent critics, and private investigators were hired to look for opportunities to blackmail them.

Three aspects of this were relevant for present purposes. First, some of the scandals caused tangible personal or environmental damage. When corporate misbehavior caused accident or illness, when new buildings full of people fell down or burned up, when there was oil on the beaches and poison in the rivers and mercury or cholera in the seafood, people grew intolerant. On those issues they would positively put politicians out, regardless of old allegiances or old religions of free enterprise. Second, the misbehavior was wildly exaggerated. Scores of thousands of honest enterprises, including many in dangerous or pollutant trades, went on doing their business blamelessly within the law. But the exceptions included some of the biggest corporations in the world and the public supposed that if a few were exposed there must be many more who were not. So a few miscreant executives of oil, chemical, mining and automotive corporations led or misled millions into thinking that they were the tip of an iceberg whose whole bulk must be menacing indeed. Third, private enterprise lost more reputation than public enterprise did. That was sometimes unjust – many offences by private enterprises included some corruption of public representatives, and plenty of environmental outrages were committed by public entrepreneurs of defence works, power supplies, airports and motorways and urban redevelopments. But most of the public offences were merely wrong-headed and could be prevented by determined democratic action. The private operators were harder to control, and personally nastier. They broke more laws, told more lies, generated more bribery, victimized more critics, and made much larger personal fortunes out of their misbehavior.

Then there were offshore scandals.

Legal immunities for the rich were nothing new. They had been built into feudal systems. Later political institutions – upper-class parliaments, privileges of nobility – often protected private wealth from government. By the nineteenth century most formal immunities had gone, but many practical privileges continued. Where property-owners' parliaments were sovereign, taxes on wealth and incomes were low. Where sovereign monarchies survived they were more than ever obliged to buy the goodwill of their richer subjects. Where popular democracy developed, it was still sometimes possible for rich individuals to buy immunities from venal politicians. But all these systems were subject to a distinction between permissible immunities (especially from taxation) and impermissible ones (which might expose the rich themselves to being robbed). Some twentieth-century innovators made the mistake of forgetting that distinction.

A century of democratic development did eventually cramp the style of robber barons. After 1940 especially, new levels of income tax and other puritan inconveniences made it hard to accumulate new personal fortunes except by capital gain and tax avoidance. Ingenuity allowed plenty of both within the law; plenty of people broke the law; but a third alternative was to avoid the law altogether. New types of immunity were pioneered when the first best-selling author emigrated to a tax haven and the first oil-tanker bought a Panamanian flag. Industrial investors began to look abroad to poverty-stricken territories where labor was unorganized, corporate taxation was lower and politicians were cheaper to buy. Thus wealth was deliberately relocated to keep it under weak government and some forms of it, for some purposes, were located technically offshore under no government at all.

These devices worked well as long as they were used to evade laws about taxes and labor conditions, laws which the rich generally permit one another to evade. Then some newcomers went too far. Promoters of offshore funds enticed investors to send billions of dollars for management from addresses out of reach of national tax laws. But out there the money tended to be out of reach of other laws too, or at least of policemen. Some of its managers mismanaged it. Others stole it. The distinction was academic in what was in any form a conspiracy against law and order – honesty between offshore investors and managers could only be honor among thieves. Many investors learned that they might perhaps multiply their money by taking it offshore themselves, but rarely by trusting it to anyone else out there. Honest or crooked, offshore and on, tax-theft soon exceeded in value the proceeds of bank-robbery, burglary and all other offences whatever against property; and scarcely anyone went to prison for it.

Meanwhile the rich suffered increasingly from another kind of offence against property. Some poor countries expropriated their foreign-owned industries and some richer ones put severe restraints on them. More and more countries learned to measure the margins which their local advantages offered to international investors, and found ways of appropriating most of the margins for their own social purposes – or at least for their own rich. Even Greek and Arab and South American dictators were driven by internal difficulties or enlightened self-interest to become greedier. In the end the only really safe havens from capitalist law were those established by contract with communist governments. Nobody robbed or expropriated western investors in Russian or Polish automobile factories. But nobody made sudden personal fortunes from them either; they were under inescapable government, as safe from tax avoidance as from other theft.

The trade in money itself did a good deal to persuade many of the rich that inescapable government might be worth its austerities. Gambling on international exchanges had once been honest gambling on real uncertainties, but the sheer accumulation of stake-money, with socially aimless oil fortunes as the last straw, eventually gave the gamblers a fatal influence on the exchanges. Their operations began to upset internal monetary stabilities and to distort international exchanges of real goods and services. These activities were no help to most of the western rich. They maddened national governments, who worked hard (and successfully, over time) to convince their electors that hardships arising from devaluations and fluctuating unemployment and costs of living should be blamed, even by the most respectable people, on lawless gnomes from Zurich and Kuwait.

Exchange problems, boardroom scandals and offshore scandals were linked by one broad conclusion which increasing numbers of angry investors and voters drew from all of them: capitalist institutions were due for a round of basic reforms. Apart from any socialist objections to them they were manifestly failing to perform their capitalist duties. For example capital markets were supposed to attract resources to the most productive uses. Fund management was supposed to make sure that sophisticated professionals did the allocating. Or so the story went. By the 1970s the story was laughable. Other people's money was not really for that sort of productive allocation. It was for buying and selling; for milking by its managers; or for investing wherever taxes would be least. None of those had anything whatever to do with productive allocation. Tax differences between alternative uses often exceeded differences in conventional productive efficiency – and in broad social efficiency – many times over. Relations between productive efficiency and take-home returns to investors grew more tenuous every year. For many years the least productive of all investment – in property speculation – was the most profitable and usually the most tax-evasive. And every investment in tax-minimization did double harm to national wealth and equity – it often replaced more productivity by less, and it always shifted more public burdens onto poorer taxpayers.

As for the sophisticated professionals, it was hard to know whether investors stood in more danger from the honest or the crooked, the competent or incompetent. In 1973 one pillar of the City of London sold assets from his unit trusts to his family companies then resold them to clear six million personal pounds – three thousand years of a workman's wages – without breaking any laws or paying many taxes. He was competent. Others – fund managers, and directors of the many conglomerates which had become fund managers in all but name – appeared to include some of the world's most inept allocators of resources bar none. Bar *none* – nothing in the misdirection of national resources by the Cuban or Czech governments (to cite the stupidest in the non-capitalist world) could rival the billion-dollar incompetence of some celebrated offshore disasters. Meanwhile many honest onshore conglomerates turned out to be expensive and indifferent managers – the components which they put together often proceeded to make marginally worse and dearer mousetraps than the little old independent mousetrap manufacturers used to make before the take-overs. (Some Right readers may dismiss these pages as Leftist ranting. So they are, but for a purpose. They are to remind readers of the flavor of the daily news of those years: incessant exposures of public and corporate scandals which by degrees shifted critical margins of middle-of-the-road opinion a moderate but vital distance to the Left.)

Except for theft from national exchequers and taxpayers, these were mostly scandals of the very rich stealing from the lesser rich. Many were literally lawless – they neither broke laws nor complied with their intentions, but exploited their loopholes and oceanic vacancies. It was harder and harder to maintain any effective control of such slippery dealing. More and more of the rich themselves were driven to recall which class was supposed to have invented law and order in the first place, and whose property it was supposed to protect. Honest capitalists – manufacturers facing jumpy and expensive interest rates, and fighting off paper take-overs – got very sick of 'the city'. They suspected that the new temptations were taking far too many financial and human resources away from solid productive uses, and raising the price of what remained. Ambitious talent was going into property and the money business instead of into the factories and industrial head-offices; funny money was spoiling the market for useful money.

Thus some each of old wealth, productive wealth, salaried wealth and small wealth came to believe in law and order for the rich, even if it had to include honest tax-collecting; and to believe in some radical reconstruction of capitalist institutions. Both were easier said than done.

Besides the conservative power of all the unrepentant rich, there were also complexity, inertia, fear of the unknown, appalling technical problems, and the difficulty of getting international agreement between governments. But it only needed some serious electoral threats to those governments, and ingenuity would find a way.

4

The historian should still be careful not to exaggerate the force of the items noticed so far. The richer ranks of society were only a little more divided, or repentant, than usual – only a little more than they had been at the time of Roosevelt's New Deal or Attlee's Labour government. Affluent radicalism could weaken some conservative solidarities, in the public services as well as the electorates, and offer some useful reformist leadership. It could be stronger if it could combine with the overlapping radicalism of the environmental movements. But by itself it was far from dominant within its own class, and could not have much effect unless there was at the same time a radical swing of opinion through the other ranks of society.

There was such a swing. Like the American swing of 1932–6, the French of 1936 or the British of 1929 or 1945, it can be generally understood as a protest against the way capitalist society was going. There was the same sense that its traditional political and business managers were losing their grip: the system wasn't even working as its own proprietors intended. But as well as that element, the swings of 1975–85 included another: there was now more confidence that well-understood and workable alternatives were available. Voting for the new regimes was less of a leap in the dark than it would have been for earlier generations.

The leftward movements of opinion still had quite complicated causes. Different issues moved different kinds of people in different countries. There was the usual 'double shift' which occurs during such general adjustments of systems. Governments were changed by shifts of no more than 5 or 10% of electors; but simultaneously all parties shifted their policies a little leftwards, so the movement of opinion and policy was somewhat greater than the electoral figures alone would indicate. Historical explanations of the changes would have to be differently detailed in each national case. Here there is room only for the most general review of two or three of the most widely occurring issues.

The most potent single stimulant of change was probably the movement of urban land and property prices through the third quarter of the

88

century – at once an economic issue, and the most basic and perennial of all environmental issues. It is worth giving special attention to that movement because its effects were underrated for so long, even by the Left. It occurred in all but a very few countries of the developed capitalist world. It was a continuous movement, accelerating through occasional booms. Its long-term promise had been understood for generations by the professionals who made their livings – and fortunes – from it. But for a long time most other people saw it chiefly as a boom (or a racket) in city office building, an isolated idiocy which need not worry ordinary mortals much. Only in the 1970s did majorities of ordinary mortals come to realize what had been quietly done to them at home, through the pricing and renting of the land they lived on.

Any society has a stock of houses and a stock of people to occupy them. The richer people bid for the better houses, and so on down the scale. But the predictable distribution of people to houses can be accompanied by widely different financial arrangements. Compared with the pyramid of incomes, the pyramid of property prices and rents may be steeper or gentler, generally high or generally low. There may be more owning or more renting; mortgage money may be scarce or plentiful, dear or cheap. Moreover mortgage money can defy theoretical expectations by being simultaneously scarce and cheap, or plentiful and dear. In most developed countries the market merely sorts the houses and bidders into pecking order. Prices and ownership are determined otherwise, by tangled mixtures of history, politics and business strategy. Similar cities with similar populations, income distributions, building costs and housing stocks can be found in fact – and in further defiance of theoretical expectations – to have quite different patterns of housing prices, tenures and debts. Those patterns can have very large effects on the distribution of wealth and spendable income.

Through the third quarter of the century the ill effects of urban land and housing developments varied widely through the affluent world. But in the bigger countries, with the nastiest effects on the greatest number of people, these trends were common:

More people had to live in bigger cities. The poorer half of them got least benefit from the special concentration of power, opportunity and high culture which big cities offer – but suffered disproportionately from the higher costs of living and daily transport which big cities impose.[7] Many, especially children, also suffered unrecorded personal costs of crowding, landless housing, asphalt schools and restricted recreational opportunities. Slum-dwelling was not usually as bad as it had been for earlier generations, but it was more expensive and its sufferers got less than their fair shares – and often less than their apparent, recorded shares – of rising standards of living. If they were tenants, their comparative disadvantages increased as owners got highly regressive tax advantages, and protection or profit from general inflation.

Most capitalist cities saw a massive rise in property prices against all other prices.[8] Through the third quarter of the century land prices rose, on average, at twice the rate of monetary inflation. The rise in housing and other property prices was harder to measure, but it was difficult to find a city in 1975 in which houses were not substantially dearer in relation to wages and other prices than they had been in 1950, chiefly because the land under them was three times as dear, or worse. The proportion of real incomes spent on housing held fairly steady until about 1960, then began to rise in most countries. Some of the increasing expenditure bought better housing; after 1960 more and more of it didn't, as private living space increased less than its price did.

The net effect of those price movements was to transfer resources from poorer to richer people. The economists of the time steadfastly declined to measure how much from how many to how few. Housing costs commonly took from a fifth to a third of working-class wages, and lower proportions of higher incomes; and wages and salaries were two thirds or more of national income. So redistributions of income via property price movements may well have been even greater than the transfers effected through the same period by the development of mass consumer credit. Both transferred income after it was received, so there was a complicated relation (also unmeasured at the time) between the official statistics of income, and the real burdens on poorer households.

Some working families escaped these effects: those who lived in small cities and towns, worked near to home, had low-rented public housing, and did not use hire-purchase. But bigger numbers in bigger cities suffered the cumulative effects of increasing inequalities of income, *and* consumer credit charges, *and* rising land and housing prices, *and* big-city costs of living and transport. So even if the money wages of many of them kept up with the general inflation, the increase of real inequality was much greater than the income figures showed. What had happened was this: by reorganizing the markets for land, housing and consumer durables, factions of the rich in the property and moneylending businesses had achieved a strategic change; they had established means of transferring to themselves a permanently larger proportion of everyman's income.

Only 1 or 2% more of it each year, perhaps; but that could be half or more of poor men's shares of economic growth.

The middle classes were supposed to be consoled by the rising values of the houses they owned; property prices shouldn't hurt the Right if they were enriching a full 50% of the population at the expense of the rest. But heirs tend to be more interested in that than owners do; and even they, often enough, sell houses to buy other houses, gaining nothing from the high prices except high death duties. When ordinary people looked at the property business in the 1970s they did not see it as a business whose gains were widely distributed to a property-owning democracy. They saw houses and mortgage rates rising beyond the reach of anyone young, while a few much-publicized individuals and private companies were known to have made ten, fifty, a hundred millions each – and paid tax on very little of it. They saw scandals, rapacious developments, environmental outrages. And they saw no excuse for any of it: it was a purely predatory branch of capitalism, producing nothing that couldn't have been produced better by fairer methods.

But for a long time it looked too complicated to reform. How could government hit the speculators without endangering everybody's property rights? The Right managed to keep that anxiety alive as long as it did chiefly because big countries are so reluctant to take notice of small ones. The capitalist world had quite enough exceptions to that sort of property business to show that it had never been necessary to tolerate it anywhere. In various parts of Scandinavia, the Low Countries and Australia there were examples anyone could imitate, and improve on. Some of those countries had brought high proportions of their urban land into public ownership. By different strategies others had distributed land and houses to make high proportions of their people, including their working classes, owner-occupiers. Either method could give people more equal shares of money, land, housing, or all three. But these achievements were persuasive to foreigners only when their causes and effects were properly understood. It had once been thought that Norwegians, New Zealanders and Australians could afford fairer shares of land, housing and ownership because more equal incomes gave them more equal capacities to pay. The opposite was nearer the truth. In none of those countries did the distribution of wealth or income give most people the means to buy anything resembling equal shares of private land and housing, if the market had been run as it was elsewhere. On the contrary, their arrangements distributed those assets more equally than they distributed almost anything else – wealth, income, education or economic opportunity. If they were in a general way more equal than the bigger capitalist societies it was partly because for half a century their electors had insisted that whatever party was in office, one basic item of wealth should be distributed with unusual fairness.

Through the same half century many land-reforming societies had become richer per head than Germany, France or the United Kingdom. Their land arrangements weren't perfect – they still had some land sharks, office booms, and high housing prices in affluent suburbs – but they were effective enough to leave no excuse for the proprietors, politicians and economists of the bigger countries to go on wringing complacent hands over 'the inexorable realities of the market'. All land markets are political creations. German, French, English and American land markets were reactionary survivals, sustained by Right government, and working with increasing social inefficiency. Wherever there was honest government or the possibility of it, those markets could be reconstructed to work equitably as soon as enough electors wanted that to happen, and grasped that it was practicable.

They grasped it at last through the boom and slump of the 1970s, and that helped to gather support for the great reconstructions of policy of 1975–85. Affluent working classes were suddenly sick of their silos. Young business and professional people rebelled against the prices and mortgage debts that went with the sort of housing they expected. Plenty of both joined in the action that stopped the bulldozers and the wholesale destruction of good townscape. The property business itself did a good deal to split the ranks of the rich. Lenders and builders, especially of housing, could not prosper unless land was plentiful at prices their customers could afford. Indeed there were formidable capitalist interests in keeping land cheap, if they could only be brought into alliance. Every dollar that everyman had to pay for his land was subtracted from what he had left to spend on things which required capitalist production – including house, furniture, car and equipment. In Australia the movement for a more radical reform of land prices and tenures was led by a remarkable trio of mortal enemies: socialist politicians and intellectuals, public housing managers, and the country's biggest speculative building developers. None of them had anything to gain from land markets which encouraged a purely extractive capitalism: a use of wealth not to augment wealth but merely to redistribute it, always in the wrong direction, always to the disadvantage of majorities, to no constructive purpose whatever.

Thus land questions helped to unite the Left, the environmentalists and other allies. Rhetorically they could join in denouncing 'rapacious developers'. More constructively they could work out new ways of pricing and allocating land, and persuade electors to adopt them. This work fell to them and to other amateurs because most orthodox economists at the time were incapable of it, for reasons built deeply into their professional ideologies.

5

The urban and environmental and land troubles were all superimposed on central problems of capitalism which continued to inspire its permanent opposition – the whole range of the revolutionary and reformist Left.

Which are the central problems of capitalism is always a matter of opinion. Among those who came together in the reforming alliances of the last quarter of the century, three general kinds of diagnosis were popular. First there was the belief, which moved many otherwise-conservative environmentalists some distance to the Left, that however well capitalism had worked for economic growth and personal freedom in the past, its greedy and competitive approach to natural resources would not do for the different environmental problems of the future. Second there was anxiety, on the Right as well as the Left, about the cluster of economic and social problems which centred around inflation. And finally there were all the evergreen objections to a capitalist system which ran on avarice, inequality, alienation and other inhumanities.

Most capitalist economists came to see inflation as the system's central technical problem. A very few had predicted this long before, in the course of adapting Keynesian theory to cope with its own success – with the management of permanent full employment. But too-rapid inflation continued for a long time to be regarded by most experts as an irritating impurity in the system, a product of clumsy central economic management, or of irresponsible political promises or labor militancy. Such simple understandings were upset by accumulating experience. It became apparent that inflation occurred in diverse forms, with diverse causes, and with accompaniments which could include plenty of unemployment and unsatisfactory rates of economic growth. Its social and international effects were more various and damaging than had been supposed. And for capitalists they were not its worst effects. Its most frightening implications were technical. The inflationary wage and price *pressures* were not mistaken or irrational. Individually, economic man was behaving with precisely the enlightened self-interest that was sup-

4-2

posed to maximize the efficiency of the economy as a whole. But complicated instabilities at the heart of the system – positive feedbacks and spiral effects – were distorting its allocations of incentives and rewards, and therefore of resources. As in 1931, the system needed some correction if it was to survive, but this time the changes might have to be more radical.

Theorists continued to disagree about the causes of these troubles. But by the 1970s everyone agreed that they called for public control: probably for some combination of price, income and profit policies. As to what those policies should be, there was again violent disagreement. Some of it was technical but most of it expressed classical conflicts of interest between rich and poor, Right and Left. If what had passed as traditional or market distributions of wealth and income were now acknowledged even by the Right to be dangerously unstable and inefficient, then distributions would have to follow deliberately chosen patterns instead. Nobody on either side was likely to choose such patterns for economic efficiency alone. There was no technical reason why they should, or indeed could. The world's richest countries, Sweden and the United States, operated at opposite extremes of the capitalist range of inequalities. The highest efficiency was obviously available at either extreme, perhaps beyond, and presumably anywhere between. The Right could point to American productivity; the Left could argue that the only *untried* way to become more productive than the Swedes was to become more equal than they were.

Through the early years of the 1970s American and British and other governments of the Right were still trying with increasing desperation to control inflation by coercive increases of inequality – sometimes by inducing unemployment, more often by wage-freezes variously dignified as income policies. Some governments tried to restrain higher incomes and profits and prices as well as wages; others didn't. They all failed. Controls on property and executive incomes were never serious; prices wouldn't slow down if wages didn't; and wage earners succeeded in resisting the wage freezes. The wage earners were sometimes helped by political sympathizers or conniving employers, but overwhelmingly the war was planned, commanded and won by the labor unions – the oldest organization of the old Left, in its oldest role.

In the short run these sometimes seemed to be hollow victories. The poor couldn't win either way – if they beat the wage restraints, they lost in other ways to the continuing inflation. But the leaders of the resistance soon had more in mind than the traditional defence of wage levels. They were stirred from the defence to the attack – and to make some peremptory demands on their political parties – by two more ominous developments. One slow fuse that had smoldered for a quarter of a century finally reached its powder keg: these were the years when it dawned on the rank and file of labor (as on the rank and file of economists) that capitalist societies were now permanently increasing instead of reducing a number of their internal inequalities, had probably been doing so for twenty or thirty years, and were now doing it at an increasing rate. And this sour awakening coincided with the first noticeable impact of environmental troubles on mass standards of living as heavy pollution-abatement costs were heaped onto retail prices, and the petroleum and coal-mining troubles began.

Thus within a very short span of time the mass of working men and women made three discoveries. For decades past they had been quietly and systematically cheated of some of their share of growing productivity. Now the tax-dodging proprietors of oil and land were accelerating that trend by forcing permanent (and voluptuously profitable) increases in the 'real' prices of housing, heating, gasoline, public transport and other oil-fuelled services. And inflation, from which the poorest of the population were already the worst sufferers, was to be controlled by policies which would permanently restrain wages and improve profits.

It was too much. Or in a larger, longer, happier, more historical view of it, it was – at long last – *enough*.

4
Second chances in theory

Here, converging through the 1970s, were the ingredients of a new time of troubles. Systems and policies which had carried the capitalist democracies through a quarter of a century of easy evolution now faced problems of environmental and economic management with which they could not cope. Popular tolerance could of course survive any number of doomsday books and gathering clouds and early warnings – but now the prices and shortages and disorganizations were actually beginning to bite. Strange shifts and inconsistencies appeared in traditional voting patterns. Fewer governments survived elections, or expected to. In these rich societies revolution was unlikely; but some drastic reconstructions seemed inescapable.

But what should they be, and who would engineer them? The situation was nowhere simple, but one way to simplify it – in analysis, and perhaps also in action – was to think of the Right, the Left and the environmentalists as three political forces, of which any two could combine to beat the third. Of course there were not three such parties in any country, or three such distinct divisions of voters. Environmentalists were scattered through all parties, and Left and Right ideas coexisted in the minds of many people in the middle. But by some mixture of party re-alignment and the re-ordering of ideas in people's minds, coherent national solutions to the new problems were likely to be arrived at (if at all) by some alliance of two of those three basic approaches.

Which two? In some countries in the past, rarely and temporarily, Right and Left had been known to cooperate to kill some third party which tried to hold the balance between them. More often, moderates of Right and Left had cooperated against extremists of Right or Left. More recently there had been attempts to unite 'old' Right and 'old' Left – the true believers in economic growth – against environmental opponents of growth. But this time such centre blocs were unlikely. Middle-of-the-road alliances could only run on middle-of-the-road policies, and it was the decisive failure of middle-of-the-road policies that had allowed the problems of inflation to become so acute. Radical therapy was needed, and neither Left nor Right could possibly tolerate the brand of radical medicine proposed by the other.

So it was a situation for the classical opposition of Left and Right, with two new circumstances to intensify the contest. Because on issues of land and inflation the middle of the road now seemed unsafe for technical reasons, 'Left' and 'Right' meant more – they stood for programs further from the Centre and from each other – than had been true of potential majority parties in any rich country for generations. And environmental and quality-of-life issues were so important to so many electors, and so closely linked with some of the strictly economic issues, that it might well be chiefly on environmental issues that Left and Right would have to compete for the vital margins of swinging or uncommitted support.

At the time it seemed unlikely that the Left could win. Their obsession with mass living standards was often difficult to reconcile with environmentalist values. Their radicalism threatened rich and middle incomes directly, and whenever those affluent classes were driven to close ranks and bring to bear all of their immense skill and influence in business, communications and government, they were very hard to beat by any ordinary democratic process. This time moreover the threat was not the traditional threat of mild doses of tax-and-welfare, from labor or social-democratic parties eager to reassure swinging voters of their extreme moderation. In all rich countries (except a few with Swedish-style distributions already) the threat from the Left now included large transfers of wealth, income and private economic control. In trying to persuade majorities to resist such threats, the Right could appeal to feelings and anxieties which were widespread and deeply entrenched, especially in the minds of women voters of every class: dislike of bureaucracy, and of militant labor; distrust of untried theoretical solutions; fears for personal liberties; fears of disorganization and breakdown.

To understand why the Left parties nevertheless did as well as they did, it is necessary to understand more than the facts of class economic interest, even including the internecine conflicts of interest which were now tending to divide the rich and weaken the Right. A grossly simplified explanation of the Left's success might reduce its causes to two: First, wherever broad parties of the Left existed, cost-of-living troubles and rising inequalities strengthened their 'natural' or traditional support, leading people on low incomes to vote Left with quite unusual solidarity – small shopkeepers, self-employed tradesmen, 'working-class tories', wives, widows and all. Second, they were joined by radical minorities from higher income levels, minorities whose movement to the Left expressed a subtle but vital change of mood. The previous chapter noticed some of the origins of that change. Urban and environmental troubles, quality-of-life issues, local and community initiatives, business scandals and property prices and the problems of inflation all contributed. It would take too long to trace the detailed ways in which those and other concerns coalesced to generate a pervasive radical mood: a mood which allowed stable alignments, coherent national programs and permanent radical gains. Rather than try to trace that complex process we shall try instead to sum up the dominant ideology that emerged from it.

2

The popular ideology of the 1980s had its most formal intellectual expression in a group of new social theories. Like the mood which they expressed, they were by no means *all* new: an important part of their function was to modernize some quite traditional liberal and radical ideas. But it is worth tracing their development at some length to make clear what the new moods actually were – how people felt, what they valued, what they believed to be 'the limits of the possible', and why they came to act politically with what would have seemed a few years earlier to be surprising daring.

As usual, new ideas began as responses to new events. For example, as noted earlier, the behavior of inflation seemed to be changing. Why should it change its mechanisms, and apparently its causes and effects and predictability, within otherwise-unchanging economic systems? Perhaps it had changed in America for technical reasons related to a particular stage of economic growth; but if so, why did similar changes simultaneously afflict European economies which had reached scarcely half the American level of productivity?

This was only one of the odd developments which prompted what came to be called the 'phase theories' or 'threshold theories' of the last quarter of the century. Their mixture of old and new ideas – of reassurance and promise – was so artful that it is worth digressing to notice some of the older traditions which they drew on.

They were creatures of their time in many ways. Intellectually they were part of a recoil from a period of unduly compartmentalized and sterile social science. They offered fertile opportunities to political scientists and sociologists who suddenly wanted to relate genuinely scientific research to genuinely useful policy-making, in academic disciplines which had seen too little of either from 1950 to 1970. In economics they marked the return to strength of the school of institutional economists who had never expected much of the purer sort of economic theory – the sort that looked chiefly for regular mathematical relationships within an abstractly isolated 'economic system'. The institutional school believed in studying the economic performance of *whole* social systems: a performance which was never likely to be intelligible without a good deal of reference to political and social structures and psychology, institutions unique to time and place, and continuous historical change.

There were other convergences. In form, threshold theories sometimes echoed the Marxist dialectic. But in substance they owed more to a growing belief among both Marxist and non-Marxist historians that history was neither simply linear nor simply repetitive; rather it created different degrees of freedom and determination, different patterns of social choice and constraint, at different stages of development. Similar ideas came from town planners who had developed threshold theories about the choices and diversifications which were open to cities of different types at different stages of growth and wealth.

At the same time the concept of 'stages' was being used with new caution. Many institutional economists had concluded that industrialization (for example) could never be understood as a standard process, performable in much the same way by one developing nation after another. Historically it was different every time, and theoretically it had to be, if only because each national modernization altered the world in which the next had to be attempted. If that was true of primitive industrialization, it was likely to be true at every stage of economic growth. So, reversing an assumption common in the 1950s, it now seemed that the one thing the advancing capitalist countries could *not* expect to do was to follow very closely in the footsteps of the United States.

For instance the Americans had been the first to produce $2,000 annual income per head. At the date when they did so, they had particular forms of organization and they perceived particular ranges of social and developmental options as viable for the future. When other countries in turn reached that $2,000 level they did it in a world which now included competitors richer than themselves, different knowledge and technology including knowledge of the American experience above $2,000, and – inevitably, in a world so changed – different perceptions of a different range of social and developmental options. As one example, when Americans looked forward from $2,000 a year as pioneers of the unknown they could not *know* what level of inequality would accompany higher productivity than that, or whether there would be any room for choice about it. By the time a dozen other national societies were passing the $2,000 level they could observe the Swedish performance at $3,000 as well as the American performance at $4,000; and some communist societies were also approaching those levels of productivity. Developing societies might not be able to choose any particular precedent as a ready-made option for themselves – every society had unique constraints of its own – but they all had grounds for believing in a wider range of workable alternatives than either Americans or Swedes had had real evidence for at their own $2,000 stages of development. Of course followers if they were unimaginative could always let themselves be constrained rather than liberated by the example of leaders; but generally, time and experience were proving to leaders and followers alike that the range of inequalities and social structures which were compatible with economic growth, and with capitalist growth, was wider than either Left or Right had once expected. And that discovery itself could be generalized: at any date, the range was likely to be wider than people *yet* expected. Instead of taking an arbitrary selection of economic trends which had operated up to the $2,000 stage, and extrapolating them to chart a course beyond that, it now made more sense to extrapolate something quite different: namely a growing capacity to perceive and choose between historical options – an increasing tendency to *alter* course.

This potent idea came from various sources. On it, the threshold theorists set out to build new structures of theory and method and useful knowledge. Historically, they acknowledged that most early industrializers had very limited choices. That phase of growth was constrained by necessities of primitive saving, by limited technology and social skills, and also by compulsory priorities – food, housing, health and elementary education for multitudes in absolute poverty. But the methods and values and inequalities which might be genuine necessities of that first phase need not be perpetuated, as so many of them had so often been, to become constraints on later phases of growth. At each later phase, as growth took them over threshold after threshold – two rooms and a bike and a village nurse; four rooms and a bus and a doctor; eight rooms and two cars and transplant surgery – societies were progressively freer to choose between different uses and distributions of their productivity, *if they only knew it.* Insofar as they didn't know it, and consequently failed to assess and choose deliberately from among the multiplying options opening for them, it could be said that objective and technical constraints on their directions of progress were being steadily replaced by constraints of ignorance and misunderstanding.

Developing these themes, the threshold theorists took some mischievous pleasure in arguing that a good deal of their parents' ignorance had been foisted on them by their social scientists. Some of the schools of social science which were dominant in the 1950s and 1960s were so anxious to imitate the abstract, universal and value-free characteristics of physics that they searched social behavior *only* for regularities capable of supporting mathematically-expressible universals. Anything else they came across they discarded as idiographic, by which they meant useless knowledge fit only for historians. Thus they selected whatever seemed least likely to change, then dearly hoped it wouldn't change, because their theories and reputations and emoluments depended on its not changing. Then they worked hard to persuade laymen and politicians that futures must inevitably unfold by strict extrapolation of going trends – and could be predicted as soon as there was massive enough investment in computerized multi-variate analysis. It was exaggerating only a little to say that through those years, many of the millions which the rich societies invested in enlarging their social options by trying to know more about them were in fact used to reduce their options by persuading them that they had scarcely any choices. The more up-to-date social scientists they hired, the more research institutions and multi-disciplinary teams they financed and the more electronic hardware they paid for, the less they could possibly hope to understand about their real social options and capacities.

What the threshold theorists tried to do instead was to establish what actual range of social options was open at each stage of economic growth, and of world history. They were specially interested in the relations between stages of growth and stages of history. Obviously a society industrializing in the nineteenth century and another doing so in the twentieth had different options; just as obviously, contemporaneous societies at any date had different options if they were at different stages of growth. What was new was the growing belief that fully equivalent societies, at some stages of growth and of history, might also have wide opportunities to differ. Societies still living chiefly on village agriculture could choose to add a bike to each household, or rapid transit to one metropolis; they could choose to put a nurse into each village, or curative hospitals (with transplant surgery) into a few cities; and the choices would affect general patterns of inequality as well as particular distributions of transport or medical services. Richer societies had wider choices, if they were politically aware and organized to take choices.[9]

Such expanding freedoms are easiest to understand for individuals or households, who can choose to spend income above subsistence in a wide variety of ways, and to use their home capital to produce a wide variety of goods. For whole social systems it is more complicated. At any specific time and level of productivity, objective constraints are imposed by existing capital, technique and human and natural resources. Other constraints are imposed by existing social and institutional structures, especially by the power and material interests of ruling classes. Further constraints, of special interest to the threshold theorists, are built into people's consciousness of their options. People will die of thirst in reach of pure water if they believe it to be poisonous. In affluent countries they don't die of thirst, but they have at times abstained from a great many workable social and economic reorganizations. Plenty of such options are rejected as genuinely undesirable. But others are rejected because of false or needless fears of organizational incapacity, or loss of freedom, or economic breakdown. Some chances are missed because social conflicts are won by the wrong factions; potential allies fail to form alliances, or potential winners underestimate their political strength and don't give battle. Such perceptions of alternatives are very difficult to test. Tests for truth or falsehood are not always appropriate; there are also gaming problems, and questions of self-confidence. A mistaken overconfidence in your own capacities can't enlarge them, or dissolve external obstacles. But a mistaken belief in your own *in*capacity can incapacitate you, and turn a mistake into a truth which may in due course be seen in retrospect as an historical inevitability. Like politicians, the threshold theorists had to mix guesses and hunches and gambling chances with their surer facts and theories.

They had plenty of material. As rich and poor societies developed through the second half of the twentieth century, many constraints arising from ignorance were eroded by experience. The copy-book case, cited so often here as elsewhere, was the Swedish/American contrast. It had once been orthodox to believe in a determinate relation between capitalist economic growth and specific inequality. Too much inequality would hinder growth by restricting mass purchasing power; too little would hinder growth by discouraging saving and capital formation. Despite any amount of public capital formation, and some expert doubts of their own about marginal propensities to save at different income levels, many capitalist economists went on encouraging those reactionary equations long after Swedes and others had begun to combine American productivity with unAmerican degrees of equality. Similar lessons were as plain in communist experience. Small communist countries representing various stages of economic growth – Bulgaria, Hungary, Poland – were more equal than the USSR, often had more personal freedom, and achieved as good or better economic growth.

Many other developments served through the same years to enlarge people's understanding of their options. The British nationalizations of 1945–50 were at first written off as failures because, as the British chose to use them, they contributed next to nothing to their supposed purpose of reducing inequalities. But in time they contributed to proving other things. Public acquisition did no necessary harm to personal liberties. Making flexible use of both public and private management, public ownership could be as efficient as private ownership for most purposes and more efficient for many. *And its capacities were obviously subject to historical change.* Public ownership had quite different potentiality in 1900, 1950, 1975; it had different potentiality in mixed or fully capitalist or fully socialist contexts; it had different potentiality under honest or corruptible governments; it certainly had different efficiency in Sweden, Russia and the USA. Once again a new social perception made its first appearance as a Polish joke: 'Only communist states can keep private enterprise honest; only capitalist states can keep public enterprise efficient.' Meanwhile under the name of 'socializing the flow' the Japanese and others demonstrated that another combination – private ownership with public management – could also work. Other developments around the world converged to show how very wide was the range of workable relations between government, public and private management, and public, private and cooperative ownership. Furthermore almost any of those ways of organizing production could be made to work in favor of either more or less equality of income, according to political taste. Scarcely any of the stereotyped generalizations of either Right or Left, about the 'intrinsic efficiency' or 'intrinsic inefficiency', the 'intrinsic tyranny' or 'intrinsic anarchy' of either public or private enterprise survived the practical experience of the 1970s.

There were many examples of that kind. But the threshold theorists and institutional economists were not chiefly interested in cataloging what had been done. They were more concerned to improve the general social capacity to judge what *could* be done – to make first-time innovation at once more imaginative and more sure-footed. We need not review their many detailed assessments of the social options open at various dates, on various assumptions, to scores of national societies. What mattered more was the mood of relaxed and confident social experimentation which their work expressed, and encouraged. Ideologists – including many orthodox economists – had once debated rival social and economic forecasts as if they were mutually exclusive scientific predictions of inevitable, historically determined heavens or hells. Now – with the lists of options much winnowed and augmented – practical versions of many of those futures were debated and campaigned for in a matter-of-fact way as workable alternatives. Extrapolation was out; choice – and with it, a more active and meaningful war of political parties and programs – was in. To the horror of one old school of capitalist rhetoricians, an ancient article of their rhetoric was suddenly believed by the Left: 'wealth is freedom'. When societies grow rich enough, they become free to do anything they like. Within broad practical limits that include choosing any mixture of public and private enterprise; any level of environmental extravagance or frugality; and any pattern of equalities and inequalities.

3

Being interested in ranges of choice, the new theorists were also interested in processes of choosing. They soon concluded that those also changed as capitalist societies developed from phase to phase. In this line of argument they were criticized by Marxists for underrating permanent realities of class, and by other political scientists for saying nothing very new. But their work offered further encouragement to reformers.

Marx (they said) lived in a world in which ownership did indeed separate the classes and determine their relations with each other. Any non-owners among the rich – professionals, salaried managers – were dependent enough to make no difference to the political role of a ruling class based on ownership of the means of production and governing in the interest of owners. But times have changed. Ownership has been diffused, separated from managerial power, and reduced to a legal right to have private title to capital and draw income from it. Except that you don't have to work for them, incomes drawn from the going rates of interest or profit are much the same as incomes drawn from the going rates of pay for professional qualifications or managerial skills. The few owners who retain the old kind of direct proprietorial control are now vastly outnumbered by salaried and professional earners, many of whom are rentiers too, so that there is no longer any important distinction between property-owning and salaried classes: they are the same people. However their incomes combine elements of investment and salary, and whether they work in private or public enterprises (or in capitalist or communist countries), these shareholding, salaried and professional rich are now the main beneficiaries and defenders of economic inequalities. But they are not distinguishable as a functional class because no line separates them from those below them. The increase and diversification of middle skills and incomes has transformed all affluent societies (capitalist and socialist) to classless societies in *one* sense: people are – and unless old class identifications survive in purely sentimental form, they *see* themselves as being – individual competitors on a perfectly continuous ladder of incomes.

Thus the atomization of society need not mean that people have no social integration at home or at work; but it does mean that most of them contend economically and politically with individual rather than class situations in mind. They do still often classify themselves, and act accordingly, as for example in labor unions or professional associations. But that is now a matter of choice. It does not mean that functionally-defined classes still exist as facts of life and determine the political role of their members. It means that people choose to classify and ally themselves this way or that way – sometimes in 'income classes' and sometimes not – according to strategic and tactical opportunity. This represents an historical change from early, class-structured capitalism. But it does not represent any change in the nature of economic man nor in his propensity to act in his own interest, alone or in alliances. Nor does it represent any reconciliation of economic interests, nor any necessary reduction of conflict or increase of consensus in politics. It merely alters the structure and method of conflict, and the possible bases of alliance or consensus. Above all it widens the tactical options open to most members of the system.

Thus a self-serving contender with an income in (say) the 40th or 50th or 60th percentile of incomes no longer wonders whether he 'really' belongs to a working class which should rationally vote Left or to a bourgeois class which should rationally vote Right. Instead he weighs the alternatives of joining a low-income alliance to soak the rich, or a high-income alliance to soak the poor, or an alliance of middle incomes to play the middle against both ends – or a Protestant or Catholic, white or black, rural or urban, or any other mutual-interest or self-defensive combination. He also weighs the likely advantages to himself of his society having variously shaped, variously flat or tall patterns of in-equality. All these calculations are qualified by beliefs about what is actually possible and what political parties are actually offering; also by beliefs about justice, the costs of social conflict, the comparative values of freedom and safety and wealth, and so on.

105

So far this sort of analysis did not stray far from conventional understandings of democratic capitalist pluralism. But these theorists insisted that pluralism itself was a choice. Different national societies had different degrees of it because their citizens, by choosing to act in particular combinations, had *chosen* different degrees of it. As a favorite historical example, they cited the ways in which low income earners had chosen to respond to the historical change from class-structured inequalities to 'continuous' inequalities. All the industrialized societies had passed through a phase – often between about 1880 and 1920 – when their new industrial and urban masses were for the first time numerous, literate, enfranchised, and substantially free to organize politically. They were all offered similar kinds of radical leadership and propaganda, just as they all suffered similar barrages of conservative pressure and propaganda. At the beginning of that phase their societies all had political systems dominated by middle- and upper-class parties. The national working classes were all offered the option of voting for those traditional liberal and conservative parties, or for new parties of their own, whether social-democratic or revolutionary. By large majorities the European masses chose parties of their own. By even larger majorities, after some decades of hesitant experiment, low-income Americans chose otherwise. The pressures on those choices – the bias of government, press and employers – were much the same everywhere. So why have so many historians tried to explain away as inevitable, or historically or economically 'determined', one of the most critically important and *free* acts of choice in modern history?

Freedom to choose was still (in this view) a variable historical condition. Those industrializing societies had offered those particular options to that particular generation of low earners. But once the choices were made and entrenched in durable institutions, the ranges of choice open to later generations were reconstructed accordingly. Europeans could now act together as income-classes whenever they wanted to; Americans could not, without what would now be a very difficult reconstruction of their party system.

The continuing European option turned out to have different value at different dates. For three quarters of a century it seemed to have very little direct value to European workers. The parties of the Left governed rarely, and achieved very little for their supporters when they did. They achieved so little partly because capitalism achieved so much, keeping its promise of growth for all, and partly because the parties of the Right had the sense to do a good deal of moderate reforming themselves. Even

106

the Left's own voters had cause to doubt the Left's capacity to do much better than that. The workers in rich countries had nothing to gain from Stalinist tyranny, and their leaders were not good at managing capitalist economies during their few early periods of office in the 1920s and 1930s. Left government threatened middle incomes and opportunities directly, and might well reduce poorer incomes by incompetent effects of unemployment or inflation, or by provoking strikes of capital or other disruption from the Right. On almost any income it was at least *safe* to vote for the parties of the moderate Right. Under their management growth continued, and for a long time so did progress towards more welfare and equality. Parties of the moderate Left acknowledged the truth of that when they ran safe too, promising not to cause any serious disturbance to the steady capitalist progress. Both parties meanwhile did what they could to pick up swinging voters and special-interest groups on non-class issues – and began to look a little like Republicans and Democrats. Soon the Right could believe that (except for some revolutionary relics) the Left had conceded its basic and original error, and joined the system. Marxists agreed: the social-democratic and labor parties had become capitalist institutions for the social control of the class they represented.

But there was one sense in which both those interpretations were wrong. In mid-century conditions, low earners may have made very little effective use of their class-based parties. But if the conditions should ever change, it might once again be very important that they still had such parties. However the conditions and wishes of American low earners might change, *they* had no such instrument and no real hope now of creating one. Because the European social-democratic parties continued to exist, rusty but serviceable, their societies retained one option which American society did not: namely government on behalf of the lower half of earners, concerned chiefly with their interests as low earners, answerable chiefly to them and their chosen allies. That widened the options for environmentalists too. Where public ownership or other types of control hostile to private profit-making promised the best environmental management, environmentalists could swing majorities for experienced parties of the Left which were already favorable to such solutions.

Meanwhile there was threshold theorizing on the Right as well as the Left, but all to the same effect: people were freer, if they only knew it, and the purpose of such theorizing was to teach them to realize and use their freedoms. Right shouldn't argue with Left about the new scope for choice, but only about the right and wrong uses of it. This was an atmosphere in which specialist reformers – urban reformers, land reformers, all kinds of environmentalists – could thrive. Their relations with Right and Left were often tense, because there were solid economic interests and passionately held values at stake. But in another way the atmosphere was cooler than it used to be. People now argued about uses of public and private ownership and management like they used to argue about sales-taxes or butter subsidies: as instrumental devices. It no longer paid to rant about your own program as the one and only possible alternative to national bankruptcy, Stalinist enslavement or global disaster. People knew better. Most parties of any consequence were recognized to be offering workable futures. The futures were differently profitable to different interests, differently attractive to different values, and most of the interested parties understood their interests and values very well. It was a long time since democracy had felt so businesslike – so like a genuine process of choice.

5
Second chances in practice

The countries which made the most of their opportunities through the last quarter of the century were those which had unitary constitutions, and political parties based however loosely on class or income. To sum up the reasons why that was so and why the Left achieved so much, three questions will serve to draw together the general explanation which has been suggested so far. How were the fortunes of Right and Left affected by differences of national political structure? By choices of political strategy? And by movements of mass and class opinion?

Constitutional forms and party structures had a lot to do with the actual capabilities of government. To distribute environmental costs and benefits with deliberate justice and to restrain inflation by any but the most reactionary means, quite complicated long-term policies had to be carried out under coherent central direction with coordinated action by executive, legislative and local arms of government. In the capacity to provide that sort of government the rich democracies fell into four general groups.

First there were those with the two characteristics noted in the first paragraph above: the United Kingdom, Japan, the Scandinavian and Low Countries and New Zealand.

Next there were those with unitary constitutions but with regional or other social divisions which made for fragmented or undisciplined political parties. In France and Italy Left and Right were each divided, few majorities were simple and many coalitions were impermanent and negative – 'you drop the crazy novelties from your program and I'll defer the contentious parts of mine'. In practice that usually left the public servants to govern. In Italy the effects were made worse by administrative weakness, corruption and poverty. In France they improved as the Gaullist constitutional reforms established a strong executive, and a developing alignment of socialist and communist parties got ready to use it. French public services and central planning institutions, though conservative unless forced to be otherwise, were efficient. But it was still difficult for the Left – even a united Left – to get control of them by simple electoral majority. The numerous, prosperous and socially stable population of the French countryside and country towns meant that rich/poor divisions were always complicated by urban/rural and other divisions. However progressive in welfare matters the rich could still muster formidable rural, regional and religious support for strong private property rights and weak taxation of wealth and income.

Third, in Germany and Australia there were federations which were however blessed with parliamentary executives so that the conservative bias of the federal structure itself could be overcome to some degree by disciplined parties acting coherently at more than one level of government; and both countries had party systems based on class, and nationally organized labor unions.

Finally there was the American federal structure with sovereignty fragmented vertically as well as horizontally. Because neither central and state governments, nor their executives and legislatures, could really discipline each other, political parties couldn't command or be commanded either. The American parties were admirably designed to give detailed attention to innumerable local needs and sectional interests but they were not designed to be masterful coordinators of federal and state policies, or to divide the political nation on lines of income, so there could be no coherent national government by and for the lower half of income earners. There could be occasional programs to relieve poverty but no effective programs to reduce wealth or the general scale of inequality. Such a restriction of choice could be seen as an effect of inherited institutions, but both were really secured by values, incapacities and conflicts of interest deeply entrenched in the national culture.

Some rich countries did not fit neatly into any of those categories. Canadian politics mixed elements of class and regional division, and of European and American style. Canada developed exceptionally good technical environmental services, under-employed them, used them without much care for class distributions, and became the best single supplier of able personnel to international environmental agencies.

2

Each country's range of choice in economic and environmental reform was thus conditioned by its political inheritance. Within that range of choice there were then questions of political strategy.

The Right's initial advantages and disadvantages simply reflected the buoyancy of existing social and economic systems. As long as those delivered full employment and rising living standards to majorities the Right stood in so little danger from any suffering minorities (or moralists) that its principles were widely accepted as belonging to Centre rather than Right, and were endorsed in practice by many labor and social-democratic parties as well. But as soon as the economic systems struck trouble, so did the Right. The richer half of society began to experience contradictions between its old free-enterprise faith and institutions and its new anxieties about inflation, land and environment. The poorer half, well educated at last, grew discontented with its diminishing share of growth. Organized labor (and disorganized capitalist pricing) blocked most of the action which governments of the Right were willing to take against inflation.

In those circumstances the best strategy for the Right would certainly have been a pre-emptive one. If capitalism was beginning to generate excessive instabilities and inequalities the rich had the strongest interest in restoring the traditional balances that had served them so well. But a pre-emptive strategy required some daring on a number of fronts – with inflation, with property rights and markets, and with threatened resources.

It was theoretically possible to break into the vicious circle of inflation by applying direct controls to prices and higher salaries only, thus avoiding direct confrontation with labor. Public industries could be made sufficiently independent to go bankrupt like private industries if they failed to pay their way. If prices were then controlled with wartime rigidity, wage pressures would bring profits back to modest levels but labor would soon learn that pressure beyond that point could only close industries down. Excessive wage demands would then become so obviously internecine that they would weaken rather than strengthen labor solidarity in the long run. If restraints on salaries and property gains were also enforced the trend to greater inequality might at last be arrested and labor would then be even more inclined to behave itself. Thus a limited adjustment of the system – not much more painful than the Keynesian adjustment had been – might restore both the stabilities and the reasonable inequalities of the golden years of Eisenhower and Macmillan.

Most countries had some would-be leaders of the Right who were willing to offer such policies. They all had decisive numbers of middle or swinging voters who would gladly have given power to any safely non-socialist party that did offer them. But no non-socialist party did.[10] Too many of the traditional leaders and supporters of the Right were

111

greedy, short-sighted or passionately or complacently devoted to traditional policies. They also missed some environmental opportunities. Whether in 'the national interest' or in the interest of capitalist proprietors, more and more problems of scarce or monopolized resources were inviting radical public intervention. If the Left did the work it would be designed to increase equality or public ownership for their own sakes. The Right could do it differently. Minerals, fuel, power, some transport and some heavy manufacturing could all be nationalized quite helpfully to private enterprise as a whole. Dispossessed owners could have lavish compensation and the state could then provide cheap energy, materials and services to the private enterprises that needed them. Land reforms could be designed to deal generously both with proprietors who were dispossessed, and with business users and affluent householders under the new arrangements. Where it proved difficult to regulate the waste outputs of competitive industries the state could take over the pollutant processes *only*, then perform them with proper care at low prices for the benefit of the private enterprises they used to belong to. Altogether the public management of physical resources and monopoly services offered enticing opportunities to a radical Right – but scarcely anywhere was the Right radical enough to sieze them.

If the proprietors and traditional supporters of the Right wanted to stick to traditional free-enterprising methods, what alternative strategies were open to them? Broadly there were two: strong environmental reform, or no change from the conservative pragmatism of former years.

Many environmentalists themselves hoped for strong environmental action from the Right. Those who wanted to stop economic growth altogether couldn't expect immediate help from either side, but they could hope that harsh events might persuade the rich to call a halt sooner than the needy poor were likely to. Those who were more concerned with local environments – people who wanted to reduce industrial pollution or private motoring, protect wilderness parks or threatened species, improve the quality of landscapes and townscapes – often accepted the orthodox theory that these were middle-class concerns with which middle-class political parties were most likely to help. And as the cold war died abroad and at home and a newly respectable Left began to pick up votes from the growing internal troubles of capitalism, leaders of the Right were aware that they also might need new supporters and that some of their old supporters might want new reasons. Could enough middle-class swingers be attracted by strong environmental programs, especially if the costs were met from regressive taxes or spread inconspicuously over retail prices and service charges under the all-party slogan 'make the polluter pay'? It was a plausible strategy but there were reasons why not many parties attempted it. However well it might have worked back in the golden age, when comfortably prospering majorities were failing to notice any gentle increments of inequality, it would now be politically quite dangerous to add heavy environmental costs to the already un-popular shortage prices and property prices, the general inflation, and the harsh wage policies with which the Right were desperately trying to restrain inflation. There were also simpler objections, closer to home. Plenty of businessmen still wanted old-style growth with no bureaucrats sieving their sewage and taxing their externalities. And conservative politicians knew that significant minorities of low wage earners and rather more of their wives, who also wanted fast growth and low prices and no nonsense, had always voted for the Right and should not be discouraged from continuing.

Between them the American parties nevertheless could and did get away with a good deal of strong but inequitable environmental action, merely taking care to avoid direct confrontations with organized labor. But the strategy only worked where there was no serious political competition from the Left. Whenever there was such competition the least dangerous course for the Right – for Conservatives and Liberals, Christian Democrats and Gaullists – was to carry on as before as middle-of-the-road pragmatists. Environmentalists need not be ignored or an-tagonized. They could expect many moderate improvements, moderately maldistributed; or when emergencies occurred, rations and emergency services rather better distributed. Such a strategy was not nearly as helpless as this jaundiced account of it may imply. These were ex-perienced parties. Over the years they had done much to ameliorate the social effects of their capitalist systems. They had nationally-trusted leaders who could often get better service than the Left could from their national public services. Despite economic upsets and some changes of popular thought and feeling noticed elsewhere in these chapters there was still plenty of support in such civilized and comfortable societies for adaptable, pragmatic, untheoretical government, moving with the times, meeting troubles as they came, attending in season to the pensions and family allowances: for the devil the people knew, and the good things so many of them had.

What options were open to the Left?

Some of the very, very old Left were still for lambasting all environ-

113

mentalists without exception as 'the new Right'. But not many, and not for long. For any cool calculator, environmentalism offered golden gifts to the Left. If, as nearly everyone believed, three quarters or more of the new environmentalists were by class and upbringing the natural property of the Right, then they were worth buying over at almost any price.

Having come to that conclusion each social-democratic or labor party had to decide whether to try for a 'strong' or a 'weak' Left/Environmentalist alignment and program. Strong meant a strong dose of both: environmental action radical enough to satisfy the mainstream of environmentalist enthusiasm, but made acceptable to traditional working-class and radical supporters by discrimination in the choice of environmental projects, by egalitarian *methods* of environmental reform, and by independent action on other fronts to reduce inequalities. A weak strategy on the other hand meant moderating the program of each movement to make it inoffensive to the other: environmental action should be mild enough to do no perceptible harm to mass standards of living, while traditional tax, income, industrial and welfare policies should continue conservative enough to cause no pain to swinging voters, whether old middle-class sympathizers or new environmentalist allies.

Whichever way they inclined the parties of the Left soon learned that the third alternative – of unequal or weak/strong mixtures – wouldn't work. Traditional radicalism with weak environmental trappings drove too many middle-class voters away and attracted too few of them back on environmental issues. That simply surrendered environmental initiative and support to the Right. The opposite mixture – strong environmental policies with weak provisions for social equity – was ruled out by the strength of organized labor, and by recent political experience. Through the mid-century summertime which had once promised to last for ever, many social-democratic leaders had lost hope of ever again winning majorities for the old programs of workers' rights and socialist reconstructions. So in the 1960s they tried to attract more middle-class support by running as classless, consensual 'parties of progress', soft-pedalling socialism and offering progressive theories of education, technological change and personal liberation instead. Those might have been good additions to the old blue-collar program but they did not prove to be sufficient replacements for it. Old supporters stayed away; new ones were fickle. Classless government is the natural pretence of the Right. The Left can only get away with it in unusual circumstances: if they can become the party of city against country, or if the Right has managed to discredit itself – and even then, only at times when labor is content with very little.

So there was nothing to be said for strong/weak mixtures. But between pure strong and pure weak strategies the choice was not always easy. Parties of the Left faced different problems in different national situations. Canada and the United Kingdom had oil they could nationalize; Japan had none. A tough attack on pollution or on urban traffic congestion might not cost Swedish or Australian consumers half as much as it would cost English or Japanese. A tough attack on inequalities might bring on more conflict with foreign owners in Canada or the United Kingdom than in Japan or New Zealand. If strong Left/Environmentalist programs were ill-conceived or ill-timed they could bite into full employment and everyone's incomes and shopping prices without enough compensations for the majorities they were intended to benefit. More than one national electorate at one time or another rejected strong programs decisively. So leaders who tried for weak programs did not always believe they had much choice and they need not necessarily be blamed for the unimpressive results. It nevertheless turned out to be the strong programs that prospered, in the double sense that they did more good for their societies and kept their sponsors in power for longer terms. This signified more than merely the rewards for valor. With hindsight, it can be linked to three economic circumstances – as can most of the success of the Left through those years.

First, the mechanisms of inflation were not in fact susceptible to weak treatment. Whole sectors of economic activity eventually had to be taken out of unequal private ownership before the new systems of wage and price adjustment would work, and be tolerated. By no means all of private ownership or management had to be taken over, as we shall see. But the transfers were large enough to make the Left a more natural choice for the work than the Right could be.

Second, as already noted, there were advantages for the Left in the nature of some of the environmental problems. The toughest environmental measures proved not to be voluntary at all; only their ways and means and equities were open to choice. Rather than being debatable programs for long-term conservation of resources, or for very high environmental quality – policies which might well have split or embarrassed the Left – they were defensive responses to involuntary dangers and shortages. For that work the Left had no special advantages. The Right were just as good at organizing rationing or emergency services. But when the work did fall to the Left, the Left could often extract more permanent gains from it. There were ways of making temporary rationing – or at least its general principles – permanent. For example in the difficult business of policing black markets governments of the Left were quick to declare sectors of private production or wholesaling 'uncontrollable' and thus to take whole industries into permanent public ownership in circumstances which made such takeovers less unpopular than they might otherwise have been. The same principle sometimes applied to more voluntary reforms. Even the most conservative environmentalists could see that some kinds of economic activity which needed to be policed for environmental reasons were by nature resistant to any control short of public ownership or management.

Finally that same principle had special implications when resource and pollution problems included, as they often did, international economic conflicts. When those were intergovernmental – state-aided trade wars, oil diplomacy, sea-bed wrangles – the Right did as well as anyone else. But where the international rights at issue were private the Left were readier to be rough with them. It may not always have been rational to dispossess foreign owners or to carve multi-national enterprises into national (often nationalized) chunks. But it was increasingly popular. That was partly because with the spread of social-democratic government it became safer. Expropriation by isolated socialist states had once been too dangerous because the retaliation could be so damaging; those who paid too little for the assets they acquired would suffer general capital flight, emigration of skills, international boycott, CIA sedition. Now there were fewer boycotters and fewer havens for capital to fly to. Social-democratic states did well, taking what they wanted on their own terms. Communist states did even better, importing any capital they wanted from rentiers in capitalist countries who were becoming more and more willing to settle for 4% with the world's only *total* safety from confiscation.

Fiction kept pace with fact. James Bond's successors still tracked their prey to private islands spiked with electronic defences and ill-gotten blondes, but they came to blow up tax havens rather than laboratories for processing heroin or controlling the world's weather. Spies who might once have stolen secret formulae now stole scarce rutile or helium or genetic stocks. Pock-marked foreigners who might once have sought with whips or hypodermics to defile our women now sought with mine or quarry to defile our landscapes. Secret servicemen who once detected security leaks now detected oil leaks. Gnome-baiting filled a void which had troubled thick-necked citizens since the sad decline of Red-baiting.

And a few of the facts kept pace with the fictions. As the Left rebuilt an inescapable taxing power it became for many the party of law and order. As the Right tried to obstruct public acquisitions of Oil for The People, Land for The People, This Nation's Heritage for This Nation's Heirs, the Left was once again, as rarely since the brave days of Garibaldi and Gambetta, the party of patriotism. 'Internationalism' now suggested offshore theft, corporate plots against national resources, or more attempts by the French Right to federate Europe against socialism. The Left still believed in peaceful international relations and brotherly cultural exchanges – but strictly by agreement between strictly sovereign states.

3

It did not matter that some of the Left regimes were short-lived. Such historical shifts forward (or leftward) are system-wide. The parties may maintain their distance from each other, relatively speaking, but they all move. The Centre moves. Basic changes are made irreversible as much by the new positions of those who once resisted them, as of those who led them. The Right no more offers to restore free markets in gasoline or land than it offers to restore chattel slavery. Instead it offers to 'call a halt', to consolidate, to administer the public enterprises better – and perhaps to relax equalities a little by tax and salary concessions.

The leaders of all these developments – politicians, labor leaders, publicists, theorists, administrators – liked to see themselves as the prime movers of history. But they were more creatures than creators. Movements of mass and class interest and opinion shaped most of the contests within and between the parties. The opinions were the same old mixture of self-interested and disinterested, though there had been some critical redefinitions of self-interest. The whole spectrum of opinion had shifted to the left, driven by obvious needs for greater public economic control. But as to the types of control and their effects on the distribution of wealth and income, Right and Left competed as usual for the small margins of support that made the difference between office and opposition. This was the competition which, outside America, the Left managed to win – not always, but often enough to build better rather than worse equalities into permanently reconstructed institutions.

It was in these contests that so much of the early, uncoordinated, often ineffectual experience of grassroots protest and local action – and love of nature and fear of doomsday – bore fruit at last in national programs and majorities. Onto cores of traditional class support the Left majorities

117

were built by attracting people who had originally rebelled not against inequalities of wealth but against the bulldozing of neighborhoods, against factory smoke and airport noise, against congested and polluted streets, against private property rackets and public housing towers, against municipal and national and offshore corruption; and against the abuse of natural environments by timber-getters, beach-miners, dam-builders, oil men and auto-makers and highway builders, and poisoners of rivers and crops and creatures. The spoliation had made people angry and often for the first time political. Grassroots action made them confident. The effects of inflation disturbed their faith in traditional economic policies and the parties responsible for them. Environmentalist philosophies and threshold theories helped to persuade them that their societies were now rich and capable enough to *choose* what to do with their skills and resources and inherited institutions.

It only remains to summarize what they did choose to do with them.

4

The ways and means of Left reform are for discussion later so this summary of their end-of-century achievements can be brief.

Some improvements were common to most rich countries whatever the color of their government. They all made technical progress. There was better information about natural resources and systems. Local, national and international services monitored air, water and soil and the ecology of the life they sustained. As routinely as the rich societies had once been sewered or vaccinated, they now conserved other things besides human life. More wilderness was protected, more land converted to country and town parks. Spoiled land was recovered for community uses. Road, rail, dam and conduit engineering paid more respect than ever to landscape design. Foliage, cobblestones, outdoor sculpture, imaginative playgrounds and intricate pedestrian networks extended to give most city and suburban streets some of the charms that had once been confined to arty urban villages. Whole town precincts were conserved because they were beautiful or historically interesting, or because they housed activities or communities of people who shouldn't be disturbed. Central agencies provided money and technical help to community groups and local governments working to improve their neighborhoods, especially where local people supplied some of the planning and labor.

Besides allocating resources to produce these public goods all the rich countries adopted some degree of deliberate scarcity. Some of it was to conserve resources over time – oil and natural gas were used less and less for electricity, domestic heat or private transport. Other resource-conservation was done to improve present safeties or qualities of life. There was careful management of industrial and domestic wastes, including more recycling and use of alternative materials than would have been chosen by least-cost calculations. To conserve good beaches poorer deposits of sand were mined. To conserve national parks some of their minerals and building aggregates were left in the ground. To conserve natural forest and moorland dearer timber had to come from the conversion of marginal farmland to commercial forest. Electric power was transmitted not always by the cheapest routes from generators which were not always built at the most economical locations. And so on – some quite expensive care for landscape, townscape and critical resources became as habitual as the regulation of factory safety or public health. People came to think of the new environmental standards as reformed uses of wealth rather than as policies of scarcity.

Other lines of action were less unanimous. There was some deliberate dispersal of office and industrial work from bigger cities to smaller ones, which were made to take any going increase of numbers. The end results were worth it but there were transitional sufferings. In the smaller cities people could have plenty of private and local community space without generating big-city mileages of daily travel; and as private transport had shorter and shorter range it was valuable to live in easy reach of work and city services. But some of the more affluent found the small cities dull. Most big cities lost some population as they were slowly re-centered, and their old slums were thinned and patched up to more comfortable standards; and a good many of their more affluent suburbs were forcibly desegregated, and populated more heavily. Public transport was free or subsidized everywhere, though there were times when it was also rationed, or just scarce. Private motoring policies varied with local circumstances and with technical developments – and offered one very important field in which private use could be separated from private ownership. When resources allowed cars or runabouts for (say) a quarter of the population, that did not mean (as it had once done) that the affluent had unlimited private transport and the rest of the people had none. Instead publicly-owned, privately-managed car-hire services rationed some private mileage to everyone for evenings or weekends, weekly shopping trips or annual holidays. Meanwhile a great deal of effort and money went to improving cycling and pedestrian conditions. Thus by slow degrees the cities were physically improved and shaped to distribute their costs and serve their citizens more equally.

Activities of that kind made up the voluntary and constructive half of environmental action. The adaptive or defensive half consisted in coping with shortages and substitutions, especially in the supply of energy. Energy soon required some deliberate allocation in all countries, both between alternative economic uses and between individual consumers. The Right tended to do enough rationing to supply essential services and to keep the citizens healthy and at work. The Left often went further to distribute the whole supply by allocation, which might of course include allocations to limited free markets, and split pricing to favor poorer consumers. Energy was a most important case of the integration of environmental with distributional policy but many other changes had the same character: egalitarian provisions were built into the distribution of environmental benefits or costs, or both. Taxation (genuinely progressive at last) financed public transport, improvements to poor neighborhoods, waste disposal, recycling services for some mass-producers of necessaries, and (to keep food cheap) a lot of scientific and technical and transport services to agriculture.

There remained the many changes whose costs and benefits could not be allocated in any direct way with deliberate equity. Rising costs of energy, and of raw material extraction and industrial processes forced to meet new environmental standards, necessarily meant higher prices for a wide range of consumer goods which it was not practical or desirable to ration or subsidize. The producer or the polluter must pay and so therefore must the consumers. Higher prices for clothing, furniture, household and gardening equipment, building and maintenance work, sweets and drinks and entertainments reduced the purchasing power of every income with effects more painful the lower the incomes were. Together with dislocations of employment arising from environmental reforms and shortages, these were the cost-of-living effects which did the most widespread harm to low earners and their families and to the pattern of inequalities as a whole. They could only be redressed by independent distributional reforms. In practice it was rarely possible to separate the unequalizing effects of environmental change from the unequalizing effects of inflation. It was to cope with both that the new methods of inequality control were developed.

Like managing full employment or rates of inflation, managing the general pattern of inequality is a complicated business. Here there is only room to notice two very general features of it.

First, distributions of wealth and income are now properly monitored. From fine-grained analyses by industry, skill, age, sex, spending pattern, family composition, region (and so on) individuals and groups know exactly where they stand and whether they are climbing or slipping in relation to a variety of ladders. But it is more important that simple graphic representations of national patterns of wealth and income as a whole have become standard information for government, opposition and electors. Just as government is held responsible for the general level of employment and the general movement of prices, so it now has to answer for the general pattern of inequalities. Politicians commit themselves to three-, four- or five-year programs to produce (or prevent) specific adjustments to the national pattern. Promise and performance are monitored, graphically reported in all the media and watched as critically as are the employment and inflation indexes, with similar political penalties for mismanagement. In the decades since this became a standard requirement of government – and unlike the other two indexes, a subject of explicit conflict of values between Left and Right – government and its advisers have learned a great deal about the interrelation of income distributions with growth rates, inflation rates and employment levels. Although the complicated machinery of national economic management which so nearly lost control through the inflationary crises of the 1970s now has to take account of the additional tasks of resource and environmental control and inequality control, it nevertheless manages rather better than it used to do even in the early, easy Keynesian decades. That is due partly to longer experience, but chiefly to the surer means of management which became available with some large transfers of activity from private to public control.

The extensions of public control constitute the second of the general adjustments of economic organization for which the Left have been chiefly responsible. Most of them have been guided by a new strategy for drawing boundaries between public and private sectors of the economy. Everyone was sick of the excessive public regulation of private business. Whether it was there to protect shareholders, consumers, tax-collectors or the physical environment, businessmen hated overcomplicated regulation and governments knew how expensive and unpopular it was and how much of it was anyway evaded. It had very bad effects on business motives and on social efficiency. Far too many business decisions had to be tactics against government, rather than calculations of productive efficiency. So instead of elaborating more and more complicated regulations for the diverse kinds of business activity that required control for purposes of national economic or environmental management, government began to apply (wherever it could) a simpler principle. Economic activities should be sorted out according to whether they could or couldn't reconcile private motivation with public interest. Those which could belonged in the private sector; those which couldn't belonged in the public sector.

For taking over what needed to be taken over the terms varied from purchase to confiscation. A lot of compensations were paid in 'wasting bonds' – unsaleable rights to income which would lose their value over one or two lifetimes. The extensions of control likewise took diverse forms: transfers of whole ownership or of majority or minority shareholdings; combinations of public ownership with private management, or vice versa; acquisitions of single firms, of whole industries, or of proportions chosen to produce public/private competition. Ideally the public took over only as much as was necessary to avoid the need for excessive regulation of the rest. Thus public ownership was used economically and public control continued to grow less doctrinaire and more pragmatic and versatile in its methods.

Though most of them aimed in a general way to simplify control, the detailed reasons for the takeovers were as diverse as their methods. Some activities were taken over for specific environmental purposes – to possess particular resources or to control wasteful or pollutant processes which resisted regulation. In a similar way specific anti-inflationary purposes prompted takeovers of types of production and distribution which could not be effectively price-controlled any other way. Then there were preventive or punitive takeovers of firms whose owners couldn't or wouldn't comply with national policies, or threatened to export capital or jobs. Money-lending and investment management – especially mortgage-lending, consumer credit and the investment of insurance and life funds – occasioned most of the new practice of applying degrees of public management to private assets. This avoided some compensation problems and allowed comparatively unoppressive public control of a lot of resource allocation, rent and interest rates, dividend policies and executive rewards.

The most radical but by far the most popular of all the takeovers were the property reforms. They varied from place to place. Some states resumed all freeholds, others diffused them more widely to all their householders. Some treated most land alike, others had different rules and markets for rural and urban, residential and industrial and commercial land. Some controlled whole properties, others only the land under them. To cope with the general social and economic task of allocating land without much open marketing, some resorted to a good deal of administrative allocation; some monopolized transactions rather than ownership; some dominated the markets by public dealing. The detailed social effects were as various as the methods. Some of the new arrangements – including some introduced by governments of both Left and Right – were oppressively bureaucratic. Others – likewise including some from both Left and Right – came near to fulfilling a conservative dream of small-holding democracy, with everyman's personal independence strengthened by a home patch of very independent ownership. But whatever their social effects the new arrangements all met one requirement which by the end of the 1970s came quite peremptorily from every European and Australasian electorate: residential land must stay cheap. It must never again be used to force massive transfers of wealth and income from poorer to richer. Just as most education, health, scientific research, road-building and passenger transport had one after another been taken ' out of the market ', so now – for the same good reasons – was most urban land.

Some very general effects of these reconstructions can now be summed up.

First, as noticed earlier, governments now had better instruments of general economic policy. They had direct control of many environmentally sensitive resources and processes of production. They could use that control for environmental purposes; they could also use it, especially by pricing and allocative policies within the public sector, to influence the social distribution of many costs and benefits of environmental reform. There was a similar strengthening of government in national resource-allocation and in the management of inflation. For the purposes of inflation control workers were no readier to submit to inequitable wages in public employment than in private employment. But in the public sector price control was simple and sure; acceptable wage policies were less likely to be evaded by reclassification and 'firing and hiring'; profit rates could be used as direct levers of central economic management; losses could be tolerated for longer periods than private enterprises could tolerate them. And the management of so much new lending and investment gave government better control of the general directions of economic growth.

The last was perhaps the most critical change of all because it meant that levels of personal inequality were at last sufficiently disconnected from levels of saving and capital formation. Within broad limits (and still requiring quite complicated tactics and machinery) government could now determine the relations between growth, private saving and inequality. The rich could no longer say 'let us keep all we can spend and then a great deal more, or you'll get no growth'. Government could determine growth policy on its merits, and independently, inequality policy on *its* merits. Private saving still had to supply some particular kinds of investment. Patterns of inequality still had to supply hopes and incentives, securities and freedoms. Income controls had to be workable without intolerable inquisitions, and acceptable to democratic majorities. But for the first time in a capitalist history full of hopeful or fearful illusions on the subject the overall pattern of inequalities could be substantially affected by democratic choice.

With that development quantitative changes added up to a qualitative change; the extension of public control reached a point at which it carried capitalist systems across another threshold. Public control and enterprise now constituted the dominant framework or structure of the economic system. That framework still defined a great many fields for private enterprise, which still accounted for half or more of conventional economic activity and allowed plenty of scope for the distinctive efficiencies of private risk-taking and management and for the types of personality and talent which throve best in private enterprises. Moreover plenty of public enterprises had to 'meet the market', producing what people wanted and allocating resources according to market indications of demand. The new arrangements did very little harm to consumer sovereignty – in some respects they improved it, through improvements in advertising and in the price and uses of consumer credit. But over all, by mixtures of direct and indirect control and competitive market influence, the public was now in command of what for democratic purposes it needed to command: the level and type of environmental care; rates and sources of saving and the general directions of new investment; and the general relativities of profits, dividends, salaries and wages.

In the social-democratic societies which built this structure of control there was plenty of conflict about building it and about the right uses of it. Most countries developed the new controls at varying rates and dates between about 1975 and 1990, in fairly piecemeal fashion. Each new lever or institution was at first used chiefly for the specific purpose that had occasioned it: to control particular resources, processes, distributions or whatever. When the new controls were also used in combination in a deliberately orchestrated way it was at first chiefly for the traditional purposes of economic policy – to control rates of growth, employment and inflation. At the same time there was persistent though still piecemeal attention to questions of equality. The strategies which succeeded in restraining inflation also reduced some inequalities. Many specific land, housing, urban and environmental reforms – including capital taxes and confiscations – also reduced inequalities. So did a number of independent tax-and-welfare redistributions which were done as pay-offs or packet-deals in connexion with types of environmental reform which were unavoidably inegalitarian in themselves. These various special-purpose policies accumulated to bring about quite radical reductions of inequality. But there remained the further possibility of making 'direct and pure' alterations to the pattern of inequalities for purposes of class interest or social justice alone. By about 1990 everyone knew this was possible. If democracies so wished, their inequalities could now be substantially reduced or increased without any necessary harm to environmental standards or economic efficiency. Long before such changes struck technical economic limits they would be limited by the tolerance of masses of moderately rich on the one hand and moderately poor on the other: by the levels of relative standstill or loss of income at which proletariat or salariat could get enough sympathy to make successful use of strike or sabotage rather than submit to majority rule. And *which* majority ruled was likely to be determined chiefly by the calculations of advantage – or the sympathies and conceptions of justice – of small percentages of people in the middle, plus some at every income level who voted for other things than their own material advantage.

Modes of conflict and levels of tolerance changed significantly through the reforming decades. As reform progressed the serious conflicts were no longer between paupers and millionaires in societies which soon had very few of either. They were conflicts for small margins of income between workers at pithead and coalface; between skilled tradesmen, nurses and schoolteachers; and so on. Even the most general conflicts – about the class shares of proprietors and professionals, managers, blue-collar workers, pensioners, students – took on more of the detailed undramatic character which used to belong to industrial wage-fixing or wrangles about teachers' or public servants' pay scales.

In this connection it is worth noticing what happened to two anxieties which had troubled many Left theorists and politicians in the early days of reform. Would flatter equalities make internal social conflicts more violent, especially if large numbers on middle incomes had to lose ground? And – reflecting some old Trotskyite fears – would free and democratic but very equal societies be able to survive in a world which still included unregenerate capitalist inequalities in the United States and elsewhere? The problems were separate but the solutions were in some ways related. Some aspects of affluent resistance to change will be noticed below. But once the acute structural conflicts were over and the new scales of equality established, internal conflicts tended to be less intense than before if only because the stakes were lower. Just as the middle classes had learned to do without their servants early in the century, then learned to share motoring road-space with the masses through the middle of the century, so at the end of the century they learned to do without a few other privileges, and the remaining conflicts about smaller and smaller margins of social reward took on the banal, sometimes squalid but not at all dangerous tone described above.

This was helped rather than hindered by the survival of affluent privileges and opportunities in the United States and elsewhere. The alternative, unregenerate capitalist world was big enough to accept most of the capital which recalcitrant Europeans might have liked to export. But less and less capital was portable under the new regimes. The alternative world did however accept affluent migrants with whatever money they could manage to bring with them. This was a significant safety valve for the reforming societies, ridding them of many citizens to whom wealth or resentment meant more than home, nationality or majority rule. Of the senior British peerage (earls and above) half soon departed. They scattered to the Bahamas, Bermuda and the United States, and especially to Spain where the taxation, hunting, government and peasantry were suitable to their tastes. From six of them plus one viscount and two upstart commoners more than three billion dollars' worth of city and country property was sequestrated. Governments remembered the prudence of Henry VIII and the Long Parliament (from whose confiscations many of the emigrant families had got the land in the first place) and once more took care to distribute plenty of it to enough new owners to resist any 'restoration'.

Through those first fifteen years the tolerance of all parties adapted to various educative experiences. Some of the early salaried strikes and strikes of capital began in a mood of high and hopeful truculence. A little disorganization, some capital flight and 10 or 20% unemployed should suffice to bring labor back to its senses, and swinging voters back to vote for sensible middle-of-the-road government. But despite some howls of 'fascism' from the Left, not many people on the Right really wanted the risks of Right revolution, though they saw no harm in reminding the Left of the fate of President Allende of Chile, brought down by haut-bourgeois non-cooperation, petit-bourgeois strikes, proletarian wage-inflation and a murderous coup by a 'non-political' army. It was never a very persuasive example. European governments had better organization, bigger majorities and altogether calmer support than Allende. Their citizen-soldiers were more likely to shoot saboteurs or rebellious colonels than the governments for which most of them had voted, or crowds of their fellow trade-unionists in the streets. These governments were also better managers than Allende, of richer and easier economies. They could draw on plenty of talent to run any private enterprises recalcitrant enough to invite takeover, and in any case European and Japanese takeovers did not provoke any general emigration of management or skill. The Left began their radical work with land, environmental and anti-inflation reforms which were acceptable to almost as many rich as poor. And step by step they confined the Right to democratic options only, as step by step they brought the rich under the rule of law.

That rule of law was simpler than many of the convoluted accretions of tax and company law which it replaced, but still far too complicated to be described in a page or two. Some of the new arrangements have been mentioned already, as means of public economic control. Here we can note in the most general way some of their disciplinary aspects. Because no fully effective controls for tax or any other purposes could have been imposed on the complicated patterns of ownership and flows of business which were characteristic of the old regime, company and commercial law were revised to force drastic simplifications of business organization. The safest form of share-ownership became personal and direct: holding-companies and structures of subsidiaries had to justify themselves before registration and accept internal supervision ever after. Directors personally were made to share responsibility for a wide range of offences by companies, and by employees of their own and their

127

subsidiaries. That and other revisions of liability caused most interlocking ownerships to dissolve overnight and made sure that any that remained were policed more watchfully by their own directors than public agencies could ever have policed them.

Limited liability continued for involuntary business failure but for very little else; and for most purposes it applied only to personal and not to corporate shareholders. Faced with that, directors and shareholders were soon inviting public representation on their boards and inside their accounting services, for their own protection. There were new types of penalty for wilful or negligent business failure and for wilful tax-evasion. They were applied to directors and managers personally for corporate violations as well as to individuals' tax behavior. They included sentences to a condition rather like undischarged bankruptcy in which the offender's wealth and income from all sources were administered – and above a parsimonious personal allowance, garnisheed – by public trustees. Assets not disclosed in returns of capital and income automatically became public property; assets undervalued could be acquired at their owners' undervaluations.

All this was accompanied by a good deal of bureaucratic nuisance, some miscarriages of justice and some damage to managerial motivation. But the damage was small when compared with the gains in simplicity of law and organization, in honest tax paying, and often in business efficiency. The effects on efficiency were not surprising. Most of the overcomplication of business organization and accounting had been done in the first place to evade or avoid the law, or for variously antisocial oligopolist purposes, rather than to make production more efficient. A great many takeovers and conglomerations had achieved more diseconomies than economies of scale and done nothing for the long-term interests of shareholders. They had been contrived by managers chiefly to inflate the rewards of the new levels of super-management which they created; or more respectably to allow inefficient managers to be replaced, and misused assets to be better used, both of which operations could usually have been done by simpler methods.

None of these administrative developments was quite as potent as the political weapon of acquisition. For the assets they acquired, governments offered graded compensations. What kept most business in line with the spirit as well as the letter of public intentions – and made shareholders watch boards, and boards watch managers, as never before – was the threat of acquisition on terms which would vary with the reasons for acquisition, which might be anything from friendly to punitive.

There were international reprisals, though with Japan and most of Europe and Australasia enforcing the new principles they could rarely be the sort of reprisals that used to work against banana republics. The need for them diminished as methods of international investment adapted to the new hazards. The less secure investors felt about conditions abroad the more they tended either to invest at home or to invest under cover of contracts with the governments of the foreign territories concerned. Contracts with governments could usually be relied on, however their laws might change from month to month. There were complicated and not always good effects on international distributions of investment. One effect was wholly good: between the propensities to invest at home, and to cover investments abroad by investor-to-government or government-to-government agreements, there was a steady strengthening and simplification of sovereignty over economic activity and less and less opportunity for anyone to evade it.

On the way to that state of affairs there were plenty of transitional troubles. For example Chrysler lost patience with their English labor, shut their English plants and got ready to supply the United Kingdom market from Spain and Germany. The Social Democratic government of the Federal Republic waited till the reorganization was complete then acquired 51% of the German operation; British and German governments prohibited Spanish-built imports, and what remained of the Chrysler English plants were acquired and split 51/49 between the Industrial Development Corporation (public) and British Leyland (private). American markets were promptly closed to British and German cars. In the trade and patent wars with the United States which followed that and various other socialist outrages, French governments of the Right at first saw advantages in joining the American/Spanish/Italian alignment but most French and Italian labor didn't. In France there was another 'week in the streets' of the 1968 kind and soon afterwards the first of the new Popular Front governments was elected, heavily patriotic and anti-Coca Cola. It failed to cope with some acute contradictions between the internal and international interests of French labor and it soon fell. A weak Right coalition returned to office at the moment when British, Dutch, Danish, Italian and Irish governments had decided to force a crisis over the European Community's broken promises of regional redistributions. Through the governing machinery of the Community the five carried a program which would have transferred about four billion dollars a year from French and German and Low Country donors to Irish and Italian recipients. Besides vetoing that, the French moved to demolish the

machinery it issued from. The German government disappointed some
of its international socialist admirers by not opposing the demolition, but
it would help it actively (and enlist the British and the new French
government of the Left as well) only if there were also other reconstructions which in effect restored all member-countries' rights to tax and
confiscate, and to control their internal inequalities with full sovereignty.
From that date the Community survived as a trade negotiator and an area
of free personal movement and cultural cooperation but it no longer
protected any businesses or any taxpayers from the sovereign requirements of their national governments. On the whole this was welcome to
the Left everywhere despite its effects, or lack of them, on poor Irish
and Italians. The Left had learned that effective control, both by voters
over governments and by governments over business, required strict
sovereignty which worked best – with least loopholing, corruption or
other obfuscation – where it could work directly, undivided, on not too
large a national scale. It was likely to be weakened by each level of
government and each division of power or responsibility which interposed
between the citizens as voters and the end-effects of government on the
governed.

7

Thus for a decade or two the Left did well. For such radical purposes
they had the advantage of mass organization and old-established rights
to strike and demonstrate; and also a new respectability. The European
and Australasian parties could not possibly be suspected of plotting to
abolish the democracy they throve on; the red menace now frightened
very few old ladies of either sex and the 'dead hand of socialism' was
now the only hold anyone of any political complexion had on the rate
of inflation.

But for direct action to be effective the labor unions always needed
some degree of public sympathy, and to hold governing majorities the
traditional Left always needed allies. But the very success of their
reconstructions tended in time to reduce the sympathy and alliances they
could attract. Once built, the new institutions of government could be
worked by either party. Right could now cope as well as Left with the
problems of inflation and environmental management which had once
driven so many middle-class people into Left alignments. The time came
when many of those people had what they wanted and could do without
their Left allies, who in turn had a good deal of what *they* wanted and
were getting lazier in office and less militant in their mass organizations.

So it was time for Thermidor. The revolution could rest, consolidate, perhaps retreat a little – though never back to the old regime. The natural candidates to do the consolidating were the parties of the Right. If they trod carefully they could often recover their old majorities, govern, and begin quietly to extend some salary scales and capital limits and tax concessions.

How far might it be possible to relax the new equalities without provoking enough backlash to return the Left to power?

Most of the reforming societies had brought wages, salaries, pensions and between 95 and 97% of all incomes within a fourfold order of inequalities (after allowing for tax, family size, patterns of expenditure, housing costs and other subtleties built into the new indexes which made these figures scarcely comparable with pre-1975 statistics.) A few judges and managing directors and star artists and performers and Nobel prize-winners took home four unskilled workers' or pensioners' wages. It was more important that 93 or 95%, including politicians and professors without Nobel prizes, were within a threefold order and 85% were within a twofold order. Inequalities of capital ownership were greater but they were diminishing, and they were less use to their beneficiaries than they used to be. Owners could still manage their fortunes but distinctions between capital and income were strict – shareholders could no more dissave or consume private capital than trustees of public capital could steal it. So (besides climbing up the fourfold income scale) what were the rewards of success? The first was to control capital – anyone who could build a business or an investment portfolio could usually run it for his lifetime. Second, these societies inherited ranges of housing from hovels to palaces, and most of them let private owners spend capital on one house each and give or bequeath one each to some number of kin. (That didn't encourage too much grandeur because nobody could afford much domestic service or exceed the household rations of energy.) Third, besides bequeathing houses and some household goods, owners could entrust capital temporarily for the support of surviving dependants.

These were better equalities than most communist societies had. That was not surprising. Democratic distributions of freedom, information and political power were good in themselves, and they were producing and policing more equal distributions of other goods which in turn (in a 'virtuous circle' of causation) reinforced the equal distributions of freedom and power. These were the achievements of democratic government by and for the lower 55% of earners. How much further could that sort of government go? Or how far back could government for the upper

131

55% go if 10% in the middle changed sides? It was hard to guess, but perhaps the limits of tolerance on each side and the interests of swingers in the middle would allow about a point of movement either way, to a three-fold or a fivefold scale of incomes. Through the second and third decades of reform the local fortunes of Left and Right took the social democracies to various temporary resting places along that range of possibilities.

Those that moved furthest right towards a fivefold scale were the big lucky countries – France and Germany. Their masses were well enough off to be tolerant and the complications of 'big' government allowed scope for the pervasive, unobtrusive kinds of relaxation at which their public servants and private lawyers and accountants were masters.

Those that rested in the middle were the small lucky countries, where life was richer and more comfortable than in the big ones but government was more direct and inescapable, upper classes had never been accorded much deference, and the Left had managed to attract more enduring national affection.

The big unlucky countries had tougher problems and more acute causes for internal conflict. Much depended on the handling of the conflicts, which in turn depended partly on political inheritances but even more on deeply entrenched habits of public, class and personal behavior.

Italy never had 51% for any line of action and was never one of the reforming societies. If the north had been independent it would probably have been taken over by its intellectual Left and its communist labor. But the old alliance of aristocratic and village Mafia went on governing the south, if governing was the word for it. Rome collected a lot more American business now that Frankfurt and even Paris were taxable. National governments governed very little of Italian life, leaving that to locals, many of whom stuffed and miscounted local and national ballots so shamelessly that nobody any longer knew quite how Italians voted.

In Japan, under pressure of the most acute and poisonous environmental dangers, there was some tautly controlled violence then a decade of extreme equalizing and constitutional 'gaullisme of the Left' before most democratic rights and press freedoms were restored. In the United Kingdom Left leadership was democratic and non-violent, but tended to be wild in technical ways. There were impulsive lurches to the Left, like the panicky nationalization of land, which achieved less than more discriminating interventions might have done. In the end the United Kingdom had the flattest wage and salary scales and the fairest distribution of most public goods and services, but also the biggest surviving property incomes and some housing which extended the concept of the 'leasehold house and garden' to include quite aristocratic acreages of private park.

Despite that, the United Kingdom and Japan had in most respects moved furthest to the Left. Because they were supposed to have inherited the stiffest social distinctions and the most biddable working classes, their radicalism surprised some observers. But acute resource troubles and falling standards of living had driven their low and middle earners to act with unusual and militant solidarity; and their class cultures were not altogether unhelpful to the new material equalities. The cultures of both countries included (in very different ways) some calm and civilized styles of class relation – even of class warfare. Family structures supported the pride and identity of many Japanese who lost influence or income. When the political crisis was over, Japanese firms in their new composite ownership continued to operate with familial solidarity, and Japanese streets – crowded or empty, by day or night – were as safe as any in the world outside China. Meanwhile finely complicated distinctions of style and status gave many an Englishman a sense of his place in society which no socialist or bureaucrat could ever take away from him.

Scotch whisky and fine woollens had always paid low wages; and there were just enough export trades like them to pay the diminished import bills. Traditions of highly educated work for modest pay had always helped London's acting, writing, talking and publishing trades to make it an intellectual and artistic market place. Fewer middle-aged American tourists came; more young from both sides of the Atlantic came. Pollsters reported that many continental Europeans, though officially richer than the English, still thought England the most agreeable European country to live in. Pubs, football and bingo don't use much network energy; nor do the world's best theatre, newspapers and television. National service in the coal mines – where the educated conscripts are the unskilled labor – does more for class relations than military service ever did. There is plenty to eat and drink and enough warmth at home – household rationing of energy makes the smallest houses the warmest, and pensioners as warm as toast. There was some panic emigration in the early days of reform. Many of the recalcitrant went to the United States, where money incomes soon averaged three or four times British incomes. But a lot of their children moved back to England ten and twenty years later, to rejoin the high and low culture and the safe and friendly faces in the street that went with buses and bikes, one plain enamel bathroom, and honest government.

133

6

Ideas and persuasions

I do not know how much of that social-democratic history may be practicable but the rest of this book is for people who would rather work for something like it than for other directions of change.

The argument must return to earth, to present time and ways and means. As it changes gear some signposts may be helpful. The next three chapters discuss general principles of action; then there are three more about practical policies. How can democrats be persuaded and organized to deal more prudently with resources, and more equally with one another? We might think better about that if we had no stereotypes of capitalism and socialism and could consequently think afresh about production and distribution, liberties and equalities, social values and social relations. But ideas of capitalism and socialism pervade our language and the beliefs on which we act, from which ideas for change must start. In conventional terms what follow are proposals for particular mixtures of capitalist and socialist organization. They bring together Left revisions of environmental programs, and environmental and other revisions of traditional Left programs.

I assume that the Left need no longer fear any old style of pure private capitalism. Private profit and productivity now depend on massive uses of state power, and private and class uses of that power are as important as the uses of private capital. Pervasive bureaucracy is unavoidable; only its purposes and methods and general humanity are at stake. Right versions of it will be oppressive and unequal. Left versions may be nearly as bad unless a reformed, inventive Left finds new ways to make such societies friendly, equal and free. One way or another, new forms of order seem inevitable: there is no way back to the mid-century summertime of capitalism. The reasons for believing there is no way back should perhaps be argued here, but because they belong to the analysis of the new inflation they are argued later, in Chapter 10.

1

There have been many revisions of Left programs. One reason for revising them is that they have not so far been very successful. Some of the New Left concentrate on that – on better ways of fighting battles the Left has always fought. Others are concerned less with how the Left has failed and more with how the world is changing. Social-democratic theory was born under a capitalism whose worst effects seemed to be industrial drudgery, poverty, recurrent unemployment and a too-slow reduction of inequalities. Nowadays capitalism is troubled more by other things: by problems of energy and exhaustible materials, increasing or unstable inequalities, and inflationary mechanisms which threaten a general crisis of distribution. Those will force radical changes whoever governs. So the democratic Left has double reason for rethinking – it has so far failed with many old problems and now it faces new ones as well.

In the history of capitalist workers' efforts to improve their social shares there have been many pendulum swings between political and industrial action. Since the Right took political office nearly everywhere after the second world war, Left efforts have been chiefly industrial. They have helped to generate the systematic inflation to which the classical response should now be a return to politics. In one sense that has already happened: the industrial bargainers have politicized the bargaining process. People bargain *with* organized power *for* rates of pay and price and profit derived *from* ideas of equity and judgments of coercive opportunity. Nevertheless the method is so nearly self-defeating that a return to governmental politics, for the purpose of constructing a less destructive economic and bargaining system, would be historically likely if it were not for one hindrance: the politicians have no convincing reconstructions to offer. The Right offers unequalizing solutions which won't work because organized labor won't let them work. The Left is weak and evasive about the inflationary competition for shares within the ranks of labor, and it still cannot attract majorities for solutions which would radically reduce inequalities. No major party in any big country is yet offering a fair and workable solution to inflation; nor a non-tyrannical way of reducing inequalities; nor a resource and environmental policy which would not increase inequalities.

But although it confuses and paralyses many Left parties at the moment the coincidence of these three problems really creates an historic opportunity for the Left. Anyone who can make progress with all three can certainly pick up enough votes to bring the traditional 35 or 45% vote for the Left up to a working majority. Progress with any of the three is likely to be popular and irreversible. They lend themselves well to integrated approaches. What so far prevents the Left from seizing its opportunity is that it doesn't yet know what to do about the problems, and too many voters know that it doesn't. It is not frustrated (as often in the past) by the superior skill and performance of the Right, or by electors lulled and contented by the trouble-free progress of the economic system, or by organizational weaknesses of its own. It is frustrated now by a lack of valuable and workable things to do: a lack of ideas, a lack of program. This chapter is accordingly about the inventive and persuasive intellectual services the Left may need if it is to reform its own capacities to reform the world around it.

2

The new problems are more political than technical. Even the ones with technical causes need political solutions because they are all aspects of a general need to correct capitalist distributions. The corrections have to be quite radical, so Left and Right will both need social and economic theories about untried alternatives, and research into projected rather than present systems. Innovations have to be integrated into going systems which of course have to be understood; nevertheless innovative research needs to be more imaginative and constructive than a lot of the sterile social science of recent decades. If it is to be technically coherent (let alone socially useful) it needs to be explicitly value-structured. That is offered as a forecast, not an incitement; but practical recommendations follow from it.

The needs to control inflation, uses of resources, and physical shares of land and housing all mean that less and less distribution can safely be left to free bargaining and marketing (of goods, land or labor). *Critically* less. Allocations and rewards have to be brought under enough regulation to control monetary inflation, and shares and uses of land, energy and other critical resources. Any machinery capable of controlling those fundamentals will incidentally be capable of controlling the general pattern of inequality too. So existing scales of inequality will no longer appear to be caused by inexorable economic laws or by imperatives of democratic freedom or free-enterprise efficiency. They will be more and more obviously imposed, or at least negotiated, by government. When majorities believe that governments really do determine the scales of inequality they will hold governments squarely responsible for them, and

137

politics will have to adapt to that divisive fact. (Of course governments have always been responsible in a broad way for patterns of inequality. But they have been able to coerce most of their subjects, or persuade them that the inequalities were in practice unalterable, or unalterable without dangerous losses of efficiency or social safety.)

There can be no single technically best, ideally efficient distribution of wealth or income – no possible basis for unanimous agreement among self-seeking economic men. Instead there are the classical alternatives of class rule, or of arriving democratically at disagreed systems to which majorities will consent and to which minorities can be got to submit without crippling resistance or breakdown. That need not be quite as difficult as it sounds. Most incomes are already fixed by political and institutional rather than market methods. But the methods need to be adapted to excite less inflationary behavior. People have to develop more direct and realistic ways of competing for shares. And the well-to-do have to be brought into this realm of law and order by means which will still keep as many as possible of them working efficiently.

That suggests what kinds of intellectual service may be needed. There is already a great deal of technical understanding of the mechanisms by which present systems take in rational individual behavior and aggregate it to produce self-destructive effects of inflation, environmental degradation and unproductive inequality. What are needed are inventive and persuasive proposals for better systems capable of attracting both the support needed to introduce them, and the individual behavior needed to make them work properly. That calls for imagination; analysis and criticism of alternative proposals rather than of existing systems; and persuasion. Inventive proposals for change, addressed in plain language to citizens and politicians, may be technically as well as politically more useful than further research into present systems, or mathematical modelling of the reasons why present mechanisms are incurable.

3

The relations between social scientists' values and the technical direction and coherence of their work may be most obvious in inventive work, but they are just as surely present in the analysis of existing processes of any complexity. Most social scientists now accept this in theory but its practical implications are not as widely understood as they need to be. Self-frustrating working rules are still common. Social research can be abstract or concrete, general or particular, quantitative or qualitative, certain or uncertain, speculative or analytical or descriptive. But none of it is value-free, or could imaginably be so. Fashionable preferences for work that is abstract, general, quantitative, analytical and certain are merely that: fashionable. They also give specific political direction (varying from field to field) to the work. So do most of the other scientistic preferences (and pretences) that often go with them.

The practical implication is this: social scientists, including many of the experts government has to rely on, ought to behave more like politicians than like neutral public servants, and ought to be hired, fired and listened to accordingly. If electors want some radical equalizing of wealth or income it is pointless to ask neoclassical economists about it. If governments want to decide between policies which would bring different benefits to different people it is pointless to call for most current types of cost–benefit analysis. If they want good housing and transport for city-dwellers it is pointless to ask most systems-analysts to supply any but some minor services to the planning. If they want better distribution and pricing of land it is pointless to ask advice from most present land economists or locational geographers. This is partly because conservative experts won't do radical work with much zeal or ingenuity. But it is much more important to grasp that however the experts see their personal duties, the hostile values and technical incapacities have been built, often without their knowing it, into the theories and procedures they have been trained to use: into their expertise itself.

Values are built into theories and methods in many and various ways. A preference for objective observation (i.e. for facts that all observers can agree about) discourages attention to many qualities of life and to the distribution of many kinds, and causes, of wellbeing. A preference for general theory discourages almost any way of understanding 'idiographic' facts, such as novel social choices or historical changes of course. Successful general theories might illuminate those; but in the unsuccessful search for them, generality becomes a principle of scientific selection, so that expertise consists in knowing what doesn't change and cultivating an expert blindness to most possibilities of changing it. Disciplines draw arbitrary boundaries for themselves, often with conservative effects on their work. And when valuation can't be concealed, scientists try hard to be seen to apply the citizens' values rather than their own. That sounds objective and democratic, but is often neither. Somebody still decides what questions to ask of which citizens, and how much weight to give to which answers. The method often confines research to

139

already existing options, and puts high value on existing distributions of opportunity and purchasing power.

A very large number of social scientists trained between about 1950 and 1970 were indoctrinated with those and other rules of spurious objectivity, and hold to them as principles of science more dogmatically than they would ever assert consciously political or religious opinions. If they have come to concede in a philosophical way that a lot of social science is value-structured, they nevertheless cling to the idea that the old objective machine can still work impartially for any party if the appropriate value-premises are fed into it. But the values are built into the machine: into its structure, perception and reasoning. To ask experts with such tools of trade to apply their neutral, objective skills to improving the quality of other people's lives is like asking personally hydrophobic workmen to shovel water with neutral, objective sieves.

At the same time good intentions are no use without good technique. The alternative to being baffled by Treasury economists or betrayed by urban technocrats is not to 'think with the blood'. The pursuit of value-freedom was one tragedy of good intentions; there'll be another if radicals decide that passion will do instead of careful counting. The proper function of a social scientist's values is to direct and organize honest work – including true observation and mathematical reasoning wherever those are useful. Observing and selecting, measuring and valuing are the necessary warp and woof of most social science. Plenty of information – about equalities and inequalities, for example – can't be known or ordered at all without mixtures of 'subjective' judgment and 'objective' measurement. The choice and structure of most causal analysis has to depend throughout on its purposes. Any understanding of complex social life has to be a texture of imagination, valuation, selection, and technical observation and understanding.

The Left need experts who relate appropriate values coherently to appropriate techniques. They can be found. But some very influential schools – especially of economics, sociology, psychology and urban planning – did for many years make a disciplinary issue of those value-free and scientistic delusions. So there are some shortages of Left expertise; and even when intellectual fashions change, it can take a long time to reconstruct educational curricula and habits of mind. What can Left politicians do about this practical problem when they have to staff their policy-making services?

The institutional problems tend to be easier than the personal ones. Parties taking office or governments changing direction can usually move experts about within the public services; most countries allow some mobility between business, government and universities; most public services include frustrated reformers eager for more radical political directions. Knowing good experts from bad is another matter. Happily there are many professional fields in which the sillier scientistics never took on. Plenty of experts in health, poverty, social work, taxation, drug control and crime control, education and a great many public economic enterprises have always known how they hoped to improve the world, and done their best to choose rational techniques for the purpose. In many of those fields moreover the values which order the work are as acceptable to one political party as another: there's no need to replace all the school teachers or statisticians after each election.

Where the values and technical options are more contentious the problems may be harder, but politicians are as likely as anyone else to have the right approach to them. For research: 'What are you trying to find out that we don't know already? Why do we need to know it? What will it allow us to do, better than we do it already?' For the design of a new law, institution, service: 'Who will it help or hurt? Who will like it and who won't? However beautiful its intentions, will it be workable by the people who will have to work it? What would we actually lose by doing it at half the cost?' And so on. Pragmatic (though not necessarily short-term) attitudes to intellectual services are usually best.

But social scientists sometimes come bearing gold bricks and politicians and research councils have been known to buy them. Parties running on classless issues – on style and technological promise – are specially vulnerable. What should they do when old experts advise that any further improvement of society is technically impossible, or when new ones offer (say) to double exports or to uncover the fundamental dynamics of poverty in return for modest millions of research expenditure? How should politicians approach intellectual risk-taking? Obviously they will look for the usual personal qualities – intelligence, common sense, technical competence and inventiveness. Sometimes the candidates will have records, having got governments into trouble or out of it before. Beyond those I can only suggest one negative, one frivolous and one temperamental test:

Negative: By all means apply political tests, but do it by finding out what the candidate has done or discovered or advocated in the past; don't trust party affiliations. People join good causes and political parties for a wild variety of purposes: to put the world right, to rise high, to show off, to make money (including research grants) and to indulge warm, warm feelings of Recognition and Influence. Only a few of those carry any special promise of intelligently directed expertise.

Frivolous: First distinguish the mass monitoring, surveying, census-taking, etc., which genuinely need expensive staff and machinery to gather social information which politicians genuinely need to know. But beyond that – when dealing with candidates who offer to solve problems, discover causes, make break-throughs, invent policies – it is often safe to rank them inversely to the staff, hardware and computer time they ask for and to the size of personal office and car they ask for. (The same can't be said of the influence they ask for: the best are often the most eager for that.) Avoid: those who talk jargon which the patrons or the people to be studied can't understand; fashion-conscious folk who promise to keep the province up-to-date with this season's sophistications at Rand or MIT; anyone with a financial interest in selling data-processing machinery; experts in multivariate analysis who call it that; cost–benefit analysts who won't forecast distributions; all urbanists from the USA; traffic planners who have to be prompted to include cyclists and pedestrians in 'traffic'; persons who believe they can lower the price of land (unlike any other commodity whatever) by increasing the taxes on it; people who say 'I just offer the expertise – it's up to you politicians to say what you want done with it'; people who use the words systemic, societal or idiographic without irony.

Temperamental: Practical policy-making usually needs practical advisers. Plenty of fertile research is done by unbusinesslike people and plenty of perceptive observations and criticism are made by politically impractical people. But politicians need immediate advisers of another kind. Life and government are continuous. They are not projects, they are flows. They don't stop and wait for studies which demonstrate the need for further studies. Politicians need experts who will give whatever advice, after whatever study, there is time for. 'Be doing *this* while I find out more about *that*.' This is not anti-intellectual advice – the more skilled and up-to-date the experts are in their professional arts the better, but they must be prepared to apply the arts *now*.

As one test of temperament, ask experts what general type of end-result they hope their work will have and listen for answers which, having made the operation intelligible, follow its consequences through to some account – the more homely and personal the better – of the kinds of people who may be helped or hurt by it and the ways in which they may be helped or hurt. Beware of people who feel that the limits of their discipline, expertise, research contract or public service responsibility should also mark the limits of their interest in the consequences of their work. (All disciplines have their equivalents of the traffic planner who thinks severed neighborhoods are someone else's problem, or a compensation-cost problem.) It is absurd to ask for holism if that means an all-embracing understanding of complex systems. But there is a more modest holism: care for the effects of action on whole people, not just people-as-motorists, people-as-labor, people-as-statistics. Any holism requires valuations (holism is simply one or another particular selection of the causes and effects thought to matter most) and it usually means tracing whatever ramifications of action seem likely to matter most. Bad scientists won't explore ramifications which their techniques can't handle with proper scientific certainty. Good scientists mix whatever methods will discover most and do most for the people concerned – however mechanized or hand-held, sophisticated or simple or merely instinctive the best available methods may be.

The simplest test is to see if experts approach their work as they approach their private problems. They are always holists at home, looking to the effects of their actions on whole people and families. At home they don't care at all for value-freedom or fashionable restrictions of method. When they want to make money or trouble, plan a house or a holiday, win a fight or a divorce, save a threatened neighborhood or a sick child, their values drive them to strictly rational choices often of exceedingly mixed methods. If their values drive them to similarly uninhibited rationality in their public work there is some chance that they love their public as themselves, or have at least learned to serve it as thoughtfully as good politicians do. The point is worth repeating any number of times: thoughtful caring is not desirable for political or humane purposes only, or for 'applied' purposes only; it also has to supply much of the technical rationality and coherence of most social science. In this field the purest corn is the purest wisdom: the best *people* are likely to be the best social scientists, and the usual double meaning of 'best' is exactly right.

4

The economists who can be helpful to Left policy are generally those who want to reduce inequalities, and also extend the scope of economic science. There are good reasons why those political and technical purposes go together.

Put most simply: if you want to understand economic activity it does

143

not usually help to try to isolate 'an economic system' for study. A great many of the present generation of orthodox economists have been taught to base their science on that abstraction. It is tempting because it seems to promise a self-contained deductive science. But it has to assume that economic effects are sufficiently explained by economic causes, while other influences don't operate, or don't vary, or don't matter. In life, economic effects arise from very diverse causes. Even if steady relations hold between economic phenomena there is no reason to assume in advance that they will always be the most useful relations to know for purposes of understanding or social control. When economic science is confined to relations between quantifiable economic phenomena only (as it is, authoritatively, in many of the books which introduce students to the discipline) its power to discover or invent is very limited, and likely to work with a strong conservative bias.

Economics should really be the science which explains economic performance by reference to whichever of its causes and conditions it would be most useful to know. This is to ask for more institutional economics, or perhaps more old-fashioned political economy. What should its scope and subject-matter be?

A reforming economics should keep itself informed of the technical inventories and forecasts of natural resources. It should then supply most of the basis for resource policies: what to use, re-use, use up, conserve, export or import, for which productive purposes and for whose advantage. Plenty of this is done already piecemeal, and governments are beginning to shape national resource policies, though not yet with much care for their distributive effects. Their experts need to pay more attention to distributions, to compare qualities as well as quantities, and to interest themselves in the domestic uses and effects of material goods after their delivery to their users.

New approaches to distributions need to include new analyses of them, new summaries, and new theories.

The existing information about wealth and income often needs to be supplemented by better knowledge of physical distributions – of land, housing, warmth, nourishment, education, communication and whatever else may (or ought to) attract political attention from time to time. Many societies need to know more about distributions within families and through their life-cycles. Statistical services should not be oppressive and should not waste money or public tolerance trying to be too encyclo-paedic; but it should cease to be easy for social sufferings or maldistributions to continue simply because not enough is known about them.

Besides more detail about who gets what, there is need for more vivid summary representations of patterns and trends of distribution. These, and the way people understand and trust them, may prove to be important in restraining inflation, and in making the distributive implications of environmental policies clear and acceptable. There can be no value-free or unanimously agreed summaries even of distributions of income, and summary pictures of other social distributions are always likely to be contentious. But the press and public of developed countries learn quickly enough how to judge, from conflicting expert offerings, how their own interests and relativities and their societies' general patterns of distribution are faring.

Besides knowing who gets what, democracies need more control of it. It will soon be necessary to arrive democratically at deliberate principles of distribution – at acceptable patterns of limited inequality enforced as indirectly and unoppressively as possible. That will call for skill as well as will. At present governments don't believe they know how to control much of the distribution of wealth and income. Better controls wait on better theories of control. In one view those in turn must wait on better theories for understanding existing processes of distribution. But that need not be so; cures don't always depend on understanding causes. New systems of distribution need not use the more mysterious or uncontrollable mechanisms of the systems they replace. We need distributive mechanisms which *do* work as intended. Their design can't expect much help from existing economic theories, which don't explain distributions of income satisfactorily[11] and don't even try to explain distributions of wealth. Moreover the processes which those theories do try to explain are already changing. Any effective control of inflation is likely to upset present theories of output and employment by altering too many of the marketing and allocating mechanisms which those theories rely on. Socially, ownership and production and exchange need to be reorganized to produce a better primary distribution of rewards and incentives; and scientifically there need to be integrated theories of employment, output and distribution.

Those theories are likely to differ from present theories in two formal ways. Integrated theories of output and distribution will have to be more institutional – they will embed some regular mathematical parts in a good deal of the more concrete and eclectic explanation characteristic of history and political science. Second, present theories are the work of observers who try to understand and model the mechanisms of processes which nobody (or if you like, too many people) designed. Which parts of economic activity can be controlled, and what deliberate redistributions can be made, are among the things to be *discovered* by passive theory of this kind. The new theories will of course include the same two elements: passive understanding of mechanisms, and proposals for intervention and control. But the balance should have changed to make the design-and-control element the dominant one. To that extent new theories should *precede* new processes: they should be more like programs, or designs with working instructions, for systems which will aim to use automatic mechanisms and relationships, but only where they can be made to work as intended. The role of the more passive or understanding type of theory will shift to understanding the context within which economic activity occurs – the politics and psychology, the democratic desires and tolerances which determine what economic performance societies collectively want, and what their people individually are willing and able to deliver.

The best discussion of this subject is scattered through the works of Paul Streeten, from 'Programs and Prognoses' (*Quarterly Journal of Economics*, LXVIII, 1954) through his methodological appendix to Gunnar Myrdal's *Asian Drama* (London, 1967) to later papers in *The Frontiers of Development Studies* (London, 1972).

5

Economics (like law, medicine and other professions) has practical work to do. Other disciplines, which spend most of their time at teaching and research, create a special problem in the relation between social research and higher education. There are neglected links between inequality and the much-criticized 'publish or perish' rules of universities – links which do some social harm as well as the academic harm which is more often debated.

Philosophy, sociology, anthropology, social psychology, political science, history and studies of language and literature have some practical branches but their main business is to enlighten students and citizens in a general way rather than to supply them with practical professional services. To attract talent and keep it lively the universities are usually right to ask their academics to give half their time to teaching and half to other intellectual activities. But that wise aim has silly consequences when the quantity of research in each discipline comes to be determined mechanically by the number of students who happen to want some education in it. There is no reason why that mechanism should allocate research resources intelligently, and it doesn't. Half the damage can be corrected – where society needs more research than the teachers can supply, additional research services are easily added. But there is still no satisfactory solution to the opposite imbalance which occurs wherever a large teaching need generates more research than is really needed.

For example a society which wants well-educated politicians, public servants, journalists, teachers and citizens may find it desirable that in any year 1 in every 500 of population should be taking a university course in history or political science. A United States population of 200m. will yield 400,000 students of those subjects which at a staff: student ratio of 1:10 demands 40,000 academic historians and political scientists. Under a publish-or-perish rule requiring one book or equivalent articles every three years that should yield 13,333 volumes of academic history and political science per year. American society does not need that amount of new academic print on those subjects.

Plenty of critics notice how dubious such industries are but not many go on to guess how high their opportunity costs may be. Newspapers, local government, local associations and action groups, specialist reformers including muckrakers, environmentalists and consumer-protection agencies, planning and administrative services, the research departments of political parties and often the legislatures themselves get on as best they can with whatever talent is left while 40,000 chosen by each other as the country's cleverest occupy their time with exercises many of which are merely ritual.

That is a misleading picture of the actual condition of a good deal of political science in American universities where non-teaching time goes increasingly to activities which nobody could call ritual. Some members of other disciplines also find valuable things to do. Sociologists can always find social activities or institutions which research, imagination or persuasion could improve. Teachers of English write for stage, screen or street-corner, act and produce, edit and encourage other people's work, argue about censorship and generally apply themselves to improving people's enjoyment of their societies' arts and communications. Some academic employers take a catholic view of all those activities but many don't; as long as scholarly criticism continues to be the surest way to academic advancement, *especially* for the rank and file of the less brilliant, so long will the supply of obscure writers to criticize be like the supply of fossil fuel (exhaustible) and soon no doubt like the supply of scarce metals (recyclable).

Just as the number to be taught won't usually match the amount of

147

conventionally-defined research that society really needs, so it won't always match the extra-curricular opportunities for specialized skills. Teachers of drama or educational theory may always find something professional to do out of class but what (other than academic research) should philosophers or historians do out of class?

Some historians might begin by diversifying their discipline *in* class (as some already do). One branch of social science should try to be the holist one which deals with the general structure of societies and with the way they change through time – accepting and learning how to cope as well as possible with all the uncertainty, methodological difficulty and ideological conflict which necessarily go with that sort of work. Perhaps historians should be the ones to try – including the present and future in the curriculum might help to revitalize a somewhat stuck-in-the-mud profession. Historians should certainly also continue to write history books, whose effects on social self-knowledge and policy are often underrated; but not $20,000 \div 3 = 6,666$ new history books per year, trebled if you count all the affluent democracies. And historians and philosophers are only the most obvious among the many intellectuals whose non-teaching activities cannot all usefully be professionally specific.

Their societies should probably maintain them as a species of critic, clergy or intellectual-at-large, using them as their talents allow for *ad hoc* research, part-time public inquiry and administration, general social and political writing and broadcasting, and so on. None of that need prevent their being effective teachers, or working at conventionally disciplined research as often as they genuinely want to. But although most academic employers think they give their employees full freedom as intellectuals-at-large, plenty don't really do so. They tolerate free speech, but strictly disciplined publication is still what many of them chiefly appoint, promote and pay for.

Both of the conventional approaches to reforming this state of affairs are well-intended but misconceived. One is to pay more for good teaching. The other is to accept more extra-disciplinary activities as payable substitutes for disciplined publication. But both are difficult to assess (as is a good deal of disciplined publication, except by weight). Some assessments are unavoidable, to fill jobs and allocate work. But many more are made necessary by habits which the universities would be better without. Universities outbid one another for staff; staff compete for steeply-graded promotional rewards. If the universities offered more equal pay the academics would compete (as many already do) for more fruitful things – for working resources and opportunities, for places at the best centres with the brightest students and colleagues, for respect, influence and intellectual eminence. If universities reduced their material inequalities some of their members would give more time to their students, some would publish less ritual print, many might put their time and talent to better uses than occupy them now. And the best theorists and researchers would continue to produce the theory and research they produce now.

That need not introduce more 'applied', bureaucratically directed or myopically 'practical' research. On the contrary it would liberate academics to choose more freely for themselves how best to use their skills. It would do more good than harm to conventional incentives. Steeply graded rewards at present motivate a lot of the ritual output of the duller members but scarcely any of the valuable output of the brighter members. Money incentives don't make academics' thoughts more original or their research more fertile. (When they do good work they expect whatever are the recognized rewards for it, but that is different and simply depends on what the going rewards and ideas of equity happen to be.) Beginners don't think 'I'll make this article brighter the better the promotional chances are.' At the other end of the promotional ladder Keynes didn't write his *General Theory* for the royalties or a smartly bargained move to higher pay at Berkeley. The best of young and old are more ambitious than that; and for those who are not, and who might respond to more equal pay by growing lazier, no good is done by bribing them to produce larger instead of smaller quantities of dull research that nobody wants.

Academics can be enticed to compete chiefly for money if institutions set out to motivate them that way. But it is not the way to get the best work from most of them. It would be more effective to offer more equal pay and more diverse working opportunities. Plenty of intellectuals would welcome both. The universities would run better and set better social examples. And the societies they belong to might be better served by intellectual resources of which too many are at present sterilized or misdirected by the penalties and temptations of the universities' internal inequalities.

There remains the most important matter of all. What sort of social theory, planning and persuasion does a peaceful social-democratic revolution need? What follows will be familiar to many politicians and public servants and variously unwelcome to many Left activists and intellectuals.

The Left must learn to be – in an intelligent selective way – conservative. It should stop associating all change with progress and all conservatism with reaction. The intelligentsia especially should stop sneering at everyman's stodgy attachment to so many familiar values and institutions. The Left should defend many working, social and family networks as it is already learning to defend physically-threatened neighborhoods, townscapes and landscapes. It should recognize the ideologue who wants to raze the whole rotten bourgeois fabric as the social equivalent of the rapacious developer who wants to bulldoze old neighborhoods to make way for arid acres of concrete and glass. Almost all change destroys some social capital, hurts some personal securities and leaves somebody uprooted and mourning.[12] Change is a *cost* of achieving better equality, freedom, social cohesion. Instead of trying to commend it for its own sake to people who know better, the Left should learn to treat it as a cost, and economize it. What new directions of social theory and persuasion does that suggest?

'Theory is thought about action.' It must debate what action is possible, what action we want, and how to go about it.

It is easiest to begin with action we don't want. Social-democratic majorities won't want to destroy the family, desert the cities, abolish property or otherwise clear the ground for a blue-printed Utopia, or to 'see what grows' praxis-wise. On the other hand they are already impatient of the mild methods by which democracies have tried for a century (or been prevented from trying) to civilize a rapacious economic system whose inequalities are once again increasing. Social-democratic paths run somewhere between those boundaries. The task for pathfinders is to think of ways to reconstruct institutions radically, by controlled transitions which test the ground as they go and keep the machinery running throughout, with all the people tolerably fed and safe and free at every stage, and not less than 51% of them demanding or consenting to the transformations.

It is not easy to replace or reconstruct long-established institutions, services or habits of behavior. Nor is it easy to sustain the popular will to go on reconstructing them. Practical innovators have learned a lesson: the more radical you want to be, the more conservative you may need to be.[13] The more drastic the changes, the more reassurance people may want. They are not wrong to want it. Social institutions exist chiefly in the beliefs and expectations which people express in their collective behavior. Their expectations of each other are complicated, slowly learned, and vital to social peace and economic efficiency. Every change makes some skill and experience obsolete, every new institution is likely to suffer some costs of inexperience. The greater the change, the harder it usually is to predict all of its effects. This is partly because people who have to work or use the new institutions haven't the time to learn too many new procedures at once, and it is partly because people are rightly nervous and distrustful of first-time changes – nervous that the new things won't work or distrustful that they may inadvertently upset equities, open floodgates, shake foundations, admit Trojan horses, etc. What people like best is a step at a time, then time to see the new things work and to check that everything else still works. These are not primitive or childlike or reactionary misgivings, they are rational precautions in any running reconstruction of complicated machinery which consists chiefly of the complicated expectations which people have of one another. And they are rational precautions if change is to help people rather than unnerve, disorganize or alienate them.

Institutional continuity and administrative economy have often been conservative concerns but radicals have a more vital interest in them. Radicals need to civilize and equalize society with *least* alarm, *least* anxiety and uncertainty for as many as possible of its members. They have the strongest interest in minimizing any needless bureaucratic muddle and tophamper. Whatever administrative capacity they can muster is bound to be strained to the limit by unavoidable reconstructions, and no avoidable loads should be added to it. Experts and intellectuals who want to help radical regimes through their initial battles and reconstructions need to get out of the mood that looks for 'daring', 'all-embracing', 'over-arching' solutions and into the mood that looks for economical interventions which achieve large effects with least disturbance. We want to fix the price of land without disturbing everyman's secure occupation of his house and garden, or producers' forward planning of the space their plant or warehouses will need. We want to limit the capital anyone can own, and perhaps make it unspendable; that need hurt less than one person in ten so how can it be done with least alarm to the other nine?

For these purposes, political moods and intellectual services need to be cooler and more discriminating than those of the revolutionary Left, but at the same time more radical and combative than the too-safe style of most labor and social-democratic parties in recent times.

The need could be expressed tritely as a need for more rethinking: for baby-and-bathwater studies, with finer separations of goods from bads. To abolish capitalism in simple Russian style would throw whole nurseries of lovable and quite reformable babies out with the bathwater. Plenty of private economic freedoms and motivations are worth keeping – but there is scope for thought about which to keep and how to make them work more sociably. The moderate Left has usually compromised with private enterprise quite unimaginatively, nationalizing some of it, tolerating some of it, strangling some of it with regulations. Too few on the Left think constructively about it – about better integrations of public ownership with private management, better reconciliations of public and private interest, better separations of the useful from the harmful functions of conventional economic motivation. All those reformist packages – 'private ownership means production for profit, public ownership means production for use' or 'banking, transport, mining and heavy manufacturing are the commanding heights of the economy from which the rest can be directed' or 'tax the betterment of land to recover the value which accrues from public rather than private action' – need to be taken apart from time to time so that their parts can be inspected for error or obsolescence, not only to prevent obsolete ideas from living on but also to prevent good ideas from being junked because of a single failure or misapplication.

Fruitful work is already done in separating questions of economic distribution from questions of well-being. Experts from physicists at one extreme to organic gardeners at the other are researching ways for people to live better on less, materially speaking. Gains of that kind are the purest gold from everybody's point of view; conventional materialists should stop poking fun at them and get into the same business. Many industries and households could live better on less if their suppliers of oil, gas, electricity, sunlight and garbage disposal could learn to cooperate better. Efficient use is as important as efficient production, and may be more important if resources are exhaustible. Economists could try to design national accounts to reflect that, which they don't now.

There is need to rethink relations between material production and the satisfaction of a great many human needs. Too many recreations have been mechanized, usually for the purpose of commercializing them. One man tickles fish; another catches them with rod and line and perhaps some rubber trousers or a rowing boat; another won't fish at all without car, caravan, power-boat and hundreds of dollars' worth of romantic clothing. If cities and countrysides were better related, if more public transport were designed with reversible weekend uses in mind, and if city-dwellers cultivated gentler images of themselves as countrymen-at-heart, then all parties (especially the fish, in cleaner seas and streams) could be happy at less material cost. When gasoline is short the king of Norway rather likes the excuse to take the tram to ski at Holmenkollen. Norwegian country cottages are said to use network energy inversely to their owners' incomes – the richest like to cook on wood stoves by the light of oil lamps, for old times' sake. Long before it became eco-fashionable, one publishing gentleman I know was bicycling around the City of London in the way of his business, overtaking many slower and consequently less affluent tycoons in their traffic-jammed Rolls-Royces. Social timetables can often economize material capital as when staggered hours spread loads on roads, public transport, power generators or family bathrooms. When schools, theatres, libraries, stadiums and parking lots serve diverse community needs through day, evening and weekend the gains are often social as well as material.

There is room for more of that sort of time-efficiency and cost-efficiency; and also for equivalents of purely social kinds. Some societies have very expensive, resource-wasteful, pollutant and also humanly cruel ways of satisfying people's desires for excitement, status, esteem or individual difference; others have cheaper, comelier, kinder, more socially useful ways of generating and satisfying similar desires. Whatever jealousies they may generate amongst themselves, people who go in for fishing or rose-growing or home carpentry don't cause much anxiety or material loss to people who don't. The same ought to be true of people who go in for success.

There is room for inventive thought about many procedures of adjudication and crime control. One Australian study discovered that two thirds of the money that changes hands after traffic accidents goes to lawyers (and is counted into GNP, so that a country with safer roads and simpler procedures would count as poorer). There is plenty of scope for improving equalities under the law. Whatever the level of 'social prevention' there could also be rich social returns to acceptable methods of catching and convicting a higher proportion of offenders. On this subject the Left is often misled by its stereotype of law and order as a rich device for oppressing the poor. There does indeed need to be more attention to the

153

class bias of law and to the social origins of crime; there do need to be more constructive ways of dealing with offenders; there are indeed police scandals; but most of the scandals of law and order are still scandalous evasions of it, and most of the victims of crime are poor. Reliable law and order are conditions for many other qualities of life which vary independently of economic productivity: honest government; many equalities; enjoyment of town and country parks and town and country lanes and byways; children's freedoms, women's freedoms, all vulnerable people's freedoms; the famous civility of English people to each other and to other strangers; and so on.

Readers can multiply their own examples. In all sorts of fields – in urban forms and timetables and manners, in education and family life, in communications, in access and attitudes to art and nature and human companionship – there are opportunities to improve the qualities of life without necessarily increasing material production. Some of them depend on consciously rejecting the equation of well-being with material income – not in order to make the poor more content with their lot, but to help people to make more efficient uses of whatever material productivity and equality their societies have.

Such analysis – the detailed, open-minded separation of goods from bads, and of real well-being from the economic goods that are supposed to serve it – is valuable for many practical purposes. In a larger way it is also valuable for purposes of persuasion. The problems of democratic reform are chiefly problems of popular belief, expectation, understanding and tolerance. Like anyone's understanding of the world beyond his own expertise or direct experience, popular belief and understanding have to be constructed of simple theories and images. Such simplifications persist or change in response to personal experience and private and public learning. If it is important for experts or politicians to keep their understandings of the world up-to-date and well related to their values, it is doubly important for the citizens to do the same. So persuasive thinkers may often be at least as valuable as original thinkers.

The persuasion of public opinion is a mixed and largely self-inflicted business. It is partly technical and educational, concerned with how the world works and how attempts to reform it would or wouldn't work. It is partly a war of interests, partly a debate about values; and people's conceptions of their interests and values change with their changing technical understandings. It is partly personal or fiduciary: people cannot understand everything for themselves, so just as they choose doctors or newspapers, so they judge which experts or ideologues or politicians to trust. Most of those professionals are in turn listening and responding to *them*. Persuasion – in the broad sense which comprehends all the activities that move opinion – is itself a large part of any process of change and a condition of most of the more formal or technical kinds of change. So persuasion has to be the heart of any social-democratic strategy.

The chief hindrances to social-democratic progress are the resistance of the rich who would lose by it and the misgivings of a great many of the rest; the two become one when as their most effective method of resistance the rich work to encourage the misgivings of the rest. But the most obstinate stereotypes are still the ones which *seem* to rest on facts of personal experience. The British nationalizations of 1945–51 did not do very much to transform society; on that and other perceptions of public services it has been possible to build widely-held stereotypes of public enterprise as intrinsically cumbersome, inefficient and oppressive to employees and customers alike. Communist government is oppressive at its best and murderous at its worst; on that foundation it has been possible to build stereotypes of socialist economic organization as intrinsically undemocratic and hostile to personal liberty. On the ruthless behavior of some private enterprises it has been possible to build stereotypes of private enterprise as always and necessarily antisocial. The activities of some immense organizations (chain stores, savings banks, health and educational and postal services) consist chiefly of very large numbers of personal transactions most of which are capable of being friendly and sociable events for all concerned. There are other activities (working on noisy assembly lines, processing routine paper) which are inevitably dull and unsatisfying whether the employer is large or small, public or private. But on *some* of those facts it has been possible to build generalized beliefs that big is always soul-destroying (or efficient) and small is always beautiful (or cramping).

It is chiefly by the survival of such stereotypes in people's values and beliefs that 'the past weighs like an alp upon the present'. Attacking, unscrambling, replacing, reconstructing and up-dating such beliefs is the central task for democratic reformers. Better education and communications help a little but they can never produce universal omniscience – a world understood without simplifications. Since nobody can understand much of the world without them there need be nothing wrong or deceptive or elitist in reformers working to replace worse simplifications by better ones. That calls for equal quantitites of art and science. The best-designed programs won't work until people are persuaded to understand them or trust their sponsors. The most artful persuasions will achieve nothing good if they deceive people about the real state of the world.

7

Between them politicians and intellectuals – theorists both, in this role – have to work out the strategies of reform most likely to succeed.

They must chiefly be strategies of persuasion based on convincing promise and performance. In affluent democracies no faction strong enough to matter is likely to try violent revolution or counter-revolution, and even if any do, persuasion will still decide who wins by deciding who fights on which side. The likelier war (if the Left manage to force a contest at all) is a war of words reinforced by demonstrations, passive resistance, strikes, blacklisting, urban sabotage and guerilla activity, lockouts, contrived unemployment, capital flight, international economic reprisals and other comparatively bloodless disorganizations. Though some of those try to persuade by coercing, the decisive gains and losses will probably still be at democratic elections.

What general character of persuasion should the Left attempt? How can it hope to attract and hold enough each of traditional, environmentalist and anti-inflation support – some self-interested and some not – to elect and drive and support it through years of radical and sometimes bitterly resisted change?

In some small countries it probably can, in Japan and the big European democracies it just might, in the USA it obviously can't. To succeed anywhere it needs a special kind of simple-but-complicated leadership. Simple values and compelling visions have to drive people and governments through a lot of patient, detailed, confusing reconstructions. Democracies manage that in wartime. In peace it is harder; and the hardest part of the package to sell may be the simple faith itself. Equality has to be the inspiring, unifying idea of the whole enterprise – but some very uninspiring images of equality are entrenched in many citizens' minds. It means revolutionary breakdown to some, dismal mediocrity to others. To millions of workingmen's wives it chiefly suggests more strikes and hire-purchase arrears and strained relations with their husbands. To many people it is simply boring.

Against all that, three things may work for the Left. The citizens are better skilled and educated than ever; anxieties about resources may make them readier to share resources fairly; and there are signs that more people at all levels of income are ready to cry 'enough' and to be choosier in the use of resources. Second, the effects of bad and increasingly unstable capitalist distributions are growing more acutely unpopular. Third, whatever may be thought of Left threats and promises, Left *achievements* are popular. Left governments usually fall because they fail, not because they succeed. They fall because they fail to deliver full employment, stable prices, industrial peace, tangible social improvements. Their successes survive. New policies of equality may be pared in detail, eroded by inflation or (very often) offset by other trends or transfers; but most specific egalitarian reforms survive because once established they tend to be solidly, invulnerably popular.

These – changing moods and values, the malfunctions of inequality, and the popularity of equalities once established – make opportunities for change. The Left has to supply simple visions, complicated programs, and competent performance. Simple values are vital to all three. Widely shared and well understood purposes (rather than formal directives and bureaucratic liaisons) have to supply most of the momentum, invention and coordination of complicated new programs. Such things are not impossible. Plenty of states, parties and corporations pursue simple aims (office; profit; victory in war) by complicated methods. But as a strategy for peaceful social change it cannot be easy. From building and maintaining agreement within political parties, through reorganizing and re-educating many arms of national and local government, to engaging the public in satisfying ways in such a single-minded but confusingly detailed enterprise, the task for Left leadership is formidable. But it is only by that sort of strong-but-complicated approach that the Left can now hope to make much way. It will need, among other things, very able intellectual services.

One task for those services has scarcely been touched on in this chapter because it is the subject of the next. As the most important of all tasks of 'separation and reassembly', what can be done to improve relations – the working relations and the relations in popular image and stereotype – between equality and liberty?

6-2

7
Equalities and liberties

Utopian thought is often useful. Marx was right to insist that futures have to grow out of presents, but he was wrong to refuse to plan or imagine what the futures might be.[14] Too many of his followers turned that into a truly crazy rule that Marxists must never think about socialism. So it was against doctrine for Russian communists to think about socialism before 1917 and against law and prudence for them to think about it after 1918 or 1928 (or to recall what some of them had thought about it in the interval) so they managed to build a uniquely thoughtless form of it. To distinguish better aims and tactics from that oppressive example the Chinese communist party set out to make revolution more deliberate: to make it step by step, province by province, with less wrangling analysis of the system to be demolished and more constructive thought about what to build in its place. The revolution was still bloody but its elements of persuasion were clearer. Besides refining the revolutionaries' planning, each communized province demonstrated the confiscations, violence, brainwashing, land reforms, equalities and honest government that the next could expect. Thinking ahead about the structure of socialism and persuading by 'doing and showing' produced a society which (good or bad) was as like its builders' forecasts as the Russian outcome had been unlike them.

It is scarcely necessary to urge democratic socialists to plan ahead. Making very clear what they want to do is usually the only way to persuade people to do it. Democrats also have to 'show by doing', making each step of change sufficiently popular to attract support for the next. But there the Chinese likeness has to end. Communist socialism may prompt some thoughts about democratic socialism, but it is still the biggest single hindrance to achieving democratic socialism. At the time of their revolutions Russian and Chinese workers and peasants had very little wealth, liberty or law and order to lose. Rich democracies have plenty of all three and will not trade much of any of them for gains in equality. It is hard to know how much of the opposition to equality is to the thing itself, how much is fear of its possible costs in freedom or security, and how much is simple disbelief that more equality is practicable; but equality won't make much progress until majorities are persuaded that the progress can be reconciled with continuing order, productivity and freedom.

2

I doubt if many people are persuaded by simple affirmations of the values of equality or liberty, or by lists of their many meanings, or by analyses of the reasons which believers in them seem to have for their beliefs. Simple statements of faith or principle don't mean much until practical programs spell out their implications. Readers who nevertheless want to refresh their idealism, or analyse it, can return to the classics of each tradition.

One can value equality and liberty equally but allow that the idea of equality has inspired better books. The liberal classics tend to be more critical than constructive, and they evade too many of the problems they ought to confront. They expect men to be better the freer they are, a belief which we contradict every day in a thousand precautions against one another. They say men should have all liberties that don't hurt other peoples' interests – but politics is almost exclusively about the other sort, the liberties which do affect other people's interests. If we had only the liberties which don't conflict and none of the ones which do, that would set new standards of slavery. But the classical liberals didn't say what should be done about conflicting liberties. John Stuart Mill – like Marx – was a brilliant critic of some existing constraints on people's liberties. Like Marx he was clear about who he thought should have power. But like Marx he said very little about what they should build with it.

Some freedoms are negative or natural and exist as long as nobody interferes with them. Others can only be exercised collectively. Others are freedoms of individuals but it takes collective action, including plenty of constraint, to create them. Taking them all together it certainly makes sense to value some societies as freer than others and to prefer the freer sort. But it never made sense for liberals to discuss *only* the question of more liberty or less – rather than which liberties for which people to do what, and at whose cost. Liberty is really a vague collective for a host of social and moral dilemmas and conflicts. Some liberties are good, some are bad, some are indifferent. People disagree which are which. Some of the disagreements can be resolved by agreeing to generally liberal institutions but when liberties conflict, disagreements about them can't

159

be resolved in that way. Many freedoms do conflict with other interests: liberty is a conflict-of-interest problem. Some of the conflicts are between rich and poor: liberty is a class problem or a race problem. Some freedoms hinder production or social organization: liberty is an efficiency problem. Some liberties-to-prey belong in the jungle and are just as deadly anywhere else. Very poor people haven't many options: liberty can be a problem of economic growth or redistribution. Most liberties have to be institutionally created and protected: liberty is a constitutional, administrative, design-and-construction problem. Though valued as equally free, different societies may offer differently detailed patterns of choice to their members: liberty is a shopping problem. Liberties are unreal unless people have will and skill to use them: liberty is a hearth-and-home, educational, character-building problem. A vote is both a choice and an influence; many freedoms for me impose constraints on you; for those and a great many other reasons liberty is always a problem of power. Freedom, power and subjection can easily be three people's impressions of the same relationship; then liberty is a question of definition and valuation.

The idea of liberty is also a wanton begetter of idiotic generalization. Consider the Professor of English who says that he wants to abolish censorship because 'communication should be absolutely free'. He doesn't really want the morning papers to print the evidence given in custody cases, or confidential psychiatric reports on juvenile offenders. He doesn't want police witnesses to tell juries about accused persons' criminal records or unwarned admissions. He doesn't want the Sunday papers to publish the yield of uncontrolled bugging, bedroom-photography or other invasions of privacy. He doesn't want unchecked commercial blacklisting for debt-collection or credit-rating. He doesn't want governments to know everybody's private affairs or to publish what they know. He doesn't want Treasury clerks to communicate freely with stock-exchange speculators, or bank clerks to publish the combinations of their employers' safes. He doesn't want blueprints for nerve gases or atomic bombs to be published to all small republics. He often wants to enforce more truth in labelling and advertising, especially of medicines and tobacco. He doesn't want his own writings to be printed without his permission or without royalty or with the 'nots' left out to reverse his meanings. He may want libraries to stop lending books until certain authors (but not others) are paid for public lending rights. In fact he agrees with almost all of the innumerable rules which restrict communication, but would like a few changes: public lending rights, less tobacco advertising, and more explicit representations of sex and violence in public entertainments. Does he therefore say 'We ought to amend two or three of the rules, thus and so'? No, he contradicts most of his own beliefs by declaring – fearlessly, on television if possible, with quotations from Milton's *Areopagitica* and dark references to Hitler, Copernicus and the Spanish Inquisition – that all censorship whatever should be abolished and all communication should be free.

Similar exaggerations afflict other movements. To liberate a country may mean exchanging one ruling group for another with gains in pride or political independence but not in anyone's personal freedom. Liberating racial minorities may mean improving their chances to unequalize their rewards or to coerce rather than be coerced. Some schemes to liberate women would genuinely increase their freedom of choice; others merely urge them to desire different things; others would equalize them with men by unequalizing them with one another. Some of those who want to free educated women from housework want a fairer distribution of work between women and men. Others think rich women deserve more of the pleasures of inequality, so poor women should go out and work in rich women's houses just as poor men have to go out and work in rich men's factories. That would redistribute some advantages from poor to rich. Others want to redistribute advantages from weak to strong – people should follow affections rather than conventions, more parents should have their children cared for by other people, children and spouses whose charms fade should be deserted more freely. Some liberators (the saddest) mean by liberty exactly what others mean by alienation: an absence of mutual bonds and obligations, a strict and usually loveless independence of other people. Often without realizing it, too many liberationists are trying to apply to human relations the nastiest nineteenth-century principles of tooth-and-claw capitalism: they preach an unfettered individualism with terminable voluntary contract as the only acceptable human relation and no protections at all for victims, dependants, weak bargainers or third parties.

Most of the best liberationists – of women, children and others – really ask for more love or equality rather than more liberty. Their programs may be good or bad, they may trade better freedoms and constraints for worse or worse for better, but the complicated redistributions they propose should scarcely ever be summed up as simple increases of liberty, though they are usually advertised as that. The wildest idiocies of all are uttered about business. It may be useful to distinguish public from private ownership, but neither would be very enterprising if enterprise were free. For private capitalism to work at all, innumerable rules of law have to shape and protect precisely defined, precisely constrained economic roles and opportunities. One thing which often has least affect on enterprisers' freedom of action is the difference between public and private shareholding. But ideologues of Right and Left still identify (say) commercial slaves like commission salesmen or petrol-station lessees as 'free' and (say) the public employees who developed penicillin or atomic energy or high-speed trains as 'bond'.

Most of these are merely silly ways of talking. Free is hooray, unfree is boo, so when people want to enlarge a freedom they say they want to increase freedom but when they want to restrict a freedom they don't say they want to reduce freedom, they say they want to reduce rape or tax avoidance or Sunday trading. Such contraints, they say, will increase freedom – women's freedom from rape, traders' freedom from overwork or irreligion, Treasurers' freedom from want. Led by Franklin Roosevelt, the 'freedom from' usage allows people to demand safeties, equalities, constraints, coercions and other unAmerican goods without ever actually naming them – *any* program, whatever its content of effective choice or effective coercion, can be expressed as a freedoms-only program. Uneducated folk who used to say we needed the right sort of freedom and not too much of it – and that people should be allowed to do some bad things but not other bad things – may sometimes have had terrible programs in detail but they were right in principle about the instrumental nature of liberty, and also of language.

Language may not matter as much as this complaint suggests – however they torture it, people generally know what they mean. By liberty they mean some particular set of what seem to them to be good liberties and good constraints. From now on this chapter will try to conform: liberty means the familiar democratic permissions and prohibitions which define familiar freedoms of belief, communication, assembly, association and movement; the prohibition of arbitrary violence or imprisonment in most circumstances; and equal and effective rights to vote. In a more personal sense it stands for the set of constraints, freedoms, values and expectations which together allow most people (brought up to that set) to feel that they can lead reasonably unfussed, uncramped and unbullied lives. Can those particular liberties and constraints survive (or be improved by) more equal distributions of material goods? Or to put it another way, can economic liberties and constraints be altered without damaging too many other valuable liberties and constraints?

3

What sort of people want equality? Overwhelmingly, free people who already have some. But what sort of people want more of it?

One economic theory says that there can never be a rational majority for greater equality. Half the people have incomes above the median income and must all expect to gain by greater inequality. Of the half with incomes below the median *some* – those who expect to climb individually – can also expect to gain by greater inequality. So it is not surprising that the vote for the Left is rarely much above 40%. Though it may be uncomfortably near to the truth in many cases there are nevertheless technical and psychological flaws in the theory. Majorities can benefit from plundering minorities of the very rich; depending on the particular pattern of distribution there may be many incomes above the median but below the average; and not everybody votes for his own material advantage, or values that above other advantages. Right and Left each like to think that their own ranks vote for efficiency or justice while the enemy votes for money. The Left suspect that the rich hang on to the money by one means or another *whatever* the democracy votes for. The Right usually insist that desire for more money is the normal and understandable reason why anyone poor votes Left, while anyone rich who votes Left must be guilt-ridden, hungry for power, or unnaturally destructive.

It is sometimes more illuminating to see those who want more equality as lovers or haters. Some lovers work unselfishly in social services, others can be found wherever they can work directly or indirectly for the better human relations which they believe equality allows. Pure haters generally hate people – those on the Left commonly hate rich or powerful people. Those who hate relationships or institutions – what the rich do to the poor or what inequality does to both – are often hating and loving at once. Some mixture of the two is usually needed to cope with the do-gooder's perennial dilemma: to be too good is often to be ineffective, while to be effective often requires guile, aggressiveness, power-seeking; ends and means corrupt each other. That has to be accepted – if good can't be done by imperfect people it cannot be done at all. We should not sneer so freely at the American folk-image of the good gunman who bloodies his hands in aid of civic peace and honest government. If Robespierre and Stalin had been better balanced haters and lovers they also might have ridden off into the sunset at correct historical moments, leaving better-governed towns behind them.

There may be a tendency for haters to be better fighters both on behalf

163

of revolutionary movements and in contests for power within them. Peaceful movements for democratic reform usually have work for all sorts. Haters can be excellent militants, muckrakers, tax collectors; lovers may be better cooperators, social workers, builders of consensus, designers of workable institutions. The best reformers are usually a complex mixture of both and anyway the classification is too simple because neither love nor hate is usually simple. Despite some Christian instructions, to love people is often to hate whoever hurts them. Nor are other political psychologies as simple as they are sometimes made out to be. There have been many historically wrong and personally insensitive misrepresentations of the patterns of feeling commonly called paternal, and of others called puritan. Joyless oppressive people are not the only ones who love equal and honest justice, or work and what it creates. Some governors and parents are permissive because they don't care too much; others because they care very much. Oppressors likewise. Plenty of stern parents or governors don't love dominating – they love their fellow citizens or their children, don't want them to prey or be preyed on, have ideals (however appropriate or inappropriate) for them, and feel responsible for the injuries they suffer or commit. If some Calvins or Savonarolas push these feelings too far or in oppressive directions that doesn't make a general case against just government, any more than the disorder of a frontier gold-rush makes a general case against liberty. In many branches of democratic government it is thought virtuous to deal equally and respectfully with people and to constrain them to deal so with one another. That mood – which majorities often endorse – commonly expresses some fondness for people and for just and friendly relations between them. To dismiss it as a love of power or a worship of work or a hatred of spontaneity is often absurd.

The way in which a love of equality is itself regarded varies greatly from society to society. The Right everywhere like to discredit such feelings as self-seeking, twisted or impractical. The American Right have had unique success in entrenching in the national culture a fundamental distinction between love of political equality (psychologically normal) and love of economic equality (wierd and probably foreign-inspired). Such stereotypes tend to verify themselves – where it is abnormal to love equality only abnormal people do it. But American intellectuals have at times gone to extraordinary lengths to authorize and dignify the stereotype. One textbook of social pathology listed 'radicalism and the radical' between 'crime and the criminal' and 'alcoholism and the alcoholic'. A generation of historians explained white efforts to abolish black slavery as psycho-compensation by a frustrated New England elite. Sociology and psychology joined in classifying radicals among the maladjusted, and in explaining desires for economic equality as envious, guilt-ridden or bottle-fed.[15] Thus it was established that the Right was sane and the Left was sick. Meanwhile in different circumstances (and with different social scientists) Norwegians and New Zealanders, Israelis and Tanzanians and Englishmen who value whatever equalities they have and work for more of them can all be as normal as apple pie – whether loving or hating, feeling or calculating, driven or enchanted by imprints of infant or adult experience.

4

Some of the best modern recommendations of equality and incidentally of liberty too are in the works of Richard Tawney and Richard Titmuss, in John Rawls' *A Theory of Justice* (Oxford, 1972) and in Michael Young's account of equal opportunity in *The Rise of the Meritocracy* (London, 1958). Moralities of equality are as various as moralities of liberty. In Young's summary: 'One could say it was wrong to pay one man more than another because there should be distribution according to needs. One could say it was wrong to pay the lazy scientist more than the diligent dustman because there should be distribution according to effort. One could say it was wrong to pay the intelligent more than the stupid because society should compensate for genetic injustice. One could say it was wrong to pay the stupid more than the intelligent because society should compensate for the unhapppiness which is the usual lot of the intelligent. (No one can do much about the brilliant, they will be miserable anyway.) One could say it was wrong to pay the man who lived a long and serene life in Upper Slaughter as much as a scientist who wore himself out in the service of knowledge at the Battersea Poly. One could say it was wrong to pay people who liked their work as much as those who didn't. One could – and did – say anything, and whatever one said it was always with the support of the particular kind of justice invoked by principles implicit in the statement.'[16]

Those questions apply at any scale of inequality. But what should the scale be? That also can be dismembered into a complexity of questions, beginning with the far-from-obvious meaning of the idea of equality itself. Consider the two patterns of income distribution in Figure 1. In the first most people are very equal with each other but very unequal with a few rich and a few poor. In the second there are no very rich or very poor but there are big inequalities where perhaps they matter most: a lot of

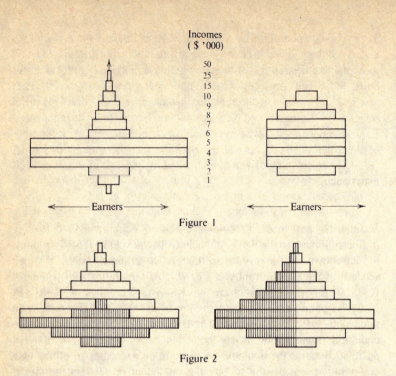

Figure 1

Figure 2

people are taking home three or four times the rewards of a lot of other people. Which distribution is 'more equal'? Whichever seems so to your values might seem different if the patterns disclosed bias between sexes, races, inheritances, etc. The patterns in Figure 2 look alike until you learn that the shaded parts show women's or blacks' incomes, or the prospects of children of poor parents; whereupon the patterns still look equally equal to some values but not equally equal, or not equally fair, to others. It matters to some values more than to others that in the first pattern all males (or whites, or professionals, or sons-of-the-rich) are rich and all females (or blacks, or laborers, or laborers' children) are poor, while in the second pattern each sex, color or trade has its own ladder of success so that men, women, whites, blacks, surgeons, laborers, children of the rich and children of the poor all have similar chances of riches or poverty.

Just as those comparisons require value-judgments so do most comparisons through time, i.e. judgments that inequalities are growing greater or less. In Figure 3 each sloping line represents the movement of a personal or class income. By all conventional tests inequality is

166

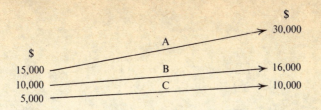

Figure 3

increasing between A and B – each year A gets a bigger increase than B, his income grows at a higher percentage rate, he gets an increasing share of national income and his income is an increasing multiple of B's. But there agreement is likely to end. Once, A got $10,000 more than C; because he now gets $20,000 more, one observer will say that A and C are less equal than they were. But their percentage relations have not changed so another observer will say that their inequality has not changed. A third observer may want to take more notice of what these incomes actually buy. He may observe that it takes $2,000 to stay alive, and that $7,000 buys a house and car, workable access to most educational and career opportunities and a statistical chance of living as long as the rich do. Because he thinks it important to have these essentials of a common lifestyle, this observer may judge that A and C have become more equal than they were. But a fourth observer may give more importance to other thresholds of expenditure: perhaps $20,000 takes A into a class which has second houses, servants, swimming pools and private schooling and rarely intermarries with those below; this observer may judge that A and C have become less equal than they were. There will be similar disagreements about the relation between B and C – if the absolute difference between their incomes matters most, they are less equal than they were; but proportionately, or by some 'common life-style' tests, they are more equal.

The life expectancy and life-style tests may attract more interest if general standards of living ever have to fall. In Figure 4 all absolute and relative tests would say that equalities had improved, though the second citizen has lost his effective participation in the society and the third just died of starvation. In most of those examples there will be disagreement about the relation between two or three incomes with steady trends. When real-life judgements have to be made about national patterns of millions of irregularly changing incomes, complicated by distributions of wealth, opportunity, land, housing, mobility and a dozen other things, disagree-

167

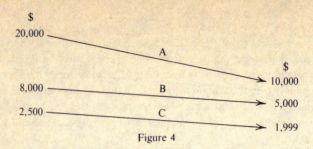

$$\$$$
$$20,000$$
A
$$\$$$
$$10,000$$
$$8,000 \quad\quad\quad B$$
$$5,000$$
$$2,500 \quad\quad\quad C$$
$$1,999$$

Figure 4

ments will multiply accordingly. And it is no easier to agree about equalities than about inequalities. Would perfect equality mean equal pay per person, per worker, per household? Per day or per life-time? Each principle would contradict most of the others. How would an equal society distribute unequal but indivisible things – unequally attractive jobs, houses, locations? *All* judgments of equality and inequality have to rest partly on objective measurements and partly on judgments of value.

From this, some Right-thinking behaviorists will conclude that equality and inequality are meaningless concepts which should be ignored in science and in life. It is more sensible to conclude that the element of valuation in judgments of equality is like the element of valuation in most social judgment and throughout most social science. Summary statements about the trend of inequalities in the capitalist democracies ought to be based on true information, and it is right to call them false if they are not. But they also have to select the assets to be compared (including what to count as wealth or income), the classes of people to be compared, the relationships which are judged to matter most, and some unprovable assumptions about the value of similar assets to different people.[17] It should not be upsetting to know that judgments of equality must have that dual character. All the judgments and understandings that we live by have it.

5

None of these difficulties need prevent widely agreed observations of obvious and important differences in equality between Sweden, the USA and South Africa or between China, Hungary and the USSR. Within the rich democracies, debates have tended to concentrate on detailed questions: what decent minimum should the poorest have, and what is the right pecking order for the rest – should bricklayers get more than school teachers, should unmarried parents get less than other single parents,

168

should investors in property do better than other investors? Those debates will continue but they should grow less important as attention shifts to consider how steep the whole range of inequalities should be. That question can be put in its least controversial form by assuming that the practical options are to extend, to hold or to flatten existing margins between incomes. Leaving most people in their present order of inequality, should incomes stay as they are, or move closer to one another and to the national average, or spread further apart to produce generally larger inequalities?

Extremes are not worth discussing. Perfect equality is not conceivable, let alone workable. On the other hand democracies won't tolerate a return to South African or pre-industrial inequalities. Practical questions are about degrees and directions of change – questions of more or less, not all or nothing.

There is nothing to be said in favor of greater-than-present inequalities. Very little *is* said in favor of them. Instead they are defended negatively – the winners say that the onus is on the losers to show 'why not?' What harm do increasing inequalities do? As long as the poor make progress why should they mind what progress the rich make? Isn't envy useless, and a sin? Or they argue democratically: majorities support the systems which deliver the inequalities, so majorities must be presumed to favor them. Or they argue technically: it would be dangerous to upset such a successful applecart, and nobody knows how to reverse the trend to inequality without disrupting the capitalist system to everybody's loss.

In fact democratic majorities scarcely ever vote for deliberate increases of inequality. They often vote for reductions – for tax-and-transfer equalizations and anti-poverty or head-start programs, many of which however don't work or are offset by other unequalizing processes. The history of these efforts, and the dwindling support for the few politicians who offer explicitly to increase inequalities, suggest that most democracies would already equalize more if they could find safe and effective ways of doing it.

The argument about envy is absurd. Goods have to be distributed somehow between richer and poorer people, and whoever doesn't get them is likely to envy whoever does. If you believe the poor need them more or will extract more well-being from them, poor men's covetousness is slightly more respectable than rich men's covetousness. But the rich view gets good publicity and has a marvellous self-righteousness: the rich are somehow the *natural* owners of their assets, so to change the rules to distribute the assets more equally would be non-economic – it would

169

be artificial, political, envious or at best charitable. Even as sensitive a moralist as John Rawls is driven to take the sin of envy seriously – in *A Theory of Justice* he takes the trouble to argue his way around it, instead of laughing in its face. Perhaps the objections to such nonsense need repeating from time to time.

What harm does the wealth of the rich do to the poor?

The simplest answer is the best: whatever the rich have, the poor could use. More for some leaves less for others. Not *much* less, the Right will always argue. 'If all after-tax income above £5,000 were distributed tomorrow' my English newspaper says 'it might increase the working man's wage by 30 pence a week.' Of all the Right's arguments, these are often the most complacently dishonest. That particular example even fiddles the arithmetic. It also ignores all spending of capital, all rich takings that don't appear on income tax returns and all public services and transfers to the rich, then distributes its notional transfer not to the poor but evenly to everyone, beginning with whoever admits to £4,999 after tax. The Right rarely interest themselves in the effect of taking (say) British income above £3,500 per family and distributing it from the bottom upwards to raise the income 'floor'. (Millions of the lowest incomes would double; millions more of the lowest wages would increase substantially.) In January 1974, when most British miners at the coalface got about £1,750 a year and asked for one or two hundred more, one estimate of all British income, after tax and reinvestment, averaged above £3,000 (i.e., above £4,000 before tax) to a statistically average family.[18] In the United States in 1970 'the income of the top fifth was 223 percent of average income, while the bottom fifth received only 28 percent of the national average...the top quintile had 41.6 percent of all family income, while the bottom quintile received 5.5 percent'.[19] So if you took five representative Americans and transferred a quarter of the richest income to the poorest, that would multiply the poorest income by three; the richest would still get 50% above the national average, and twice as much as the poorest. Meanwhile if private housing land in most affluent cities in the northern hemisphere were distributed so that the richest had only twice as much as the poorest, all the urban poor could have outdoor space, workshops, storage, gardens; if cars were distributed equally every household could have one; and so on. It is true that the taxable part of the incomes of the richest 1 or 5% would spread thin if distributed to everyone. Significant gains depend on shifts from the richest quarter to the poorest quarter (or thereabouts). Remarkable numbers of the Right conclude from this that even if substantial class transfers *were* made, the richest 1% need not really contribute at all because their contribution would make so little difference!

Apart from the money it brings, is there anything to be said for equality for its own sake? If a family has to live on $100 a week does it matter whether its richest fellow-citizens have $200 or $2,000 a week?

It can matter materially. Distributions of income affect what goods are produced and the prices of some of them. If the rich are still poor enough to prefer public transport, the poor can have cheaper and better transport than they can have if the rich can afford to desert public transport for private cars. If for any reason an economy can only produce (say) a million tons of private vehicles, the distribution of income may determine whether it is most profitable to make two-ton cars for half a million people, half-ton cars for two millions, motorbikes for five millions or push-bikes for forty millions. If half a million rich have plenty to spend, the poor may have to spend their money on something they want less than they want vehicles; their freedom of choice and their real wealth are reduced by the presence of the rich. *Even in crude material terms they would be better off on the same incomes in a poorer society*, i.e. if rich incomes were reduced and the social product reduced by the same amount. This might not be true of an imaginary world of free markets, adaptable capital and unlimited natural resources but it is true of land, transport and many other goods in the real world, and may soon be cruelly true of energy. Rich Arabs, Americans and Europeans may soon price poorer countries out of access to oil. Within any society, if there is only half as much house-warmth as people want and could afford at cost, then if incomes are unequal enough the richer half of the people can push the price to the point where they can take the lot (further enriching the very rich who supply it), leaving the poor to freeze and spend their money on things they want less than they want warmth. Some such pre-emption of limited resources is already true of warmth in some rich societies, food in some poor ones, and private housing and land in many of both. Scarce goods can of course be rationed – but that amounts to reducing real inequalities, and if it is right to do it at all why is it wrong to ration income or capital ownership?

Inequalities do plenty of other damage. They affect government, usually in the direction of reinforcing themselves. (Equalities likewise reinforce themselves.) Inequalities probably bias social and political research and persuasion – overpaid intellectuals become content with societies whose critics and innovators they ought to be; if more economists had been poor they might have tried harder to explain distribu-

171

tions. As argued earlier, steep inequalities often encourage corruption in government and business, and to the extent that they do so they limit society's collective political, administrative and economic options. Some of the competitive ambitions which propel cost-push inflation might operate at any level of equality but the anxieties and fears of falling behind which also propel it are more imperative if inequalities are great, and quite desperate if they are thought to be increasing.

For all the harm that steep inequalities do to material shares and efficiencies, it may be that the other harm they do is worse. Private capitalism is in many ways exploitive, divisive, degrading. It makes a good accommodation with the irreducible selfishness of man, turning some of it to productive use. But it makes too little social and productive use of the loving and cooperative propensities of man, and frustrates and discourages too many of those propensities. If competition is too tempting and punitive – if the differences between success and failure from top to bottom or from grade to grade are too great – competition can easily force more avarice, enmity and alienation and (often) less rather than more productive enterprise. Harsh penalties for failure often penalize co-operative, gentle, generous or forbearing behavior. But although it is fair to blame capitalism for encouraging various vices, they wouldn't necessarily disappear if capitalism did. Competition between capitalists is important, but nine tenths of the competition in capitalist societies is for wages and what they buy; it is an effect of inequality and would continue under any other system of inequality. A compulsory respect for wealth or success (because the alternatives are too painful) will usually leave less respect for love, individuality, cooperation – and sometimes also productivity. More equal incomes on the other hand allow more common experience, more of the community that depends on compatible life-styles; but paradoxically more freedom and diversity too. That relation is discussed later, but any society is likely to be freer in proportion as differences of life and style can be freely chosen as effects of faith, taste and individuality rather than as the automatic accompaniments of success or failure in conformist competitions. Harsh competition forces many conformities. Anxious competition for very unequal rewards – often more savage, corrupt or otherwise unproductive as the inequalities increase – may have zero-sum effects in money (what one loses another wins) but not in other things. Ruthless rich breed ruthless poor, rich crime breeds poor crime. Bitterness below and anxiety on the way up-or-down don't usually increase serenity at the top. Steep inequalities degrade many human relations, intensify most social conflicts and – at least above

172

Swedish levels – do nothing for growth, productivity, conservation or any other good thing.

6

If not many people argue openly to increase present inequalities, plenty on the Right argue against reducing them – against making South Africa more like the USA, the USA more like Sweden or Sweden more equal than it is already. Of the commoner objections to trying to improve equalities, two or three deserve a paragraph each.

More equality is said to reduce incentives to work.

This scarcely needs to be taken seriously. The most equal democratic societies are among the hardest working; the most unequal are not. This holds for most levels of income and types of work. Private management is probably as good in Sweden as in the USA and public management is probably better. In the United Kingdom there are grounds for believing that public management of big business is on average at least as good as private, though rewards in the public sector are a little more equal. Government, administration and police are always better in more equal democratic countries. The professions need be no worse and their services can be better distributed. English doctors who are paid more equally are as good as English lawyers who are paid less equally; English or Scandinavian doctors who are paid more equally are as good as American or Australian doctors who are paid less equally. More equal Sweden and the less equal United States have identical percentages of people living partly or wholly on welfare doles – the Swedes do it in a more settled fashion and probably give better chances to the children of the doled populations. Similarly unequal and equal societies (Australia and Norway, for example) have fuller employment and smaller welfare populations. In all four the productivity of labor seems to be about the same, i.e. productivity varies with resources, capital intensity and management rather than with national scales of inequality. There is no evidence at all that steeper inequalities make the poor work harder. Or the rich either – though tougher taxation sometimes drives them to work harder. Some each of rich Americans and rich Swedes work very hard. There have been cases (in England and Hungary for example) of secure rich growing lazy and pleasure-loving then working again when they were more effectively taxed.

Besides working hard, people in more equal societies tend to work more usefully. They produce fewer luxuries and more necessaries and usually have less incentive to con or prey on one another or to get rich by

173

transferring wealth rather than creating it. Swedes complain that people fiddle their taxes and welfare allowances; however bad that is it is not as bad as its 'private enterprise' equivalents in countries whose poor are prey to gambling and protection rackets, police graft and police-assisted drug traffic. Wherever the rich can make property or share-gambling gains or lend usuriously to consumers poorer than themselves or distort their productive activities to minimize taxation, a proportion of them will direct their energies to doing those things. They will hire some of society's scarce professional skills to help them. Society will hire more of the same skills to try to stop them. Poorer aspirants will hire yet more to try to imitate them. These are harmful activities in themselves and they divert skill and resources away from productive uses. Altogether there is overwhelming reason to believe that all capitalist countries could use flatter equalities to *improve* their economic incentives and efficiencies.

More equality is said to discourage productive investment.

This poses several questions. Will investors try to do their best? Will equalities drive capital away to other countries? Can equalities be enforced without cramping the productive kinds of business freedom and flexibility? The first question is easy. The personal motives of investors need not vary with the amounts they have to invest. The desire for profit animates small and large investors alike, and the performance of firms is not usually affected by differences between few big shareholders and many small ones; except that rich investors can usually cheat, avoid taxes, and export capital more freely than small investors can. Investors' circumstances may affect their preferences for risks, income, growth, short and long terms; but there seem to be all types among investors of all sizes. In any case owners' motives and skills are not very important. Most of the decisions which allocate resources and form and maintain capital are made not by owners but by salaried members of corporate boards and managements and governments. Those who make the decisions may expect personal advantages in reputation, appointment, promotion, share or salary income if their decisions are good, but there are no persistent differences between the track records of public and private boards or between directors who hold shares and directors who don't. There are also circumstances in which decision-makers can do their personal fortunes more good by bad investment decisions than by good ones. Directors can make more money for their friends and relations than for their shareholders; politicians can invest in electoral rather than economic returns. Both may be more tempted the bigger the available rewards.

It is no defence of very high rewards to show that some corporations

174

can afford to pay them or that some good decision-makers earn them. Rewards tend to be higher in private business and in less equal societies, lower in public business and in more equal societies; but there is no convincing evidence that the bigger differentials generate better performance. Americans have invested very ably in many fields, but others who pay their decision-makers less have often done better in other fields – for example in energy, shipping, railroads, mass housing and urban infrastructures and services. Within national histories some of the most productive capital formation (both public and private) has been done during periods of Left government or high personal taxation, notably in Israel and Scandinavia. Make your own judgment of the comparative success of investment in and by Renault and Leyland, Volvo and Rolls-Royce; then remember which is public and which private, which pays its decision-makers most and which pays them least. Likewise compare British and Norwegian policy and investment in their offshore oilfields. Opposite examples could just as easily be found. Whatever good investment may depend on it does not appear to depend in any regular way on private ownership, on steep inequalities between owners, on steeply unequal rewards for decision-makers, or on steep inequalities in the surrounding society.

Does equality drive capital and skill away? Some rich natives in equalizing societies may invest abroad if they can, some international investors may stay away. The first problem diminishes as private wealth is more equally held and more surely anchored and taxed. The second may be serious in some poor countries, but self-financing is a small and easy price for rich countries to pay for economic sovereignty. The richest are already almost entirely self-financed and most of them now worry about too much foreign ownership rather than too little. Countries which tax rich investors heavily may have problems in attracting some very specialized skills, and in differential treatment of native and foreign employees, shareholders and taxpayers. The Left sometimes underestimate the good that some multi-national enterprises can do in well-governed countries, just as the Right underestimate the harm that others do in ill-governed and very unequal countries; the enterprises themselves can operate adaptably to national conditions and from most of them governments get the performance they deserve.

Equality is said to make for monotony and mediocrity.

Partly it has to, partly it doesn't, and often it has the opposite effect. Some of the diversities which tourists like to see – in landscape and townscape, in the passing parade of faces in the street – can only be

175

generated by extreme inequalities. Poverty and disease diversify faces, poverty and wealth diversify neighborhoods, houses, cars and personal arrogance. In equal societies Breughel and Hogarth and Goya – and Lawrence and Gainsborough – might have lacked subjects. (They might have painted more like Leonardo or Rembrandt or Cézanne.) It is more important to remember that if equality monotonizes some things, inequality monotonizes others. Harsh competition forces many conformities and reduces many differences of taste and individuality. In any case the fact of monotony matters less than its character. Nobody minds monotonous standards of health, safety, efficiency – or wealth and good taste. 'The similarity of tastes and choices is all right if they are good tastes and choices. Even if not, the similarity is often and above all a sign of *freedom*: more and more people are at last getting what all of them have always freely, independently, identically wanted. Before we all got the same houses, the contrasts of mansion and slum did not signify individual differences of desire, nor a tenth of the free choices we have now...At the heart of the trouble is a tension inherent in identical human desires to be individually significant. You and I, similar creatures, want too many of the same things; one of the same things we want is to be different from each other. We seldom achieve it by innocent difference of taste. But there is one difference which is consistent with identical tastes: the difference of better and worse, more and less. The quest for individuality loses its innocence in competition and politics. I get more money and buy more difference for me. I get more power and force some difference on you.'[20]

It is true that equality standardizes some things. But it is not true (as often alleged) that art, architecture, entertainment, or social or scientific or industrial ingenuity are among them. In various free and unfree ways, Scandinavia and Israel and Poland and China are inventive enough. Equality doesn't standardize taste or patronage. Some rich are good patrons. Many more are terrible patrons, like the French who left all the best painters of the Third Republic to starve. Even the Medici were more often public than private patrons; so were most of those who maintained the eighteenth-century composers. Church and state have often been good patrons, perhaps because the rich spend other people's money more daringly than their own – as private patrons they more often stick to boardroom portraiture and the commercially guaranteeable work of living conformists and dead masters. Nowadays even the dead masters sell more originals to public than to private galleries, and they sell more copies, prints, records and performances in the more equal societies, which also generate more than their share of adventurous new work. Very few of the high arts rely much on rich private patrons. They live on mass and middle-class customers and on public subsidies. As rich societies grow more equal the audience for *avant-garde* work does not contract, it more often expands and diversifies – the 'advanced' markets expand when affluence and higher education are widely spread, not when they are restricted to a few. Meanwhile the flood of what elitists condemn as crass, conformist, commercialized, degraded and degrading art and entertainment comes most copiously from the most unequal of the rich democracies. The Danes have least censorship but it is the less equal Americans who sell the biggest quantities of the most degrading sex-and-violence pulp to their (richest, least equal, most degraded) proletariat. Australians are almost as unequal as Americans but it was not their rich who built the Sydney Opera House – a Labor government commissioned it, public lotteries paid for most of it and the parties of the Right confined themselves to sacking its inspired architect. (A Right government then tried to degrade its environment with car stacks; a communist-led labor union prevented it.) Except in necessaries like health, plumbing, housing and transport there is no reason to expect more equal societies to be more monotonous. As long as they are free as well as equal they are more likely to elevate and diversify tastes and to educate, recognize, encourage and patronize more individual excellence and originality per head than less equal societies do.

Finally there is the commonest objection to trying to reduce inequality: *it is impractical, it simply can't be done.*

Some pessimists believe that existing inequalities have defences as automatic as the laws of motion. Every action brings an equal and opposite reaction. At one extreme a dollar added to poor wages or pensions returns to the rich via rent or price adjustments. At the other, communist revolution may lop a few tall poppies but it leaves fewer people than ever in control of the means of production and where inequalities matter most – between manager and worker, or between factory worker and fruit-picker and charwoman – Russian inequalities are not much different from American. Dreadful expenditures of blood, freedom and efficiency have bought negligible gains in equality.

This objection can't be answered in a paragraph (or a book, for that matter). If an answer had to be headlined in a few sentences it might be this: it is not true that inequalities are the same everywhere. Many countries already make effective transfers from very rich to very poor. Inequalities of capital ownership vary widely from country to country and are technically easy to alter if ever there is political will to alter them.

Inequalities of income have changed through the industrial era. Wealth and income even have some independence of each other – American wealth is currently more equal than English, English incomes are more equal than American, and there are different relations between different distributions of each in Scandinavia. Other inequalities vary rather more. Racial minorities fare differently in Holland, New Zealand and the USA. Norway and Australia distribute domestic housing, land and privacy more equally than Sweden does though Sweden distributes income and some other wealth more equally than they do. Distributions of influence, esteem, safety and other immeasurables vary widely and so does the possibility of controlling them. Most 'inexorable' inequalities of the economic kind are maintained chiefly by choice – by the influence of the rich, by popular preference, or by popular illusions of impotence. As new problems and malfunctions force some radical reconstruction of present systems, any democratic majorities who wish to do so should be able to develop fairer and flatter equalities than any dictatorships do.

7

Just as liberties conflict with one another, so do equalities. For different reasons the friends and enemies of equality both tend to neglect this problem. It can be simply stated. There is only one way to make pure improvements to human equality: it is to flatten the whole world scale of inequalities by moving everyone nearer to the average. *Any* other redistribution though it reduce some inequalities must increase others. If you take a dollar from the richest man and give it not to the poorest but to the second poorest you increase inequality between those poorest two; and so on.

Real life is full of problems of that kind. Should working-class wages be raised to reduce inequalities between the workers and the rich but increase inequalities between the workers and the very poor? Should the poorer classes of the richer countries be net givers or net takers? Everyone's compassion has limits beyond which good intentions don't extend, or can't be made effective. By conscious or unconscious mental mechanisms nearly everyone segregates these questions from one another and applies different and often very inconsistent principles of justice or compassion to different compartments of his life and relationships.

Besides such moral questions there is a practical one. When groups are more equal within themselves, will they tend to be more generous towards others, or less so? Does any general relation hold between people's behavior in relation to near and far, 'home' and 'foreign' equalities? If miners are paid more equally with one another, will that increase or reduce their hostility to the rich, or their fraternity with pensioners poorer than they are? Will equally paid professions be more generous or less generous towards other trades? Will equal societies tend to give more international aid than unequal societies give?

Some internally equal groups deal very harshly with outsiders. On the grandest scale the whole rich white world stands in that relation to the rest – however imperfect, its internal equalities are better than those which hold between rich and poor countries, or within most poor ones. On the smallest scale, internally affectionate families or tribes sometimes contend ruthlessly against each other. Internally solid-and-equal labor unions have sometimes followed exclusive, racist or otherwise uncharitable policies toward groups poorer than themselves. There is a familiar social mechanism which often enough links external conflict to internal solidarity.

Nevertheless there are some signs that 'far' and 'near' equalities do increasingly go together. It is in the most equal societies that organized labor most often bargains as one, the stronger helping the weaker and both showing some forbearance towards the unorganized poor. In less equal societies strong unions more often bargain alone, for steeper margins within their own pay scales and with less concern about where the money comes from; and more of their leaders are personally corrupt, and rich. There are similar contrasts between richer groups whose wealth also depends on collective bargaining. Doctors and other professional groups bargain with least conscience in the most unequal countries; Norwegian ship-owners submit to more social redistribution of their wealth than Greek or American ship-owners do. More equal societies tend to have either bigger or more genuinely disinterested and sacrificial programs of international aid. It may not matter which causes which; the 'near' and 'far' equalities go together.

Because poverty can force people to be selfish it used to be feared that mass democracies in which the comparatively poor had a share of political power might be collectively more selfish in their dealings with subject peoples or poorer countries, while the rich ruling classes of less equal societies might be more 'generous' in giving away some of their poor subjects' resources and living standards. But experience has provided few historical contrasts of that kind and more of the other kind. There are likely to be more yet. Wait a year or two until more North Sea oil is flowing. Then compare the internal inequalities of the USA, the

179

United Kingdom and Norway; compare the internal uses which they make of their oil revenues; compare the proportions of those revenues that they give away to poorer countries. It is predictable that the Norwegians will be the most equal among themselves. They will use least of their revenue at home but apply what they do use there most equally. They will spend most on conservation and environmental protection and on long-term investment and foreign-exchange policies which deserve to be called intergenerational aid. And they will give most away, and will give it to the most internally-equal recipient countries where it is likely to be used to do most good for most poor people. The Norwegian policies will probably be administered by parties of the Left and supported by organized labor; but they won't change much if the Norwegian Right (which is usually some way to the Left of the British Left) takes over government.

Some people think that any concern for equality within rich countries is hypocritical while they continue so much richer than the world's real poor. But to do much about that maldistribution requires three revolutions: one in the rich world, one in the poor world, and one in the relations between them. The third depends on the first two. European and American majorities won't send much aid abroad while they have prior claims against their own rich, and anxious competition for very unequal shares within their own societies. In most of the territory to which aid goes, powerful minorities use a good deal of it to entrench themselves, building enclaves of heavy industry and metropolitan service for their own class and doing very little to improve slum life or peasant productivity. Between nations as between generations, aid won't do much of what it is supposed to do while it is managed at both ends by rich minorities.

Aid is anyway a minor matter. Rich countries face harder and perhaps more hopeless questions about their relations with poor countries. Distributing financial and material capital doesn't by itself distribute productivity; with the most ideal aid programs, it would still be fanciful to expect any very quick development of the mass skill and culture which would be needed to wring efficient production and equal distribution from 'equal ownership'.

Material and cultural thresholds have great practical importance. Equalities which might work above them can't work below them. A lot of the necessary work of science, business and government couldn't be done in practice by people with (say) India's average rations of education and sustenance. People can't be expected to share fairly if that may cost their children health or life. (Cultures of poverty are sometimes full of

180

generosity; but people escape them if they can, and their elites always do.) So there is little enough that rich countries can do, in the short run, for poor countries. They can stop defending Right (or multi-national) regimes from internal revolution. Some policies of aid or trade can improve the circumstances in which poor countries try to mend their own fortunes. And rich countries can improve their own equalities. That may at least *allow* some future generosities even if it doesn't guarantee any. It seems likely to be a condition of their ever willingly limiting their gross shares of world resources, and their citizens' personal ideas of the amount of material wealth worth having.

That is a main point of some earlier references to thresholds. In affluent societies there is a level of material wealth and skilled mutual service at which – if they are in other ways capable of it – humans can realize most of their capacities for love and good life. They can live comfortably and securely to old age, with no material hindrances to whatever fun and companionship they're capable of. They can spend more waking hours at leisure than at work. They can enjoy (or if able, create) art from the lowest to the highest. The critical material level which allows all that is (within modern societies) quite modest. A hundred years ago most of their people lived below it. Now most live above it – in material terms most of their people live more comfortably and securely than Phidias or Plato, Shakespeare or Beethoven or most of their audiences did. So there is deep good sense in the preaching that now says 'enough is enough'. People should be content with sufficient comforts (as a great many are already content with a sufficient house) and turn their energies to generating more and better love, companionship, art, fun, skill – and equality. But the equality is a first condition of the contentment, and of any general environmental self-restraint. So it is likely to be a first condition of any willing sharing of surplus resources, on a significant scale, across national boundaries, for the benefit of the billions still fighting nature and each other to scramble nearer to a tolerable minimum of material security. Rich whites should equalize their societies for their own sakes, but also as a first step towards improving their relations with the world's poor.

All societies are likely to be selfish in adversity; and most improvements of equality are likely to be achieved within rather than between sovereign areas. But those who once predicted that the most equal societies would be the meanest seem to have been wrong. The most equal democracies at present run the most equalizing aid programs. The least equal democracy does its best – by war, economic sanctions, corruption, assassination and civil disorder – to kill any equalizing governments that appear in poor coun-

181

tries. The values of equality are habit-forming and where their costs are not too high they tend to flow over from one policy to another, and from friends to strangers.

8

Even if they are not necessary, conflicts between equality and freedom are certainly possible. Equalities can always be ill-designed, or enforced by oppressive methods. When they are, they may reduce productivity as well as freedom. Some communist countries have flattened their margins for skill or hard work too far, with apparently bad effect on economic efficiency. It is hard to know how much of that effect is caused by the equalities and how much by other sins of government. Czechs who resent flat pay scales also resent bad bureaucracy, fluctuating terror, and some inequalities which their ruling minorities continue to enjoy; they might respond differently if there were more incentive margins within trades and less between them – and free speech and effective democracy.

Most matter-of-fact evidence of conflict between equality and freedom, or between equality and productivity, comes from comparatively poor countries. Free India had not much of either equality or productivity; the dictators of Taiwan have done more to improve both the productivity and the income shares of their poorest 40%. When the Yugoslavs were allowed to be a little freer in the 1960s their inequalities increased a little. But Scandinavian/Australasian/American comparisons do not suggest that the same relations hold in richer countries. Even if they did, it should be possible to change them. Many non-class equalities – between young and old, healthy and sick, people with and without children – are easy to improve without much increase of bureaucracy. Freedoms may be infringed by the bureaucratic control of incomes, but all rich countries are now driven by their inflationary troubles to attempt such controls. Fixing incomes more equally need be no more oppressive than fixing them less equally, and seems likely to be more successful.

Finally there are equalities in the distribution of housing, urban land and other domestic resources. These are comparatively easy to contrive; they have no necessary costs in freedom and they offer large gains in productivity; and they tend to be undervalued in theory and neglected in practice by the Left almost everywhere. They are the subject of the next chapter, which tries to offer one example of the rethinking which the intellectual services of the Left should be applying to many more of the fields in which problems of liberty and equality overlap.

182

8
Ownership and alienation

The purpose of this chapter is to develop some social and economic implications of Michael Young and Peter Willmott, *The Symmetrical Family* (London, 1973).[21]

Most people and many of their politicians understand the relations between ownership and alienation. But some social scientists don't, and (with varying success in different countries) minorities of experts and intellectuals work with theories which encourage technical misunderstanding and discourage good government in this field.

In affluent societies (as in most others) much more than half of all waking time is spent at home or near it. More than a third of capital is invested there. More than a third of work is done there. Depending on what you choose to count as goods, some high proportion of all goods are produced there, and even more are enjoyed there. More than three quarters of all subsistence, social life, leisure and recreation happen there. Above all, people are produced there, and endowed there with the values and capacities which will determine most of the quality of their social life and government away from home. So the resources of home and neighborhood have commanding importance. Home may be the scene of some general exploitation of women by men and children, but those relations tend to improve as the resources improve, and most other uses of domestic capital are capable of being wholesome. It is in the activities of home, neighborhood and voluntary association that there is least money exchange, least division of labor, least bureaucracy, least distinction between production and consumption, least occasion for oppressive or exploitive or competitive uses of ownership, and most of the best opportunities for cooperative, generous, self-expressive, *unalienated* work and life. Anyone interested in building a more cooperative, affectionate or equal society should therefore look first, and centrally, to the resources of home and neighborhood.

But that whole domestic economy – a third or more of every developed economic system and two thirds or more of every social system – tends to be systematically undervalued and consequently starved of resources by the orthodox economic thinking of both Left and Right.

What should Left theorists think instead? Instead of finding domestic ownership guilty by association with commercial ownership they should recognize it as potentially the benign opposite of commercial ownership. They should stop thinking of private corporate ownership and state ownership as the basic alternatives for productive capital. For most purposes those two should be lumped together as institutional ownership. Whoever the shareholders are – whether public or private or cooperative, capitalist or socialist, equal or unequal – institutional organization must necessarily divide and specialize and alienate a lot of the labor it uses. We nevertheless need a good deal of it for productive purposes. It can be half-civilized in various ways; and it need not occupy more than a third of anybody's week, or between a sixth and an eighth of conscious life if you count everybody's waking hours from birth to death.

Institutional ownership characterizes most of both of what are commonly called the public and private sectors of the money-exchange economy. Together with private small-business ownership it uses perhaps three fifths of a developed economy's capital and about the same proportion of its labor. The domestic economy, using chiefly home capital and free labor, accounts for the other two fifths. *Those two should be perceived as the basic divisions of the economic system.* Allocating resources between the two, and between households within the domestic economy, should be the subject of the most careful economic policy-making that any government does.

This chapter argues that it should be socialist policy to shift more resources into the domestic sector, and as far as possible to equalize household capital. The likely effects of that are widely desired by the masses, and widely misunderstood by their economists and ideologues. It need not lead to the 'private affluence and public squalor' condemned by J. K. Galbraith, if resources in both sectors are distributed with productive intent, environmental care and proper equality. A more generous and equal provision of domestic resources is what can now do most not only for the private life of affluent societies, but for their public and social life as well. It can probably assist their real economic growth, in environmentally tolerable directions. It can do most to reduce alienation and replace it by more self-expressive and cooperative activity and by more of the living unities which the critics of alienation dream of. And it offers the most effective single strategy of equality for capitalist *or* socialist societies; whereas without it, more equal distributions of money

184

and services (which are anyway harder to achieve) will be much less valuable in their effects.

2

The subject can be approached by understanding the history of changing relations between commercial and domestic resources, or more directly by observing how people in developed societies use space and time. Michael Young and Peter Willmott do both in *The Symmetrical Family*. That book has been received as a quiet exercise in sociology. Together with the various lines of social inquiry which it draws together it ought to be understood as the basis for a general reconstruction of about half of all socialist theory and practice. One of its historical themes can be crudely simplified as follows:

Before the coal-and-steam revolution, most of the people who were able to live in settled households at all lived close to land and home. They farmed, or worked at other trades as close to home as farmers do. Most members of most households helped to produce any goods that were produced for market, as well as goods for their own subsistence. So however poor or exploited they were, families were often cooperative producers with some control of their tasks, their timetables, and some at least of the goods they produced.

The first industrial revolution broke up that co-op. Work moved out of the family into the factory. Labor still had to live in walking distance of it, so millions moved into the crowded slum housing of the early industrial cities, where they found neither space nor spare time to do much more than eat and sleep. Members of the family went off singly to long hours of low-paid wage labor. At home they had to live on what their wages would buy. They were slaves of the commercial economy right around the clock. Scarcely any work was done except for money; almost everything produced was sold for money; so to a modern economic science which counts *only* work and output which exchange for money, that era's statistics of economic growth still look wonderful. Even housework was commercialized – the practice wasn't new but the scale soon was. With the primitive equipment of those times it took long hours of labor to keep home up to any genteel standard; so to look after the rapidly rising numbers in affluent upper and middle classes, domestic service became the biggest single occupation in the commercial economy. But there wasn't much house-keeping in the warrens the laboring classes lived in. Child-rearing was short. Children went to work young, and

185

learned most of the little they needed to learn on the job. Many of their mothers as well as their fathers worked long hours for wages. Off work, without time or space or opportunity to do anything constructive, personal skills and versatilities didn't develop. Housing was merely shelter. The family wasn't together much, and didn't do or produce much. It was at its most degraded and unimportant as an institution.

Then came the second industrial revolution: mass-produced household goods, network water and gas and electricity, ubiquitous transport; and another great shift of productive resources. The first industrial revolution had moved production out of the family into the factory; the second industrial revolution moved a lot of it back again. By 1970 the British housewife was using the horsepower the British factory worker had used in 1910. Households could *make* and *do* things: a steadily increasing number and variety of things. With equipment and materials supplied by the commercial economy, they were soon producing a good deal of the twentieth-century standard of living for themselves.

Productivity in one sector bred productivity in the other. As the factory economy grew more efficient it used less labor for shorter hours, so it did the double service of giving people more domestic capital, and more free time to use it. We think of washing machines and vacuum cleaners and do-it-yourself tools and materials. But the thing people wanted most, for itself and as a condition of most other blessings, was space: bigger and better houses with more rooms for more diverse activities, with working and storage and garden space around them, and with space for schools and parks and community services in local neighborhoods. Affluent minorities may value modern transport as a means of personal mobility and busier, wider-ranging communications. But to most people the richest gift of powered transport has been private space: the enlargement of home. Since the first railway London's population has multiplied fivefold, and also increased its private space per head several times over, so that the metropolis has sprawled over twenty or thirty times its old area. But the average time it takes a Londoner to get to work or city has scarcely varied through all those years. People have converted each improvement of transport into an increase of private space.

All this suggests that the flow of consumer goods has been overrated as the characteristic product of industrialization. The most profound achievement of modern industry – of the forty-hour week of organized, alienated labor – has been to give people at home energy, equipment, materials and communications, and time and space and freedom, to

186

produce for themselves: to make and do what they want, when and where and how they want, working together or apart as they feel inclined, and enriching their time and social experience in all sorts of ways freely chosen by themselves.

In celebrating most of this historic liberation, and the wholeness and self-determination of life that it allows, Young and Willmott are scarcely regarded by other socialists as being socialist at all. As head of the British Labour Party's research department a quarter of a century ago, Young once tried to persuade the leaders of the party that socialism could and should begin at home. They were (he reported long afterwards) merely baffled and embarrassed by the idea.

3

Most of the new freedom and productivity depend on (among other things) distributions of private space. Distributions of space don't follow at all automatically from distributions of income, and their effects are scarcely noticed in most contemporary economic and urban theory. Five kinds of effect are specially important: effects on life at home, on public and social life away from home, on environmental policies and possibilities, on economic growth, and on equality.

The effects on life at home are dramatic enough to generate universal desires for better rather than worse home space and resources. More people than ever now choose to live in family households, and they want private housing on private ground if they can get it.[22] The middle classes get it everywhere. Whether the urban working classes get it depends very little on their market preferences or capacities to pay, and almost entirely on public policy. In most English-speaking countries and in Norway a good many of them do. Through the rest of continental Europe most of them don't.

Whether or not people are getting it, their desire for the small house and garden is fully intelligent. For most people under 18 or over 30, private housing on the ground is incomparably more resourceful and adaptable than landless apartments can ever be. If land prices are under control, small houses are usually as cheap as other housing forms to build and service. As time goes by they can be replaced, altered, enlarged or modernized according to individual need, without the wasteful private and social costs which usually go with the mass demolition and replace-ment of apartment housing. They can be shaped and grouped to meet diverse tastes, as freestanding houses, pairs, rows, clusters. Compared with most modern 'landscaped apartment suburbs' they can often house people almost as densely on the land and almost as conveniently to services. They can generally allow more freedom from 'house rules' and other constraints by landlords or neighbors, and their occupiers are freer than most apartment-dwellers to control and vary their privacy or publicity in relation to neighbors and visitors and strangers; and to allow individuals similar options of privacy and community within households. Many small housing forms can be built in stages and most can be altered – often cheaply, by do-it-yourself methods – to adapt to changing tastes, means, family numbers and interests (or injuries and handicaps) through households' life-cycles. Their indoor, outdoor and out-house spaces can be adapted to allow a marvellous variety of sociable or solitary activities, productive or enjoyable and often both, including a very large number that are not possible either indoors or in public places and are therefore denied altogether to apartment-dwellers. All sorts of payable part-time and full-time trades flourish in back yards, especially where the working classes are allowed to have back yards. (Those are often the *only* opportunities for under-aged, over-aged and part-time tradesmen.) People of every age and class can grow flowers and fruit and vegetables and green shade; they can keep birds and animals; they can work with wood and clay and metal and chemistry sets; they can make more noise and more mistakes; they can dismember cars and cycles and other machinery, and make toys and build kennels and hutches and boats and dolls' houses and walk-in cubby-houses – all with more freedom than any communal workshop or public park can ever allow. And a wide range of social possibilities goes with those private freedoms.

Those resources are used. Most of the hostile stereotypes of house-and-garden life are unresearched. There are some unhappy and some inactive people in every kind of housing; but 'suburban apathy and isolation' predominate only in limited and atypical circumstances. (Those attract most of the researchers.) Whenever they are fairly sampled, most urban and suburban people don't think of good housing either as convenient shelter, or as something chiefly to display in a competitive or conformist way. They think of it as ample, versatile, *useable* private space, indoor and outdoor: their own bit of the world where they can live as privately or sociably as they like, and do as many and varied and interesting things as possible. They perceive their houses and gardens as resource centres, use them accordingly and very often use them well. And although the material things which people make and do and enjoy in their private time and space are a large fraction of all economic activity, they

188

are often less important than some other effects: the human relations which develop in resourceful households; the scope which their intricate, alterable, home-designed indoor and outdoor spaces offer for art, self-expression, fantasy and imagination; and the skills, capacities and values that people develop in the course of using them.

Those skills and capacities and values also have powerful effects on life away from home. That is one of many reciprocal relations between private, commercial and public resources. An understanding of those relations ought to be at the heart of almost any general social or economic theory; but in most contemporary theory they are neglected or falsified.

Two mistakes are very common. One simplifies (and perhaps misrepresents) the argument of J. K. Galbraith's *The Affluent Society* (New York, 1958) to assert that capitalist societies oversupply people with private property and undersupply their public services. Some public services are indeed undersupplied, in the USA and elsewhere, but doubling their budgets doesn't usually get them used by the people who need them most. The main cause of that, and of the other effects Galbraith complained of, is not an excess of private resources but their unequal and unproductive distribution. An absurd extravagance of private space and superfluous equipment for some people contrasts with the crowded and unproductive squalor of big-city slums and out-of-town shanty towns, and the caravans and prefabricated 'mobiles' in which a sixth of all Americans have to live. The same maldistribution of private resources helps to account for the maldistribution of public services which was first noticed by Richard Titmuss: resourceful middle-class households are able to seek out and use more services than ever find their way to the landless, barely-equipped shelters of the poor.

The second mistake, common in older orthodoxies of Left and Right alike, is to see private and public resources as alternatives. 'You don't need private gardens if you have public parks' (or laundries, or kitchens, or crèches, or workshops, or libraries). That is about as sensible as seeing husband and wife, or bolt and nut, as alternatives. The real need is to understand the reciprocal, mutually necessary relations of domestic, commercial and public resources, and to allocate resources in the way that allows each to do most to nourish the use and productivity *of the others*. The fertility of each does not depend chiefly on its getting more than its share of the available capital; it depends at least as much on its exchange of services with the other two. Homesteads – however affluent

7-2

– are underused if they are starved of public and commercial services. Commercial capital is unproductive unless a developed domestic culture supplies it with highly developed human capacities. Many public services are underused, and some are quite unuseable, if they are offered to people who do not have appropriate domestic resources.

The interdependences between home, neighborhood, public and commercial resources run all the way from the rooms inside a house to the most central services of cities and nations. Inside the house, diversity of activity depends on stimulus from outside, *and* on space and storage at home. People cooperate more, and usually like each other better, if they can escape each other sometimes. Gardens help them to do that; so do separate indoor and outdoor spaces which allow different activities to go on at the same time. People with resourceful rooms of their own are often the best contributors to common family life. In the garden, children with plots of their own take more interest in the garden as a whole. People who work urban land of their own take more knowledgeable interest in public gardens and parks, and they go (more often than people without land of their own) to enjoy any accessible wilderness. Community workshops and trades and crafts get used where people have space to practise the crafts at home; people practise the crafts at home where there are community workshops to attract them to meet, learn, use common equipment, and compare work. Similar relations hold between neighborhood and central city services. There tend to be good local libraries where there are good central library services. Local craft centres do best where there are central craft markets and training schools. There is most amateur and local theatre where good professional theatre and training are within reach. Reciprocally, the first-class central and professional activities do best where there is plenty of home and local activity to generate interest and custom and recruits for them.

Home is where most people now hear most music, read most books, watch most drama, read and see and hear most of the world's news and most analysis and commentary on it. If the 'alternative' theory of resource allocation were true, public and community life should have dwindled correspondingly. But the theory is not true, and the 'isolation of home' is not happening. Since young people got tapes and transistors they play more instruments of their own and go out to more live pop gatherings. The people with most gramophone records at home tend to go to most live concerts. The people who have most books at home make most use of libraries and educational services. The people with room to play most games at home also play most away from home. These relations are general. It is where home space and resources are *poorest* that poor people spend most time at home, but do least there, and watch most of the poorest television. There is no truth in the theory that it is possible to fill the streets with sociable life by stacking the people into tower flats. The ground around tower flats is usually the most arid, unsociable and unused of all urban space. There is no way to nourish public social life by starving and overcrowding private life. On the contrary, the better the resources and opportunities are at home the more versatile the inhabitants are likely to become, and the more active and sociable and interesting to one another they will be away from home. Reciprocally, diverse experience away from home stimulates more interesting and creative activities at home, as long as there is space for them there.

So even if the enrichment of leisure were the only purpose, there would be two good reasons for distributing private space generously and equally. In all the places sampled in the international time studies reported in *The Use of Time*, people spent at least three quarters of their purely social time with kin rather than with other acquaintances or strangers. That by itself would justify a generous and equal distribution of private space and resources. But the same policy will usually also do most to nourish the use of commercial, communal and public social places and resources. As long as the away-from-home resources exist and are reasonably accessible, they in turn will stimulate the fullest use of the domestic resources. Life may still be arid in new outer suburbs and new towns before their public services arrive and their community networks and activities develop. Studies of those pathological situations account for some of the professional dislike of house-and-garden forms and low residential densities. But the cure is to develop the support and stimulus that will get the private resources used; it is not to turn the clock back a hundred years by taking the private resources away.

There are similar relations between domestic resources and environmental values. Environmentalists should stop thinking of cities and suburbs as enemies of the countryside, or as worse land uses than farming. It wouldn't enhance human happiness or improve anyone's diet if the people of Paris were housed in one cubic kilometre (as they could be) while the rest of the town was ploughed under to grow maize instead of people. People are the richest of all crops, yielding much the highest value per hectare; but as with other products the quality may decline if the land is sown or grazed too densely. Instead of complaining about suburban sprawl, its critics should get it better planned, better centred, better served. Instead of wanting less room for private gardening in town they should try for more. Generous private houses and gardens *can* degrade the environment if people fill the houses with machinery and drench the gardens with chemicals. But the same relaxed housing forms also allow the best scope for *good* environmental behavior. It is in private houses with storage space and some land around them that it is easiest to use more human energy in satisfying ways, and to manage with less powered commercial services. It is also easier to adapt to many kinds of environmental and industrial breakdown. People in landless apartments suffer most when the rubbish truck doesn't come, pipes burst, the lift and clothes-dryer stop; and at other times, especially if they are affluent, they tend to make the most insistent demands for powered commercial services including passive entertainments. And they are likely to bring up children like themselves.

That points to the most important relation between home resources and environmental values. Environmental policies will always be determined chiefly by people's values; and urban houses and gardens are the nursery of most of the best environmental values. People who live in town but grow some foliage of their own, and keep a cat to deter mice, are the mainstay of all the movements which work to protect larger landscapes and ecosystems. Private residential land is both an environmental good which ought to be fairly shared, and a vital educator: a classroom for work-skills, play-skills, nature study and environmental values which an environmentally careful society would be mad to deny to any of its people.

Though they are rarely noticed in orthodox accounting, there are obvious relations between domestic resources and economic growth. Through the first industrial revolution the organized use of paid labor contributed most to the growth of productivity. Now that the factory and transport revolutions have transformed about as much of daily life as they can, commercial growth is slower because more and more of it has to be in labor-intensive services. With full employment and a limited working week those services cannot grow much more except by attracting people back from domestic activity to work for wages. But a great deal of commercial output has meanwhile gone to build and equip houses and connect them to services and communications. That equips people to do more for themselves. With the domestic economy as well capitalized as many commercial services are, it can often contribute more than they can to growth, especially because it can draw on reserves of underused labor. Plenty of that is not hard labor but quite welcome activity, with the double value that the work and its output are both enjoyable and both deserve to count as goods. But the domestic growth is necessarily slow. It depends on the development of skills and interests and incentives, and on the distributions of space that arise from the slow growth and reconstruction of cities. Plenty of European and some American city-building is still designed to give ample private land to middle-class households but none – and also less indoor space – to poorer households. That restricts national productivity, distributes its output more unequally than conventional accounts will ever show, and confines the poor to forty hours of alienated work for others (often by one member only of the household) and very little for themselves.

That is only one of the relations between housing and equality which tend to be ignored by experts of almost every persuasion. Left experts dislike the private ownership of productive property. Right experts treat housing as a consumer good and expect people to buy as much as they want of it out of income. Both are obsessed by money flows, and by the money-exchange transactions which are the only things their one-eyed accounting systems are designed to record. Both – if they think about it at all – suppose that distributions of income determine distributions of private space just as they determine distributions of other goods.

In practice, present capacities to pay have comparatively little effect on distributions of private space. Most subdivisions, houses and apartments are indivisible and last for several generations. *Past* capacities to pay, *past* politics and *past* uses of landowners' class advantages have constructed most of the present housing stock; rich and poor now occupy respectively the best and the worst of it, and have to accept whatever equalities or inequalities are built into it. Grossly unequal capacities to pay could not now house the New Zealanders very unequally, because they inherit a stock of very equal houses. Perfectly equal capacities to pay could not now house the Swedes equally, because a third of their stock of urban housing has private land and two thirds doesn't.

If private urban space were subdivided and distributed freely in open markets it would usually be distributed (in cities of any size) with extreme inequality. That would happen because land ownership is somewhat monopolist; because suppliers have many bargaining advantages over buyers and tenants; and because for various reasons the mass of would-be house-buyers have very little chance of borrowing the price of a house if they must bid for money in open capital markets. So all affluent societies rig and regulate the business to some degree – though not always in the interest of equality. Government everywhere fixes or influences the type, size, land allowance, safety, sanitation and general quality of the new housing that may be built; supplies some public housing; taxes owners and tenants differently; and controls or influences mortgage-lending in various ways. It thus determines much of the basic distribution of new capital between the domestic and commercial economies, and by its influence on the distribution of private urban space it does a good deal to determine domestic productivity. Over most of the affluent world government does this in substantial ignorance of many of the effects of its policies. In most European cities a few dollars' difference of household income allows one household to rent an apartment, another to buy one, and a third to buy a capacious house and garden. Differences of domestic productivity then act as a powerful multiplier to increase the original inequalities of real income. Meanwhile in many English-speaking cities different policies give the poorer household as much space as the richer; the same multiplier then works to reduce their real inequalities – but painlessly, at little or no cost to the richer.

Domestic investment probably has an up-and-down curve of marginal return. Varying with local values and circumstances, people generally identify a level of housing which allows them to do most of the things they are likely to want to do. Beyond that level they don't typically use additional income to move house or buy more space, they spend it on other things. If a house can give each of its inhabitants a room big enough for some work and hobbies and storage as well as a bed; if a house for more than two or three people has common spaces to allow more than one common activity to go on at once; if it has some each of covered and open outdoor space for work, storage and gardening; and if it is insulated and equipped to heat water, cook food, wash clothes and keep people at tolerable temperatures – then it can accommodate most of what most people of ordinary means are likely to demand of it. Bringing it up to that standard is likely to be productive investment. Expenditure beyond that is likely to be more like expenditure on consumer goods – it buys margins of comfort or luxury or display which may increase the pleasure with which people use the house, but won't usually extend the *range* of activities they can use it *for*. A principle of very rough justice might define investment up to the sufficient level as mostly productive, and above that level as mostly for consumption, or anyway of less marginal value. There is some alternative support for that principle in one of Young's and Willmott's arguments. They think that many high-income households try, both at home and away from home, to do too much for their own good. Individuals suffer strain, uses of time and space conflict, cooperation deteriorates. So even if extravagant housing does extend the range of household activity, the marginal output may not be worth its personal and social costs.

In summary: private indoor and outdoor space is not quite like any of the three conventional categories of goods we are accustomed to distributing and accounting for. It is not like commercial capital whose output can be measured by its money returns – though it usually has to bid against commercial uses for its resources. It is not public goods like roads – though in equipping people with productive capacities it is a little like education. It is not ordinary consumption goods – though it is an enjoyable possession whose owners should contribute to paying for it. It is best understood as productive capital whose output can never be fully accountable because it ranges from measurable economic goods to quite unmeasurable social and personal goods and qualities of life. The distribution of existing stock will generally be ordered by inequalities of wealth and income; but the equality or inequality of the stock itself is everywhere determined (directly or indirectly) chiefly by government. That stock is a large and fertile part of any developed society's capital, but its fertility depends almost entirely on its degree of built-in equality. It can be most productive only if it is distributed in sufficient shares to all households. We are quite accustomed to insisting on commercial full employment: a job and a basic wage for everyone willing to work. Since almost as much investment and output are at stake, we should learn to insist in the same way on domestic full employment: on sufficient private space and opportunity for every household willing to use them.

When houses and gardens and local neighborhoods are perceived in this way as 'resource centres', and their inhabitants as producers, it becomes obvious that land and housing policies can be potent equalizers or unequalizers. That is true of relations within households, between households, between classes and between nations. Within families, traditional housing reformers have probably been right to see housing as an asset more likely than most to be shared well. Unlike money income it can't easily be monopolized, lost, gambled, mis-spent, over-committed to the hire-purchase of over-sized cars, or taken away altogether by absconding husbands. Like the housing stock as a whole it can have physical equalities built into it, for example in the form of labor-saving equipment for housewives or generous space and storage and privacy for children. Between households and classes with unequal money incomes, a stock of physically equal housing can be a specially practical equalizer. Unlike most other distributions of wealth or income, distributions of space can be arranged so that the rich don't have to lose nearly as much as the poor have to gain. Good housing and land policies don't merely transfer income or services from one consumer to another. They give otherwise-poorer people useable capital: the means of producing for themselves goods and satisfactions which would otherwise never be produced at all to be enjoyed by rich *or* poor.

Once again, there are reciprocities. Over time, unequal capacities to pay do exaggerate inequalities in the housing stock if government allows them to do so. In turn, the terms on which private space is occupied will usually increase inequalities of wealth and income if government allows them to do so – it usually happens that private tenants pay most for the use of private space, public tenants pay less, and (over time) owners pay least and gain most: effects which are compounded by most countries' tax systems. So every consideration of national productivity and personal and class equality converges to support the conclusion that private space should be distributed very generously and very equally, and should wherever possible be owned by its occupiers.

Some orthodox economic objections to that conclusion follow.

4

Summary of this section for economists. Capital markets are efficient when commercial production (in proportion to its efficiency) earns the means of bidding for the capital it needs. Domestic production cannot do that – it is the commercial wage-income of the domestic entrepreneur, *not* the productivity of the domestic use, which has to bid for domestic capital. So there is no reason whatever why an open capital market should arrive at optimal (i.e. most productive) allocations either between the two systems, or within the domestic one.

Think of developed societies as having two economic systems, a commercial one and a domestic one. The commercial economy, using institutional capital and the forty-hour week of paid labor, is best at producing some of the things people want. The domestic economy, using free labor, home capital and some public capital, is best at producing others. Some goods can be produced equally well by either. Each system depends on exchanging goods and services with the other. People should therefore decide collectively (because the market cannot rationally decide it for them) how much of each kind of work they want to do, and what

196

balance of the two kinds of goods they want to have. They will then need some economic theory to tell them what allocation of resources to the two economies will produce the desired balances of work and goods.

No orthodox economic theory of Left or Right does that. Economists did once debate the merits of 'use' theories and 'exchange' theories of value. For various purposes of scientific ambition, spurious objectivity and capitalist profit, exchange value won. With trifling exceptions orthodox economists now ascribe value (in working practice if not in theory) only to things which change hands for money. This does not mean that they ignore the domestic economy; it means that they keep massively false and misleading accounts of it. Most of the inputs to produce domestic capital are paid for, so they count as costs. Scarcely any of the work and output of the domestic economy changes hands for money, so most of it is officially valued at nil. Thus a third or more of all capital is made to appear unproductive, by the elementary method of pretending that a third or more of all work and output are worthless. Housing (the most expensive and productive item of domestic capital) is represented by some as the least productive of all uses of capital, and therefore an active enemy of economic growth; or else it is represented as an extravagant consumable item whose distribution has no productive implications at all.[23]

These distortions have been built into the structure of much orthodox economic theory, capitalist or socialist. Those who reject them must often do it by rebelling against their education. Governments which adopt productive housing policies too often have to adopt them as welfare policies, on their social merits only, believing they have serious costs in economic or urban efficiency. The following are some of the ways in which bad economic theory can obstruct good housing policy:

Houses take so long to pay for out of household incomes that the price to most buyers is affected more by interest rates than by building costs. Orthodox theory says that the way to decide the most productive use of any dollar of capital is to see who bids most for the use of it; so people who want houses ought to outbid commercial competitors for their resources. The cost of a house combines with the distribution of income in capitalist countries to prevent a majority of households from doing that. One orthodox solution is to make those households tenants, so that a larger proportion of what they can afford to spend on housing can go as interest/profit to some investor. Another orthodox solution is to sell them a poorer asset, so that a larger part of what they can afford to pay can go as profit to the supplier. Instead of selling or renting houses to the

American poor, American capital sells them caravans. That has three orthodox advantages. The manufacturer can usually take more profit than could be got from building houses for people who could scarcely afford to pay for them. There is also more profit for the moneylender, who takes hire-purchase interest at two or three times the rate of mortgage interest. And there is more profit for landowners – instead of selling land for housing, they continue to collect both rent and capital gain from the land under the caravans. Compared with selling houses and land at whatever rates of mortgage interest the poor could afford, the caravan strategy reduces domestic productivity and possibly all productivity. But orthodox accounting says it is a more efficient use of resources and will usually record its effects as contributing more to economic growth.

It is quite irrational to expect an open capital market to distribute resources efficiently between housing and other uses. The output of housing doesn't bring direct money returns, so it is the commercial wage-income of the user, *not* the comparative productivity of the use, which has to compete with alternative uses of the resource. Similarly between one house buyer and another: the highest bidder for the bricks and mortar is the household with most money to spend, *not* necessarily the household which can use the resource most productively. The more affluent house-buyers often spend capital, and include elements of unproductive luxury in their houses, so they preempt real resources without which poorer households can't make their free time and labor productive at all. So in unequal societies an open market for housing resources will usually distribute the resources in a fairly unproductive way. Orthodox theory will declare that to be the most productive way.

Similar arguments apply when housing resources are not skimped but misused. It costs Germans and French and Swedes rather more to build and service small landless apartments for their working classes than it costs Norwegians, English, Australians and New Zealanders to build and service capacious houses and gardens for many of theirs. The different domestic productivity of their working classes does not then appear in their national accounts. It may even happen that the apartment-dwellers, being able to produce less for themselves, are driven to work more for wages and to buy more commercial goods and entertainments. National accounts will then show poorer populations as richer, and vice versa. The relevant quantities of time and activity are so large that these distortions are probably quite significant. On a common-sense valuation of the goods and satisfactions which they are equipped to produce for themselves, Norwegians may well be as rich and equal as Swedes, and English may still be as rich as French or Germans – though orthodox accounts say otherwise. Norwegians and English average as much as 50% more domestic capital than Swedes, Germans or French, and they have more generous and equal shares of private urban land. It may well be that their private productivity more than offsets their lower commercial productivity – and does so in the goods and activities on which they put the highest value.

The same bias is reinforced by some other theorists, especially the town planners and traffic planners who think that dense housing can make cities work more efficiently. Many of the alleged transport and service economies are not real, but even if they were, their advocates *never* compare the gains with the losses: they never compare the dollars and minutes saved from the worker's daily hour or so of travel with the dollars and satisfactions lost by constricting what he and his wife and children can do with the six or eight hours which (on average) they spend at home or in walking distance of it. Multiplying the time by the numbers, the opportunities for gain or loss are probably ten or twenty times greater in the domestic system than in the transport system. Almost all the efficiencies claimed for dense housing depend on treating housing as nothing but shelter, and leaving its output out of the accounting. 'Efficiency' is thus defined to mean producing more commercial goods, less domestic goods, and often less goods altogether. Like the orthodox economic theories, these are built on the expert value-judgment (it is certainly not the people's value-judgment) that the work of the domestic economy is worthless.

Practical politicians, especially in English-speaking countries, have often ignored or overridden this professional nonsense. But not often enough – it is a dangerous mistake to underestimate the influence of bad theory. Orthodox economic theory compels any genuinely productive housing policy to appear weakly as a welfare policy laced with 'uneconomic' subsidies. It authorizes many mean-spirited restrictions on the amount and style of public housing. It encourages governments to allow private housing resources to be distributed unequally and unproductively in open markets. It encourages them to permit as 'economic' the wholesale destruction of serviceable housing wherever someone can get more profit from other uses of the land. It strengthens the resistance of national Treasuries to many humane and productive housing expenditures. It distorts national accounting, and builds a great destructive blindness into the education of many young economists.

Socialist experts make most of the capitalist mistakes about the domestic economy, then add some of their own.

The first industrial revolution allowed its town workers scarcely any private space or time or equipment at all. They lived like twentieth-century battery-chickens, for the same reason as the chickens do: a ruling class owned all the means of production, including the bare tenements the workers slept in. Instead of the twin economic systems we have now there was only one, and the masters owned it. So in the world Marx knew, scarcely any ownership was innocent.

That miserable phase didn't last long, but it lasted long enough to beget one true socialist insight and one fatal socialist mistake. Marx developed a perceptive and compassionate theory of alienation. It described the condition of workers who did not own or control their land or tools of trade or their time or anything their labor produced, and who could express nothing and see nothing of themselves in what they produced. They were denied the means of developing and enjoying most of the potentialities that humans are born with. They were fragmented and denatured: kept alive like animals to serve a single purpose of somebody else's. The institution which enslaved them seemed to be the institution of property. So Marx and his heirs identified ownership itself – instead of its wrong distribution – as the root of evil. That may have been understandable at the time, but it was about as sensible as attacking the maldistribution of food by abolishing food.

The mistake was the more remarkable because Marx and some of his contemporaries understood very well what those suffering masses needed. They needed to replace unequal, impersonal, exploitive relations of production by more equal, affectionate, cooperative and voluntary relations. They needed the living unities they had lost or never had: to live whole lives as whole men and women, dignified and many-sided, able to work at tasks and by timetables and with companions of their own choosing, making and doing things for themselves and one another – things which expressed their own intentions and satisfied their own tastes and needs. *They needed precisely the unities and freedoms which the domestic economy now allows to the more fortunate of their greatgrandchildren.*

At the heart of the critique of alienation was the idea that the worker ought to control his resources: his capital and labor, his time and his product. His work lacked meaning and his life lacked fullness and unity because he did not own those things. Why didn't the early socialists therefore decide that he *ought* to own them? Some Utopian socialists did. But in their programs Marx could see only the sacrifice of industrial productivity and a reactionary retreat to the poverty and 'rural idiocy' of peasant smallholding. The promising technology of his time could be made productive only by the institutional organization of divided and alienated labor. Max Weber thought that complex organization, under *any* ownership, must unequalize men and degrade their lives to some degree. So did Marx, often enough; but like Weber he couldn't think how to civilize the monster so he designed his practical proposals to correct its other sins, especially its distributions of money and power. About the problems of alienation under socialist organization he was usually evasive.

It was a technical mistake to expect that the new technology would go on reducing the amount and importance of domestic production. In fact it soon began to do the opposite: to equip the new domestic economy. In that economy, which among other things produces every society's supply of labor, independent smallholding is technically efficient. Free choice and voluntary cooperation come naturally. So can the dreamed-of unities. And productivity does not depend on competitive motivation, 'incentive inequalities', institutional ownership or bureaucratic organization. It depends instead on the most equal possible distribution of domestic land and capital into private ownership. So the new domestic economy (complemented by appropriate communal and public services) offers socialism a historic opportunity to resolve most of its internal dilemmas and contradictions, to reconcile productivity and freedom and equality, to be truly popular – and even perhaps to get elected.

Institutional production must obviously continue. Much of it needs to be reorganized, often by traditional socialist methods for traditional socialist reasons. But whoever owns its capital, it also needs to be 'humanized'. A lot of that has been done already, and more is in hand here and there – job enrichment, workers' participation in management, the organization of smaller and more stable working teams. But that sort of improvement does not depend only on institutional arrangements at work. It also depends on the cooperative or uncooperative capacities and values which people bring to work. Most of those capacities are built into people by their upbringing, which in turn can depend a good deal on the resources with which they are brought up – a good domestic economy is a necessary condition for civilizing the institutional economy.

By no means all institutional work has to be soul-destroying. Some of it will always be challenging, inventive, absorbing. A lot of it can be tolerably interesting and sociable. The worst of it can at least have fair pay and short hours. But for all that, it must always be heavily regulated and only half civilized: the institutional economy can rarely offer the best or most important scope for either the freedom or the brotherhood of man. It needs to be tamed and deprived of as much as possible of its power to corrupt and unnerve and unequalize people. It should then cease to be the centre of socialist attention. It should become a service: a banal but necessary supplier of goods and services, mostly to that other economy in which men *can* be their own masters. Its necessities need occupy less than a third of the week of most workers, less than a sixth of conscious human time. Socialists should concentrate on equalizing and improving the other five sixths.

That is not what most socialist leaders and experts and ideologues have concentrated on. They have concentrated on the institutional economy and the distribution of money. They are rightly obsessed by the task of getting institutional capital out of unequal private ownership. But too many of them have been wrong about nearly everything else, and intolerant of any women or liberals or Utopians who tried to put them right. In most of the liberating and potentially equalizing growth of the domestic economy which Young and Willmott trace, 'hard' socialists can see only a monstrous historical mistake: a capitalist victory and a class betrayal: a worthless and corrupting *embourgeoisement* of the masses.

Seeing the masses seduced by capitalism, 'hard' socialists respond by doubling their distrust of ownership. It does not occur to them that the house and garden and car turn people away from the party of equality chiefly because the party of equality officially despises the house and garden and car, and the life they allow. The heart of the trouble is this: most Left ideologists have never worked out what they should do with the institutional economy when they *do* capture it. What should it produce, what should it enable the ordinary worker and his family to *do* with the five sixths of life that are, or ought to be, their own? A good test of any ideology is to insist that it answer that question *in detail* – minute by minute, hour by day by year, what should ordinary people be able to do with their time, and what are they likely to want to do with it? Most of them do not wish to divide most of their time between cocktail parties and *avant-garde* theatre; nor between watching television in a landless apartment and socializing in strictly public places. They want a much more complicated pattern of diverse activities, private and familial and social and public, including a great many active, productive, creative activities. They also know, as Left ideologues don't, that their outgoing social lives will be better in proportion as their home resources are individual and good, *not* standardized and poor. They want to *have* things so that they can *do* things, including many of the things they do socially with other people – as Marx in his wiser moments understood.

Besides the general distrust of ownership, socialists are prevented from understanding this chiefly by the Marxist theory of class. I believe that the least misleading way to understand modern inequalities is to see them as continuous from richest to poorest. Values and attitudes are also distributed continuously, though lumped and layered and clustered in patterns more complicated than patterns of income and occupation can (by themselves) explain. Some of the richest and most reactionary people are employees, some of the poorest (and some of the most radical) are independent tradesmen or proprietors. Parties of equality have the difficult task of persuading majorities of middle and poor to act together. The 'natural' working class, for which Marxists see a natural common interest and political role, is no longer distinguished by the fact of wage labor. It is distinguished in practice by low pay, blue collars and (very often) mean rental housing; and it has long been a minority class. Its 'lost' numbers – skilled or white collared or otherwise prosperous – are enjoying their possession of houses and gardens and cars and are unlikely to vote for anyone who wants them to trade all those for a standardized apartment near a jolly public park. But neither on the other hand do most of them love their employers much. They'll vote socialist again when socialist policy offers them what they correctly recognize as the material conditions for equal, cooperative, unalienated work and life. If the leaders of the Left can't learn that from the obvious sources – from the evidence of their own eyes, and from the living experience and aspirations of the masses they are supposed to represent – but must learn it from books instead, they should begin with Michael Young's and Peter Willmott's book.

With economic growth, whole classes cross thresholds of income. When workers can afford education, cars and resourceful housing, they use them much as middle-class people do. But because Rightist minorities had those resources first, Marxists call the resulting culture 'bourgeois' and identify it with class-exploitive politics. (Because aristocrats installed the first water-closets, it should follow that every modern WC endows its users with aristocratic values.) That kind of determinism is absurd. Even on Marxist assumptions, political values relate to class position, not material culture. In most countries the spread of common life-styles *increases* the vote for more equality. And not only for class equality – Young and Willmott notice that as household resources improve, men and women grow more alike, exchange more tasks, do more together and share more fairly. Given equal resources, productive households promise to reduce both class and sexist exploitation.

Meanwhile ideology continues to determine policy. Attitudes to private ownership determine which socialist policies can be good and which cannot. Industrial, income and tax policies can be good. Many public, welfare and personal services can be good in themselves because they can run on public capital and wage labor. But they cannot be fully fruitful if they are offered to people with very unequal domestic resources (which are chiefly human, but depend in various ways on material resources); and because it runs best on private ownership the domestic economy (and therefore a large fraction of national productivity) has generally done poorly wherever 'real' socialists have governed. Communist governments do their best to confine productive work to the institutional economy, and to prohibit production outside it. Socialist housing is the affluent world's worst. Socialist cities (including Swedish cities) give private land to the lowest proportion (and exclusively to the richest) of their people. Pathetically, Russian town-dwellers go out and comb the countryside for patches of neglected land they can plant, visit, enjoy, 'make their own' however tenuously. Their masters, who own everything just as the masters did in Marx's day, discourage this petty-bourgeois practice. In that and other ways they do their best to build for twenty-first-century Russia the urban fabric of nineteenth-century Manchester. Plenty of Left as well as Right technocrats are doing the same for the working-class quarters of west European cities. The hard Left – Marxist and technocratic – thus works as hard as any capitalist to kill the most promising of all socialist opportunities, and to perpetuate the alienation which Marx condemned as the worst effect of primitive industrial capitalism.

Voters know this. Women know it all too well. 'Next thing, they'll confiscate hearth and home.' Not many of the democratic people who vote against socialist parties are in love with big capitalism, or in fear of revolutionary bloodshed. They are in love with private life, and afraid of *any* contempt for it; and even in the milder parties of the Left they see some contempt for the furniture and security of the private space and time in which all people are born and formed, and ordinary people then suffer or enjoy the greater part of their experience of life. The ideologues are wrong, the people are right, and more than any other single cause it seems probable that this explains why most democratic socialist parties have got fewer votes from women than from men, and have spent most of the twentieth century out of office.

That has allowed the Right to get most of the credit for the imperfect but nevertheless prolific distribution of the new domestic resources. Right governments and capitalist markets distribute them very unequally. To extract profit from the domestic economy they do their best to infect it with commercial values and competitive anxieties, and to persuade households to see themselves as consumer-cooperatives rather than producer-cooperatives. But however they try to corrupt the domestic economy, they do not threaten to starve or abolish it. Right rhetoric celebrates the family, promises to nourish and protect it, and recommends that it *own* all the private space and resources it can. When Right leaders say that people want to be equipped to do things for themselves, rather than 'expecting everything from the State', they may often be hypocritical but they are nearly always right. And besides prudent politicians, the Right has its share of honest and generous reformers. When they want to reduce inequalities their traditional philosophies positively encourage them to do it by improving the distribution of do-it-yourself resources – by redistributing domestic rather than commercial capital ownership. Good housing policies (though seldom *very* good) have come more often from the Right than from the Left. For all its faults, the Right approach to the domestic economy has generally been more intelligent, productive, egalitarian and popular than the usual approach of the Left.

So the Right has deserved its victories, and the Left its defeats. But the suffering citizens haven't really deserved either. Wrong options face them at election time. If they want good private resources they have to vote also for the rapacities of commercial capitalism. If on the other hand they want that monster reformed, they have to vote for parties which appear to threaten their private resources. The options need to be reconstructed. Social-democratic parties should be radical at work and liberal at home. The main purpose of the radical reconstruction of the institutional economy should be to put it to work to enrich and equalize the domestic economy and its complementary public services. The domestic share of social capital could well be raised to half, and distributed with physical as well as financial equality.

Not much of that will be achieved merely by tinkering with housing and town planning policies. It needs a fundamental change of socialist philosophy; new symbols of what the Left stands for; changes and replacements within the industrial and party machines; and decades of persuasion and public commitment to convince the citizens that the change of heart is real, and based at last on true instead of false understandings of the economics of freedom, equality and productivity.

6

In summary: institutional and domestic ownership should be perceived as the basic alternatives for productive capital. Much of the institutional economy needs to be taken out of unequal private ownership, and civilized as far as possible. But that may never be very far: elements of alienation and bureaucratic inequality are bound to go with any complex division of labor and coordination of effort. That will matter less as institutional production occupies less of life, and loses its power to unequalize the rest of life. Much of its output should go to equip, serve and complement the domestic economy, more equally than happens now. The distinguishing purpose of socialism should not be to reduce private and increase public ownership. It should be to tame institutional and increase domestic ownership: to attack inequality and alienation by giving to every household (as far as scarcity and environmental prudence allow) the fullest control of the most versatile resources it can use.

Nothing in that need make any household – or any society – more settled or suburban than it wants to be. It is consistent with a society as footloose, sociable, crowded, adventurous and away-from-home as any other. But life-styles and the habitations they need should be open to choice by poor as well as rich, so that urban densities and diversities don't have to mean a free choice of private pastures for most of my life, and a box in a battery for most of yours.

Most capacities for love develop (or don't) in childhood; the largest quantity of willing human cooperation occurs within and between households; cooperation there is the pattern, and has to be the continuing basis, for cooperation anywhere else. To put it in the most shocking possible language, socialism should cease to be the factory-floor and chicken-battery party, and become the hearth-and-home, do-it-yourself party.

PROGRAM

9

Shares of space and services

Distributions of capital, income, services, and private space and resources all depend to some degree on one another and on the organization
of production, and need to be understood in simultaneous relation to one
another. But the subject has to be ordered somehow. To sketch the
substance of a social-democratic program I begin (briefly, because I have
nothing to add to the conventional wisdom) with some questions about
doles, public and professional services, and the control of pollution. The
chapters then deal in turn with urban planning and land and housing, the
control of inflation, the distribution of wealth and income, and the
organization of as much production as really needs institutional
management.

1

How do public services compare with distributions of money as aids to
equality? The question is too general. The best way to supply dentistry
won't be the same at different times, in different societies, or for people
who live respectively in cities and on offshore lighthouses. It would be
pointless to debate the general merits of money and services, if there were
not a faction of the Right arguing for the money principle in just that
general way: for a universal basic income to replace *both* specific-purpose
welfare allowances *and* a number of services, even including (in the
de-schooling movement) public education.

The case for money is summed up in the slogans 'what the poor need
is money', 'money is freedom' and 'all dollars are equal'. Money is a
liberator and equalizer. It enables poor people to judge their own needs
and allocate their resources as freely as everybody else does, with
dignity and independence.

The case against money is that it is often the easiest resource to lose,
misuse or steal, and of all people the poorest tend to have the weakest
defences against those mishaps. Services can be good equalizers inside
households. Doles, like other incomes, don't go to everybody, they
usually go to one member of each household. That doesn't necessarily

distribute freedom or anything else to the other members. Schools educate children; dental services protect their teeth; libraries lend them books to read; summer camps give them holidays; playgrounds and hobby workshops give them company and creative scope; counsellors widen their choices and chances of jobs; alert health and welfare officers may protect a few of them from corrupt or violent parents. If the state withdraws those services and distributes cash to parents instead, not all the parents will spend the cash on dentistry, books, holidays, etc. – or on anything else for their dependants, in some households – though some may spend it on things they need more than they need those services. Most of those services won't be as cheap, or won't be there at all, if private investment has to supply them. It does not necessarily do most for freedom and dignity to give the most vulnerable people nothing but shark bait in shark-infested seas – nothing but money in societies with money-lenders and debt-collectors, landlords who keep rents up to capacities to pay, old folks' homes and hospitals which do likewise, alluring advertisers, hire-purchase offers you can't refuse – and any number of bars, betting shops, poker machines, commercial religions, over-priced tranquillizers and other addictive attractions. Among the customers, more men want money and more women want services; and some change their minds when better experienced. Among their Right-wing mentors, some want to give them nothing but money because that gives them free choices. Others want to give them money because it may be possible to give them less that way; or because commerce can get more of it back; or because it helps to shift investment (profitably) from public to private sectors.

But services also have their problems. If the model of money-only welfare is the shark-infested sea, the model of service-only welfare is the nursing home which takes the patient's whole pension then treats him however the management thinks best. Sensible solutions lie somewhere between, in thoughtfully detailed mixtures of money and service – differing only in detail from the mixtures of income and public service which everybody demands in a modern society.

There is another aspect of the problem. Most services involve human relations between those who use them and teachers, child-minders, health and welfare officers, housing officers, counsellors. Money allowances involve other relations, especially if they are means-tested and claimants have to deal with clerks and investigators. Many of the relations can be helpful; others can be felt as oppressive or humiliating. The experience of the old, the poor, the sick, and of single parents and neglected children, may be better understood by the healthy and successful classes if some of them have to deal professionally with those sufferings – though those effects will vary, as some of the professionals conceive reforms and agitate public opinion, and others are conservatized, and learn to despise their clients. But whatever the personal understandings and misunderstandings, formal records accumulate. Unlike universal doles, means-tested allowances and personal services generate good statistical knowledge of poverty and other miseries.

In theory, Right and Left should both favor strict means-testing. For the Right it economizes welfare expenditure; for the Left it makes sure that every dollar does its best to improve equalities. In practice both parties divide about the principle, and its application to particular services. Means tests are expensive to administer, and humiliating, and they can reconstruct people's options in damaging and corrupting ways. To qualify for pensions people have to spend their savings and sell their houses (or under other rules, hang on to houses they no longer want); windfalls, casual earnings and help from kin have to be taken in cash and lied about, as the poor learn from their betters some of the law-breaking arts of asset concealment and tax evasion. (As welfare cheats they are then caught, convicted and punished five or ten times as surely and a good deal more severely than affluent tax evaders are.) Universal allowances avoid some of these troubles but they rarely improve equalities, and they are paid blind to plenty of people who really need personal help or protection rather than money.

All societies, however governed, will continue to have 'welfare populations'. These will include varying proportions of villains, addicts, voluntary and involuntary unemployed, victims of crime, illness, accident and old age, orphaned and abandoned children, and single parents and their families. There is no short satisfactory way through the dilemmas they face themselves, or present to governments; and their problems are so various that most generalizations about them are bunk. But one conventional attitude and one Scandinavian institution may be worth remembering.

Some social problems are intractable, but that doesn't mean that the whole welfare population should be 'accepted', doled and forgotten. It means that detailed, perceptive, individualized aids are not only best in themselves, they are also likeliest to sort out those who can be helped from those who can't. Even the lives and deaths of those who can't can sometimes be made more tolerable – to themselves, or to their victims or neighbors or kin. The Left should not write off services to troubled

209

individuals and families as 'support for the system', or lose patience with types of aid in cash or kind which include some possibility of personal contact. Nobody should be put off by sneers at 'paternalism'. If social workers or pension clerks behave badly they should be replaced by better ones, not by shark-infested seas. In a more general way it would be good to reconstruct the conventional image of paternalism. There are good and bad fathers and good and bad occasions for fathering. The bad ones don't justify abolishing the rest. (The most numerous of all classes of disadvantaged children are those without fathers when they need them.) The literary Left who made 'paternal' a politically abusive word were doubtless thinking of some misuses of authority or benevolence. But they made a weapon for the enemy – 'paternalistic' is now any winner's convenient, dismissive swearword for any love, help, care, compunction or responsibility toward losers. It is good to base equalities on public right rather than winners' benevolence, but public rights (or doles) can't do much of what needs doing for many of the young, old, overworked, sick, anxious, lonely and weak members of the welfare population. Whatever its pattern of rights, the most equal society will still be a society of people unequal in many respects; and responsible, helpful, understanding relations between unequals will usually be better than uncaring ones.

There is probably no escape from means-testing (or other tests of entitlement) for some kinds of 'sudden victims' – for each week's crop of freshly widowed or deserted mothers, evicted families or sick or unemployed workers. But means-testing doesn't stop there. If housing and educational and superannuation policies are to do much for equalities, much larger numbers have to put up with what are always, to some degree, undesirable inquisitions. For these mass customers, it might be best to marry an idea from the American Right with one from the Scandinavian Left. Those on the Right who want to replace most welfare allowances by a negative income tax argue that it has the virtue of subjecting everybody, without class discrimination, to the same annual inquisition. Unfortunately a once-a-year retrospective assessment can't be adapted to most purposes of emergency aid and weekly shelter and sustenance; but it can be adapted to other purposes which affect much larger numbers of people, if tax assessments are *public* (as in some Scandinavian countries) and therefore available to every branch of government. If the annual assessment of each citizen's income, capital and net worth goes into a public register, most stable non-emergency entitlements can be derived from that: pensions, children's and students' allowances, housing entitlements and anything else that an equalizing society may add to the list: entitlement to low-interest loans, low-rent holiday housing, public transport concessions, theatre free-lists, and any other split-pricing of goods and services. If all Norwegians from paupers to shipowners can put up with the publication of their incomes before and after tax, so can anyone else. The publicity is worth while for its own sake: assessment is surer, evasion and tax-theft are more difficult, contrasts of wealth and poverty are dramatized and the rich find it harder to disguise their rate of capital enrichment. As people get used to it the cost in privacy is not great, and is mostly confined to property incomes and a few professional and self-employed incomes. (The salary and wage-fixing arrangements of modern societies mean that eight or nine incomes of every ten are well enough known already.) And once that particular privacy is sacrificed a lot of others can rest untroubled. Most other mass means-testing can cease, while social research, policy-making and administration can be more flexible, effective and uninterfering than before.

2

There are familiar difficulties with services. Some don't reach all the people they are meant for. The hindrances may be locational, psychological, financial, libertarian. People live at varying densities so their physical access to services can't be equal – or equal access can have very unequal costs. Should city and country people get equal services, or equal shares of public expenditure? Should people who are personally skilful at using the services be able to get better service than those who are not? Governments have to compromise, doing their best to bring service to the customers or customers to the service and unavoidably doing better for some than for others.

Questions of freedom range from easy through difficult to spurious. The spurious ones are raised by a few professions whose representatives insist on equating professional independence with the right to unlimited loot. Some doctors are worst, with some lawyers close behind. National medical and legal services can be organized in a variety of ways. In most of the existing or proposed public medical services in democratic countries, doctors remain as free as before to work where and how they want to; they can choose their patients, who can choose their doctors; even specialist and hospital doctoring don't differ much from private services in any professional way. They are merely paid for in different ways. To make medical service equally accessible to all, the one constraint which doctors do have to accept is price control. Wherever government subsidizes demand for a limited resource it must usually also control supply, or price-control it, whether the demand is for land, housing, transport or anything else. There is no good reason why doctors should be excepted. Their own incomes benefit from the restraint of other people's freedoms (to practise medicine, for example) and from the regulation of prices and incomes which most of their fellow-citizens submit to. Plenty of professional work, including teaching and scientific and social and medical research, is already done with full professional independence but for regulated rewards. Doctors who resist price control do so merely as hard bargainers of an unusually rich and ruthless kind. If the conflict is about freedom at all it is about the freedom of a very few to get rich by the private exploitation of a state-educated, state-subsidized, state-enforced monopoly of an indispensable skill. But if price control is conceded, very few other doctors' or patients' freedoms need be threatened by well-designed public provisions for equal access to medical services. Medical Associations could well be asked to design those services, subject only to the contraint that they produce a specified pattern of doctors' incomes.

Legal services present different problems. People need to be deterred from using some of them – unlimited opportunities to litigate would have hilarious consequences. But free advisory services are safe enough and can be organized and paid for (at controlled prices) without reducing lawyers' independence. There are more difficult problems of equality in the unequal risks which have to be taken by litigants of unequal wealth, and in the costs of legal services in matters (like conveyancing, motoring, matrimonial and family affairs) which might often be managed better without such expensive attention. I need not summarize the reams that have been written about the effects of legal costs on equalities under the law. Some are obvious whenever rich parties, who are usually directors or officials risking other people's money, confront poor parties risking their own money and facing the ruinous costs of both parties if they lose. Rich parties often have gross advantages of action and bluff. But to redress the balance by enabling poor parties to go to court without *any* costs or risks would expose too many branches of business and government to a whole new hijacking industry. Tinkering with costs, legal aids, ombudsman services or inquisitorial procedures can ameliorate the trouble in various ways but some part of it remains intractable. Some social problems of unequal wealth or fighting or bargaining power would disappear if personal incomes were more equal but this is not one of them:

even if the odds were fairer between individuals, there would still be unequal contests between individuals and corporate bodies including arms of government.

Three other directions of reform are being explored in many parts of the world. One is to substitute public for private action where rights to civil action don't in practice protect poor people adequately – for example in collecting maintenance for deserted wives and children. Another is to economize by substituting one lawyer for two or three (two adversaries and sometimes a judge) wherever one could sufficiently advise and protect the parties. Many routine agreements and transactions could safely be done by a neutral negotiator/draftsman with a duty to see that each party understood what he was doing. A third direction of reform is to simplify laws and procedures to make more of them usable with less professional help. Some states register the ownership and encumbrance of land as simply and cheaply as the ownership of motor cars, and prescribe forms which allow citizens to sell or mortgage land and buildings to one another at a fraction of what such transactions cost in time and money in (for example) the United Kingdom. Simple land ownership can also improve the fairness and efficiency of town planning, taxation, price control and other functions of government – which is a main reason why many lawyers and proprietors resist it. In some countries the legal costs of motor accidents are higher than the sum of all their other costs and various experiments are in train to try to simplify and cheapen procedures of adjudication and compensation. There is no need for the costs, complexities and corruptions of workmen's compensation if there are adequate general provisions for people widowed, injured or unemployed. Many matrimonial and family disputes could be settled better by family arbitrators than by adversary actions in court.

Law reformers can add many more to that list of possibilities. Laymen need to approach them with caution. It may be hard to reform procedures (or their costs) alone; the law itself often needs to be reconstructed to make it more cheaply or easily useable. If that reduces precision or certainty in difficult cases it may nevertheless be worth while if it cheapens large numbers of simple cases or transactions. The costs and benefits of simpler and surer law will become very important in attempts to reduce primary inequalities of wealth and income, or to redress them by more effective taxation. Tax-theft needs to be as surely punished as any other theft. Both aims could be helped by some radical simplification of the permissible forms of business organization and responsibility.

Those changes might reduce some business freedoms and efficiencies, and increase others; but whatever their net effect on production they might be worth while for other reasons.

Meanwhile laymen should not 'take life out of the lawyers' hands' too impulsively. Laymen's law can be as oppressive, unequal and uncertain as lawyers' law. For example well-intended reforms of the treatment of young offenders have sometimes given social administrators dangerous powers to imprison children – including wrongly-accused children – without trial. Do-it-yourself title and transfer systems for land, tenancy, motor cars or sales on credit need some safeguards for ordinary citizens against professional dealers. Many contests between parties of unequal wealth or skill are fairer if both have lawyers than if neither has. And so on. Law reform is cooperative work for lawyers and social reformers. When lawyers – even social-reforming lawyers – do it alone they tend to concentrate on making the law more workable by lawyers and courts. It is also desirable to make more of it workable without lawyers, and for the rest, to make lawyers and courts as cheaply and equally accessible as possible.

3

How should pollution be controlled and how should the costs of controlling it be distributed? Professional discussions have concentrated on three alternative approaches: by taxation, regulation or public ownership.

For dealing with the business chiefly by taxing pollutant emissions, various advantages are claimed. The method leaves private enterprise free, private and profitable. Depending how the tax is applied, it may encourage producers to develop less pollutant techniques. Costs are incorporated into the prices of the relevant products instead of being unloaded (or instead of the pollution being unloaded) onto the community at large. Objections to this approach are of two kinds. Environmentally it may not be effective enough. Socially it means that traditionally free goods and evils are withdrawn from the free list and transferred to the list of things which are priced – and therefore distributed unequally according to people's unequal capacities to pay. But the existing inequalities of income were established when those goods were free, and expected to stay free. When anti-pollution taxes raise prices or transfer goods from the free to the unequal list there is usually therefore a double increase in inequality. If the goods are necessaries there is the ordinary regressive effect of indirect taxation; and in addition the whole basis and effect of monetary inequality is made harsher by increasing the range and number of goods which have to be paid for out of income.

Historically such transfers from the free list to the unequal list are not unknown. They happen when the rich decide they want some of the poor's common property, or when the poor actually begin to use some free good which the rich have formerly monopolized without paying for it. So commons are enclosed, or parking meters appear where formerly parking was free. But in rich democracies the balance of change has been in the opposite direction for a century or more – what used to be unequally distributed market goods like toll-roads, health, education and housing have been moved wholly or partly to the free list. The Right environmentalists who now want to preserve a threatened environment *chiefly by pricing more and more uses of it* are trying to reverse a long historical trend, and to return from the distributive principles of the twentieth century to those of the eighteenth. If they prevail, so that threatened resources are rationed chiefly by price, and the control of pollution is financed chiefly by 'internalizing' social costs into product prices, then majorities may experience environmental reform chiefly as a sharp increase of inequality.[24]

The second alternative is to regulate pollution directly, i.e. to ban it or ration it or set standards for it, on the model of factory regulation, pure food laws and other traditional protections of public safety. If the requirements raise costs of production their distributive effects may be much the same as those of a taxing system. Regulation at least allows the old prices to continue until the pollution is reduced. Regulation and taxing can both be inflationary. If emission taxes are high, to overcome manufacturers' inertia and force them to re-equip quickly, prices often go higher than they need to – and then stay there. But regulation may also make opportunities for prices to be fiddled a little more artfully than usual. Both methods make consumers of particular goods pay most of the cost of environmental improvement.

A better variant where the technical facts allow it may be to separate the production of pollution from the disposal of it. If public agencies look after the disposal (by supplying sewerage, or recycling wastes) public policy can decide which costs to charge to particular consumers and which to distribute more progressively, for example through income taxes. This is one example of the third general approach to the pollutant industries, which is to take them into public ownership. Any desired balance of production and environmental forbearance can then be applied by public management, and the costs can be distributed through prices or taxes as seems most equitable in each case. There are three main objections to this policy. First, it doesn't reduce any costs (though it may avoid or redistribute some profits). Second, it may increase costs wherever public management is less efficient than private. That often suggests mixed approaches: the public needn't mine the ore or mill the timber, but it may own the land, minerals or forests and control the extractive and processing industries by contract. But, third, public ownership does not by itself guarantee any improvement of environmental care. Public agencies have been, and many are still, as bad polluters as any. Radical reforms of some of the public agencies may be needed if they are to perform efficiently, responsibly and equitably. (Some reforms are discussed in Chapter 11.)

Between taxation and regulation and public ownership, and pricing and rationing and subsidy, different problems will attract different solutions. But in choosing them two general points are worth remembering. Professional advice is likely to be systematically biased against serious consideration of the distribution of costs. Environmentalists give priority to the effective reduction of pollution; orthodox economists tend to favor market mechanisms and disregard social distributions. Between them they will often propose methods which combine effective control of pollution with continuing efficiency of production. Both those aims are important, but politicians and administrators may have to tramp on their experts to insist that distributive equities are also given the weight they deserve.

Second, the problems of equity would be different and simpler, and many problems of environmental management would therefore be simpler, if wealth and income were fairly distributed in the first place. Many pricing and taxing approaches to the control of pollution ought to be resisted while present inequalities of spending power continue. But those pricing and taxing methods do have some of the efficiencies claimed for them. It would be good to be able to use them without injustice. That is one more reason for making radical redistributions of wealth and income.

4

The remainder of this chapter is about shares of space.

Where people live, and the uses they can make of the land around them, can have profound effects on their experience of life. Shares of space matter for their own sake. They also affect uses of time, and shares of wealth and work and opportunity. But the markets for space – private and public, indoor and outdoor – are quite 'imperfect'. The goods are not as divisible or interchangeable or reproducible as most economic goods are. The prices matter, but the choices offered to particular households and classes may matter even more. Land, housing and cities need to be understood as a single complicated field of public policy. The following sections are about cities, housing and land markets. This section offers some preliminaries about land uses.

Most big capitalist societies allow land to be a double unequalizer. They distribute it unequally, often less equally than income. As economic growth stimulates demand for accessible urban land, its price increases faster than the price of labor or anything else, so its unequal ownership further unequalizes wealth and income. There are direct transfers via rents and prices to inheritors and investors in land, and indirect transfers from those who don't own land and houses to those who do. There is often some further unequalizing among investors. Those who lose (especially in periods of inflation) are the institutions which lend on mortgage at fixed interest for long terms. Those are chiefly savings banks, building societies, life assurers and superannuation funds, and governments – i.e., institutions which chiefly lend the small savings and taxes of large numbers of people with low or middling incomes. Rich investors don't lend on land, they do better by buying and selling it, often with money borrowed from savers poorer than themselves.

There have been three general approaches to the government of land uses. One is to let owners of land do what they like with it. That leaves it all in a single market and tends to keep most of it cheaper than other methods do. But it can allow bad urban development, bad neighboring, expensive and wasteful services, and various commercial uncertainties and social inefficiencies.

So governments try a second approach: they draw maps and codes to regulate what owners can do with their land. Zoning distributes the land to a number of separate markets: each city has so much office and commercial land, so much industrial, so much dense residential, so much house-and-garden land, and so on. This also has plenty of disadvantages. It is hard to do well; it has often made for needless monotonies and inconveniences of land use; it has often been used to perpetuate privileged segregations. Any zoning plan creates many small monopolies and hands out capricious gains and losses to owners who find their land zoned for differently profitable uses. The quickest way to get rich is then to buy land zoned for low-valued uses, get it rezoned for more profitable uses, then sell it again. Skilful operators can do a good deal of that wherever

217

the regulations are careless or the authorities are 'flexible'. Forward planning of urban growth becomes a speculators' guide. There has to be reliably puritanical government to keep the system honest at all. Honest or not, bigger and unfairer fortunes are often made in regulated land markets than in open markets.

Some governments have concluded that they had better try a third method: they should own most urban land themselves, and control its uses by contract with private users. This style of control can be as corrupt as any; it can be a bureaucratic nightmare; but it *can* work well if rightly-designed public agencies take the trouble to learn the business and practise it with skill and good social purpose.

Varying with circumstances, the best administration will usually mix those three methods. The mixture ought to be as uninterfering as possible. It should allow as much private ownership (or similarly unbothered occupation) as it safely can. That is likely to vary from use to use.

It may often be worth while for the public to own a good deal of office and commercial land. This need not increase bureaucracy if it means that zoning and regulatory planning are replaced by contractual controls, which are often simpler and more popular. Leasing policies may be designed to control the location of jobs, to reconstruct the options of those who choose business locations, to take a public share of profits and capital gains arising from good locations, or to keep useful but 'uneconomic' activities where they're needed for social reasons. Metropolitan distributions of shopping and over-the-counter services could often be improved by this style of control. Goods have to be distributed from warehouses to a million home addresses; as more suburban retailing concentrates into fewer and bigger drive-in super-centres it pulls the 'point of sale' further back from the home addresses towards the warehouses, so that the suppliers contribute less and the customers contribute more of the transportation, handling and delivery. That suits customers who have cars, time, and a liking for a wide choice of goods. But it can have social costs and class costs. There are absolute increases of private travelling time and petrol consumption and traffic damage as longer shopping journeys replace shorter, private transport replaces public, and thousands of three-quarter-empty cars replace a few full delivery vans. There are also some split-pricing effects. If the supermarkets capture most of the trade, local shops have to survive (if at all) on lower turnover; so choices narrow and prices rise for the poorest shoppers who have to depend on their local shops. Some of this reactionary effect is unnecessary. Chain-store methods *can* distribute many bulk buying and handling economies to quite local shops (in the delightful language of the trade, 'walk-in superettes') which carry the point-of-sale – if not all the breadth of choice – close to the customers' kitchens. Department and discount stores *can* do almost as well in town centres on good public transport as they can at out-of-town locations remote from public transport routes. But left to themselves, many big retailers will bias their operations to attract car-driving customers to fewer and bigger drive-in centres: the land is cheaper, and however many walking and cycling and bus-riding customers they lose, the motoring customers have most of the spending money. But if sites for retailing are available only from public agencies, the agencies don't find it hard to reconcile cheap and profitable service with some social efficiencies and equities. They can allow some of all kinds of service while insisting on cheap local supplies of necessaries for the poorer half of shoppers – though that poorer half may have only a quarter of the spending money and very little of the private transport.

There may be less need to insist on public ownership of industrial land. Unless there are shortages or private monopolies its location and uses are easy enough to regulate by gentler methods, including conventional zoning, and the price of industrial land rarely rises high enough to have much effect on the prices of factory products.

Agrarian land reform has a long history which need not be reviewed here. Any country which wants to do so can, over time, distribute rural land in the smallest parcels consistent with family support and productive efficiency (or in inefficient parcels, if the social gains are thought to be worth the commercial losses). It is not hard (if you want to) to insist on owner-occupation; to encourage producer-cooperatives; to prevent tax-farming by absentees or weekenders; and to lower the efficient unit-size of many types of production by providing technical, advisory, handling and marketing services. Especially in the prairie countries, some kinds of farming will still be done best by private management of very big holdings. But those tend to be the areas where private *ownership* is least essential to good management; they also tend to use least labor and to have least to do with the support of settled village populations. They could often be publicly owned, with private managements competing for leases or management-contracts. If some public management teams can also compete for the business the public and private contenders may help to keep each other lean and honest. Depending on local circumstances, management contracts can be drawn to take public profits from the land, to keep its products cheap, or to have it farmed consistently with environmental standards or recreational uses.

Awkward problems arise between farming, mining, recreation and conservation on country land. Solutions must certainly vary with circumstances – the weekend-cottage, summer-holiday, outdoor-loving and seaside-boozing businesses must differ sharply between the climates of Norway, the Mediterranean and Japan. The management of national parks and of coastal and country conservation is attracting increasingly skilful and subtle attention. That needs to be matched by more care for the fair distribution of benefits. The Left should generally be concerned to see that if access to the countryside has to be rationed, it should not be by price. Caravan camps should go where the local ecology or farming activities can tolerate them rather than where the affluent cottage-owners can. If an unspoiled coast has room for a compact holiday village, should the flats and cottages be owned by people who leave them empty for most of the year? Or by landlords who will rent each one to many families in the course of the year? If a forest or lakeside or countryside can stand a weekend shack every two or three hectares – i.e. if it can stand the use which that density of people will make of it – can the shacks be kept sanitary and unobtrusive without requiring that they be expensive? If such locations are scarce should they sometimes go by lot or waiting time or means test, rather than by auction to the richest bidders?

Most experts agree that there ought to be a great diversity of local and national parks, some easily accessible and some not. To protect the wilder ones, it may sometimes be fairest to make them difficult (rather than expensive) to reach, and to survive in. Powered vehicles could be banned from most of them, and from most beaches. Their curators might be recruited from the rising numbers who would now be willing to care for them from horseback and horsedrawn wagons. (In some countries state foresters, mining and fire wardens and park rangers have cut more roads, triggered more erosion, shattered more silences and generally degraded more wilderness than miners, hunters and holiday-makers combined.)

In these fields there will still be some unavoidable conflicts between the values of conservation and equality, and also between different readings of equality. Each has to be resolved on its local merits. Despite the bad record of many public agencies it will often be safest to get threatened wilderness into public ownership or under effective public control – then reform the public agencies as necessary. Instead of confrontations between environmentalists on the one hand and profit-seeking owners and developers on the other, with no representation at all for the town or country poor, government should try to referee confrontations between those who want to protect the land, those who want jobs working it or processing its products, those who want to enjoy it unspoiled, those who want the enjoyment to be widely and cheaply shared, and those who want to mine, strip, pollute or otherwise damage the land for profit – but also to provide cheap goods for needy consumers, or revenue or foreign exchange for needy taxpayers. The knowledge that they must confront that range of interests will often prompt some of the parties to think inventively of ways to make the land work better for everyone. There will remain some irreconcilable conflicts, and it won't always be right either to prefer fine landscapes to cheap power, or on the other hand to prefer cheap sewerage to clean seas. What matters is that the distributive implications be *understood*, and the poorer parties represented as they have seldom been in the past.

Environmentalists need not usually be afraid of the poorer parties. The 'local interests' they have learned to fear have commonly been employers, shopkeepers or landowners. If wage workers have a share of the decision-making they are often saner conservationists than their betters. (Plenty of their betters made the mistake of supposing that Australian miners would want coal loaders on their beaches, or that Norwegian workers would want to cut more forests, dam more waterfalls and refine more bauxite.) Once above the breadline and into the decision-making, many urban working classes have a respect for natural heritage and an impartial suspicion of both public and private developers. Many also hunger for two kinds of green environment for themselves and their children: for private land at home, and for quiet country or coast, preferably with fish, on holiday. Working-class youth generates some litter, and some Coney Islands and Sunny Rhylls, but through most of their lives working-class families tend to use land and sea – if they're allowed to – more gently than many richer people do. Over too much of Europe, the United Kingdom and the United States they are still locked out of a good many private woods and rivers and beaches, and are thought to love squalid overcrowded caravan camps because they are not allowed to camp cheaply anywhere else.

5

The government of cities is as complicated and conflict-ridden as the government of whole societies.

People in cities have both common interests and conflicting interests. Town planners and urban theorists have a chronic tendency to talk only about the common interests – or about conflicts between vehicles and

8-2

pedestrians, or between rival land uses – as if conflicts of class interest were not their business. In fact the structure of cities distributes costs and benefits as drastically as the structure of incomes does. It is chiefly as distributors that cities ought to be understood and governed.

By connecting everybody to pipes and wires and standard services, and by allowing some concentrated education and organization of working classes, modern cities have helped to improve some equalities of income and lifestyle. But in other ways they have been powerful unequalizers. They have often distributed their costs and benefits to increase the concentration of wealth and to aggravate inequalities of income. If one family earned twice as much money as another it could often spend a lower proportion of income to get more than twice as much land, housing, privacy, clean air, urban travel and public goods and services. Having less, the losers could earn and learn and do less, so the differences increased.

Many of these effects continue. They do so for various reasons. The most powerful are the self-interested politics of the winners, but the most intractable are the inequalities which have been built durably into the urban fabric. Plenty of the poor still live in neighborhoods built to the inequalities of 1870, while in other parts of town the broad streets and ample public and private gardens which the rich could buy or legislate for themselves in 1870 are the shares of space the rich have still. Progress can supply old slums with new services which are not too land-hungry: power and sewerage, teachers and social workers, transport and television. But it doesn't give their people private land, or public space worth having, or room for track and field games – or green shade – at school. Deliberate distributions of urban space are commonly made only once, at the first conversion of open field to urban use. After that, change is piecemeal and (except by thinning the occupation of overcrowded housing) rarely does much for anybody's rations.[25] Physical inequalities persist; and social attitudes are entrenched, by self-perpetuating segregations, to be imposed on new suburbs as well as old.

These iniquities are technically easy to avoid in new urban development if there is political will to avoid them. Plenty of new towns and suburbs have given rich and poor people fairer shares of land and local services than their unequal incomes could have bought in free markets from unregulated subdivisions. But that wholesome will has too often given way to the influences noticed in previous chapters – especially to Left, Right, technocratic and environmentalist desires to condense cities by housing their working classes at battery densities. As fast as the people

222

vote with their feet to lower the densities of the old slums, misguided governments try to rebuild the old densities vertically. (Note 27, below, describes their reasoning, which never refers openly to the class distribution of urban space, but would always in practice distribute it less equally than ever.)

What should the Left do instead?

All parties should of course try to make city life as efficient, safe, interesting and sociable as possible. Beyond that, the distinctive aims of the Left should include these: Cities should keep their central and local attractions and services in reach of their poorer as well as their richer people. Where that can't be done by locating the people it should be done by locating the centres. Taxes and services should be distributed to redress differences between richer and poorer neighborhoods, and there should be persistent efforts to get rid of such segregations. Land should be kept as cheap as possible, and payment for its use should be arranged to reduce, not increase, financial inequalities. The stock of housing and private land should have strong equalities built into it. The stock should also be various, to allow a full and interesting diversity of life-styles and types of housing and places to live; but the diversity should as far as possible reflect differences of taste rather than capacity to pay. Every household which wants the city's average ration of house and private land should be able to get it, and preferably own it, without too much locational disadvantage.

Most of that is easy to achieve in new urban development. As higher proportions of people get their fair shares of private space, and demand more public space for schools and sports and other activities away from home, many cities will continue to grow even if population numbers don't. Their new parts can be made to distribute benefits equitably. Their old parts are harder to reform. Improvement has to contend with built-in inequalities, and with the politics which defend them. When cities grow too big, i.e. when too many people are forced (by those who locate their jobs and housing) to live and work in reach of a single centre, there are also unavoidable conflicts of locational interest. Cities which are already too big may need some recentring; and a good deal of their land may need to be taken out of the market, and allocated by other means than competitive bidding.

In most industrial societies, except a few which inherit unusually good urban patterns, government should do what it can to limit the size and improve the centring of cities.

There are both common and class reasons for this. When cities grow above a million or so of population (more or less, depending on shape and geography) too many of their problems intensify. They usually cost more to run. They generate more travel, congestion and local pollution per head. They force wasteful rates of demolition and rebuilding on their inner parts. Intense competition for central and accessible locations makes it much harder to solve problems of density, shares of space and – above all – land prices.

These effects may depend as much on the distribution of central activities as on gross metropolitan numbers. London does, and Paris could, do better than some cities with half their numbers, because both have usable land in all directions from their centres. They can be more compact than (for example) lopsided cities with coastal centres. London and Paris afford great pleasure and efficiency to many of their inhabitants. They also exact high prices from others in the cost of services, in money transfers to landowners, and in housing so many of their service populations at battery densities. Most other very big cities do worse, and distribute their costs and benefits with strong class bias.

The size of a city is of very different interest to different classes of its citizens. The richer people are, the more valuable big city centres usually are to them. They are likelier to work in downtown centres. They have more money to spend, and they spend less of it on necessaries available locally and more of it on the specialized shops and services and entertainments which can only be supported in centres with catchments of many millions – i.e. in catchments which include hundreds of thousands of the comparatively rich, including free-spending visitors and tourists. Poorer people may depend as vitally on their cities, but usually on a narrower range of commoner jobs and goods and services. Most of what most families want can be provided, in an affluent telecommunicating society, by a city of a quarter or half a million. Most ordinary people have comparatively few and minor interests in their cities being bigger than that. But plenty of affluent people like cities to be bigger because they are the chief investors in, and users of, the additional diversities that can be supported as cities grow. The rich are also the chief gainers from the rising land values of big cities. They can usually get whatever they want of private land or central location. And they make the public and private investment decisions which affect cities' growth – and often their overgrowth.[26]

'Strong' decentralization – not a rural scatter but a pattern of good small cities – should usually be the policy of the Left. Decentralization isn't easy, but it is one of the fields in which a few early failures have too often led reformers to give up, rather than to improve their methods and try again. It usually takes both push and pull – some restraints (for example on new office or industrial investment) in overgrown cities, and positive public action to develop good alternative locations. The alternatives need to be attractive, interestingly-centred towns or cities. Too many attempts have failed because they concentrated on decentralizing industry and very little else. Towns built on the principle that 'jobs attract people' are generally company towns at worst and one-class towns at best. At good locations on attractive land, where investors and managers and professionals as well as captive employees would like to live, people and jobs can usually attract each other about equally. Public efforts to build new towns, or to attract growth to existing towns and small cities, should rely less than they have often done on tax and transport incentives to industrial investors, and more on providing good education, services and housing in naturally attractive places.

At the same time government should work to improve the distribution of jobs and centres and services through existing metropolitan areas. London works as well as it does partly because even its middle is many-centred, and much of the rest of it houses people at comparatively low densities in districts of distinct character, many with strong centres of their own. Younger metropolitan areas should imitate that as far as they can. 'System cities' and 'new towns in town' can do quite well if they are developed carefully, with attention to where people actually live, work, play, and want to travel, and with some re-focusing of transport and some redistribution of institutions and services. In North America and Australasia too many hospitals, universities, technical and teachers' colleges and high schools and trade schools, suburban office developments, supermarkets and filling stations, theatres, cinemas, pool halls, squash courts and other high and low entertainments have been scattered like confetti along main roads through characterless expanses of housing, in the name of decentralization – or more often in the uncoordinated pursuit of cheap sites. Not houses and gardens, but that formless uncentred litter of facilities on and off public transport routes (which anyway lead only to one dominant downtown centre) is the true and disastrous meaning of 'suburban sprawl'. Policies of recentralization should try to gather those activities to support each other – whereupon they will support other things as well – in strong town centres with their own local transport, local government, day-and-night life, and sense of identity.

For these purposes public planners have more resources than they have usually been allowed to use. One resource is government itself, which constitutes as much as a third of the office work in many cities. It often clusters into metropolitan centres because the public servants rather than the citizens want it there. Nor is the location of private investment always as profit-seeking as it pretends to be: it goes where it suits its directors to live or work, often enough. Without much loss of public or private efficiency, government (if skilful) could be more forceful in directing both kinds of investment to the places where they will do most good for the pattern of urban growth.

Old commitments are obstinate; change is necessarily slow; it shouldn't be hurried by bulldozing houses or people, or forcing mass migrations (even of public servants). But wherever a big metropolis goes on growing, whether by increasing its population or by shaking out its densities, its new growth at least should be made to take a good town-centred form, so that people can live well locally, and be free to use the larger metropolitan networks and centres as much or as little as they like. Where existing commitments and the lie of the land allow them, linear metropolitan forms may sometimes serve these purposes best. They can help smaller centres to compete with big ones, intercepting custom and economizing transport as common routes serve both metropolitan and local travellers; and they can keep most town-dwellers in easy reach of countryside.

Good city shapes and systems and centring *allow* a lot of equities, but don't guarantee them. The detail of the fabric is just as important – and often harder to reform.

Most people like to see interesting new activities appearing in their city and local centres. Most of those who feel cramped like to get more private space, and more public space especially for children. But those are almost the only changes which settled urban communities can be relied on to welcome. Structures of local law and representation should generally be designed to arm rather than disarm people to resist other changes, except where principles of equality dictate otherwise. Local electorates should generally have strong powers to resist compulsory clearances (especially of housing), physical invasion (by motorways and other bulldozers) and some kinds of social invasion (by office developments, industries, supermarkets). The exceptions – when central authorities should sometimes be able to override local opinions – should be for public transport, pipes and wires, and people. People are the likeliest to cause trouble. Government shouldn't force unwilling neighbors on one another; but subject to the respect which any new building ought to pay to its immediate surroundings, neighborhoods should not be able to exclude newcomers on grounds of poverty, color or public housing.

People are one thing, but their numbers may be another. It is scarcely ever true that cities can be made more efficient by subjecting their poorer parts to compulsory redevelopment at high residential density.[27] If that ever does appear to be true of a particular city the Left should apply three rules of thumb. One: deliberate residential redevelopment should include the upgrading of schools and services to the standards currently required in new developments. Two: new inner-city housing should as far as possible displace old industries, warehouses, railyards, coalyards, etc. (as long as they don't employ many locals), rather than displacing existing housing. Three: if denser housing must displace existing housing it should do it where the scope for increasing density is greatest. That will usually be where the existing density is lowest and the existing residents are richest.

But increasing density is rarely a sensible aim for government-aided urban renewal. Overall densities are falling in all affluent cities, for good reasons. Public renewal programs should usually have other aims: to replace incurably bad housing; to improve poor neighborhoods *without* displacing or overcrowding their people; and to improve the general class distribution of residential space, location, work and services. For the first purpose new housing needs to be patched into old neighborhoods or built street by street in 'rolling renewals' which allow people whose houses are to be demolished a genuine option of moving directly into new housing already built nearby – with whatever rent aids or other subsidies are required to make that option real. The second aim, in big cities, should be to take more of every kind of living space – dense and less dense, in each of inner and middle and outer suburbs – out of the open market, to be reserved for classes of people who would otherwise be priced out of many of them. Public agencies need to build or buy plenty of all types of housing, at many and various locations, for rent or sale to appropriate occupiers on terms which prevent resale to richer bidders.[28]

That is also the best way to apply public money to the physical rehabilitation of old housing. Since the recoil against the bulldozer, rehabilitation has become fashionable and a number of governments have offered public grants or loans to private owners to do up their own houses. But such policies face a dilemma. If (as for a time in the United Kingdom) the provisions are liberal, they are taken up by affluent owner-occupiers and landlords more freely than by poor ones; and directly or indirectly they cause a good deal of the upgraded housing to pass from poorer to richer occupiers. So they transfer resources in the wrong direction and may actually raise the price and reduce the stock of well-placed housing available to low incomes. If on the other hand (as in Norway) the aids are offered on strict conditions, they are not used much. The best way through the dilemma is for the public to *buy* whatever it wants to rehabilitate, do it up, then rent or sell it on terms which prevent its re-sale into richer hands. This combines rehabilitation with an accumulating low-income share of inner and middle-suburban living space.

Various other things can be done to reduce the built-in, inherited inequalities of existing cities and suburbs.

Many of those inequalities are related in one way or another to residential segregations. The facts and problems of social mixture and segregation can be infinitely complicated. They provoke intricate argument about the definition, 'grain', type and effect of different degrees and kinds of mixture and segregation. But the segregations which affect equalities are chiefly crude, large-scale segregations by income. Though they are attributed to snobbish social feelings, these gross segregations often arise at least as much from market competition for physically attractive land, accessibility or capital gain. Moreover 'coarse' and 'fine' segregations often arise from different causes and have different effects on equalities. Social, neighborly, face-to-face relations depend heavily on local facts and feelings; but there can be any amount of petty segregation from street to street, within districts where people with widely different incomes nevertheless share shops, services and local taxation and government. Where there is evidence that rich and poor don't want to be immediate neighbors, that may justify segregation from street to street; it doesn't justify segregation from suburb to suburb or from west side to east side unless the hatred reaches a New York or Belfast intensity. Ethnic minorities should ideally be able to find options to cluster or disperse; rich and poor should ideally be able to choose between rich, poor and mixed streets; old people should be able to find old or young, quiet or lively neighbors; people of every income should be able to choose between sparse and crowded, quiet and busy, plain and arty quarters; and so on. All those options are compatible with a rule of thumb that the average income in any local government area, and if possible in any primary school catchment, should never be far from the national average income.

There are a number of reasons why that would be a good rule of thumb. First, taste: I observe that many closely mixed districts exist; they are usually the most interesting; it seems to me that people who like them tend to be more interesting and good-natured than people who don't; and some of them nourish more direct and good social relations across class and income lines than most sociologists suspect (or ever go looking for). Second, democracy: it is usually only the winners who *want* major segregations. Poor neighborhoods sometimes resent rich invasions as they resent other invasions; but wherever poor people have a choice they tend to prefer public housing in mixed or rich neighborhoods to the same housing in ghettos. Parents especially prefer it. Meanwhile one of the most active ambitions in many ghettos is to get out of them, so that the selective emigration of the ablest leaves the rest poorer still. Third, justice: the grosser segregations intensify inequalities of money, land, opportunity, services, local organization and leadership and communal self-defence. Fourth, responsibility: large segregations don't just happen, they are contrived or encouraged by private wealth and public power. Anyone who has any influence on the growth and government of cities must use it in favor of one pattern or another. There is no way to be neutral, and the open market certainly isn't neutral. In the present state of social and economic understanding there are stronger presumptions in favor of encouraging mixtures than of encouraging segregations. Fifth, futures: mixtures are likely to work better as wealth and incomes grow more equal, and they seem likely to make the equalizing easier.

Where segregations persist various things can be done to redress their effects. Rich and poor districts can never have equal (or equalizing) schools – but their schools can have equal money, plant and playing fields. Parks and playgrounds can be distributed equally to rich and poor neighborhoods. Local government is an excellent field for the rule 'from each according to his capacity, to each according to his need'. Local taxation ought to be progressive *both* within *and* between districts. This can be achieved by making transfers from one local government to another, based on the average rateable value per head of population in the area of each. The boundaries and transfers should be designed to put a punitive tax on affluent segregations, so that a rich income or property in a rich district pays higher rates than the same income or property would pay in a mixed district. (At present opposite relations hold almost everywhere in the capitalist world.) Money should go to districts which need it until their public investment reaches equality with others' and sometimes beyond that – poor districts without much private land need *more* public spaces and resources than do districts full of private houses, cars, gardens, pools, workshops, bookshelves and stereos. Poor districts need positive discrimination in the provision of public services, local outdoor and indoor recreations, consumer-protection and tenant-protection services. The distribution of social and advisory services should often be biased in favor of populations which need them most, rather than the (often richer) populations which demand and use them most.

Some of these distributions may be improved by means of area surveys and improvement programs.[29] Good area surveys can do more than list local needs. If they are done cooperatively by citizens and voluntary groups, local government, officers of national agencies and some independent professionals brought in to help, they can often generate better ideas than any of the participants would produce by themselves. Somebody looks at the range and accessibility of local shopping and services. Somebody looks at every kind of movement in the area, finding ways to tame or divert noxious or dangerous traffic and to improve pedestrian safety, public transport and delivery services. Somebody looks for underused land, from industrial yards and fouled river-banks through underused warehouse and utility land (and any surplus churches) to parks which might be better used and streets which might be closed or narrowed to restrict traffic and provide land for other uses. (It is sometimes enough to mark all the underused land on a slum map for whole new networks of movement, recreation and green landscape to suggest themselves.) Somebody compares surveys of local employment and unemployment – if there are wives wanting work close to home, does the area lack any social or child-minding services that might employ them, or private or public employers who might be attracted? If the district needs meeting places or recreations which are not strictly public responsibilities, might they nevertheless be attracted by some public renting or land-dealing? Besides material gains such surveys can have permanent effects in livelier community organization, and they can improve the education of all concerned, including the politicians who presently hear imaginative demands for money, land, shopfront services, street closures, and old rope and timber and locomotives for new styles of playground.

These participant methods work for districts and neighborhoods. On larger scale there are other ways of surveying and redressing inequalities of wealth and opportunity between regions. They have usually concen-

230

trated on jobs and welfare services; they should be developed to include direct aids to city centring and services, and to education and housing.

6

All affluent societies need to attend to building durable equalities into the housing stock. They all need to allot more land, materials and building capacity to housing the poorer quarter or half of their people. North Americans could do enough (though they probably won't) by rationing and redirecting existing flows of new building. Most other societies need to build more than they do now, diverting resources from other uses.

The poorest new housing should be built to much better standards than poor incomes can at present pay for. The half-life of housing is a generation, so it should be built to the expected needs and capacities of the second generation who will occupy it.[30] Plenty of other investment anticipates need in that way. If housing investment doesn't, no later improvement or equalization of incomes can save the next generation from living in spaces designed to the poverties and inequalities of the past.

Government can influence new building in various ways. It can supply research and information. Its planning arrangements can locate and timetable the development of new housing. It can regulate sizes, qualities, standards (but should take care not to do it monotonously). It can ration resources – if basic housing needs labor and materials, government can ban or tax or license less necessary building, including the building of offices and luxurious houses. In the course of its regulation of banks and building societies and insurers it can require them to lend proportions of their funds at specified rates, or to specified classes of customer, or for houses of specified value.[31] It can itself borrow and lend for housing purposes. Above all it can buy, build, deal, rent and sell housing in more diverse and flexible and competitive ways than any governments have yet attempted.[32]

Scarcely any democratic governments have developed an effective role as suppliers of housing. The British are best; but most of their effort was until lately confined to building standard rental housing for a standard type of household. Other governments have built for small proportions of their poor, or financed cooperatives to do so. The housing has often been mean, monotonous, segregated and landless – which has discouraged the poor and the policy-makers from calling for more of it. But it is quite possible to design and staff public-interest trusts and companies to do the business well, if government is determined that they shall

231

do it well, and learns how to choose and direct managers capable of doing it well. The right role for them will vary with national and local circumstances. It should scarcely ever be limited to providing rental housing for the poor. Public housing agencies should be equipped and empowered to buy, build, rent and sell housing; borrow and lend; and where necessary supply other things which neighborhoods need if their housing is to work well. They should often supply some of almost every kind of housing, for families and couples and communes and single occupiers, old and young, settled and transient, poor and not poor. The wider the range of their business, the *less* call they are likely to make on tax revenue. In many of their activities they should compete with the private sector – they should never be confined to the residual role of doing only what the private sector fails to do. Keeping the private sector competitive should be a main part of their business.

That range of activity can serve a lot of purposes at once. It helps to keep the public agencies well informed of needs and market movements, and attentive to customers' preferences. It forces competitive tests of the efficiency of both sectors. It identifies the public-interest operators as suppliers of a wide and respectable range of housing so that public housing need not (of itself) attract hostile feelings. It keeps private enterprisers' rents and prices moderate. It gives government a flexible capacity to add whatever needs to be added to the general housing stock. And it allows plenty of public influence on the allocation of housing to particular classes or needs.

As far as it can, government should usually try to manage the supply and distribution of housing without owning too much of it, just as (for example) it manages national levels of employment without employing everybody. The analogy is appropriate, because distributions and prices of space can affect as many fortunes, for good or ill, as distributions of jobs or taxes do. Land and housing are not as hard to manage as national levels of investment and employment are. But the management has to be skilful and responsive, and the traditional public housing business is only a small part of it. What to buy and build, who to house and how, what pressures to put on which markets, must depend from year to year on changing local facts and forecasts. Market effects are always changing. From time to time particular kinds of private rental housing are allowed to decay; or sold off to their occupiers; or emptied and upgraded and sold to richer buyers; or converted to rooming or boarding uses; or converted from rooming and boarding to other uses; or turned into offices; or demolished because their land is worth more without them. Money markets and mortgage arrangements and rates of inflation encourage new building for one class at one time, for others at other times. These trends help or hurt particular types, groups, classes of people. It is the business of national and local housing managers to see that the short-term effects of the markets leave somewhere for everyone to sleep, and that their long-term effect is to build better standards and equalities into the stock. The public agencies may have to build a good deal; they may buy low-income housing to prevent its demolition or transfer to richer occupiers; they may buy land or housing in affluent districts for transfer to poorer people; they may buy non-residential land and use it for housing, or use it to supply poor neighborhoods with public spaces and services. They may need to apply elements of subsidy for particular purposes. But over time, most of what they do should (and can) be done in the ordinary way of business, costing the taxpayers little or nothing.

Most of these operations need to be managed locally by people with local knowledge. Central authorities are perpetually tempted to 'think big' – to prefer big sites to small, big deals to a dozen small transactions a week, big clearing and rebuilding, and mass movements of people. Central authorities do have to monitor the business, manage its macro-economics, allocate resources to particular purposes and areas and agencies. But most of the practical operations need to be committed to agencies local enough to know their areas well – to know which shopkeepers are prospering, what housing is coming onto the market and what is not, which landlords are thinking of upgrading or selling out, what the local supply of cheap rooms and lodging is like, where alcoholic old men can sleep. They must usually also work knowledgeably with local government, local welfare services, local action groups: and they need to understand local lifestyles and social tolerances. Local and national circumstances will determine whether the best people for the work should be employed by local government, by independent housing agencies or cooperatives, or by public development or renewal corporations. But it will always be important to establish the right divisions of function between central policy-making and locally-sensitive management.

The nature of the work may often call for some deliberate pluralism. Big public housing authorities are often good at dealing fairly with waiting lists of 'standard' families who have to be classified, means-tested or otherwise ordered and served with visibly impartial justice. Different talents may be needed to help ethnic or other minorities to stay together in old neighborhoods if they want to; or to decide when to buy up old lodging houses and make sure (unobtrusively) that they go on housing the diffident or impecunious or disreputable characters they have always housed. Housing the people who need public help most – the poorest, least competent or least popular people – has special difficulties for public agencies precisely because public agencies are, however distantly, arms of government. It is very difficult for bureaucratic housing authorities to offer genuine 'housing of last resort'. This is not usually because public housing officers have (as their critics often allege) stuffily respectable standards; it is because the respectable majority of their customers have them. If customer B has debts, a conviction or two, stinking breath, a different woman and child from the ones he had last year, and a history of unpaid rent and aggrieved neighbors, and if he never thought to put his name down for his next house until he was evicted from his last one, how does any public official get away with housing him ahead of customer A, who can pass the relevant means test but owes nothing and pays on the nail, has a lawful wife and three tidy children, joined the waiting list two years ago, has kept in touch punctually, and knows the relevant local editors and clergymen and the telephone numbers of his representatives in local and national legislatures? There may have to be different agencies for those customers – and even then, subtle deterrents to keep A out of B's way. As private landlording of cheap housing declines (or grows extortionate) public agencies have to develop new roles and tactics. They must sometimes (for example) buy the sort of old housing the poorest customers are used to, improve it but not too obviously, then distance themselves by leasing it to the kind of management the customers will accept – charities for some purposes, commercial landlords and landladies for others, welfare officers for others again. Agencies which are themselves managing some properties can be ground landlords of others, without detailed powers to interfere. They can then house A themselves, and tell B where to try instead.

Some comprehensive agencies may manage to run big quantities of all those lines of business from one head office. Others may do better to divide and specialize. Their success or failure will depend mainly on the people they choose for the work. It demands right mixtures of sympathy, commitment and skill. But those are not too hard to find, and the work is not too hard to do (though some traditional public housing authorities would find it impossible, or quickly make it so). All the detailed lines of action suggested above are being done well somewhere, on large or small scale, already. To orchestrate them, and get the scale right, and begin the build more deliberate equalities into the whole stock, should be no harder than plenty of the work that governments already do well enough in other fields.

How should such policies be financed? The answer depends on the way capital markets are managed in conditions of inflation.

7

There has been a mistake in the response of many capital markets to inflation; but unlike most ill effects of inflation, it is curable by institutional action.

When money values are stable, debts maintain both nominal and real value over time. When money is unstable they can do one or the other but not both. There are then two options. Lenders and borrowers can agree to go on specifying their capital obligations in nominal terms, and cope with inflation by raising interest rates. Or they can specify debts in real terms (for example by indexing capital debts to a consumer price index) whereupon interest rates can behave as they do in stable conditions. To continue nominal lending in conditions of inflation is to 'innovate by inertia'. Obligations become unpredictable; components of early capital repayment are built into interest rates; all credit effectively shortens. The economic effects of this change are devastating. Firms and industries are sorted out as they never were before, according to their capacities to adapt to short credit and steeply sloped requirements for real repayment. Differences which never mattered in stable conditions become critical. Some industries can live on share capital and customers who pay cash. Others sell cash goods but need long credit for producers. Housing needs short credit for producers but long credit for investors or consumers. Inflation therefore changes many competitive relativities. Industries which depend on long credit at continuous prices over time lose resources to others, or to unemployment. There are consequent changes in the structure of the economy. But the new competitive test ('Who can do best on least or shortest credit?') has none of the social efficiency of the test it displaces ('Who can use the capital most profitably, however long he needs it for?'). Economists can think through the implications; they will find that the classical link between consumer preference and efficient allocation of resources is no longer there. The machine is likely to produce less than it did, and is certain to produce a less-desired schedule of goods.

From this distortion, housing is the worst sufferer. In stable conditions there are level, dependable relationships between personal incomes, capacities to pay for housing, and long-term rates of interest. Small

235

depositors in banks and building societies, and many of the same people as borrowers for housing, are able to run the bottom third (or so) of the capital market to their mutual advantage at low rates of interest. But if the institutions insist on nominal terms of debt under inflation, rates of interest rise and require high early rates of repayment. That excludes poorer households from borrowing, or paying enough rent to service the debts of landlords using borrowed capital. Because a house costs three or four years' income there is a multiplier – each 1% of interest adds 3 or 4 to the % of income which the household must pay for its house. If repayment at 3% interest takes 20% of income, repayment at 7% interest takes 30% of income; 10% interest takes 40% of income; and so on. Those who *can* still borrow are encouraged to buy more housing than they otherwise would; so the terms of debt have the double effect of reducing allocation to housing, and redistributing it in a reactionary way.

Capital markets should be reformed to offer real as well as nominal terms of debt. As lenders and borrowers bid for the terms which suit them best, interest rates can sort out the volume of each flow in an ordinary market way. If that is done, a great many housing problems should cure themselves as households recover effective capacity to bid for capital and pay for its use at continuous prices over time. Many public housing programs could then be financed from the market without subsidy, and the rest (for the poorest households) would need revenue subsidies on quite modest scale.

By itself, that capital reform would not remove inequities between those who own their housing and those who rent it. The inequities are great. Between households with equal incomes, spendable income after taxes and housing costs can differ by as much as a quarter or a third over the households' life-times. Some reformers want to tax owners in various ways, most severely by counting the notional rents of their houses as taxable income. The technical case for doing that is derived, partly by mistaken reasoning, from some bad value-premises concealed in the structure of orthodox economic theory. To understand the issue, economists can read the work of Patricia Apps, *Child Care Policy in the Production–Consumption Economy* (Melbourne: Victorian Council of Social Service, 1975). Pragmatists can meanwhile attend to helping tenants rather than hurting owners. Tenants can be helped by housing allowances, tax concessions, low rents, rents which buy equity. Scandinavian and Australian public housing agencies have effective ways of delivering equity and ownership to public tenants. Extending ownership to everyone who wants it is a main part of the answer to this problem – and easy to do, in any equalizing society.

8

How can land and housing markets be reformed without intolerable measures of confiscation and bureaucracy?

There is no doubt that they need to be reformed, and to run under deliberate public influence. Free markets cannot be expected to arrive at good allocation and pricing of urban land and location. Even the most extreme believers in the efficiency of market mechanisms will usually concede that open markets may work badly where there are significant externalities, monopolies, or bad distributions of spending power. Many transactions in land have elements of all those inperfections, and of others as well. There are unproductive risks when investors have to gamble on other investors' locational decisions. Processes of urban growth often motivate landowners to behave in socially inefficient ways. Professional readers who want to understand the business will learn it best from the works of G. Max Neutze (published in not-very-accessible form by the Organization for Economic Co-operation and Development; the Centre for Environmental Studies at 62 Chandos Place, London; the Australian National University; and the Department of Urban and Regional Development, Canberra). For people who are more impressed by practice than theory, some British new towns manage their land well, by the method of public monopoly. Swedes apply good principles to the pricing of residential land, but distribute the land itself very unequally. Germany develops urban land with technical efficiency, but distributes it to aggravate inequalities and segregations. Some Canadian provinces are developing urban land banks for negative purposes of 'avoiding shortage'. The best current performance may be that of the state government of South Australia. For a generation it managed its urban land markets indirectly, without compulsion. A change of national government allowed it to adopt in 1973 the methods recommended by Neutze which include some compulsory acquisition, but still no confiscation or 'nationalization'. Urban land is distributed with unusual equality and serviced with unusual efficiency. A high proportion of it is owned by its occupiers. Land prices are about half, and housing rents are about two-thirds, of their levels in comparable Australian cities.

So how should these markets be managed? What follows is a review of alternative approaches to the task, beginning with some over-simple ones which ought to be avoided.

237

Price control of housing sales and rents can usually work well in a permanent way only if it is used gently in support of other, stronger policies. By themselves severe price controls tend to breed black markets, and evasive devices to transfer the use of land without transferring title to it. Rent controls also can sometimes be evaded, and they encourage private landlords to maintain their houses badly or to sell them or turn them over to other uses. Regulation *by itself* can't achieve much, for long, for the mass of poorer tenants or would-be buyers.

I don't believe there is any way to reduce or equalize the price of land by taxing it differently. Some economists believe that people have fixed sums to spend on land and location, so that if taxes rise, prices have to fall. In real life that doesn't seem to happen; buyers pay the old price plus the new tax, and spend less on other things (or set about increasing their incomes, or changing their governments). When property taxes go up, rents go up – but rarely come down if the taxes come down. Sales taxes go onto sale prices. Special taxes, for example on undeveloped land, rarely induce owners to develop land copiously enough to depress market prices; instead the taxes go, as 'holding charges', onto prices. Some town planners want to tax the betterment of land as it first comes into urban use, then use that revenue to finance comprehensive and compulsory redevelopments in older urban areas – a scheme fairly described as raising the price of new urban land in order to raise the price of old urban land. The desire to 'capture the betterment for the public' is understandable but it can't really be done by taxation. If the tax is set to take most of the betterment it restricts the supply of land and raises its price; if it is set to avoid that effect it simply goes onto the price of 'bettered' land. A correct approach to betterment should try to reduce it altogether by keeping land cheap; and to take any betterment that does occur in the form of profit on public dealing.

Subsidizing the demand for land is usually as foolish as taxing its supply. Equalities can rarely be improved by providing bigger mortgage loans, or by subsidizing tenants to pay higher rents to private landlords. Government should always take care how it operates on the demand side of the housing and land markets. It must – and everywhere does – have a good deal of direct or indirect influence on mortgage lending. The amount lent to each buyer should ideally be geared to the desired housing standard and to the costs of an honestly competitive building industry. But wherever the land-price element of house-price is much above zero – i.e. wherever new houses are priced much above what it costs to build them and develop and service their land – bigger loans are more likely

238

to enrich the suppliers of land than to improve the houses or reduce the buyers' deposits. Similarly, rent subsidies should usually be applied only to public housing or to other housing under effective rent control; otherwise they enrich landlords rather than tenants. It may be possible to get *more* houses built by the indirect method of stimulating demand – but only if the demand for bricks and mortar can be separated from the demand for land or desirable location. (There are various ways of marketing the two separately, and of getting competitively priced private building onto publicly supplied or price-controlled land.) So whether it chooses to stimulate building directly, or indirectly by financing demand, government should never try to attract more land into the market by helping people to offer more money for it. Most public operations in the land market should be on the supply side.

To some reformers that suggests nationalization. 'Nationalizing' land can have various meanings, none very helpful. It can mean general confiscation and conversion to leasehold. That produces more bureaucracy and seems massively unnecessary for most people's housing and for many rural smallholdings. Confiscation also works unfairly between people who happen to own land and those who happen to own other capital. It makes sense only in the context of a revolutionary confiscation of all capital – and even that would do well to exempt most private houses and back yards.

Those objections need not apply to a 'top-end' confiscation. The next chapter discusses a type of confiscatory, once-only capital redistribution which would take assets only from the richest five or ten per cent of citizens. That would have the double advantage of flattening the pyramid of land prices, and of giving public agencies a bank of business and residential property for various uses and redistributions.

Nationalization can alternatively mean compulsory purchase with full compensation. That makes no sense as a general policy: the mint could scarcely print enough paper to pay for it, and it would still leave most of the population occupying the land it occupies already. But if on the other hand compulsory purchase is applied only to big holdings – to investment properties rather than owner-occupied properties – it pays all big owners at price levels established by the recent transactions of a very few of them; so it secures and realizes immense private capital gains many of which need never be realized at all if the pyramid of prices could simply be deflated. It also misses the chance to discriminate between richer and poorer owners; and it does nothing immediately to deflate prices or improve equalities – those effects have to depend on the procedures

239

which are introduced to replace free buying and selling. Similarly, because it applies to everyone, mass conversion to leasehold may in itself do very little to restrain the prices at which the citizens can buy and sell rights to occupy land. Any attack on the pyramid of prices may have to include *some* replacement of marketing by administrative allocation; but the less there has to be, especially for the mass of ordinary housing, the better. The market works well for exchanges between people with comparable resources.

A better strategy than nationalization or universal leasehold might have three elements.

(1) Countries which don't have general registration of land titles should introduce it. A public register records all titles, and debts and encumbrances on them, so that rights which are not registered don't exist and aren't enforceable, and any unregistered land becomes public property. The register can also record sales, prices, and current values for purposes of rating and taxation.

(2) Public agencies should be big dealers in real estate, and should deal with the over-riding purpose of keeping most residential land cheap. In some cities steady public dealing is enough to achieve that. Where it is not, the dealing may need to be strengthened by some price controls, some compulsory purchase, and some measures to kill the business of private speculative investment in the inflation of land prices.

In most small cities it should be enough to adopt the practice of buying land for urban conversion at rural-use valuation, compulsorily where necessary. It should then be sold *cheaply* into urban use. If that is done on small scale it merely hands capital gifts to the lucky urban buyers. So it should be done on big enough scale to establish the low prices generally.

In big cities where big operators or intense locational competition have already built a high pyramid of prices, it may be necessary to be radical, i.e. to break what capitalists regard as the rules of the game (or the laws of nature). Public agencies should buy whatever already-urban property they need for housing or public purposes, with or without compulsion, at market prices. They should lease or resell it cheaply – which means that they may often have to allocate it to users by need or waiting time or other social considerations. The terms of sale or lease can protect it against resale at higher prices. The public dealers will lose a lot of money. Those losses should be met from annual capital taxes on defined categories of real property in that city or region: income-bearing property, and owner-occupied houses above defined values, which stand on land

240

valued above a defined value per hectare. The taxable levels of value should be set to exempt a high proportion of owner-occupied houses and smallholdings, and to give proprietors an incentive to keep the land prices of their properties below the taxable threshold. The rates of tax should vary annually as necessary to recover the public dealing losses. If the public dealers do their business properly, rich proprietors as a class should supply the land the public needs at prices the public can pay, while (as a class) sharing their losses fairly. When such policies are introduced there may be serious transitional troubles and inequities. There may need to be 'small claims tribunals' to compensate people who can show that they are personally poor losers as shareholders in rich properties. But – compared with the billions transferred from poorer to richer by the operation of (say) the London or Sydney land markets – I believe the trouble would be worth while. Most land would soon be owned by its users and occupiers, or by public agencies.

(3) The state should create for itself a power to 'close' particular land markets, i.e. to become sole buyer from private parties and sole seller to them in proclaimed areas, or types of property. Its agencies could then apply, at some strategic points, a type of price control which is proof against black marketing, though it would sometimes have to be reinforced by some compulsory purchase.

The more drastic of these powers should be used sparingly. Where they're not needed they should not be created at all. Private marketing has most of the advantages claimed for it. As long as the bidding is between user and user, without speculative investors bidding to buy monopolist advantages *against* the users, open marketing won't usually push residential prices too high, except in some specially attractive parts of the bigger cities. Those can be somewhat mixed and desegregated by public developers; and for the remainder, affluent people can safely be allowed to pay one another high prices.

If they are intelligently managed, these policies can be quite unoppressive to most of the citizens. Except for some poorer expectations of capital gain, a majority of households and other productive users of land need scarcely be disturbed at all.

9

In summary: Land and housing should be traded in managed markets, with public agents operating wherever possible as competitive rather than monopolist suppliers, and using their tougher powers sparingly, under legal and political safeguards. They should work to distribute land and housing first, money second; but both equitably. Their dealing should aim to make owner-occupation of houses, workshops, small shops and other smallholdings as secure and widely available as possible, at prices as close as possible to building costs; and to make absent ownership and business investment *in land as such* less attractive than productive investment in building, manufacture, commerce or services. Most of the unequalizing type of capital gain and rent-taking from property should cease.

Would people vote for these reforms? Most of those who make a business of gain from real estate would oppose them. Most people who own more real estate than a house or a family farm would lose some wealth to levies or price deflation or both. What would be the responses of the much larger numbers of owner-occupiers who would escape levies, but lose some expectations of capital gain from their houses? Some are affluent or conservative folk who would vote Right in any circumstances. But most people don't buy their houses chiefly to make money from them; if they spend three or four years' income to buy a house they'll be content to know that they can expect that real value back when they sell it. Many – enough to defeat reform in most countries at present – could doubtless be scared into voting against 'socialist confiscation' even though they would be in no danger of suffering any. All would need to learn by experience that they were offered good rather than bad administration of such novel schemes. But as the effects of property booms and bankruptcies, and of housing shortages and battery housing policies, and of soaring mortgage interest rates and other inconveniences continue, some such policies as these may become acceptable to majorities before long, if the Left can design and present and manage them well enough.

Much of the argument of this chapter has assumed that reforms of environmental management and urban planning and land and housing have to be attempted in societies which still have their present inequalities of wealth and income. If wealth and income were more equally distributed some of the suggested reforms would be unnecessary and many could be done more simply. Redistribution of wealth and income would not solve all the domestic problems – the richest people will still get the best houses even if they're only richer by a dollar or two – but it would transform a number of them.

10
Shares of wealth and income

To share goods more equally, democracies must control prices and incomes and the distribution of capital wealth. Current attempts to do those things don't work, and some of the dynamics of inequality which need to be controlled are themselves changing. The most obvious is the mechanism of inflation.

1

The new inflation is not a simple malfunction of the economic system. It is better understood as a new phase, characterized by new distributions and uses of power, in the history of social organization. Its economic manifestations may so far have been resisted most successfully by communist dictatorships, and least successfully by capitalist dictatorships, but in varying degrees they afflict all systems. For the democracies there is no way out of the new trouble by retreat to the past, though there may be some disastrous attempts at that, with or without some years of world depression. From the threatened war of everyman against everyman the democracies must work their way forward to some new principles of order and social distribution. If the distinctive personal freedoms and securities of democracy are to survive, there is not much doubt what the new principles will have to be. When they have been established, the change may not be regretted. But the transition is bound to be dangerous and if it is too chaotic or protracted it may have terrible human and social costs.

The troubles arise from accumulating changes in the amount and distribution of bargaining power, in a broad sense which includes public and private coercive power as well as pricing, hiring-and-firing and wage-bargaining power. Owners and employers have always bargained with a good deal of governmental help and protection. Through the present century political equality, technical change and accumulating skill have enabled some of the ranks of labor to attract some of the same help and protection. Employees can now organize with some security from

243

private and state coercion and from theft of funds, victimization of leaders, and strike-breaking or wage-lowering by non-union labor. So workers can strike without starving, or restrict production without striking. These rights were built by slow steps then strengthened by the management of fuller employment. The result is not an equal social distribution of bargaining power but the power is more widely spread than ever before and it is not fanciful to say that there has been some absolute increase of it: as labor has gained strength, capital has not lost strength correspondingly. Instead it has learned to deflect some of the force of labor's bargaining onto consumers and other third parties; and at the same time the hard bargainers, stronger in attack than in defence, generate a dynamic instability by continually over-succeeding against each other. Wage claims are met and passed on in prices, which prompt more wage claims. Capital-intensive or otherwise profitable industries pay wages which others then claim on grounds of equity regardless of their industries' capacities to pay. But capacities to pay have a new adaptability. Market leaders set prices which others soon follow; consumers confused by incessantly changing prices pay them; producers and distributors learn how often it is now possible to push prices up a little sooner or further than costs. Modern economies have such imperfect competition and non-interchangeable capital that pricing responds less and less to classical considerations and more and more to arbitrary ideas about the margins on turnover or the returns to capital that are 'reasonable'. All parties – wage bargainers, shoppers, borrowers, lenders and investors – learn to add double margins to their forward calculations: one margin for the expected inflation and a bit more (as a rational response to greater uncertainty) for the unexpected. Hallowed relativities are upset; anxious wage claims leapfrog one another. And there are other mechanisms of wage-leading, price-leading, hedging, cheating, emulation and anticipation which institutionalize inflation and help to accelerate it. If the old demand inflation was too much purchasing power chasing too few goods, the new social inflation is too much baffling and bargaining power chasing not only too few goods, but also too few certainties and securities.

It is worth considering how an extreme or pure model of such a hard-bargaining system would work. Imagine a society with a perfect division of labor. That means perfect interdependence: every single member's contribution of capital or labor is essential if there is to be any production at all, so every member has an individual capacity to stop the whole productive machine. Each if he understands his interest will refuse to let the machine start unless he is promised a high price for his contribution. The asking-prices will inevitably add up to more than the total that the machine can produce. In the wrangling that must therefore occur, *economic* bargaining power is equal: every bargainer can effectively withhold the whole social product. So the share which each gets will have to be decided by force or (in this free democratic model) by capacity to hold out. As starvation drives one after another to lower his asking-price in the hope of getting the machine to produce something for him to eat, those who can afford to hold out longest for most will do best. If the contenders have equal capacities to hold out (equal selfishness, obstinacy and hoarded resources) they will eventually agree, just before they all starve to death simultaneously, to work for exactly equal rewards. They will do so because they have equal bargaining power, not because their contributions to the productive process have equal value by any other standard. In practice people don't have equal coercive or holding-out power so the weak will agree to work for less than the strong, and the product will be distributed in proportion to unequal bargaining power rather than to unequal values (by any other standard) of the members' productive contributions. Such a system rewards hoarding, ruthlessness, and nothing else. It motivates scarcely any of the *better* work or management or allocation of resources which unequal rewards are popularly supposed to motivate.

Real life differs from that model in a number of ways. There is great interdependence in advanced economies; many trades are essential trades; substituting organized groups for individuals, there is indeed the over-supply of bargaining power which the model depicts. And it is not confined to economic bargaining. Students combine to coerce their educational masters. (One effect is a general 'grade inflation'.) Young men combine to defeat systems of military conscription, or to make military forces ineffective in wars they don't approve of. But despite the general increase and the wider sharing of coercive power, not everybody has a share of it. Some people (capitalists, solvent subsistence farmers) can hold out for a long time, living on their own resources. Some (power suppliers, transport workers, policemen) can disrupt society very quickly by stopping work. Some (miners, commercial farmers, builders, factory workers, many investors) supply things that can be banked so if they stop work the effects take longer to bite. There are also many weak bargainers, and beggars weaker still. Dependants, pensioners and people in marginal trades have nothing essential to withhold. A great many people whose work *is* essential are not organized to bargain. For example farm laborers, housewives or women workers in food processing and distributing industries could stop the productive machine but they are not organized to do so. The presence of those and other weak bargainers allows strong bargainers to gain at the expense of the weak instead of at the expense of one another. They do it indirectly through the mechanism of inflation. Strong bargainers compromise by promising each other more rewards than the machine can produce. Partly this makes no difference – people adapt their bargaining to the inflating currency. Partly it helps to keep the machine at work – inflation is a face-saver for bargainers, and there may even be some value in the hopes and illusions which people accept as substitutes for material goods. But chiefly inflation helps the rich to fleece the poor, the strong to fleece the weak.

This happens in three general ways. Inflation adds to the traditional advantages with which the strong get money, spend it, and save and invest it. In getting it, competition becomes more continuous and dynamic. When money was stable (or even when the rate of inflation was a predictable 3 or 5%) people could choose to rest content with what they earned, stirring themselves occasionally to demand some share of growth or to defend their incomes if directly attacked. Now that money values move continuously every income is under continuous attack, and can only be defended by active counter-attack. The effect of this is to increase the rewards for strength and skill and the penalties for weakness. Most of the traditional protections of the weak consisted of established rights and rates of reward which were safe once they were won. Inflation erodes such established positions – including many freely conceded, widely agreed relativities. Established positions now have to be recaptured every six or twelve months. Even in the few societies which peg some weak wages and welfare allowances to price indexes, inflation erodes other resources of the weak and the poor. It erodes poor savings faster than most rich savings – poor savings get the lowest interest, poor borrowing (mostly through consumer credit) pays the highest. People have to teach their children not to save but instead to be clever debtors – and a few more foundations of personal security and social trust dissolve. The weak also suffer as spenders. Housewives and pensioners used to know exactly what everything in the shops was worth. Now that prices leapfrog confusingly, unskilled shoppers are easier to deceive. Market knowledge obsolesces overnight. Shopkeepers exploit the confusion to push their margins up a point or two higher than necessary, a week or two ahead of wholesale movements. Corner shops do it, dealers in land

246

do it, multinational oil companies do it – anyone in a position to fiddle a price does it to a public stripped of what used to be its knowledgeable market expertise. As in getting income so in spending it the strong, clever and knowledgeable do even better than they used to do and the weak and poor do worse.

Besides its strictly economic effects inflation also erodes some political and social decencies. If the currency were stable it would often be hard (in welfare democracies) to reduce poor incomes or even to stop them getting some share of growth. But when to hold their real incomes people need (say) 15% more money income each year, weak bargainers can be 'given' a 'generous' fraction of that rate of 'improvement' while the strong bargain their way a point or two ahead of it. Employers, affluent salary-earners and well-organized workers might not have the face to demand standstills or cuts in other people's pensions, welfare allowances or public services or in the wages of women's and other weak bargainers' occupations for the purpose of pre-empting or transferring income directly from poorer people to themselves. The indirect mechanism of inflation allows them to do it without appearing to do it and often without wanting to do it. While appearing to bargain chiefly against each other the strong bargainers together take – at the very least – an unfair and unequalizing share of any growth.

Sometimes there appear to be compensating effects. Ordinary people can pay off old mortgages more easily – but most of the losers from that are small savers rather than rich investors, and the poorest quarter or half of most populations can't buy houses at all, or share in the capital gain of the land under them. Wages take an increasing share of national income – but the poorest wages get a declining share, and if profits lose a point or two, plenty of profit-earners make up for it with high salaries or capital gains.

So there are class transfers, and some increase of inequalities within the working classes. There are also general losses of social efficiency and personal security. From troubled managers to anxious pensioners, people of every class 'wonder where it will end' as their skills become erratic and their old certainties are shaken. Habitual bargaining routines and expectations are upset. Traders prosper or not according to the payment delays they can get away with. Traditional economic theory is less and less useful. The quality of a good deal of government and public and private business management declines as fine estimating becomes impossible, long-term planning and lending and contracting become hazardous, contingency allowances have to increase, and investment decisions –

sometimes distorted already by tax considerations – are distorted further to take advantage rather than disadvantage from the inflationary process. Gold, land, commodity futures, and 'confidence markets' in anything from art to postage stamps attract capital more busily than useful manufacturing or services do. Houses are built five years behind demand, offices three years ahead of it – and the rents of both rise faster than the price of anything else.

If they stand back from the confusion to look for underlying causes of it, many people – with philosophical help from the Right – are inclined to blame greedy materialism in general and organized labor in particular. 'Suddenly everyone thinks he can get a ten per cent raise out of a two per cent increase of productivity' and 'the labor unions have simply taken over the hijack business – they're clean out of hand'. But most of the greed is compulsory and defensive, driven by a rational anxiety to 'keep up'; and so is three quarters or more of anything labor gets from its hardest bargaining. Organized labor is no more selfish than most of the other parties; and among the hard bargainers its interests are the least hostile to equality. With a few comparatively rich exceptions, when labor bargains against private capital it almost always bargains for poorer against richer – for a result which would reduce inequalities if the rich didn't pass the bill on to other poor. When labor bargains against public employers its gains could often reduce inequalities if public pricing, taxing and salary-fixing policies cooperated to that end. When labor bargains chiefly for parity with other labor, that need injure equality only if the parties are already richer than they ought to be. Some strong trades bargain for rates above the national average of incomes, but most organized labor still bargains from below it. The exceptions – some engineers, printers, builders, automakers – are comparatively few, and still positively self-restrained by comparison with higher public servants, academics, doctors and airline pilots; and unlike those toughs they are usually bargaining for *local* equality, i.e. against executives and shareholders richer than themselves.

Workers can rarely defend or improve general social equalities by bargaining in any other way. If they abstain from an available gain it is likely to be snapped up by employers or other hard bargainers; it won't often go to lower product prices, to raise the wages of charwomen or pensioners or to improve public services. In a war of everyman against everyman the strong labor unions can't help being the men in the middle. They have no power to determine who shall lose what they gain, or gain what they lose. They bargain directly against capital or for parity with

248

others who bargain against capital. They don't control the mechanisms of pricing and inflation through which public and private employers choose to deflect the force of their bargaining back onto themselves and poorer sufferers.

Often enough those who do control those mechanisms succeed in pretending that they don't, and that it is the strong unions alone who propel inflation, squeeze the poor and endanger national currencies and exchange balances. One trouble is that the various contributors to inflation have different visibility. Even under current policies of price- and profit-control, many prices and executive rewards and most rates of profit, dividend and capital gain can be adjusted without much bargaining or publicity at all. So the only action by which organized labor can try to improve its own shares or defend general equalities is deftly deflected by employers not only to increase inequalities but also to divide the Left and reduce political support for it. Labor unions become unpopular with pensioners and other weak bargainers. They lose middle-class sympathy. Most fatally for the Left, they become unpopular with their members' wives. Parties of the Left find it harder than ever to get elected. Politically secure, the salaried and propertied and self-employed classes continue to work the mechanisms which assure their own percentages of economic turnover, leaving the poor to get ahead only at the expense of one another.

And the poor do sort themselves out at the expense of one another. It is in this way, bedevilled by mechanisms which they can't control, that the groups of low earners who can and do bargain hard – the strong labor unions – find themselves in an alliance of the richer 55% against the rest. (I use that expression often and never mean it literally. There are usually minorities on both sides voting 'out of their class'; there are loners, do-gooders, cross-bench voters and unselfish voters at every income level; and '55%' is shorthand for any sufficient margin of numbers or influence.) However unwelcome, the hard bargainers' alliance is a Right alliance whose successes increase inequalities between middle and poor incomes.

This uneasy alliance of enemies, though desired by neither, is quite likely to become, for want of better, the program of the more intelligent and realistic Right. If you can't lick 'em, enlist them – or at least corrupt them. Upper classes have often responded to changing balances of advantage by making prudent extensions of privilege. Old upper classes have recruited new middle classes. Rich white South Africans have recruited poor whites. And despite their hard-bargaining appearances, many rich industries are doing their best to buy good relations with labor at consumers' expense, with higher wages, fringe benefits, participant arrangements, worker directors and shareholders. More and more of the Right may come to see a tacit alliance of all the hard bargainers as offering in the long run the surest defence of inequality.

Though it works, that unloving alignment does not work very smoothly. First, the continuing competition for shares within the upper 55% may propel inflation faster than is really convenient for either capital or labor. Second, labor is scarcely a willing ally and is always likely to be dissatisfied with the share it gets of the loot. Third, democratic government doesn't always help as much as it might. The winning alignment has to rely on government to limit the general rate of inflation to less than the winners' rate of advance, i.e. to restrain weak bargainers' incomes and public services while the strong forge ahead. But government has an independent and stronger interest in restraining inflation because unlike the members of the winning alignment it can be thrown out if too many losers unite against it. So it often tries honestly enough to apply wage and price restraints to strong and weak alike. Many of the strong evade many of the restraints. Strong capital evades more than strong labor does. But government itself employs some strong labor, and is a tougher employer than most private employers are, because unlike them it cannot afford to pass too many wage claims on to consumers and taxpayers. Strong labor in public employment nevertheless wants to keep up with strong labor in private employment. So wherever the public is a big employer of strong labor the toughest confrontations tend to occur in the public industries.

At the same time the winning allies continue to be enemies in politics. Both use government against the losers but each also wants to use it against the other. Property, business and salaried wealth get various advantages from Right government; strong labor can usually extract some advantages (if only in the form of fuller employment and weaker wage restraints) from Left government. Because organized labor tends to be specially strong under Left government and business tends to be specially irresponsible under Left government, the Right alignment of the two may often do well enough under weak Left government.

To sum up: labor is quite right to bargain hard in its continuing competition with capital. But one effect of such hard bargaining, in what is unavoidably a war of everyman against everyman, is that strong labor deserts the possibility of a Left alliance of the poorer 55% and instead – however uneasily, unwillingly or abusively – joins a Right alliance of the richer 55%. Inflation continues at a fast rate and the 55% who survive it best use it (however voluntarily or involuntarily) to exploit the rest. The winning factions meanwhile serve their interests and perhaps their consciences by voting for opposite political parties. That allows the losers some influence as arbiters in national elections, so life is uncomfortable for politicians who are likely to be put into and out of office at minimum constitutional intervals by a chronically dissatisfied public. But whichever party governs, capital gains are never restrained as effectively as incomes are; strong bargainers' incomes are never restrained as effectively as weak incomes are; the Right alignment prospers and the inequalities which hurt most continue to increase. So do all the evil social and personal consequences of continuing inflation, insecurity and unequalization.

Most of that is happening already. To call it a scenario is merely to foresee it continuing until the Left succeeds in stopping it. Nobody else can stop it. Though the Right did not plan or desire it, it is the process which the Right has to tolerate and continue as the best defence of inequality in the circumstances.

The best way to understand the nature of the trouble is to read Aubrey Jones's *The New Inflation: The Politics of Prices and Incomes* (London, 1973). That is also the best way to understand the limits of the Right's very best intentions. Aubrey Jones's intentions are much better than most others on the Right. *The New Inflation* is a penetrating and illuminating book. It assumes or implies that the bulk of neoclassical economic theory is bankrupt because the economic system no longer works as described (if it ever did). The author believes that we must now move decisively from bargained incomes and prices and profits to regulated incomes and prices and profits. He believes that the regulation must be seen to be independent – independent of government as well as capital and labor, since the parties who govern often have associations with one or the other. He wants to make adjudication work by making it acceptable to the strong bargainers, and he wants to make it work humanely by having weak bargainers more strongly represented. But – reading between the lines and noticing what the book does *not* say – the whole balancing act is designed to restore *traditional* stabilities: to arrive more realistically and without inflationary side-effects at the distributions and shares that we have always been accustomed to.

The full significance of this proposal is much more remarkable than its author makes it out to be. It amounts to this: wages, prices and profits must from now on be fixed by public tribunals. That requires that we give up whatever free-enterprise efficiencies have up to now been achieved by free bargaining, free pricing and marketing and profit-maximization. *We should nevertheless perpetuate the particular inequalities which those freedoms used to generate.* The freedoms and efficiencies were the only excuses for such cruel inequalities. Without the freedoms most of the larger inequalities will perform no useful economic functions at all. Nevertheless it is the freedoms and efficiencies that we must now *give up*, and the inequalities that we must now *perpetuate by direct state control.* Of course Jones does not recommend these illogical cruelties so explicitly. He hopes that good as well as bad trends will continue: that there will be more of the ameliorations and protections for the poor that have often characterized democratic progress. But he does not expect or recommend any radical redistributions of either capital or income, and his proposals would as far as possible take the present distributions of capital and income 'out of politics'. Summarized, his book recommends full socialist bondage with full capitalist inequality: the bureaucracy of socialism without its equalities or efficiencies, and the inequalities of capitalism without its freedoms or efficiencies.

I don't believe that the Left will fall for this – least of all that militant labor will. There are immediate and long-term, practical and theoretical reasons for expecting and hoping that they will not. The most immediate reason is that labor is not likely to surrender its bargaining strength while the rich retain theirs and continue to get richer. Many of the rich may very well evade new income controls at least to the degree that they already evade attempts to control or tax their inheritances, gifts, gambling and property and other capital gains, business incomes and perquisites, lease-backs and tax-farms and extra-territorial devices. Ineffective control of those is now to be coupled with effective control of mass wages. A tough version of that program, as it would be applied by many less tender than Aubrey Jones, amounts to capital owners and the rich salariat saying to the stronger unions: 'Join us. Let the middle classes keep two or three or four workmen's wages each; let those with property keep five or ten or a hundred; let the very rich continue to do what they like – and in return, the toughest labor can have one-and-a-half or two wages each.' Aubrey Jones's more civilized version would try to prevent further unequalizing within the lower three quarters of incomes, while still putting no very convincing restraints on high incomes or capital wealth. His control of prices and profits might be no more effective than other controls on rich gains have been, and they are in any case intended to perpetuate past rates of profit, not to reduce them.

If organized labor submits to either type of differential control – if it accepts *any* cure for inflation which institutionalizes past inequalities after their economic justifications have disappeared – it will have lost a critical battle, and a critical opportunity. (It may well also in the long run have lost money.) On Jones's terms it will have surrendered to Russian-style state-enforced scales of inequality. On the tougher terms to be expected of most Right governments it may not have helped its own fortunes much but it will have elected to help those above it against those below it, towards American patterns of inequality and perhaps of personal ruthlessness and internal working-class strife.

There remains a more fundamental objection to Aubrey Jones's program[33] and to all others like it. Either it is spurious – merely a ribbon-wrapped wage-freeze – or else it destroys capitalism and supplies nothing workable to replace it.

To control inflation it is already obvious that it is necessary to control prices, profits and a majority of incomes. To control those it will probably become necessary to control distributions and uses of capital too. Even without that – even if controls remain as partial and conservative as Jones recommends and most democratic governments already accept – such controls must drastically alter the fundamental mechanisms of capitalist organization, allocation and motivation. What will remain of the dynamic of capitalism when its profits, prices and personal rewards are state-controlled? There will still be differential pay within and between occupations. There may still be economic penalties for badly conceived or badly managed investment. So there will be incentives to work. But the positive mechanisms on which capitalism relies to motivate cost-saving competition and innovation, to attract labor and skill to the most productive uses, and to attract investment and allocate resources to the most productive uses, *must simply cease to operate.* Jones insists – and the current governmental schemes won't work unless they also insist – that rates of profit on turnover and return to capital must be pegged. Any efficiency-gains must therefore go to lower prices instead. That means that private capital must become a strictly public servant. If it is not allowed to improve its rate of profit, public-service motivation must from now on be its *only* motivation to improve the efficiency of its performance. But none of these schemes of control includes any of the machinery which motivates public-service efficiency, or non-profit inno-

253

vation. Instead they offer an exactly wrong mixture of capitalism and socialism – the worst of each without the dynamic principle of either.

Capitalism ran on the principle that people should maximize their assets, whatever those were – land, money, machinery, labor (and also of course, any available brute force or political influence). Governments have long intervened to restrain some kinds of maximizing, especially to protect some weak bargainers and to restrain some unproductive types of strong bargaining by brute force or by monopolists. Most of those interventions adjusted the conditions of competition but encouraged competition to continue. Efficiency still paid. Because it did – because lowering costs and maximizing profits still paid – capitalism still had animating motives. The profit motive has become less *directly* important in a good deal of big business, where the operative motives have become more like those which motivate managers and bureaucrats in any big organization. (Banks and insurance companies with private shareholders behave much like banks and insurance companies with public share-holders or with none; motivation is much the same in British Airways, Shell and British Petroleum, respectively public, private and half-and-half.) But the classical maximizing principle did directly animate a great deal of small and medium business, and a certain amount of wild-cat innovation; and in big business, both public and private, it supplied socially acceptable *conventions* of competition and tests of performance and efficiency.

A good deal of that must now change. In one vital respect the new controls are different from earlier public controls of capitalist behavior. Their central purpose now has to be to *limit* gains, to *prevent* maximizing, and especially to prevent maximizing by the *most efficient* businesses and the *most productive* labor. Most of the maximizing mechanisms will have to be replaced by governmental methods of allocating, pricing and wage-fixing. Those will then need to be backed up by governmental methods of motivating economic efficiency (methods which discipline most public industries already) or there will be nothing at all to motivate it.

That much – the basic transition from capitalist to state-socialist regula-tion of production, by means of all-embracing controls of profits, prices and incomes – is already the program of the moderate anti-inflationary Right. The 'middle' Right seems to accept freedom, with hard bargaining and fast inflation, as the least of the evils. The reactionary Right wants to restore the old industrial disciplines by applying doses of deflation, unemployment and coercion. Many see income policies as a useful new method of coercing labor: old-style capitalist freedoms can thrive on the use of state-disciplined labor, as they used to do in serf or plantation economies and still do in South Africa.

If state-socialist control is unavoidable, the Left would like to accompany it with socialist distribution. The Right would not. In the coming political contest each side has something going for it – some helpful tendencies in the social and economic processes themselves.

Habit and precedent work for the Right. In the development of modern mixed economies plenty of public enterprises have been built, and plenty of private ones have been taken into public ownership. Public takeovers have usually paid full capital compensation to the former owners. Public enterprises have imitated private wage and salary diffentials. Public borrowing pays interest to private lenders. The new controllers of prices and incomes already try to fix wages to perpetuate past margins, and prices to perpetuate past rates pf profit. They don't interfere with private rights to accumulate, inherit and draw income from capital, and dissave and spend it as 'tax-free income'. Thus capitalist democracies already have very large elements of 'administered inequality' and their new economic bureaucrats can easily administer more of the same.

Those possibilities help the Right, but others may help the Left. 'Administered inequality' is not likely to stop the inflation. As people become more desperate to stop it, some balances of strength are likely to be tested. Neither business nor government can now coerce organized labor as a whole. But if organized labor insists on it, it may be possible to impose 'unacceptable' restraints on higher salaries; and any democratic majority, if it is desperate enough, can install a government which will take possession of recalcitrant capital. The critical question is whether organized labor will act directly against the salaried and propertied rich – or indirectly *with* them, at the cost of continuing inflation and at the expense of all weak bargainers. I believe that in the less corrupt societies, time will teach them that inflation is not worth whatever short-term gains it allows the strong. It is also likely that hard bargaining will reduce differentials among the hard bargainers themselves: miners and auto workers, petroleum and power workers, technicians and managers and even doctors and academics and pilots can expect to move a little closer to one another. It is of course possible that they will simultaneously move further ahead of everyone else. But their avarice is chiefly fuelled by their own inequalities; as those are reduced, they are likely to be less ruthless towards people poorer than themselves. Meanwhile the attack on inflation – however ineffective at first – must increase the power of government over many more things than prices and incomes; and that should bring *some* increase of influence to the weak bargainers who have nothing but votes to bargain with and no-one but government to represent them.

Finally, any progress is likely to be self-strengthening. If inflation is slowed a little – if only by hard deals among the strong – people may bargain less ruthlessly. Militant unions who command fuel, power, transport or other essential services may still bargain hard when they know they are bargaining chiefly (or at least, more than before) against people no richer than themselves; but I do not believe that most of them will bargain quite as hard as they do when they see enticing and punishing inequalities all around them, and the prices of necessaries rising every month. Consider what they see around them now: fortunes made through booms and held through periods of depression and mass unemployment, while ordinary people's savings shrivel whatever they do with them; executive and professional rewards several times greater than theirs, buying children's chances several times better than their children's; outrageous double standards in the trial and punishment of rich and poor offenders against welfare, tax and other income-control laws; million-dollar gains (sometimes assisted by million-dollar bankruptcies) for operators in property and other socially useless lines of business; and for themselves meanwhile an anxious race to keep ahead of inflation until they retire to pensions which are very likely to fall behind it. If you *added* those conditions to societies which had lacked them, you would expect strong labor to respond by bargaining harder. If you subtract them, then however habit-forming the hard bargaining may have been it is likely to moderate to some degree. It is also likely to be more effectively resisted wherever it deserves to be. The surer the progress towards a closer equality of incomes, especially between trade and trade, the less public sympathy or political support there will be for groups thought to be bargaining unfairly.

That suggests the only conditions in which it may be possible to tame the beast. *Controlling cost-push inflation ought to be an integral function – almost an incidental function – of a general social control of inequalities.* That would need to include four elements. One – the distribution of domestic space and resources and public services – was discussed in previous chapters. How should the Left approach the other three: the control of prices, incomes and the distribution of gainful capital wealth?

Some prices are easier than others to regulate so price control should be versatile, not confined to regulation alone. For these purposes goods and services fall into four general categories:

Some things are by nature easy to regulate: commodities with uniform or easily graded quality including most minerals, fuels, timber, raw wool and cotton and synthetic fibres; grains, milk, eggs, carcass meat; mileages and tonnages of passenger and goods transport; postal services and telecommunications; some bulk-processed materials including steel and other metals, soap and detergents, alcohol and tobacco, and standard grades of bread and butter and some other processed foods; some entertainments including cinema and stadium admissions; receiving licences, driving and road licences. It is comparatively easy to regulate the prices of most of those things without much increase of present bureaucracy. The effects of the controls will vary but for most products they need not interfere with competitive efficiency in design and processing and marketing, or with cost-cutting price competition in some cases.

Second, there are prices which are automatically controlled if incomes are. For many professional and personal services a single control of fees or salaries serves both purposes.

Third, prices of land and houses can't all be directly regulated but they can be strongly influenced, for all but a few people in the biggest cities, by methods suggested earlier.

Those three groups of goods and services account for three quarters or more of most people's spending, including a high proportion of spending on necessaries. So the hindrances to controlling that large part of the cost of living are political rather than technical. If price control were geared to appropriate land, housing and income policies (to which also the hindrances are chiefly political) it could be quite effective.

There remains a fourth group of retail goods and services whose prices are genuinely difficult to regulate because of variable quality, variable demand, multiplicity of design, model-changing, etc.: machinery, furniture, clothing, some seasonal and perishable foods, and a great many publications and arts and entertainments. Cars and some other machinery could be regulated more than they already are if models were standardized more than they already are. But for most goods in this group standardization would be undesirable because people choose and use the products for individual purposes of taste, self-expression or 'social signalling', purposes which are important to personal identity and (in arts and communications) to basic freedoms. After the revolution Soviet women had to wait forty years for a choice of colored underwear; they are still waiting for much free choice of housing, words, music, pictures or opinions.

Although its policies may have to be cautious or partial, government need not let all prices rip throughout these awkward fields. Some (consumer durables) may be good fields for public/private competition. Others (broadcasting, publications, entertainments) may be adaptable to independent non-profit enterprise which might sometimes be more co-operative about price regulation than profit-seekers can be. In some industries government may be able to influence prices by taking over segments or 'horizontal slices' of industries. Private enterprisers already use plenty of public oil, steel, transport, and bulk-purchased imports; private contractors build most public housing, offices, roads and bridges. In some of these composite industries (especially public housing) the public intervention has always been intended to control prices. That principle could be extended. Private producers who use public goods and services might be subjected to contractual price controls. The ease or difficulty of applying regulatory price controls could become one among the standard considerations which guide decisions about public ownership.

Where – as with clothing and furniture, some entertainments and some machinery and appliances – detailed regulation of prices is impracticable it is sometimes possible nevertheless to judge if prices generally are too high and profits or rates of reinvestment or executive rewards are undesirably high. In some of these fields there could be some mild resort to terror[34] if public acquisition of particular firms, processes or whole lines of business were a regular (though perhaps little-used) weapon. And so on. As observed earlier, 'to nationalize or not' is often too crude a question. For purposes of price control as for other purposes it is usually better to ask what minimum, most economical intervention (appeals for voluntary cooperation; regulation; public/private competition; part-ownership; horizontal or vertical public monopoly; or guidelines enforced by threats of selective public acquisition) will achieve what the public wants to achieve with least loss of freedom or increase of bureaucracy.

Price controls still have obvious limitations. Unlucky countries will always be vulnerable to international prices – the best they can do is to distribute their internal effects as fairly as possible. And in all countries incomes are a chief cost of production, and enough economic activity is exempt from the discipline of bankruptcy to make sure that national patterns of income can't be restrained by price control alone. Controls of prices and incomes have to support and depend on one another.

3

Government cannot hope to dictate more than a very few wages. In most democracies rewards have to be negotiated trade by trade and industry by industry, in diverse ways which must depend a good deal on the nature of industrial relations and wage–price relationships in each industry, and on the patterns of organization and representation which employees choose for themselves.

But for one vital function there is perhaps a role for a new and dictatorial central authority. The authority should be established to regulate the numbers and rewards of all jobs – public and private, without exception – whose pay puts them in the top 1 or 2% of incomes. It should regulate them entirely – salaries, perquisites, fringe benefits, share and superannuation entitlements and all – and should probably manage the taxation of self-employed and property incomes in the same bracket. Employers who want to create jobs above the defined level should have to justify them and get permitted rates of reward for them before filling them. Such a central office shouldn't be 'responsive', i.e. its business should not be to keep top people's margins moving in punctual response to movements of mass wages. On the contrary it should operate somewhat independently of other wage-fixing, as government's strongest single instrument of inequality control, doing its business with full publicity so that all the other wage-bargainers can know to what summit their own aspirations might hopefully be related. A good deal of middle-management and salaried-professional wage-fixing would look after itself if that one touch of brutality at the top became routine. It is not an impractical notion. The highest public salaries are already fixed by legislatures, tribunals or public service commissioners. Some of the highest private salaries are also subject to public regulation; the control is usually ineffective, and purports to hold or moderate existing differentials rather than to review them in any radical way, but the principle of control and the offices to exercise it already exist over a good deal of the capitalist world.

For the rest – for the mass of middle and lower earnings – methods have to be adapted to circumstances. In a few industries price control alone may serve. Many industries may continue to bargain within central-government guidelines as they do now. Others may need new

259

machinery. Whatever its form, employees won't only demand to be heard; they must have as much influence as anyone else in determining *how* they should be heard. In some countries that may produce very diverse, pluralist modes of negotiation. Others may move towards model machinery applicable in all industries, and towards some sort of central 'wages parliament'. The latter might be best in the long run – but harder to achieve.

Whatever the machinery, it will continue to be bargaining, conciliating, adjudicating machinery. Government will be no more able to dictate wages (except at the top) than it is now. But in the different atmosphere of an equalizing society it may become possible to use some methods which labor doesn't tolerate now. Piece-rates may become more acceptable. Labor may be willing to sort out more of its own differentials within collectively bargained price limits and block-allocations of wage money. If labor bargains centrally, i.e. for a wide range of trades at once, it tends to bargain for flatter differentials; it may take more notice of the interests of workers as consumers; rewards for productivity can be more widely spread; 'price for price' deals may become interesting (for example cheap transport fares for cheap fuel and power). All this assumes that equalization really has begun from the top down and what labor does without, shareholders and retailers can't pick up; so that wage-bargainers can no longer hope or fear that they are competing with profits, unless perhaps with profits which get such wide social distribution that they attract the same universal interest as prices do.

So – except for a few of the highest incomes – the business of a national central office of inequality control is not to regulate a nation's wages and prices penny by penny. Part of its business must be to mediate between government and the detailed negotiating machinery which does that detailed work, and to help to develop that machinery to represent all the interests it ought to represent. A central office must take part in the policy-making which determines national scales and trends of inequality, and the allocation of the national product between incomes and other uses. It must turn national policies into guidelines for use in detailed price and income bargaining. It must cope as well as it can with particular conflicts important enough to get national attention, doing its best to encourage real rather than phoney confrontations, i.e. to encourage confrontations between the real gainers and losers – whether those be worker and worker, worker and consumer, low and high earner. As a conciliator or tribunal of second last resort it may have to intervene in disputes which the regular machinery can't resolve, or in negotiations in which big wage-leading or price-leading effects are likely. (The latent power of the hard bargainers will always make sure that the tribunal of *last* resort is the national government, or its electors.)

At the same time a central office of inequality control needs to be accompanied by a very active information service. This should keep the citizens informed, in professional detail and in popular summary, of the progress of their equalities and inequalities. It should make sure that major negotiations about wages, prices, welfare incomes and upper incomes and wealth taxes get plenty of publicity, including detailed and summary representations of the interests and inequalities at stake: wage–price relationships, relativities within and between trades, rates of profit and dividend and the incomes of the people they go to, implications of particular issues and conflicts for the general social pattern of inequalities. Governments themselves won't do much of this; they hate to be caught 'setting citizen against citizen' or confessing that their generous wage awards or tax cuts will actually be financed by inflationary subtractions from the real value of the old age pension. So public information services may need some of the independent status which electoral offices or census offices or national broadcasting commissions have. If government has to answer in the end for any severities to consumers or shareholders or labor – and for reprisals by any of them – it needs to answer to a public well and vividly informed about the issues. As a fanciful example: *'Ten dollars on the basic coal-mining wage will move miners from rough equivalence with shop assistants, junior clerks and railway porters into equivalence with teachers, drivers of tracked or articulated vehicles, laboratory technicians, draftsmen. It will allow individual miners' incomes to range from the 60th up to the 25th percentile of all incomes, instead of the 70th to the 45th as now. It will put $50 a year in energy costs onto average household costs of living. Except for the bottom 20% of incomes the government intends that this extra cost of living shall not be compensated or allowed for in other income-fixing. It is proposed as a straight social transfer to miners, as a matter of justice, and to help recruit more miners and save more oil.'* Or: *'The government intends to close the relevant airlines* (or hospital wards, or universities, or nuclear power stations) *rather than meet the striking pilots'* (or surgeons', or professors', or control engineers') *demands for three* (or five, or seven) *coal miners' wages each – not because the relevant price increases would matter much, but because those wage increases would break faith with the millions of workers who do comply with wage–price guidelines.*

Nobody is going to defy this society's inequality-limits, which have full electoral mandate, except by throwing this government out and voting for other men and other measures altogether.' And so on – with graphics, national income charts to show who wants to climb how far above who else, popular job-evaluation of miners' and professors' skills and pleasures and responsibilities, interviews with dying hospital patients and emigrating surgeons and liberated students – and doubtless, display advertisements by all parties in a free press. (And harder arguments about other trades when, instead of coinciding, considerations of recruitment and fair rewards conflict.)

If some of this sounds intolerable to organized labor, and therefore unworkable, it is once again necessary to remember that these are arrangements through which a mature democracy, sick of rich tricks and disruptive strikes and scarred once by runaway inflation and sobered by all those experiences, might manage its internal competitions for social shares *after* it had rid itself of the worst of the treadmill-anxieties and unequalizing mechanisms which bedevil a good deal of wage-bargaining at present.

4

How can labor and the Left go about the political task of building a determined majority for the principle of regulating *all* incomes, and making them less unequal than they are now?

Social-democratic politicians are understandably nervous about the bargaining behavior of organized labor in times of accelerating inflation. Nevertheless I believe that most labor should go on bargaining as hard as hell as long as gross inequalities continue and there are no effective controls on high incomes or capital ownership. The immediate costs of such bargaining must include continuing inflation, more hardship for the poor, and some danger of intensifying the isolation and unpopularity of organized labor itself.

To contain that danger, and to turn from exploiting unstable inequalities to reducing them, labor needs to move away from cut-throat, leapfrogging tactics towards a different strategy for which there have been some partial precedents in Scandinavia and Australasia. Unions should try to bargain centrally so that they can bargain for more equal rewards within their own ranks; and they should create opportunities to bargain for unorganized incomes poorer than their own. They should thus set examples of equality, and insistently and publicly connect their self-interested bargaining with broader national aims of equality. At the same

262

time they should positively embrace the *principle* of income control, rename it inequality control, and insist that it extend to all rewards without exception (or at least, without rich exceptions). They should continue to wreck all Right or weak-Left attempts at biased and incomplete income controls, while at every step demanding and promising to comply with *complete* inequality controls as soon as those are seen to be at work, and to be actually improving equalities.

For these purposes the unions need to develop their bargaining in two particular directions. First they should do more for the very poor. In a year which sees 15% inflation and 2 or 3% of real growth, British coal miners or transport workers bargaining against a state employer might offer options: *either* 20% on their money wages instead of the 17½% offered, *or* 17½% on wages and also 17½% (instead of the 12½% offered) on national old age pensions. Those moves come best from central labor councils on behalf of organized labor as a whole. Workers may need to remind each other from time to time that such generous policies aren't entirely sacrificial. They reconcile generosity with self-interest if they attract electoral support for broader programs of equality.

Second, if there are no effective national controls on higher incomes, some unions could try bargaining for contractual controls within their own industries. They might bargain for wage and salary patterns which would reduce differentials all the way from messenger boys to managing directors, and for reduced rates of profit and dividend, so that it should be seen to happen that some part of their wage gains were at the expense of the industry's owners and executives, rather than the consumers of its products.

Put in one way, labor needs a share in the control of the mechanisms by which the force of its bargaining gets deflected onto the poor. If it can't yet share in a national political control of those mechanisms it can try to get some control of them industry by industry, letting the public know that it is doing so in the joint interest of workers and consumers. Put in another way, strong unions should say to their employers 'The price of peace and productivity in this industry is no longer going to be more for both of us at the expense of the consumers. From now on part of what *we* gain comes from *you*, at least until we are equal enough inside this industry. From now on the price of peace is going to include more equality right here, between you and us.' It is true that on a national scale not much is likely to be gained in this way. Not many industries would be susceptible to it, not many unions would be strong enough for it. But any honest attempts could help to win friends where the unions need them most, within a broad alliance of the Left.

The main architects of that alliance and of its policies must still be the political parties of the Left. But inflation has so far made paralysing difficulties for them. In the national interest and in the class interest of half their electoral supporters they should restrain inflation. They have so far tried to do it – where they have tried at all – by precisely the partial and unequalizing methods which organized labor (the other half of their electors) won't tolerate. Social-democratic governments try wage-and-price controls for a while, until labor ceases to trust them; then the wage restraints are relaxed or broken, inflation accelerates and everyone else ceases to trust them. Fatal numbers of electors conclude that the parties of the Left can't control inflation 'because they can't control labor'. The truth is that they can't control either because they do too little to control owners, managers, capital inequalities and high incomes generally.

The correct approach, however hard to apply in practice, is easy to define in principle. Unlike poor relief, equality has to start at the top. Whatever else income-controls aim at, they must first aim to reduce differentials, beginning with the biggest. It is easier – economically and politically and psychologically – to do that by reducing a few high incomes than by increasing many low ones. Nobody below the top third of incomes should be asked to submit to any limitation of his income until he first sees higher incomes move nearer to his own. To vote for income-regulation a poor man needs to know that it will operate from the top down in his society; to submit to it himself he needs to see it operating from the top down in his industry.

The progress needs to be genuine and visible. It should develop simply-understandable rules – guidelines which gather strength as policy-makers recommend them, bargainers base their cases on them, arbitrators apply them, and they build themselves into everyman's definition of 'fair and reasonable'. At least until substantial improvements in equality have been accomplished it would be reasonable to define equality for official purposes in absolute terms: i.e., incomes are to be considered more equal when the difference between them is absolutely less. Equalizers can try for other rules. For example gains can be distributed in progressive quantities and losses in progressive percentages; or there can be no money gains (i.e. there can be inflation losses) above certain income levels; or gains can be applied to levelling up to particular floors or averages. Other biases, 'scissors' and 'ratchets' are imaginable. Meanwhile Left publicists should keep attention on general summaries of distribution, nation-wide and industry by industry. Whenever patterns of inequality change in the wrong direction it should be the business of organized labor to disrupt the industries concerned, or it should be the business of the poorest 55% of voters to change the government.

But it will not be possible to flatten the general scale of inequality very far if controls (including conventional taxation) apply to earned incomes only, or even to all incomes only. The direct and indirect effects of unequal capital ownership, capital gain and capital spending are too strong. To be effective – perhaps to begin at all – any general control of inequality will have to include some redistribution of capital ownership.

5

Democratic majorities have never yet been willing to confiscate or redistribute capital, or even tax it much during its owners' life-times. Action has been limited to taxes on personal and corporate incomes, gifts and successions, land and buildings, and (sometimes) annual capital taxes at rates low enough to allow most of them to be paid from income. None of those devices does much to equalize the ownership of capital. Even where they work best they fall far short of their legislators' intentions. Swedes and Norwegians of most parties tend to agree that their countries have pushed tax-and-transfer rates to their effective limits; and their best efforts can now scarcely hold their existing inequalities. In Sweden inequalities of wealth and after-tax income are now either stable or increasing and inflation is restrained only with the help of some underprivileged foreign labor and some old-fashioned unemployment. Norway has neither of those special deflationary influences. It has capital and income taxes on corporations and individuals so that the richest private flows are hit four times at rates which add up to more than 50% of corporate and 105% of personal income. Nevertheless inequalities of income and productive wealth (as the Norwegian government measures them) are now increasing; there is fast inflation; it has driven labor to break ranks and let unions bargain more independently than in the past; there is difficulty in getting labor to agree to any incomes policy to which there would be rich exceptions; a good many of the political Left have moved further Left and electoral support for the Left has broadened.

If rising inequalities and rates of inflation can't be stopped by conventional means it seems likely that as their effects become less and less tolerable to more and more people they will induce some change in the political attitudes which at present limit methods of redistribution. As people are driven to the conclusion that nothing less will work, it may become possible to redistribute capital wealth. So it is time to begin thinking about the most practical and least oppressive ways of doing it. There are no models of a peaceful democratic kind to copy – the Left will have to invent. A lot may depend on the skill and humanity of the invention. Workable, equitable, unfrightening proposals may help to create the political climate for their own implementation.

Methods of capital redistribution must vary with circumstances. Their success or failure may depend as much on their small print and their detailed adaptation to national values and administrative capacities as on their broad principles. But their broad principles are all that can be discussed in general terms. What follow are sketches of the merits and demerits of some alternative possibilities.

Should there be a once-for-all redistribution or a slow ongoing process of capital transfer? How small or large should the transfers be and how flat the equalities aimed at? On what flat or proportional principles should private capital be taken from those who have too much of it? Should different types of capital goods be treated differently? Should all redistribution necessarily be from private to public ownership, or are private-to-private transfers worth considering? Or public-to-private transfers, for example by turning tenants of public housing into owners, or workers in public industries into shareholders? Are there uses for 'intermediate' receivers of transferred capital – cooperatives, non-profit trusts, charities, etc.?

A once-for-all capital confiscation is usually dismissed as a revolutionary act for which there is no sign yet of a democratic majority. Even revolutionaries usually think of it as a way of transferring ownership to the state, or perhaps (somewhat inequitably) to worker-cooperatives. Nevertheless it is so orthodox to think of income tax as transferring *income* from rich to poor that it seems surprising that so few people have thought seriously of transferring *capital* from rich to poor. It is worth thinking of now, for three reasons.

First, confiscation to the state is doubly unpopular. Taking the stuff is thought to be dangerous or unjust; giving it to bureaucrats is thought (outside official socialist circles) to have other hazards. Transfers from citizen to citizen might make at least one half of the transaction popular.

Second, majorities who jib at general confiscation may nevertheless be willing to apply the principle in limited ways to particular types of capital – for example to big holdings of forest or pasture land, to mineral rights, or to some categories of urban land, housing, commercial and office property from which clearly antisocial fortunes continue to be made.

Some quite conservative societies have been willing to tax large land holdings very heavily; some national land reforms have included elements of confiscation; some national housing policies already subsidize the distribution of one kind of capital to some of the poor.

Third, it is worth considering a more drastic and general redistribution of private productive capital because *once done* it offers gains in liberty as well as equality. Consider some present troubles about which, for different reasons, both Left and Right complain. A grossly unequal distribution of income-earning capital[35] (which majorities still tolerate) combines with unequal wage and salary scales to generate a primary distribution of income which no free majority anywhere is willing to tolerate. So majorities everywhere insist that their governments try to limit and redistribute higher incomes by steeply progressive taxation. Legislators and administrators are driven to multiply the regulations which try to prevent businesses, and the private companies into which rich individuals and families transform themselves, from further reorganizing and complicating themselves in order to evade the fiscal intentions of the democracy. Control is so difficult that detectives are hired, business records are sieved, onuses of proof are reversed, administrative fines are exacted. Any rich man can be forgiven for resenting such cruel and unnatural invasions of his privacy and freedom of action; but observing how successfully he nevertheless wriggles his way through a good many of the constraints, any poor voter or honest tax-collector can be forgiven for wanting to refine the torture and screw it tighter. Plenty of the controls moreover have to apply to everyone; in order to check what a few dodgers do, the red tape and form-filling have to afflict many more people than they are primarily aimed at, and they often succeed in taking more freedom and taxes away from the law-abiding many than from the tax-dodging few whose tactics provoke them. It becomes faintly absurd to talk of 'free' enterprise or even in some respects of a free society.

The trouble is likely to grow worse. Processes of growth and accumulation increase capital inequalities while other trends strengthen the popular demand that land and incomes and welfare be distributed more equally. To reconcile the two would take more steeply progressive taxation every year – with more ingenious and corrupting evasions and more oppressive attempts to frustrate them. (Other evils also increase: for example capital export, tax-evasive distortions of investment, 'capital inflation' and speculative hoarding in commodities and real estate.) The process as a whole must increase tension between diverging patterns of capital and income inequality, or else it must increase the tensions which

267

go with rising inequalities of income and rates of inflation. In practice it does some of both. Not even Swedish extremes of conventional taxation can quite stop it. Rising energy and environmental costs will make it harder than ever to reconcile people to it by means of easy economic growth. And it contains no self-limiting mechanism. However slowly (and whether the capital wealth is monopolized by five, ten or twenty per cent of the population) the process of private capital accumulation is set to take us towards Arabian scales of inequality, with some attrition of liberty as we go. Moreover it is the traditional middle of the road which points that way. The political interventions which will certainly come in time to stop us short of Arabia will have to deflect us sharply to Left or Right; and the strength of organized labor and popular expectation make it hard to imagine how a Right alternative (if effective) could be very free or democratic.

So it may be worth considering a once-for-all capital redistribution as the least bloody, most workable and most humane option for the Left. It may also offer a safer and freer socialism than the universal bureaucratic ownership described by its enemies as 'state capitalism'. If privately owned income-bearing capital could be distributed equally, or in some pattern consistent with the limited inequalities of income which majorities actually want, then some of the inquisitorial activity of government could cease and so could some of the antisocial behavior which occasions it. Many people could be marginally freer than they are now. Except for being freer, most share-owned business could continue as if nothing had happened except some name-changing in the share-registers and some regulation of executive incomes. A nation of $1,000 to $10,000 shareholders could easily develop more of the institutions which already offer diverse options of risk and return to small investors and organize their holdings for use in big enterprises.

It might then be possible to make the personal limits permanent. That would require some complicated regulation, whose chief effect might be merely to redistribute nominal ownership within families or within the most affluent class. It might be easier and almost as effective to set no permanent limit but to rely on strict taxation of gains, gifts and successions, and on the possibility of further 'once-only' transfers if capital inequalities should ever again grow to be seriously inconsistent with desired distributions of income or lifestyle. The pattern of ownership would certainly change over time. That doesn't matter – an unstable but widely shared distribution would still be very much better, in itself and in its effects, than the present unstable but grossly *un*equal distribution.

Making such a confiscatory transfer would be a complicated and painful operation. There would be some rough justice and many hard cases. There would be some serious economic disruption, capital flight and concealment, and talk of revolution and international reprisal. Foreign ownership of home assets and home ownership of foreign assets would pose acute problems of policy and administration. So would the 'capital rationing' of small farms and businesses and self-employed tradesmen. But there is worse and rougher injustice in our present maldistributions, and the costs of a general redistribution have to be compared with the gains that would flow from it.

The gains could be far more valuable than the material transfers themselves would suggest, chiefly because of the effects which capital redistribution would have on so many reactionary mechanisms of income distribution. Most of the land price problem would disappear overnight (leaving a messy task of reconstructing debts secured on land). Many ways of hoarding, concealing and augmenting personal wealth would disappear with the disappearance of the capital-rich minority and the artificial 'confidence markets' which such minorities maintain. It would become much easier to regulate inequalities of income as big unearned incomes disappeared, and with them most ways of living off capital gain, disguising income as capital, and avoiding taxation of both.

Some psychological changes might be the most valuable of all. The assumptions which at present guide most salary and wage-fixing, and many profit and dividend policies, are influenced by powerful chains of envy and expectation. Top people who get to the top by merit want to share some at least of the 'top life-style' established and displayed by those who got there by inheritance or chicanery; the second rank of executives and bureaucrats and professionals rate themselves in relation to the first (as do the corporate boards and public tribunals who fix their rewards); and so on down, with public servants wanting parity with 'what they could be getting outside' and executives wanting parity with 'what they're getting next door', preferably in the form of company cars and share options. Thus the unearned incomes at the top and the unearned supplements enjoyed by many share-owning and capital-gaining salary-earners do a good deal to inflame ambitions, self-estimates, and bargaining and salary-fixing and fee-setting assumptions throughout the upper reaches of *earned* incomes. If there were no enticing examples of excessive wealth – no mansions with staff, no Ferraris, no private Picassos or twin-screw yachts – many professional men and salary-earners would moderate *their* images of success – of status insignia, creditable life-style and spendable income – as they distanced their ambitions from the more modest levels of luxury available to the highest wholly-earned and honestly-taxed salaries. It is bad that capital-rich minorities get unfair shares of unearned income. But they do much greater damage to equality by the direct, indirect and psychological influence which they exert on the distribution of *earned* incomes. Working ambition will fix its sights on whatever differentials there are. What matters socially is the *scale* of the differentials; and between them the capital-rich and the welfare poor set that scale.

Getting rid of the spire of wealth from the top of the pyramid of incomes would have other psychological advantages. The present confrontation between steeply unequal incomes and steeply progressive personal taxation is oppressive, corrupting, psychologically stupid, and difficult and expensive to administer. It wilfully creates self-righteous feelings of worth and expectation then wilfully affronts and frustrates them. Nobody in his senses would choose to introduce such a system. Low earners would not feel freer or better treated if instead of earning $100 a week they were paid $200 then taxed $100 of it – so why irritate high earners in that way? There will always be functions for income taxes, to adjust take-home pay to household need and to impose income policies on the 5 or 10% of earners who are self-employed or otherwise unregulated at source. But for the other 90 or 95 it would be better to regulate pay directly, then raise most public revenue by selective employment taxes and other devices which take money from much the same sources as now, but take it without first creating illusory personal entitlements to it. Such taxes can also operate (as selective employment taxes did for a short time in the United Kingdom) as more useful instruments of economic policy than income taxes can ever be.

Shareholding by everybody has various attractions. It allows the rich to be dispossessed without forcing any more disorganization of industry, or creation of new public corporations, than may be desirable for other purposes. It allows most work and management and investment to be motivated as they are now, with a few less antisocial temptations. With appropriate wage differentials and family allowances, and with share income as a very minor proportion of nearly everybody's income, the primary distribution of rewards could achieve most of the effect which we vainly try to achieve at present by the mad method of distributing huge differentials then trying to claw most of them back. The idea is adaptable to any level of equality. Even for those who want to keep the present pattern of after-tax inequalities, it would be good to redistribute enough capital and revise enough wage and salary scales to provide a primary distribution which could be allowed to stand, without clawing.

After a general redistribution of capital the hard-bargaining convergence of wages and salaries which happens already might well deliver a slow improvement of equality within the upper half or two-thirds of incomes. Though not entirely easy, it would still be easier than it is now for government to regulate that distribution, and for the poorest third to use their votes to get a fairer share of it.

Altogether a once-for-all redistribution should in theory allow capitalist systems to run with more efficiency, more liberty, and in some departments a little less government. If the redistribution were fairly equal it could establish a less bureaucratic version of the mixed economy, high welfare, fair sharing and personal freedom of many social-democratic dreams. It might also allow some elements of an old radical/conservative/ Catholic vision of small-holding independence to be combined with a modern scale of business organization, and with mixtures of private, cooperative and public ownership chosen chiefly on grounds of efficiency, social peace, and satisfying conditions of work. And the anticlimax which is often cited as a knock-down argument against redistribution – the comparatively small capital gain which it would yield to everyman – would really be the most fertile of its virtues. A nation of small shareholders would have no big capitalist villains – and no myths, excuses or scapegoats of that kind; and it would have an additional latent power against bureaucratic villains, in the form of an organizable owners' vote as well as an electoral one. Those prospects can be contrasted with the losses of personal and business freedom which are threatened by current attempts to restrain inflation by controlling incomes *against* the pull of capital inequalities and the inequalities of income which they help to generate. True believers in personal freedom and private business efficiency (as opposed to true believers in Arabian inequality with Byzantine bureaucracy) should rationally vote to equalize the private ownership of income-earning capital tomorrow.

So why not?

Majorities won't yet do it. Three things deter them. First the present owners do, helped by salaried and professional rich who know that high rewards from all sources depend a good deal, directly and indirectly, on capital inequalities. The rich still own or manage most of the media of persuasion, and 55% of the people can usually be persuaded that if confiscation starts at all it won't stop short of stripping us all bare and very possibly shovelling us into ovens. It is ironical that people, most of whom own no productive capital at all and have far more to fear from government in other ways, should have such special fears of capital confiscation. Democratic governments can conscript any number of young men to die in jungles; they can create instant millionaires by licensing predators to bulldoze whole neighborhoods for office sites; they can deflate a million families off work onto welfare; they can take a third of the national product in taxation, mostly from ordinary people with very ordinary incomes. But if they take capital from the rich – a danger from which eight or nine people out of ten are absolutely protected by reason of owning none – then freedom will be at an end, gutters will run red, civilization will crumble. I suspect that these richly assisted nightmares owe a good deal to one underrated way in which inequalities reinforce themselves. In unequal societies, low earners have less cause than most to love or trust government. A lot of the contact they have with it is cold, unhelpful, bureaucratic or downright hostile. Even its favors bring trouble – pensions, public housing and welfare services come with varying degrees of suspicion, means-testing, invasions of an already skimped and sometimes ashamed privacy. So it is not too hard to plant the idea that a government of superfat experts and mean-spirited clerks now wants to take fundamental possessions from the people. (*Them* taking it from *us*; policemen taking things from our houses; banks handing over our savings.) Poor people's possessions are few, precious and often precarious. So plenty of poor as well as rich vote for inviolable property rights.

Second, it is hard to apply capital taxation or confiscation fairly between owner and owner. Some assets are divisible and others are not. Different markets fix the values of farms, factories, goodwill businesses, city properties, life insurances. They yield different patterns of income and capital gain and very diverse effects would flow from taxing them all impartially. The values of some of them, especially some speculatively-priced assets, would be drastically affected by redistribution itself – should they be assessed for confiscation at pre- or post-tax values? (But existing taxes have comparable difficulties and capital levies could be designed, as income and property taxes already are, to discriminate between types of taxpayer, types of asset, degrees of hardship, etc.)

A third hindrance to capital transfer is more serious. Changes within accepted types of taxation may annoy people and provoke angry political exchanges but not many people feel that they threaten the foundations of social and personal security. Any general transfer of capital, whether from citizen to citizen or from citizen to government, would touch quite different feelings *the first time it happened*. Most of the people likely to lose by capital transfers have acquired their wealth by inheritance or by other means which their fellow democrats have always defined as useful and respectable. They have been positively encouraged, often as a duty enjoined by their culture, to build self-respect, life-styles, feelings of safety and hopes for their children onto foundations which many think of as the foundations of society itself. If the democracy suddenly reverses course, takes some of their capital property and by doing so creates uncertainty about the safety of the rest of it, then many owners and their families will feel personally violated. It is *not* just like paying taxes, or losing money in the way of business.

Both sides talk in large half-truths on this matter. On the one hand capital transfer would indeed break some solemn social promises and upset some deeply-held and widely-shared conceptions of social justice. On the other hand it could bring immense social benefits in the long run to large majorities of people. The long-term benefits in social justice and cohesion and in government and economic management would be out of all proportion to the sums of money transferred; *but so also would the short-term costs be.* As any loving Left ought to assess such things, the short-term costs would certainly exceed the short-term benefits. Some of the losers would suffer betrayal, anger, hate, anxiety and mourning more intense than any sum of satisfactions which the transferred goods could give, directly and immediately, to those who gained them. This does not contradict a belief in the diminishing marginal utility of wealth or income – an extra dollar will still usually do more for a poor man than for a rich man. What it does mean is that losses are felt more intensely than gains, the more so if the gains are windfalls and the losses strike the losers as wilfully unjust. It does not matter whether losses by confiscation are perceived as losses of privilege, or inalienable right, or freedom, or inner personal security; what matters is that if they are not expected in the ordinary course of taxation they will frighten, unnerve and *hurt*. They may not hurt the property shark or exchange gambler or tax-avoider who took his risks (including this one) deliberately – or it may not matter if they do. But it matters if they hurt the parent who has saved for his children's sake; the widow whose inheritance allows her and her children to stay on in their family house; the doctor or lawyer or architect who has had to invest for his retirement; everyone who has converted personal achievement – part of his working self, really and symbolically – into capital; everyone who has saved (as many savers do) to give rather than to have.

There would be heart-rending cases down every street. Consider a couple who work hard – she works full time, he works time and a half – to accumulate a stake to which perfectly wholesome dreams soon attach. Suppose they have pleasure-loving neighbors who work less, earn less, owe plenty and save nothing – but who one fine day with the flick of a ballot-paper take half of their hard-working neighbors' savings. Or consider another pair of neighbors who (unlike the former pair) have done much the same work and earned the same money through their working lives; but one couple has spent it all and the other has put some into life insurance and savings certificates. If a capital transfer now equalizes their savings it *unequalizes* their whole-life rewards. So would capital transfers which ignored the size of households and families. In these cases 'equalization' would outrage the egalitarian values which sustain democratic society, including the values which ought to inspire any capital redistributions.

It is simultaneously true that plenty of those who would gain by capital transfers are hard-pressed people who never had any chance to save – millions who work for low pay for rich masters at difficult, dirty or tedious tasks in mines, mills, assembly lines or very boring offices and services, and at caring for one another and bringing up children in hard-working households, sometimes with heartless landlords in unhelpful neighborhoods. And plenty of the capital they would gain would come from owners nobody need weep for – owners who inherited it without effort, or earned it with skills educated at the expense of poorer taxpayers, or saved it without difficulty from privileged salaries for privileged work, or got it by holding land or avoiding taxes or deceiving people poorer than themselves as to the merits of used cars, slow horses or offshore funds – or had otherwise conned or skinned or sweated their fellow men and done nothing to improve their needy neighborhoods. Just as there are no satisfactory tests for separating the deserving from the undeserving poor, so there are none for separating the deserving from the undeserving rich.

The least bad approach to a once-for-all capital redistribution might therefore gentle it in three ways. First it should be generous in exempting *bona fide* personal possessions – house, garden, furniture, and even jewellery and pictures up to reasonable limits of value. Second, losers should be compensated (up to a flat limit) by means-tested pensions for life and perhaps for surviving widows and minors (or capital losses

274

should be taken into account in the operation of national superannuation schemes). Third, it is not worth attempting *either* a total equalization *or* a percentage levy on all capital. Even a progressive levy which takes half the small saver's savings, and meanwhile leaves the millionaire with a quarter of his million, has heavy personal and political costs and does comparatively little social justice.

So, instead, a once-for-all redistribution might go as follows:

Government should set a flat limit to the value of income-earning capital retainable on transfer day by any individual;[36] but the limit should be set high enough to exempt the holdings of a very high proportion of the population, including most 'primary savers' and hard cases of the kinds noticed earlier, and also the working capital of most tradesmen, professional men and one-man businesses. (It might be set at a figure somewhere between one and three times the national average family income.) Personal holdings above the limit should then be confiscated. Most of them should be redistributed into private ownership to bring everyone in the society (who is not already above it) up to an equal 'floor' of capital ownership (or alternatively of net worth, i.e. capital ownership plus one year's income). Thereafter, taxation should be designed to make it difficult to accumulate new fortunes above the limit.

Under those rules most of the redistributed capital would go to children. If it had to be held in trust by parents or others until its owners turned twenty-one that would be a useful barrier against sudden inflationary dissaving.

What could such a limited redistribution do for equalities? As argued earlier its main purpose would be to improve justice, social relations and social and economic controls, and to rescue a workable democracy from inflationary strains and conflicts, rather than to enrich those who gained from the transfers. Nevertheless the direct transfers would not be negligible. The income earned by transferred capital might add five or ten per cent to large numbers of the lowest household incomes – less than the gains available by reconstructing wage and salary patterns, but a useful addition to those gains, and a necessary condition of achieving many of them.[37]

It will be obvious that capital redistribution – even from no more than one citizen in twenty – could not go as simply as that simple sketch suggests. There would be complications, exceptions, exemptions, problems of eligibility and extra-territoriality, problems with divisible owners and indivisible assets, problems of detailed assessment. It is also unlikely

275

that the whole yield of such a levy would be transferred directly to other private citizens. Some might well go into public, cooperative or other ownership; some of the private gainers might participate through intermediate institutions of various kinds. There might well have to be anti-inflationary rules against dissaving and spending capital. And so on. Patterns of ownership are the subject of a few pages in the following chapter, but the practical design and administration of a capital redistribution would have to be the subject of many man-years of planning and volumes of detail. Here the purpose of the sketch is merely to introduce some summary comparison between once-for-all levies and regular annual capital taxes, and between transfers from citizen to citizen and the more conventional Left program of transfers to public ownership.

As against a drastic levy, there is this to be said for regular annual taxation of capital or net worth: it is less shocking, so in the short run more practicable. It accords with accepted ideas of progressive taxation – in practice it doesn't differ much from an additional income tax. It already operates in a number of capitalist countries. It does not force sudden, perhaps disruptive changes of management. And it accumulates (without frightening people or provoking capital flight) the systematic information on which larger levies might one day be based.

On the other hand: it is *too* normal. In countries which already have regular capital taxation it may have slowed or arrested some further unequalization of capital ownership but it has nowhere reversed it. It does comparatively little to reduce big fortunes and offers nothing except some minor tax relief to those with no fortunes. In a larger way, regular annual taxation of capital presents a dilemma. Either the rate of taxation is low enough to allow most investors to treat it as an income tax and keep ahead of it, in which case it doesn't do much for equalities. Or alternatively the rate is heavy enough to condemn most private fortunes to slow but sure extinction – which puts the nation's capital into what must thereafter be dubiously-motivated hands. When the best personal efforts can only slow down an inevitable process of loss, some capitalists may respond by investing more usefully and productively than ever; but from most, other responses seem likelier – evasive, despairing, destructive responses, with all sorts of efforts to export capital or the formal ownership of it, or to dissave and spend it before it's all gone. Those latter responses would be the rational ones in the circumstances. It doesn't seem prudent to put a country's capital resources, for many years, into the hands of an indignant, rebellious, jewel-smuggling, uncooperative, spendthrift class. By contrast a 'top end' confiscation which transferred

276

resources to many millions of (say) $2,000 shareholders under (say) a $10,000 or $20,000 shareholding limit would put those resources into fully ambitious and traditionally motivated capitalist hands. A drastic transfer does distributive justice more immediately. It immediately stops the worst effects which unequal capital ownership has on earned as well as unearned income. It allows the anti-inflationary regulation of earned incomes to make quicker and fairer progress. And it is irreversible, as annual capital taxation is not.

Conventional nationalization has rarely done much harm, and has often done good, to productive efficiency. But it has not been carried far enough in democratic countries to monotonize ownership and management. Public and private enterprises continue to interact with each other and set standards for each other, and whether or not they compete directly in a business way they often compete for personnel and public respect, and sometimes for capital. Nothing in communist experience suggests that the democratic world would be wise to go in for universal nationalization and monolithic state capitalism. Though democracies might run such systems more liberally and efficiently than dictatorships do, they would still bring needless problems of national planning, many bureaucratic rigidities and inefficiencies, and dangerous opportunities for the entrenchment of bureaucratic inequalities. Inequality, alienation and 'compulsory avarice' are the chief offences of capitalism. None of them is necessarily cured by bureaucratic monopoly of ownership and control. It would be better – more productive and more popular – to combine as much as possible of the freedom, diversity and market-responsiveness of the present system with measures which enforce effective equalities, while allowing a pluralist economic system to make full use of traditional motivation, but *also* to accommodate as much cooperative, independent and generously-motivated enterprise as people may come to want when inequalities are decently limited and 'ambition is optional'. So it is very desirable that people should relax about public ownership, as well as diversifying its forms. They should use it instrumentally as often as it is expedient, which it often is. But they should not identify socialism or equality, in a doctrinaire way, with exclusive public ownership. Even under democratic government monolithic state capitalism is likely to encourage less freedom, less efficiency and more bureaucratic inequality than will a pluralist system which includes widespread private shareholding *chiefly by poorish people with Leftish inclinations*, whose share incomes will rarely exceed five or ten percent of their whole incomes.

Widespread shareholding may give democracy some better anchorage.

277

It need not necessarily disturb much current management. It seems likely to have more straightforwardly productive motives than many of our present proprietors have, or will have if annual capital taxes condemn their fortunes to steady attrition. And it brings into being a classical entrenchment against 'restoration'. I don't believe it need corrupt many of the small shareholders. Family allowances, insurance policies and small savings don't corrupt people; nor would shareholdings of the same modest order, though some natural gamblers and frustrated success-seekers might get a good deal of pleasure and pain from master-minding their portfolios.

It may be objected that shareholding becomes pointless if it becomes universal. When shares are taken from the rich, why need they go to anybody? Why can't firms run without owners, as for example many universities and perpetual trusts do? Answers to this objection are perhaps more psychological than logical. If private shareholders exist, they help to prevent other parties from acting like owners. If government can act as if it owns everything (because nobody else owns anything) the freedoms and efficiencies of pluralism are harder to maintain. If workers can act as if they own the capital they use, there will be gross inequalities of wealth between workers in capital-intensive and labor-intensive industries. Private shareholders can resist either kind of takeover, especially if they support each other as a large majority of political voters. Firm by firm they *can* be organized, in extreme cases, as an indepedent voice (for good or ill, but at least for independence) in the firm's affairs. And a private capital market is useful to various kinds of small, wild or otherwise unsafe-looking innovators who are unlikely to attract support from public or institutional investors.

6

Used together, the suggested controls should allow unequal rewards to perform their usual functions – to reward merit, motivate work and attract skills to appropriate uses – within a general scale of inequality limited by democratic political choice.

In earlier chapters I have dealt evasively with that general scale by writing of 'threefold or fourfold orders of inequality'. What should that mean? If it means income per head it allows very great inequalities; if the lowest income is (say) the single apprentice's wage or the single old age pension, a threefold order allows as many as eighteen pensions to a high earner with a wife and four children: $50 a week to the pensioner's household, $900 to the other. And there are other prohibitive objections to 'per head' distributions. They don't match incomes to needs; they encourage dependence, and discourage work by more than one member of each household; either they force employers to prefer workers without dependants or they require excessively low wages and high welfare allowances. On the other hand a threefold order of *household* incomes, besides encouraging too many family separations and mock-separate households, would be unworkably flat in its differentials. Top people with families of six would be reluctant to work for three single pensions; low earners with families of six couldn't possibly live on *one*, as household equalities would require. Workable arrangements have to mix individual, household and 'time and life-time' considerations – as wage and welfare systems do, to some degree, everywhere. Every consideration of simplicity, efficiency and personal independence works in favor of a rate for the job, operating regardless of family or other need as the main monetary means of motivating and rewarding work. Taxes, public allowances, direct services and housing arrangements should then adjust resources to needs, chiefly by taxing those who don't have dependants to finance allowances and services to those who do.[38]

When wages and allowances, public services and housing and educational provisions are taken into account it again makes sense to talk in a general way of 'a threefold order of inequalities' *meaning* 'for standard families', with roughly equivalent standards and styles of living for other households according to their numbers and needs. Two thirds or three quarters of the households in most affluent societies already live within that range. It already motivates most people's work and ambition quite efficiently, and suffices for some at least of the rarest talents and ablest performances. If the threefold limit were applied to all incomes without exception the highest and lowest incomes need go to comparatively few: to a handful of stars at the top and (to be realistic) perhaps 15 or 20% – imperfect workers and non-workers and lowest-rate age pensioners – at the bottom. Between those two extremes, in societies rich enough to allow long life and physical comfort to all, eight people of every ten can cooperate or compete, motivate each other to work and support each other in retirement, within a twofold order: if laborers get $100 a week (and $20 or $30 per child), run-of-the-mill managing directors and medical specialists and professors get $200 (and $20 or $30 per child, and a better house, and a better pension on retirement). To impose those limits in practice would be much, much easier than is generally supposed *as long as the limitation began at the top.*

Some cynics and some idealists will still spit at the idea of a three-fold order of inequality – because of the self-interest it still encourages and the class differences it still allows. Nevertheless it could make us more equal than communist societies are, or any dictatorial societies are ever likely to be. Housing, land and domestic resources could be distributed more equally than income, to allow people very fair shares of whatever they wanted of common lifestyle or individual difference. Within the suggested range of incomes most trades could offer some 'success above average' to their most successful individuals. Between trades and within them differentials could be at once big enough and small enough to make ambition attractive but optional, and to make the interest of the work and the human company there (or the dirt or danger or monotony there) about as powerful as the money in inclining people to one job rather than another.

The purpose of equality is not to abolish differentiation – of pay or anything else – but to free people from its anxious and punishing and corrupting effects so that they can enjoy its liberating, individualist and sociable possibilities. Better than any other writer, Richard Tawney understood the relations between material equality and personal difference, and between the radical and conservative purposes of egalitarian reform. 'All decent people are at heart conservatives, in the sense of desiring to conserve the human associations, loyalties, affections, pious bonds between man and man... What makes the working classes revolutionary is that modern economic conditions are constantly passing a steam roller over these immaterial graces and pieties... What they want is security and opportunity...a fair chance of leading an independent, fairly prosperous life... They want to 'conserve' the home, the property, the family of the worker.' So he wrote in his commonplace book in 1912; then in a famous passage of *Equality* (1931): 'What is repulsive is not that one man should earn more than others, for where community of environment, and a common education and habit of life, have bred a common tradition of respect and consideration, these details of the counting house are forgotten or ignored. It is that some classes should be excluded from the heritage of civilization which others enjoy, and that the fact of human fellowship, which is ultimate and profound, should be obscured by economic contrasts, which are trivial and superficial. What is important is not that all men should receive the same pecuniary income. It is that the surplus resources of society should be so husbanded and applied that it is a matter of minor significance whether they receive it or not.'[39]

So inflation and the maldistribution of money, and the strains they impose on democratic life, might be attacked together by means of a capital transfer, regulation of incomes to reduce inequalities and to influence wage-costs of production, and diverse methods of price control. The last two seem unlikely to work well without the first.

Most leaders of the democratic Left don't yet offer to do all of that, because they think it would scare more electors than it would attract. They know their business and their electors, and they know how vividly the Right would dramatize that program as a program of tyranny, confiscation and economic breakdown. They believe they must still compete chiefly for the support of swinging voters with middle incomes. It is fair to say that those who hold office from time to time in Germany, the United Kingdom and Australasia hold it all too often by favoring the middle against the poor, with little but symbolic harm to the rich. But the troubles in sight down the middle of the road may soon make it politic for those parties to write a genuine program of equality, try to build a broad alliance of the Left around it, risk losing an election or two – and see what sweet persuasion (and bitter experience of the ongoing alternatives) can do to attract a majority for it.

Besides being free, an equalizing society has to be productive. People worry as much about bureaucratic inefficiency as about bureaucratic oppression. Whatever a reforming society may want in a productive way – whether conventional economic growth or austere conservation – its economic life needs to be efficient. A no-growth or low-energy economy, or a self-sacrificing society working to give grain or machinery or expertise to poor countries, would have *more* need, not less, to extract most output from least resources. Could an equalizing society organize and motivate production as efficiently as we do now?

11
Organized production

More than half of modern production – the work of the domestic economy, and of plenty of trades and small businesses – can look after itself as long as it can get the resources it needs, and operate under sensible laws. Difficulty sets in with scale – with work that needs complicated organization and breeds hierarchy, inequality and alienation. It has to be done because we'd starve without it, but what could a more equal society do to reduce its bad by-products?

Readers don't need a description of the existing organization of production. It will do to notice some ways in which it may have to change. They are of three general kinds. The productive system needs to act as a better distributor, especially of incomes and 'home capital', as discussed earlier. It needs to be more responsive to changing environmental and social priorities. And both those requirements have to be met by efficient arrangements for organizing and motivating work. The following sections deal in turn with reformist purposes, productive priorities, public institutions, and the ownership and management and motivation of the more complicated kinds of production.

I

Ends and means constrain one another: democracies can only choose changes they are capable of carrying out. Some necessary new aims can't be achieved through existing structures of ownership, management and government. Nor could many of them be achieved through monopolist Russian-bureaucratic structures even if democrats would accept such structures. Would better methods therefore mix elements of both those standard patterns? Some Right realists and Left cynics used to forecast a converging similarity between the vast private and public bureaucracies of the USA and the USSR. Softer socialists have dreamed of closing the gap between two friendlier models. Sweden seems the most socialist of the capitalist democracies. Among communist societies Yugoslavia perhaps allows most petty-capitalist freedoms. Democracy and state socialism had an all-too-brief trial marriage in Czechoslovakia in 1968. I once thought of calling this book *The Road to Liberec*, after the Czech town with the free-sounding name which happens to lie midway between the boundaries of Sweden and Yugoslavia. But affluent social-democracies won't want Yugoslav tyrannies or inefficiencies, and plenty of Swedes want to improve a good many Swedish institutions.

Social-democratic economies should generally aim at the lightest, most flexible central controls that are consistent with decisive democratic sovereignty; and – subject to the same sovereignty – at pluralism, independence and market-responsiveness in industrial and commercial management. They should allow as many private economic freedoms as they safely can, and wherever they can they should offer double or alternative motivation: conventional sticks and carrots where justice or human frailty require them, but also the widest possible opportunities for people to work, without penalty, for cooperative or generous reasons, and for the interest of the work and the social relations that go with it.

Reformers should be prepared to forget some Left rules of thumb, and remember how serviceable many capitalist mechanisms could easily become. The profit motive can be quite a brotherly bond among cooperative producers. Making the polluter pay could have many of the advantages claimed for it if it distributed equal increases of price to people with equal incomes. Many dilemmas of environmental management are dilemmas chiefly because spending power is so unequally distributed. Many capitalist mechanisms should work with admirable freedom and efficiency when there is a socialist distribution of income. (By contrast, the currently-developing socialist institutions of wage, price, profit and environmental control promise to work with oppressive inefficiency and inequality while capitalist distributions continue.) There is real social and material economy in every bit of work that can be done in an independent way without having to be planned, approved, coordinated or supervised by somebody else – in the work of every household, shop, workshop, skilled trade and family business that can work independently without danger of exceeding the permitted limits of income. And a managed pluralist system which allows market success to perform a good many of its traditional functions should be able – as state socialist systems are not – to allow plenty of experiment with cooperative and communal methods of production.

Economic freedoms are immensely valuable for personal and social as well as economic reasons. Everyman should have the widest possible options of job, employer and type of work. Tradesmen should be free to work for wages or to risk setting up on their own. Innovators should have chances to innovate, not only by kind permission of public or private monopolists. Families prepared to work long hours for the sake of independence and risky chances of raising or lowering their incomes should be able to take on corner shops, restaurants, quick-food bars, caravan camps, boarding houses, round-the-clock service stations. There should be delivery rounds, night and weekend and vacation work, overtime and moonlighting for other eager beavers with more ambition than love of leisure. At the same time there should be good enough basic pay and housing and family allowances for forty hours of unskilled labor to keep a family in the essentials of a common life-style so that after that basic stint of work by one of them, husband and wife and children can choose freely between work and leisure, or between paid work for others and do-it-yourself work for themselves. All those freedoms are consistent with a range of personal incomes limited by regulation and taxation; and with managed markets and prices, big public and cooperative sectors, and other necessary paraphernalia of central economic management and inequality control in a social-democratic society. None of those freedoms has to include or depend on any right to get excessively rich. Opportunities for choice and independence and innovation need to be reconciled with requirements of equality, not sacrificed to them.

2

Decisions about what to produce and what resources to use must adapt all the time to changing technical understanding and social values. Non-experts can't contribute much to the technical part of the business. But there is a prior need to adapt institutions so that environmental policies *can* be chosen for their technical and social merits. The examples which follow are not a technical program, they merely illustrate some organizational problems.

One faction of experts says (in effect) Stop Knowledge Now. Chapter 1 expressed an opinion about the likely effects of that in rich countries; in poor countries the effects would be worse. People in lifeboats fish if they can, however they may quarrel about the catch. Of course it is likely that some scientific advances will be misused. But the effects of trying to feed and shelter the world population of A.D. 2000 or 2100 within the technical limitations of 1975 look so predictably horrible that they surely justify quite dangerous gambling, even for those who see science as a sorcerer's apprentice. Research has to be economized, it can be better or worse directed, and there is room for better social control of its output; but there has never been a time in history when the risks of advance and the risks of retreat looked so unequal. Even standstill conservatism would now have to depend on radical innovation. For some of its advocates, stopping science is a despairing way to stop rich extravagance; but whatever its motives its first effect would be to quicken the deathrate of the poor.

By no means all environmentalists want that. In *The Closing Circle* (New York, 1971) Barry Commoner sums up the case for intensified scientific effort and technical substitution. Changing ways of using materials have done at least as much as rising numbers and living standards have done to increase pollution and to exhaust resources, i.e. pollution and resource-use have increased faster per head than consumption has. Some conservative environmentalists see that as a law: more production per head will always have diminishing marginal efficiency and increasing environmental cost. But it does not seem necessary to accept the work of one thoughtless generation as irreversible. It makes more sense to develop different directions of growth and principles of substitution. Products and processes should be chosen for their costs in energy, materials and pollution rather than for their money costs only.

That will require some changes in social accounting and in patterns of private and public control and ownership. Suppose for example that it is decided that most new industrial, commercial and housing development should have integrated energy arrangements wherever possible, and that most existing systems should be replaced through a steady program of conversion. Suppose it is also decided to divert substantial resources to research into the uses of sunshine as the likeliest source of harmless and plentiful energy. Those policies might pay in the long run but in the short run they have heavy costs. Many trades have to be reconstructed, and consumers must live on less for a decade or two. Suppose the policy goes further: wider ranges of production and service are made to modify their methods to economize energy and scarce materials, and to improve conditions of work. Simple cost criteria have to give way to multiple, often contradictory criteria. Industries can't be made over all at once, so expensive new methods come into competition with cheap old methods. This must often reconstruct relations between government, public and private enterprise, and the public as voters and consumers. A Left/environmentalist alliance will want them to be reconstructed with continuous care for wages and conditions of work, and for consumers' shares.

10-2

As national resource policies develop they are likely to affect production in one or other of three ways which could be crudely characterized as simple economy, expensive substitution and deliberate gambling.

Some restraints might always have been sensible. Smaller, tamer, less pollutant cars could be as efficient for most purposes as many of the cars made now. Powered transport might well be banned from most off-road uses. Forests, oil and human talent could all be economized and some litter and pollution reduced if we did with less packaging, brand advertising and commercial promotion. (Those who want to minimize other changes could then propose that television be financed by taxes on soap and breakfast food, while those who want to reform television and taxation as well as packaging could think of other arrangements.) Investments in public transport and pedestrian arrangements could become less competitive and more directive. Many changes of that sort can be done by regulation or public investment and if the transitions are managed well they need not do much harm to mass standards of living.

Then there are economies and substitutions which would bring social or environmental benefits, but also serious costs. Some production would suffer and many people would live less well if private cars were banned altogether before a generation of work had first been done to prepare cities and rural communications to run without them. Many substitutions which might be made to spin out reserves of scarce materials would raise costs and reduce consumption in one way or another. So would some water filtration, sewage treatment and smoke abatement. So would some restraints designed to maintain stable balances of use and replacement, e.g. of soil or timber or fish (though with most of those the alternative higher consumption couldn't last long). Action against pollution sometimes improves yields, as when energy is used more efficiently, or wastes find profitable uses, or rivers are cleaned for water supply or recreation; but higher costs and lower outputs are commoner. Most of these policies have divisive elements of social substitution or self-denial. The easiest to adopt are usually those which improve environmental quality immediately (e.g. water filtration, smoke abatement). Next may be those which promise to perpetuate supplies (e.g. of timber or fish) through the life-times of those who take the abstinent decisions. It may be hardest to attract majorities for self-sacrificing policies of generational or international aid.

Third, there are resource policies which have to gamble on chances of technical progress: how much to invest in which lines of research, how fast to deplete resources meanwhile, what risks to take with radioactivity, insecticides, herbicides, vulnerable monocultures, and so on. Should people go hungry in order to conserve 'irreplaceable' resources which may turn out to be replaceable after all? Conflict multiplies conflict, as technical uncertainties confuse the political competition of conflicting interests and ideologies.

Oil illustrates most of these problems well enough. Should we replace its replaceable uses, at some cost to everybody and at high cost to those who must mine and handle more coal? If that merely hurries substitutions which must be made sooner or later, there may not be much point in it. But it might spin out reserves for what are at present irreplaceable uses – for free-steering transport, aviation, farming, drugs, plastics. If the benefits of those were distributed to be enjoyed by absolutely more people through more generations, it would be good to replace the replaceable uses quickly. But existing institutions won't distribute benefits in that way, or distribute the costs of replacement fairly either. And all the odds are complicated by the international distribution of the oil. Lucky countries could keep their own reserves in the ground for as long as they could afford to buy and burn other people's; unlucky countries might as well consume all they can get now, since abstinence now will do them no good later. Current efforts to 'internationalize' supplies are all brutally self-interested. Only two policies seem to choose themselves. One is research into alternative sources of energy. Big science will go for the glittering prizes of solar, geothermal or cleaner atomic energy. It may be well to hedge those bets with equal money for research into ways of collecting or economizing energy locally, or living well with less of it. Meanwhile international flows of oil are already being interrupted by earlier and less predictable events than the exhaustion of the reserves. Countries with coal should rebuild a capacity to mine it and use it, even at some cost in local pollution. Of course it would also be good if the owners of the reserves of oil would split prices to rich and poor buyers. But dictators who run unequalizing policies at home are not likely to run any other sort abroad.

Whatever else they are, these are all problems of distribution, and most of them are superimposed on older problems of distribution. The mixture of old and new issues often reconstructs traditional political options. The rest of this section draws examples from the business of preparing the cities to run without oil. It neglects technical questions (of transport systems and building technique) in order to notice three more general aspects of urban policy. First, some city forms seem likelier than others to reconcile requirements of equality and minimum environmental risk.

287

Second, that way of thinking illustrates a general decision-making bias for minimum risk and maximum future adaptability. Third, small changes in environmental or political facts can be as important as large ones if they happen to affect critical balances. Urban problems include many reminders that the unsuccessful programs of the past didn't always fail to get elected because they were 'wrong'. Some of them failed for want of some small margin of technical advantage or political support. Whenever old programs were good programs it is worth watching for small changes in technical or political conditions – for moments when old environmental programs can pick up new support from the Left, or old programs of equality can pick up new support for environmental reasons.

Urban policies have to be chosen in the face of multiple uncertainties. There is uncertainty about future population numbers, energy sources and transport techniques. When the cities have to live without oil there may or may not be other-fuelled private cars. There may or may not be new modes of public transport. For a time at least there should be network electricity for light, heat, transport and industrial power; but it may or may not come from sources so cheap and plentiful that people will be happy to use it to run a lot of elevators, coolers and air-conditioners, ventilating systems and water pumps.

Urban fabric takes so long to build then lasts so long and is so expensive to alter that structures planned now should be adaptable to as many as possible of those uncertain futures – and also to some other possibilities. Some imaginable scientific advances could realize the optimists' visions of rich societies with abundant energy, leisure and mobility – and large demands for private space. Alternatively, environmental constraints could force longer working hours, less leisure and no private transport. Other kinds of constraint could bring poverty and high unemployment – with millions of people short of work, money and personal resources and likely to make some resentful uses of their 'leisure'. In all those cases people will want plenty of local space. There may also be public disorder; and all parties may have reason to worry about the urban fabric in which it occurs. A big metropolis dependent on a single, complex, high-cost centre encourages its dominant minorities to dig their heels in and go on extracting, somehow, the human and money and energy costs of servicing the only viable centre of their operations. Such over-complicated institutions are the hardest to reform, the hardest to capture undamaged in a revolutionary way, but the easiest to wreck. If New York and Chicago are any guide it would be prudent for the rest of the world to stop overbuilding metropolitan centes which depend from hour to hour on overcomplicated physical networks and energy supplies, and from day to day on huge mileages of commuter transport. Besides their ordinary problems of anonymity and law-and-order, such centres positively invite military, technical and social disasters. No urban form is so vulnerable to shortages of energy, to 'complexity breakdowns' or to aimless summer riots or deliberate sabotage.[40]

What sort of cities seem likely to be most adaptable to the widest range of those alternative possibilities? Networks of smallish self-containable cities, or conurbations organized in a many-centred way; cities which distribute housing, work and central places in spatial patterns which would allow reasonably frequent and accessible public transport to run on network power if necessary; walk-up cities with gravity-borne water and sewerage and as much natural light, ventilation and warmth as the climate allows; cities with low-to-medium residential densities arranged to allow plenty of housing on private land especially for their poorer families, plenty of ground-level housing and service for the old and the lame, and some denser central housing (still served by stairs and gravity systems) for those who want it; cities which combine old-fashioned capacities for localization with plenty of new-fangled telecommunications; cities (in short) which can adapt, inconveniently but without breakdown, to varying supplies of power and private transport, to walking and cycling, to natural ventilation, local waste disposal and other temporary or permanent improvisations, and in which home is a tolerably resourceful private realm if public systems (technical and social) are interrupted from time to time, or permanently impoverished.

It happens that those are not characteristics of freakish cities designed for nothing except coping with unlikely crises. At worst they are the characteristics of the more comfortable of the 'suburban train and tram' cities built through the first half of the twentieth century. At best they are the characteristics which generations of urban planners and philosophers recommended for reasons of health, safety, efficiency, sociability and equality until the profession was briefly captured by 'Right realism'. Except for some missing equalities, they are also the characteristics of the best-loved quarters of some of the world's great cities; and of many of the smaller cities and towns whose old-fashioned fabric still houses majorities of most rich countries' populations.

The adaptable crisis-capacities of cities of that kind don't hinder their comfort or efficiency in normal times. The careful relation of centres, work and housing to one another and to public transport routes is quite

289

consistent with good road systems. With or without private cars such cities can offer comparatively short journeys, pedestrian and cycling possibilities, 'human scale' at home and street level, and reserves of physical and social tolerance which are as enjoyable in good times as in bad. Being cheap to run, they leave their people richer. Even central-city life can often be more interesting within walk-up distance of the streets than it can when extravagant commitments of money and power hoist it forty floors into the sky. The medium-sized, medium-dense house-and-garden cities may be less exciting to some rich minorities (though they often bring up more high talent than the biggest cities do); but they are simpler to plan, govern, reform or reconstruct, and to many of both rich and poor tastes they have always been the most agreeable to live in.

The point of this example is to notice how helpfully old and new issues can sometimes mix. Many of those easy-living cities have been threatened from two quarters. Private motoring encouraged their suburban sprawl to take on shapes and relationships which could never be served very well by any technique of public transport. Some people including most town planners always opposed that *type* of sprawl; now at last the environmental costs of overbuilt centres and too much private motoring, and the foreseeable exhaustion of the oil, are generating majorities for saner policies. The second threat to those efficient urban forms came from the behavior of capitalist land markets under Right government. Public and private developers overbuilt the centres, and starved the sprawling suburbs of local centres and services and communal activities, because in such unequal societies a few capital-rich minorities and central-office bureaucrats found it convenient to do so. Landlords and public administrators meanwhile crowded the cities' service populations into dense housing because for their poor customers, land prices seemed to prohibit better housing closer to the ground. Minorities had social objections to both types of development; other minorities had environmental objections; other minorities disliked the fortunes made from the business, and the land prices and class transfers of wealth which accompanied it. Only now when new issues and anxieties are superimposed on the old do those various minorities increase and come together to constitute majorities for saner and fairer policies: for relaxed densities, public transport capacities, smaller and more accessible centres, and fairer shares of more resourceful private space.

Thus the same sensible urban fabric promises the best accommodation for any of the likely alternative futures. Faced with other uncertainties in other fields, policy-makers should be alert for similar least-risk solutions, and useful reconciliations of old and new programs.

3

The existing means of central economic management were designed chiefly to finance government and to influence levels of employment. They now have to regulate prices, incomes and the use of resources. Grafting those new functions into the old ones will multiply the complexity of the business and make it harder to coordinate efficiently. It also requires central government to answer to its electors in confusing new ways. For policies of national solvency and full employment, governments have answered chiefly through national elections. They must still answer in that way for the general success of their new income and environmental policies; but those policies also introduce a lot of day-by-day dealing with wage-bargaining groups, environmentalists, grass-roots democrats of many kinds. There are likely to be more conflicts than ever (for national politicians) between general and local policies, and between national and local popularity.

Cabinet government operates coherently enough through national treasuries, central banks, controls on other lenders and borrowers, taxes and tariffs, import and exchange controls, public capital and current expenditures and other familiar institutions to control national levels of credit and consumer demand and through them, levels of employment. This machinery can't cope with hard-bargaining inflation but it is still serviceable for its own purposes and it also plays a part in the delivery of various social policies. It needs to be further refined so that controls on trade and credit, while doing their traditional work, can at the same time help to implement more detailed policies of selective investment and resource-use. Such detailing happens already through the planning of public investment, through selective taxes and trade and exchange controls and through the public direction or limitation of a good deal of private finance to particular uses, e.g. to mortgage-lending, consumer credit, particular regions or types of industry, etc. It should not be too hard to refine the controls themselves to implement other discriminating policies, but it will of course be hard to reorganize and re-educate government to do the work in effective and coherent and responsive ways.

For the control of inequality and cost inflation there need to be (besides some reallocation of public investments and services) four kinds of institutional action. Two of them – the redistribution and ongoing

291

taxation of income-earning capital, and the regulation of self-employed and other irregular incomes – must chiefly be the business of taxation offices, with some new agencies to handle transfers of capital property. A third – the control of profits and prices – belongs partly to new responsibilities of public and private business management to be discussed later, and partly to the fourth arm of inequality-control: the machinery for arriving at the mass of salaries, wages, fees, conditions of work, and related prices. Most of this machinery can be somewhat independent of the existing central machinery of national economic management, and should affect its work chiefly by simplifying it. Standard methods of contriving full employment and just-right demand should work more surely and safely when they can be operated with less anxiety about cost inflation.

The most difficult task of all may be to achieve the necessary coordination between the existing central machinery and the complicated new requirements of environmental policy, and sometimes also of participant planning. These problems need be no worse in an equalizing society than in any other; but they are difficult in any circumstances. Central government will simply cease if it has to stop the clock twice a day, and several dozen times in the preparation of each national budget, to wait six months for another Environmental Impact Study, or Participant Dialogue. But it will cease just as surely if it allows secretive, domineering, single-purpose bureaux to carve the highways, dam the rivers, alienate the minerals and the standing timber, locate the power stations and comprehensively devastate the citizens' neighborhoods in the masterful manner of yesteryear.

What can be done about this? Government is a *flow* – of decisions, and the works and events which follow from them. Most of the decisions have to be rule-bound, and many of the rest have to be taken by educated instinct; deliberate, well-researched and well-discussed decisions can never be more than a very few. Even for some of those, I think there may soon be some return to the old democratic device of electing servants whose skills and intentions can generally be trusted. That isn't the present tendency. Most current efforts to reform the machinery try to make the homework more reliably encyclopaedic (Impact Studies for Everything), and they multiply opportunities for scrutiny and adversary action. Though their intentions are good I believe the 'encyclopaedic' and 'adversary' tendencies will prove to have been educational phases in the development of new styles of public and private management, rather than permanent trends in either. To get an efficient flow of business, officials will have to be trusted again – but with some new arrangements to encourage them to behave in trustworthy ways, and to see to their own coordinations, participant arrangements, environmental studies, etc. When an engineer understands that his job and prospects depend on that sort of performance, rather than on getting the road built fastest and cheapest, then road-building will go more economically and sensitively than any number of adversary confrontations are likely to make it.

This is not an argument for benevolent dictatorship. Rules, routines, education and administrative discretion will always be related to one another in subtle ways. It rarely does to trust any one of them alone. There will continue to be specialist agencies for environmental management and elaborate patterns of formal and informal communication between them and other arms of government, to coordinate their business. But for adding environmental dimensions to the business of most arms of government, Departments of the Environment may not be the most important agents of change. In the long run the whole machine needs to be staffed by people sensitive to environmental values, as many are already sensitive to citizens' rights, constitutional limitations, rules for financial probity, etc. Anyone responsible for sensitive enterprises is likely to protect the citizens and their environment better by committing business to people with appropriate personal and professional qualities than by laying down foolproof procedures, then leaving the business to any fool chosen by Personnel's computer. Government must always mix those methods; the sensitivities will only be reliable when the latent sanctions are reliable; but to get business done efficiently and acceptably there will probably have to be some shift of emphasis back from extravagantly cautious and time-consuming routines to redoubled care for the education, selection and motivation of the people concerned. That need not be undemocratic if the necessary sensitivities and tastes for participant decision-making come to be a public servant's most promotable qualities. Citizens, flora and fauna will get more attention from servants aware of that, than from rule-bound operators conditioned to regard citizens as enemies with strictly defined rights to appear at statutory moments with writs. For similar reasons the most valuable kinds of environmental education may not be the most specialized kinds. Four-year courses which educate people in nothing but 'environmental studies' may prove to be less valuable than shorter courses, part-time courses and in-service courses which give otherwise-qualified specialists a better sense of the complexity and interdependence of social and

293

natural systems. In the long run that sort of awareness should be built into many of the specialist and technical studies themselves – and into everybody's second nature.

4

To sketch the organization of a reformed economy in a few pages is already difficult enough without complicating the attempt with future hypotheticals. If only to allow simpler syntax, the reader is asked once again to step ten or twenty years into the future. This is how it might look:

Ownership means what it always did.

Production and services are still carried on by large numbers of independent firms and agencies. Plenty of them – almost as many as ever – are share-owned capitalist firms or independent cooperatives. Each has to keep a public register of its beneficial shareholders, who may be individuals, or other firms which keep such registers, or non-profit institutions, or public agencies. There are severe restrictions on non-resident shareholders, i.e. people and corporations who are not subject to home sovereignty for all tax purposes. From time to time there are restraints on dissaving. Otherwise, shares are traded in open markets.

Public business is carried on as in the past by trusts and corporations which own their plant and do their business much as private firms do, under the same regulation of prices and incomes. Public management has always had to meet changing and contradictory requirements as to profit, public interest, etc.; more private enterprise now has to do more of the same.

There is plenty of taxation through prices, for reasons of economic and social and environmental policy. After tax, wages and prices in many industries are set to allow comparatively little self-financing out of earnings, beyond maintenance and growth in step with population numbers. From those norms the more efficient firms wring a little additional expansion and the less efficient don't. That helps to motivate management and to tell investors where the good managers are. But most substantial growth has to be financed by new capital from investors – private, institutional or public. This helps pricing policies and selective growth policies to be judged independently, each on its merits; and for purposes of inequality-control it prevents much capital gain by investors. Firms can't usually price their outputs to yield large margins for reinvestment;

294

but if they do make windfall profits, what remain after corporation taxes have to be paid as dividends to shareholders, to be handled and taxed as income before they can be reinvested. The margins for growth and capital gain, though small, are still significant for incentive purposes between firm and firm in competitive industries.

Besides share-owned firms and public corporations there is more than there used to be of cooperative ownership, or cooperative management of trust-owned assets. Some old-style consumer cooperatives and producer cooperatives continue. Some big retailing has elements of both, as well as ordinary shareholding.

Because issues of free speech and political independence were involved, it is worth noticing some arrangements which were made for newspapers and book publishers at the time of the capital transfers. It was unthinkable that government should acquire any proprietorial influence over the press, even through the semi-independent public unit trusts which were created to redistribute many of the confiscated shares. Most news companies fell into one of two classes. Those which already had large numbers of small shareholders were left like that, with many new small shareholders on their registers. But the old proprietors' chains were broken up to put each paper into the hands of a producer cooperative. Journalists, printers and deliverers elect the board and live on shares instead of wages. If they prosper, price and income controls stop them getting too rich. If they don't, they eventually get so poor that they lose staff and close down. Their land, buildings and machinery are ultimately the property of regional newspaper trusts – non-profit, non-government bodies whose trustees are elected by registered newspaper companies. The trusts perform various services for the trade; besides leasing plant to the big producer cooperatives they lease at variously commercial or uncommercial rents to specialist, experimental and other small papers. Thus all concerned have options: journalists and printers can look for work for either wages or shares, and capital can be raised on the market or leased from the trusts. It would thus be a difficult industry for any government to censor in a political way, though in most countries a democratic consensus still imposes some criminal-law restraints on incitement to crime, and on some kinds of pornography and exploitation of violence.

Book publishing has a different history and offers another example of the ways in which economic controls have been adapted to the idiosyncracies of particular industries. The old family firms had already been through one round of trials before the capital transfers, when some did

295

and others did not sell out to the conglomerate corporations which went after them in the 1960s and 1970s. Most of the proprietors who survived the takeovers survived the capital transfers too: they liked the trade well enough to accept some capital losses and stay on as managers with limited shareholdings. As a matter of policy most of the conglomerate-owned firms became independent again. Shares in them were offered first to employees and their dependants, as their personal transfer quotas. That was enough to give effective control of most houses to their employees, as the only concentration of small shareholders likely to turn up to annual general meetings in an industry in which government or other institutional shareholding (except by some non-profit institutions such as universities) is prohibited. Meanwhile price controls apply formulae which drop the price of a few best-selling books in step with their sales, but beyond that the nature of the trade is such that price and income controls cannot pin firms to the fine-but-steady profit margins which apply to more predictable industries. So they are pinned to limited rates of dividend and (as one of a small category of artistic and design industries which are treated in this way) allowed almost unlimited self-financing growth. Some successful publishers therefore devote their gains to growing at the expense of the less successful. Others don't – being the people they are they earn up to permitted personal limits and beyond that they use their successes to finance less commercial things which happen to interest them. Poetry and experimental writing, some religious writing and a good deal of political and social criticism get published in that way (as they always did). So the trade as a whole is as diversified and competitive as it ever was.

These are special cases, and so are a number of other trades for special reasons. But the bulk of manufacturing, wholesaling and retailing is still done by the familiar old pattern of firms (minus most of the old conglomerates) from billion-dollar extractive and manufacturing corporations through share-owned processing, wholesaling and retailing chains to independent tradesmen and family-owned corner shops and delivery rounds. Rather than describe the working of the private sector in detail it will be enough to summarize some of the ways in which it has had to adapt to changing patterns of public control since about 1975.

All shareholders are small shareholders, or institutions which represent small savers or shareholders, or governmental or other non-profit institutions. Salaries and wages (except a few of the highest, for which some special arrangements are described below) are negotiated under the guidelines and through the machinery sketched in earlier chapters. And into most of the private sector there has been inserted a network of public rules, employees and services designed for various purposes of scrutiny, control and assistance to private enterprise. This network is the practical expression of four general principles: selective public ownership, 'open-book' accounting, administrative justice for corporations, and two-tiered corporate management.

Public ownership (or in some cases public management of private assets) is applied where nothing less can assure good environmental performance, or distribute the costs of environmental care equitably, or impose effective price or income controls. Some of the public takeovers are permanent, as with the public ownership of some threatened resources and a good deal of waste processing. In some industries, notably land development and housing and office and factory building, the public does enough business to keep the industry competitive or to 'manage the market'. Other interventions are temporary or punitive, as when individual firms are expropriated or taken under public management for persistently breaking price or income or environmental guidelines.

The second general principle requires public accounting by firms above defined sizes (defined differently in different industries). Directors direct these firms with most of their former freedom; they authorize all receipts and payments of money; but the people who make and record the payments have public responsibilities. Private enterprise hasn't been nationalized but some of its accountancy has – accountants are licensed by a public office, under rules worked out between that and various other branches of government. To keep their licenses they must keep corporate accounts in approved form and be responsible for relevant tax, income, cost and price returns. (Many of those aren't 'returned' or subjected to much bureaucratic scrutiny; they amount to permanent public records, for reference only when necessary.) Firms can run as much additional and independent management accounting as they like, as long as it also is open. The open books have done more good than harm to productive efficiencies, and they have done away with a lot of obfuscation, double book-keeping, industrial espionage, and adversary relations between business and government.

Those arrangements are a part of what its critics regard as the most oppressive of the new principles of control. Corporate status is not as comfortable as it was. Except in a few matters of taxation individuals continue to enjoy the civil rights and protections which the courts always afforded them; but in some of their relations with government, corporations don't. Corporate property and management are open to administrative direction, and most appeals against that sort of administrative action

297

go to ministers or policy boards rather than to courts. (As one result, no individual or family now assumes a corporate personality for purposes of tax avoidance.) Several arms of government are 'indicative planners' and business is expected to comply with their guidelines and regulations. If a firm doesn't appear to comply, the relevant agency can ask a central Industrial Board to exercise one or other of a range of disciplinary powers. The Board can order that the firm's accountants be replaced by nominees of the complaining agency. It can 'proclaim' a firm and replace some or all of the members of its supervisory board with public nominees, temporarily or permanently. It can empower the relevant public agencies to particularize their guidelines by issuing specific price, income, environmental or other directives to specific firms. As an ultimate weapon it can take firms into public ownership, with or without compensation to shareholders – though the mere existence of that power is enough to ensure that it needn't be used, and it rarely is. The Industrial Board exists to make sure that any of these powers are used with care and consistency; in these areas the planning arms of government don't have coercive powers of their own. The whole apparatus would once have appeared as an intolerable threat to property rights. Now that ownership is so widely distributed it appears rather as a power over management. As a power of occasional intervention – a power to govern by exception – it is used as often to protect shareholders' interests as to injure them. More people own shares than own houses – it would be political suicide to confiscate either capriciously.

The fourth principle requires two-tiered direction of most corporate enterprises, public or private, above defined sizes. The two-tiered pattern developed from origins in European business structure, and in some Anglo-American types of public trust. A typical corporate board consists of full-time executives with as much security of tenure as such people are allowed these days. But that board answers to a supervisory board which has ultimate control and legal responsibility for the firm's performance. Some supervisory boards have one or two full-time members but most of their members are part-timers. They are nominated by shareholders, employees, management (through the working board) and where appropriate by consumer councils, environmental agencies and offices of government; and they may coopt members for special reasons of expertise, or liaison. Members are removable by those who nominate them, and in practice are removed freely enough because they don't depend for their bread on such part-time appointments. Whether the supervisory boards govern masterfully, or rubber-stamp the work of their executive boards, varies widely with circumstances and personalities.

The two-tiered arrangements were developed in response to two types of experience, one private and one public. In many of the old private corporations management had become a self-perpetuating caste, all too secure from interference by anybody. Boards perpetuated themselves as they pleased, as long as they avoided bankruptcy or takeover; one of the nuisances of the system was that poor management often couldn't be replaced *except* by takeover. Life assurance corporations weren't even exposed to that; and plenty of other managements had as little to fear from their shareholders as the Life managers had from their policy-holders. Any shareholders big enough to be heard were usually also insti-tutional – i.e. other managers with managers' interests uppermost. As the chairman of one of the first national share-buying commissions put it as long ago as 1974 'the directors are killing the old capitalism. They treat labor as the enemy, consumers as prey, share-holders and governments with contempt. They run the machine for the satisfaction of manage-ment'. Means had to be found of making those cliques answer to people with interests other than their own.

Public business also suffered, often from bureaucratic rigidities under irremovable management. Public service structures had been designed long ago to deliver honest, experienced government under changing politicians. For that purpose their bureaucratic structure, with orderly irreversible promotion and security of tenure, had merits. But delivering government is different from delivering other goods. The best of the business operations of government were often the nationalized industries which kept some of their original business structure and flexibility but accepted political direction and new severities of audit and investigation. The worst were often transport, road-building, water, power, housing and public building monopolies staffed on public service principles and com-manded by bureaucrats entrenched against any serious interference by their quick-changing political masters. Business in those fields often had long lead-times. Work committed under one government had been planned under the one before and would be completed under the one after; and its implications were often too complex to be mastered in the time that politicians could give to them. The independent strength which this gave to the public servants was sometimes used by good men to excellent purpose. But it was just as often used to perpetuate stodge, inefficiency and the worst oppressions of high-handed bureaucracy. It was responsible (for example) for many of the mid-century urban reconstructions. Irremovable public service engineers committed the urban motorways; irremovable public housing administrators bulldozed the slums and built the tower flats and the ghetto estates. Politicians could block such things but they couldn't get radically different and better things planned merely by giving different instructions to the old machine. They needed to be able to put different people in charge of it – people whose values and intentions they could trust; who could collectively bring to bear a wider range of skill and sensitivity than can usually be developed in the service of any single-purpose bureau; and who had the time and expertise to master the industries concerned, and reconstruct them where necessary.

Supervisory boards now have those responsibilities. The board of a public corporation typically includes some regulars from that and other branches of public service; some independent expertise; nominees of employees, consumer councils, environmental agencies, etc., as appropriate. Public corporations take policy instructions – usually in very general terms – from their ministers. Depending on the nature of their business they may be linked into the central policy-making machinery at political, administrative and technical levels. Some of the coordination is elaborate and sometimes cumbersome, especially for monopolist functions like energy supply and urban planning and engineering. Different coordinations are required of the investing and lending agencies – general and specialist banks, public investment trusts and some agencies which supply permanent or temporary public management of private assets.

At the heart of the public machinery, for purposes of government in general and central economic management in particular, there is the modern descendant of the traditional central civil service. Its nature, and its relation to the bodies which carry on most of the productive and trading business of the public sector, resemble the Swedish more than any other of the mid-century central-government services. But there are also important differences from that model, some of them pioneered by the Swedes themselves.

As in the old Swedish model the central service is small in number, powerful, and something of an elite corps. But it is not the closed service that it used to be. People circulate into and out of it at most levels.

Some movement occurs at change of government. More happens in an ordinary career way through open competition for jobs, and through some limited-term appointments. Regular servants who want to rise high in the economic departments usually leave the service at least once in their careers, to notch up some experience in public trusts, in private business, or in universities or research institutes. Ambitious people do this, then compete their way back into the service. Those who never leave the service tend to be regarded as worse-qualified and less venturesome – or more interested in golf or gardening – and less likely to rise high.

The other significant development has been a rough-and-ready distribution of democratic responsibilities between the central service and the public trusts and corporations. The central service is above all the instrument of national government, centrally responsible for the national economic management of levels of employment, general price and income policies, general environmental policies, and the policies which in a general way allocate national resources and determine directions of growth and conservation. The central service answers to central government and therefore (with as much sensitivity as it can) to the mass movements of interest and opinion which are expressed in the election of national governments. Meanwhile it distances itself as far as it can from local and detailed democratic responsibilities. Those belong either to local government or to the trusts and corporations. Those must see to the social and environmental studies and the participant processes which produce decisions about *which* coal to mine, *where* to build new town centres, *whose* old housing to acquire and rehabilitate – and so on. The need to produce those decisions acceptably, with full forbearance and sensitivity, has brought subtle changes to the three-cornered relations between central government, its business arms, and the local publics they deal with. Politicians know the penalties which they themselves will pay for insensitive performance. They and their central services therefore circulate the membership of the public business boards quite ruthlessly; to that extent the public trusts and corporations are less independent than they were. But they in their turn derive strength from their new responsibilities: as the experts in sensitivity they often enough tell central government what *can't* be done, or *must* be done, if the central government is to avoid confrontation 'on the site' and backlash at election time.[41]

So central government answers to the people at national elections, while public business (like most private business these days) answers day by day down every street to local government and local people for the social and environmental planning and impact of whatever it has to build, make, buy, sell or regulate. When public business fails in those responsibilities it is subject to much the same devices of 'government by exception' as private business is. Both are subject to the guidelines of indicative planning, but are left alone – filling in very few forms and

301

needing no prior approvals for most of their business – as long as they do their business in a tolerably efficient and popular way.

Innovation and new investment have survived the equalizations well enough. That is partly for negative reasons. With little to gain any longer from property, commodities, exchange movements and other unproductive gambling, investors have to think about making more mousetraps. With a blight on law-avoidance, tax-avoidance and 'pure' money-handling, inventive minds have to think about *better* mousetraps (or substitutes, when old mousetrap materials come under new restrictions). But there have also been positive adaptations to the new conditions. With less self-financing, big enterprises have to get more of their new capital from institutional investors. These include banks, insurers and various private, cooperative and public investment trusts, most directed in ways (see below) which encourage them to balance requirements of earning efficiency with attention to the guidelines of central economic and environmental planning. Those requirements don't have to be too restrictive because central governments have other holds on the volume and direction of new investment. Central banks do most of their traditional services, and central economic managers can adjust most of the capital balances that interest them through public investment trusts. These are financed from various sources, including selective employment and corporation taxes, and their business includes supplying capital to publicly-approved sectors which the regular capital market fails to supply. Their trust structure enables them to do it with more expertise, and discrimination between firm and firm, than politicians or public servants could usually bring to bear.

Resources and incentives for technical research and innovation are similarly diverse, with public agencies doing whatever others can't or won't do. In many industries innovation comes chiefly from within, as it always did; but inventive individuals can hawk their skills or ideas from firm to firm or investor to investor, and plenty of new companies (especially small ones) are built with small investors' money from the open market. Pricing policies allow different industries varying latitude to finance their own research and development.

A wide variety of work, from ad hoc technical research through planning and design to organization-and-method operations on management, is done by the expanding 'consultant sector'. Private consultant firms were traditional in architecture, engineering and some other professional fields. The principle has extended in one direction into scientific

302

and technical research, and in another into many branches of management (not merely advice to management). Independent professional partnerships and cooperatives compete for public and private business. They work on a time–cost basis, or by tender. It's a popular way to work, the field is crowded, and plenty of the tendering is severely competitive – so in most fields it's by no means an easy way to wealth. Interesting motives develop. Members of successful teams can earn up to personal income limits. In some lines of work they can build up shares of plant or goodwill to personal capital limits. Beyond that (and often before that) they can choose between various other uses of success. Some choose to grow – whatever your income it's good to lead the big teams that do the big business (as any public-service hierarch knows). Others stay small and grow more selective, picking and choosing the most interesting or self-expressive or innovative work. Some have turned themselves into salaried teams working for self-governing trusts whose profits go to good causes which interest the team members. One consortium of architectural firms runs a successful atelier school. Some successful management teams and management consultants put their spare time and money into public-interest research, producing criticism of the kind pioneered by earlier muckrakers and consumer-researchers, of which the stodgier public and private corporations are rightly nervous. One big building firm devotes its efficiently-won surpluses to planning and building non-profit holiday villages for low-income families, and uses that business to pioneer some radical and romantic styles of fishing village and mountain village design. Successful professional people still compete for the traditional honors available from governments and professional institutes; but to those ambitions many more interesting ones have been added now that success brings surpluses which must be surrendered to taxation, or disposed of by distribution of shares to people qualified to receive them (i.e., to people not too rich already), or put to non-profit social uses which can often be developed and controlled by the successful earners themselves.

One of the most valuable services of the independent professional sector has been to shake up a number of branches of public business and bureaucracy. Independent teams get a good deal of public work; and they supply competitive pressures and standards of comparison for the work which the bureaucracies continue to do for themselves. National and local governments used to have some very stodgy departments of public buildings, public works, public housing, etc. Many of them could reasonably keep the work to themselves as long as the alternative was to shop it out to private planners, designers and developers whose professional rates and profit margins transferred altogether too much public money to affluent private pockets. Nowadays the competition between public and private professional services is fairer and less inhibited. There are no longer any ideological objections to private enterprise. The public services and corporations continue to do plenty of their own professional work – and some of them get cheeky and compete with the independents for work from private corporations. Meanwhile the private teams get whatever public work they can do better or cheaper than the salaried professionals of the public corporations can do it. (The ultimate judges of that are often the public corporations' supervisory boards, which commonly include members from both public and private sectors.) Thus there is widespread competition between public and private enterprise, and their hiring habits make for less individual movement by promotion, and more by selection and job-changing. Skills earn their opportunities in a competitive market.

From these various souces, ideas and innovations flow at least as freely as before. Critics can still point to some industries, especially some quasi-monopolist ones and some public utilities, in which there is not as much as there ought to be of the less showy kinds of efficiency – the insistent day-by-day attention to cost-shaving and competitive pricing which does at least as much as 'big' innovation does for general productive efficiency. The criticism is fair, but not much of it is occasioned by any recent diminution of 'the profit motive'. Long before the capital transfers it was already conventional for corporate presidents to make speeches about the multiple social responsibilities of private capitalist management. Business had duties to its shareholders, certainly; but also to labor, consumers, government and the environment. Sometimes those orators meant what they said. Occasionally they even did what they said. Nevertheless what they often enough meant and did was to put *all* the mentioned interests firmly in their places – telling shareholders to respect labor, and labor to respect the interests of consumers, and consumers that labor costs were uncontrollable – while they quietly jacked the prices up and ran the business for the profit and pleasure of directors and executives answerable (in cold practice) to nobody but one another. But whatever those orators meant, their virtuous visions came true sooner than some of them expected. Most public and private business is now directed and managed by men who judge one another – and promote and demote one another – according to the dexterity with which, in the course of their work, they balance the diverse interests of

304

small shareholders, taxpayers, employees, consumers, and politicians aiming to stay elected. In that atmosphere most managers put a high and grateful value on the few comparatively objective tests which they *can* apply to one another, and can cite to justify executive appointments and disappointments.

In the upper reaches of business and government two impressions of the new arrangements are common: Public and private business are more alike than they were. And it is bracing but windy at the top; some of the climbers who get there don't want to stay too long.

That second impression arises from the reforming societies' efforts to amend some 'iron laws of organization'.[42] Must all large organizations rigidify, and substitute their hierarchs' interests for the interests they are meant to serve? The reformers were practical people. They couldn't expect to revolutionize the human natures and expectations of very many of the millions of employees who did the organizational business of modern industry – and must go on doing it. So to this day, many of the motives and working arrangements in the salaried bureaucracy of (say) a private oil company or a public power utility are much as they always were. But could something better be done at the top? Must elites always entrench themselves and use their *necessary* organizing powers to contrive *unnecessary* wealth or privilege for themselves?

In a general social way there have been some discoveries in this field. People compete for whatever differential rewards and advantages there are and for whatever interesting or commanding jobs there are, but the *scales* of difference – as long as they are nationwide – don't matter much. Also – given some basic guarantee of comfort in old age – most very able people (that is to say, people who are very able at tasks which egalitarian societies judge to be valuable, rather than merely at self-enrichment) are more interested in the work than the pay, and care more for their children's security than for their own.[43]

When income differentials narrowed and came to matter less, and when income-related superannuation was pegged to peak earnings at whatever age they were achieved, it became easier to move top people about from job to job, and downwards when necessary, more flexibly than would have been tolerable before. So the famous 'exposure thresholds' were introduced. As with other reforms they succeeded because they attracted support from a number of quarters for a number of different reasons.

Three sources of support were most important.

The first was the mass political support for general policies of equality.

Once the Left alliances had mobilized the numbers and will and skill to impose the capital transfers and high-income limitations it was not hard to persuade the same majorities that even under the new regime, some special stringencies should continue to apply to the highest earners.

Second, many of the experts – Left politicians, administrators and intellectuals – who planned the institutional reconstructions were well aware of the malign potentiality of 'iron laws'. They had direct experience of bureaucratic abuses in their own public business and services, and they knew of the worse experience of many communist states. Some central European communist states tried from time to time to loosen their structures of management and political control. China wrestled with problems of elite entrenchment through one cultural revolution after another. But those exercises were not very convincing – entrenched ruling groups were merely attacking some of the lesser entrenchment of those below them. None of their dictatorial efforts – even when Czech or Chinese leaders fell out and tried to mobilize mass action against one another – had the vital ingredient of free-speaking electoral support from a sovereign alliance of 55% (including most of the poorest) of the citizens. With the aid of that sovereign force, the democratic Left's intellectual services set out to design conditions of work at the top which might reconcile flexible management and efficient motivation with reasonable requirements of equality.

The third and decisive force came from the political leaders of the alliance. Party structures being what they are, politicians had fairly secure tenure of their seats in the legislatures; but they were accustomed to insecure tenure of anything above that. Elections put them in and out of office; ruthless considerations of personal efficiency and party advantage shuffled them in and out of cabinet, and from job to job within it. Whatever they earned in office, they could always return without hardship to backbench parliamentary salaries – which were not excessive, in relation to other incomes, anywhere in the democratic world. Backbench legislators earned 'middle management' incomes and accepted the fact that any pay or tenure above that was insecure. Moreover, in the early struggles to reform the structures of wealth, income and government, nobody obstructed the Left politicians as tenaciously or from such close quarters as the two groups it was now necessary to reconstruct: affluent corporate directors, and bureaucrats entrenched at the top of the public services. After a few betrayals and frustrations at those hands the political leaders were less and less willing to allow such enemies to go on enjoying incomes or securities which they themselves had always done without.

So the property, income and tenure thresholds were introduced. Their purpose was to let conventional motivation work as it always had for ninety seven or ninety eight of every hundred producers; but beyond that, to sort out some types of temperament and ambition from others by making *sure* that it would always be windy at the top.

If independent share-owned enterprise was to continue after the capital transfers it was not practical to impose absolute limits on personal capital ownership. There *is* a limit and capital and corporate taxes make it quite hard to exceed. But exceeding it is still lawful, and still happens, often involuntarily as a consequence of the successful growth of share-owned businesses. But wealth above the limit is subject to some different rules, and less protection. It is taxed 100% at succession. When government acquires property or shares for any reason, losses from above-limit holdings are not compensable. And there is some general expectation that if there ever has to be another 'top-down' levy it is likely to take holdings above the limit and spare those below it, as happened the first time. So (by analogy with the rules for income) personal capital above the limit has poor security of tenure. It may be scarcely worth having but nobody has to fear acquiring it, and successful businesses and share portfolios can grow without misgiving – though when they do, their owners usually redistribute them to below-limit personal holdings or to permitted non-profit uses.

To jobs and incomes the threshold rules apply somewhat differently. With a few specific exceptions (including some judges and ombudsmen) they apply across the board to all public and private employment and contracts for personal services. There is a personal salary threshold. It is expressed in money terms and revised from time to time but has the effect of drawing a line at the second or third percentile of incomes, so it separates the richest 2 or 3% of earners from the rest – roughly, the few who earn more than twice the national average. The rules which apply to jobs above that threshold thus apply to upper but not to middle management; to the first division or two of most public services; to the top quarter or so of the highly-qualified professional staff of universities, research institutes, hospitals; to some directors and principals in educational services, newspapers and publishing houses, broadcasting services and permanent theatrical and orchestral companies; but not to most of the ranks of teachers, journalists, engineers, technicians, orchestral players, etc. Anyone can therefore achieve – or dream of – a comfortable

307

sort of success very close to the top of his profession and his society's income structure, with the whole of whatever security of tenure and income is traditional in his line of work.

Above the line the rules are simple. *All* above-limit salary scales (and some austere general rules about perquisites) are fixed by a single national office. Interested parties are heard in the course of negotiation, but have no right of appeal, no right to strike, and no security of income or appointment. There can be appointments for limited terms. (Most countries allow as many years as the constitutional life of their legislatures.) Appointments can be renewed. Those who hold them can have secure rights to revert to permanent tenure at or below the threshold. But there is no permanent tenure of jobs above the threshold, and in some lines of business people move one another about fairly freely.

So it is windy at the top. Some step down after a term or two. Others are demoted, or moved sideways. Both are common enough to be ordinary and in most cases undisgraceful. Those who step (or are pushed) down keep the superannuation and survivors' margins they earned at the top, and don't usually lose much income. Some step down to give themselves more time to serve (if they're asked) on supervisory boards. A few serve on numbers of boards and make their whole livings that way. Meanwhile others can leave exacting jobs to go out to grass for a while. Young or otherwise daring appointments can be made without too much danger that a mistake may blight the organization for a generation. When a young man jumps to the top he may be back in a year or two – or he may earn himself the long decades of influence that have allowed some of the best of all performances in business and public service. It is easier than it was for versatile people to have two or three careers one after the other; or to make sensible descents to easier jobs in their later years. So the new flexibilities are quite widely used, and give a new meaning (different from Pareto's) to 'the circulation of elites'.

Of course people still compete, and connive and cabal, to advance themselves or the policies they believe in. Rival do-gooders can contend as viciously, sometimes with as ill effect, as rival wealth-seekers ever did. But on balance – in a pervasive atmosphere of personal and financial equality, with watchful criticism from very many quarters – public interests are better served.

Conclusion: Everyday life

Life at the top matters only as it affects life for everyone else. For that I return to present time, put the books away, and write of what I know face-to-face, chiefly in the life of my own street.

Here are half a dozen next-door houses, one with a corner shop, in an old quarter of a middle-sized provincial city in a lucky country. Some of the houses are very poor, none is very rich; the one with the shop is owned by local government and rented as cheaply as necessary to keep it going. All six have some private land, but less than the national average of it – this is old city housing, there are versatile public parks, the balance of private and public resources is good.

The households have various relations with one another. Some know each other only by sight. Others exchange tools, fruit, kittens, baby-sitting, gossip. The children are in each other's houses often, the adults rarely. There are one or two close friendships, a good deal of minor mutual help, and occasional frigidities. Altogether it is one of the comfortable social mixtures which happen easily in old cities and suburbs whenever the housing stock allows them and there are no sociologists about.

A sociologist could nevertheless classify and rank the households. They sample the national population well enough: two are working class, two lower middle, one upper middle, and one unclassifiable working-class capitalist. Four are native-born, two immigrant. Even the ages of people and households happen to be representative. There are more earners than households. They include unskilled, semi-skilled and highly skilled blue collar; unskilled, semi-skilled and highly skilled white collar; a prisoner's spouse and a pensioner. The orders of class and occupation do not coincide with the orders of income or capital wealth. The lowest incomes go to one blue and one white collar; so do the two highest incomes. The only capital-owner wears a blue collar on shift and a white collar off it. Two other breadwinners – one of the poorest and one of the richest – put such a high value on independence that they work hard at occupations that interest them, for less money than they could be getting for shorter hours of conventional employment. The order of financial inequality is

309

about threefold before tax; less after tax; and less still per head if you divide the incomes by the numbers in the households. If the scales were somewhat flatter, all the earners would probably be working as hard at the same jobs; but if the men had been paid more equally some of the richer women might have spent more time working for pay, and some of the poorer women might have spent less.

The two richest households and the two poorest own their houses or are buying them. They make extremely diverse and often constructive uses of their back yards. (They make pleasant but more similar uses of the streets and parks.) There are interesting reasons why the lowest-earning family, with less income than a London bus driver or a New York welfare family gets, was nevertheless able to buy a house. Thirty years of massive public dealing in land and houses had kept all the city's land comparatively cheap, and it still had old cottages so small and decrepit and rent-controlled that, with some luck and determination, a bedrock income could still buy one. (That family has just traded its hovel as deposit on a house and garden out in the suburbs, to become the only household of the six to own a little more than the national average of private urban land.)

As people moved in and out there have usually been three or four households with children and two or three without. Facts of class affect the children's future prospects but not their face-to-face relations, which reflect quite individual differences of taste and temperament. The only stand-offs have been between children of similar class. The two richest households have both faced decisive choices of nationality and personal opportunity. Both seem to have traded some adult tastes and chances of wealth for what seemed to be their children's chances, not necessarily of getting rich but of growing up to live and work among friends in a peaceful and sufficiently prosperous society.

There are various things which this idyllic sketch is not meant to suggest. It is not meant to suggest that all is well. Within the street, securities are threatened from various quarters. Outside it, life is richer for some, and tougher and poorer for many; and from the general hazards of capitalist life – from inflation, industrial monotony and commercial temptations, from polluted streets and fast cars and hospital wards full of young paraplegics, from record corporate bankruptcies alongside record corporate profits – the people inside this cocoon are no better protected than the rest of the affluent world is.

But some protections we do have. A partly managed housing market

310

brought us together by choice and accident. It wouldn't have kept us together for long. Market pressures threatened us with a general 'gentrification'. Engineers and others thought to bulldoze us for highways, car parks, supermarkets and housing towers which nobody but profit-takers wanted. Together with other indignant electors we had to replace three levels of government. Policies of urban conservation are now being applied with deliberate care for pedestrian and public transport, class shares of urban space, and local participation in local planning. City Hall is about to ask us whether we'd like to dig up a good deal of our street, which is wider than it needs to be, to grow more trees and give more space to a land-hungry old primary school. Where the engineers had begun their bulldozing a state trust – with national money, on land supplied by local government – is now building terrace houses with private gardens for low-income families and pensioners.

These gains are insecure. All of this city's land is 'under-priced', i.e. twice or three times its current price could be extorted from us for the use of it. Roving capital from London, Hong Kong and other centres of realism has cased the prospect, and so of course have local predators. We are protected only by unorthodox policies which hang on two governments' tenuous majorities. If those governments fall, perhaps because they can't cope with monetary inflation, our land may well inflate a hundred per cent and resume its ancient function of segregating social classes, maldistributing living-space, and transferring wealth from poorer to richer.

But there are one or two things which my idyllic sketch *is* meant to suggest. Life-styles like these should not be written off as irrelevant because they are untypical, lucky, over-protected – or bourgeois. They should be seen as the end of the whole Left enterprise, which should have no other purpose than to extend and improve the conditions which make such patterns of life possible. Our street is not extravagant. It uses a fraction less than its share of national resources. It gets a lot of its work done freely and willingly, for nothing. What paid work it needs is done (as far as its own inhabitants go) for comparatively equal rewards. They could be more equal than they are; and what inequalities there have to be are more necessary within trades than between them.

But streets like this are islands, and very imperfectly protected. One cutting inequality invades ours. The children of the richer households are likely to do better, materially, than the rest – to become managers, professionals, proprietors. In the unregenerate world outside their street these childhood friends will grow up, and apart, to fivefold and worse financial inequalities, and unmarriageable differences of life-style in severely segregated suburbs. That prospect is sad, unnecessary and certainly unproductive. The children would all develop their talents, and work as well and live as happily, if the range of inequalities were somewhat less than exist within the street. Among their parents, at least three are possessed by ambitions as obsessive as any tycoon's: one for material security, one for influence, one for a cranky kind of independence of landlords and employers. The incomes of those three range from the highest to the lowest. They are all as usefully, industriously productive as their talents could possibly allow – only the bit of capital wealth is antisocially employed. Further down the street there are doubtless occasional cheats, layabouts and bad neighbors but (given the ordinary discipline of having to work for a living) steeper inequalities wouldn't get any better performance from them either.[44]

The changes which are needed to make everybody comfortable in streets a little more equal than ours are (as far as production and distribution go) quite modest. In affluent democracies sixty or seventy of every hundred households already live and work within reasonable limits of inequality – though their lives are often enough made anxious and competitive by the possibilities beyond those limits. They need move very little closer to make room for twenty or thirty to join them from below, and ten or so from above. Some of the ten may not resist the changes too bitterly if they can join in managing them.

As well as money and materials, influence also needs some better distribution. It is easy to call for more equal shares of it, but unfashionable (except on the Right) to worry about the whole quantity of it. The most equal society will not escape the classical problems of faith, order and authority. Without a tough structure of all three, any democracy is in danger of jungle war as everyman is driven or enticed to exploit the power which freedom and political equality offer him, not just against governments and ruling classes *but against every other man*. The last is what Left and liberationists find it hardest to think about coolly. Liberal democracy has allowed more and more of both the best and the worst to exploit the new superiority of minority attack against majority defence. Participation makes conflicts fairer, but it doesn't resolve many of them; and an equal society will have to police its equalities. It won't stay equal for long if – as with monetary inflation – the aggregate effect of sectional success is a self-defeating 'inflation of influence': a general disorder in which organized interests leapfrog each others' gains, nobody can succeed against government without succeeding against everybody else, and the strong can knock the weak about with more success than ever.

To police equalities in a free society, there have to be institutional and technical means of enforcing democratic control of the use and distribution of resources. There has to be enough legitimation of government to make it a forbearing but sovereign arm of majority rule. As a main part of that legitimation, political practice has to rest on a good deal of popular faith. The last requirement is new, at least in degree. Whatever romantic historians may imagine, most old social orders were maintained more by class coercion than by shared faith. We have to reverse that relation. For that, some people say we need a new faith. I think we need to give better effect to the faiths we have already. Down our street and millions like it there are plenty of corruptions; but also, desires for peaceful and affectionate relations, solidarities, conceptions of fair dealing and yearnings for security in quite sufficient strength (it seems to me) to rescue order from the new disorder. Those aspirations may look more practical as the alternatives to a regime of equality become more menacing and ungovernable. Material equalities may not by themselves generate much brotherhood, but they are a necessary condition of it. They may soon be a condition of government by consent: the only workable basis left for social arrangements between political equals.

Notes

1 All the questions asked in this chapter owe a great deal to Paul Streeten's suggestions and criticisms. That is especially true of the discussion of relations between conservation and growth. It is sometimes argued that disagreements about those two could be reconciled simply by changing what counts as growth. Conventional accounts count too many useless or harmful things and fail to count many good things. They often give no credit to good distribution and very little to quality of life. They don't count most of the goods which people with well-equipped houses produce for themselves, or the goods which unspoiled coasts and countrysides afford to those who enjoy them. But they do count the production of a lot of rubbish then add (where they ought to subtract) the costs of cleaning it up. They count building bad cities then add (where they ought to subtract) the costs of trying to make them livable. They count the fattening industries, then the slimming industries, then the medical and psychiatric services; while people who eat better, stay healthier and spend less of their leisure at clinics count as poorer. And so on. Better social accounting which measured real net welfare might allow environmentalists to join in favoring growth as a general principle. But still not to agree about it in detail – people with different interests and values would still want to count different things as 'real welfare' and weight them differently according to who was to enjoy them. It is a mistake (quite a fashionable one just now) to pin extravagant hopes to the development of better economic and social indexes. Indexes can't alter the fact that one citizen sees as goods what another sees as costs or wastes; what one wants to consume, another wants to leave in the ground. Indexes of net welfare have to be constructed by controversial judgments of good and bad. They are still worth having (though every man may want his own). Better accounting can serve all sorts of good purposes, and reconcile some mistaken conflicts of opinion, but it can't reconcile real conflicts of interest and value.

2 Some experts doubt if there was ever a trend to greater equality in this century. Others think that there was and that it still continues. It depends on what they choose to count. There is bound to be disagreement because *any* method of comparing equalities requires value judgments. Most of this book's judgments are based on percentage comparisons between the wealth and income of the richest 20% and the poorest 20%, or similar 'symmetrical' samples. That is to say, they accept the very conservative assumption that

314

equalities should be judged on a percentage basis (though personally I don't accept it). Judgments that the figures reveal improving equalities since 1950 have to be based on Right values; they often base judgments of general equality on changing relationships within the richer 20 or 50% only, and apply different percentage principles to wealth and income. (See Chapters 7 and 9.)

3 For these and other second thoughts about class demands for environmental quality I thank Sol Encel, Professor of Sociology in the University of New South Wales.

4 Some institutional economists including Gunnar Myrdal and Paul Streeten used to put great emphasis on relations between inequality, corrupt or 'soft' government, and hindrances to the development of undeveloped countries. Relations between corrupt government and economic growth vary with circumstances – corrupt government accompanied fast growth in England in the eighteenth century and in the USA after the Civil War. But those economists did not mean the same things by growth and development. Development means modernizing life and equipment at every social level, which must nearly always involve some increase of equality. Among developed countries the honesty of government does not appear to be regularly related to national wealth or rates of growth as conventionally measured. But another relation holds, and not many social scientists have yet grasped its strength and importance: *the honesty of government varies with equality of income, or with movement in that direction.* The USA was for a long time the richest democracy; its inequalities are great, and increasing; among developed democracies it appears to have most corruption, from big to small business and from central government to local police, and the corruption is increasing. But it appears to be related to the inequalities rather than the affluence. The next-most-corrupt countries are not the next-richest, while on the other hand the richest countries include the small Scandinavian and Australasian democracies which are in many respects the most equal, have least ongoing increase of inequality, and appear to have least corruption in government. It may of course be a matter of size. The biggest rich democracy is the most corrupt, the smallest are the cleanest, and the medium-sized states of Germany, France and the United Kingdom lie somewhere between. But within the history of each of them there seem to be relations between the directions of change, of corruption and of inequalities. The United Kingdom was corruptly governed while its inequalities increased through the eighteenth century. Then for a hundred and some years, to about 1950, it moved toward greater equality, and through that phase it developed outstandingly honest government; both trends were probably at their zenith under the austere regime of Attlee and Stafford Cripps. Both trends were then reversed. As inequalities increased after 1950 there was bigger corruption in local government; there were more objectionable business connections and tax avoidances by national politicians; and there was an increasing passage of

high public servants to jobs with private corporations which they had dealt with, and sometimes favored, in their public capacities.

In the USA early in the same post-1950 phase of increasing inequality some sociologists and political scientists wrote theories of the social functions of corruption, often dignified as 'economic theories of democracy', which suggested that money *ought* to be able to buy power, and that corrupt government might in some ways be harmless or positively rational as one way of achieving that. Even David Riesman, deprecating financial puritanism along with other forms of puritanism, noted complacently how many public contracts were now routinely greased with 'gravy we can well afford'. Consistently, writers who did not recoil from corruption did not seem to dislike inequality either, if they ever noticed it. But people who *do* dislike either inequality or corrupt government should take note of the strong relation between them. Old-fashioned conservatives for example have sometimes believed in economic inequality and scrupulously honest government, almost as twin ideals; but those twins seem now to be incompatible. The mechanisms of action and motive which link corrupt government to increasing inequality are reciprocal and not hard to understand: the two nourish each other in a classical example of the circular causation or 'vicious spiral' which Myrdal described in other contexts.

5 Like other excuses to increase inequalities the argument was irrational. Its authors knew well that birthrates generally *fall* as incomes improve. Consigning a few millions of the poorest children to their own devices and to the streets does not reduce national rates of reproduction, as the same economists were the first to insist when they wrote about underdeveloped societies. An early and strong recommendation of the new brutality appeared in Allen V. Kneese, Sydney E. Rolfe and Joseph W. Harned, *Managing the Environment* (New York, 1971). Kneese was the leading environmental economist of his day. He was a strong advocate of market methods of environmental control, i.e. of methods which would spread costs through prices. He always recommended that environmental programs should ignore distribution (unless as with the children, to unequalize it further). From time to time he also recommended that there be independent action to improve distributions but he never suggested what it should be, or who should fight for it.

6 Through various tax, housing and industrial policies Chancellor Barber (1970–4) supervised one of the briskest transfers of wealth from poor to rich in British history. One of its minor effects was to enrich (lawfully) plenty of his Cabinet colleagues. For example the government had allowed housing construction to fall by a third, then made an emergency grant of £100m. to local authorities to improve their municipal housing programs. Most of the money went to those who sold land to the municipalities. One vendor was a Cabinet colleague of Barber's and Chairman of his party. For 140 acres of inherited land, he personally got about one twelfth of the £100m. grant. Other colleagues had meanwhile shared in a £300m. supertax handout.

7 These differential effects vary from place to place but operate to some degree in most big cities. Some of them were explored in Max Neutze, *Economic Policy and the Size of Cities* (Canberra, 1965) and H. Stretton, *Ideas for Australian Cities* (Melbourne, 1970).

8 See Max Neutze, *Land Prices and Urban Land Market Policy*, Centre for Environmental Studies (London, 1973) and other work reviewed therein. For housing provisions and expenditures up to about 1960 see David Donnison, *The Government of Housing* (London, 1965) for the best general account of west and east European housing problems and policies up to that time.

9 Of course it is misleading to talk thus of whole societies 'knowing' and 'choosing', and the more Leftist of the threshold theorists did not talk so. Social decisions issue more often from conflict than consensus, and throughout capitalist history there have always been minorities – or battened-down majorities – arguing for radically different social options. But the predominant opinions – the conventional wisdom of the winners, of which they often manage to convince a lot of the losers too – are what this oversimplified summary is about.

10 One Australian state has .maintained price controls continuously since the 1940s: formal controls on petroleum and various items of food, clothing, equipment and other manufactures, and mixtures of regulation and public dealing to limit land and housing prices. The policies were developed by governments of the Right for the explicit (and successful) purpose of restraining money wages and therefore export prices, by methods indirect enough to be tolerable to organized labor. The same governments used public ownership quite freely, monopolizing coal mining and power supply and much of the industrial land and factory-lease-back business, for the same purpose of supplying private enterprises with cheap resources, in ways acceptable to labor.

11 For an excellent survey of the sorry state of the art see Martin Bronfenbrenner, *Income Distribution Theory* (Chicago, 1971).

12 See the thorough and original discussion of this subject in Peter Marris, *Loss and Change* (London, 1974).

13 The Bolsheviks came to believe that the novel state power and industrial disciplines they were trying to build would be helped rather than hindered by reinforcing old patterns of authority in family, factory, army and elsewhere. Hitler's earliest speeches offered to reconstruct most established institutions but he began to attract serious support only when he learned to narrow and specify the proposed changes, and to enlist and work with as many established institutions as possible – President, army, courts and any other available symbols of legitimacy. Clement Attlee could make nationalizing mines or railways or steel sound like a minor rearrangement of clerical responsibilities. He also symbolized some reassuring continuities in himself. Conservative politicians can afford to get about in beards and cloaks but radicals who mean

317

business often do best to look as safe and predictable as quiet suits, short-back-and-sides and wife-and-three-children can make them.

14 Of course he did think about futures to some degree. The best account of his contribution to the theory of communist society is in Graeme Duncan, *Marx and Mill* (Cambridge, 1973), which still concludes that 'Marx and Engels wished to retain the advantages of large-scale industrial society . . . Yet they themselves did not make clear what institutional form, what political–administrative organisation, would be necessary to manage the large and complex industrial societies which they envisaged' (p. 190).

15 There were always honorable exceptions – see for example the works of C. Wright Mills and Melvin Tumin. There were also some reciprocal attempts to show that the Right was sick too, but they concentrated on attitudes to authority rather than to economic inequality and were done chiefly by immigrant refugees from Nazi Germany rather than by native Americans.

16 Michael Young, *The Rise of the Meritocracy* (Penguin edn), pp. 155–6.

17 It will always be possible to design methods of comparison to show that most societies are growing more equal. A few economists argue that distributions are fairly stable. To believe that, it is usually necessary to emphasize the public services and welfare payments that the poor are supposed to get; to ignore what they lose after their incomes are received, to rising property prices and rents and costs of consumer credit and very local shopping; and at the same time to underrate the extent to which the rich disguise their incomes, and enjoy capital gains, perquisites, and various buying and borrowing and bargaining advantages which don't appear in statistics of distribution. Even without such allowances, comparisons of wealth or income between the top and bottom 10% or the top and bottom 20% over the last twenty years show increases of inequality in most rich countries. In relation either to the rich or to the whole national income the poorest 10 or 20% are worse off than they were in 1950 and possibly worse than at any time in this century. Many judgments that equalities are improving rest on the fact that the richest 1% or 10% have a declining share of gross personal income. But the corresponding gainers are mostly in the next two or three deciles – the middle classes whose incomes are below the top 10% but within the top 30 or 40%. Because the comfortable have inproved their relation to the rich, Rightist analyses often assert that overall equalities are improving – as indeed they would assert if Mr Rockefeller's fortune moved into closer equality with Mr Getty's.

Of the 'mass inequalities' through the middle ranks of incomes, a lot are attributable to age, and to inequalities within trades, rather than to the differences between doctors and dustmen. It is also true that comparisons of net worth – capital plus life's earnings – show inequalities up to and beyond a thousandfold in most affluent societies.

For a Right interpretation of the figures, which concludes that equalities are improving and that there is no need to improve them further, see George

Polanyi and John B. Wood, *How Much Inequality* (London, 1974). For a Left interpretation of the figures see S. M. Miller and Martin Rein, 'The Possibilities of Income Transformation', a paper delivered to a Nuffield Canadian Seminar in 1972, revised as a Centre for Environmental Studies Working Paper (1973) and published in the journal *Public Interest* (1974). For a general review of the literature by a conservative economist whom nobody could suspect of Left bias, but whose conclusions tend to agree with Miller's and Rein's, see Martin Bronfenbrenner, *Income Distribution Theory* (London, 1971). For similar questions about capital inequalities see note 35 below.

18 A calculation by Ivor Pearce of the University of Southampton.

19 S. M. Miller and Martin Rein, 'The Possibilities of Income Transformation', cited in note 17 above.

20 Stretton, *Ideas for Australian Cities*, p. 11.

21 See also A. Szalai and others, *The Use of Time* (The Hague, 1972). Some of the issues were raised by Colin Clark in 'The Economics of Housework', *Bulletin of the Oxford Institute of Statistics* 20, 2 (1958) and have been explored by others but neglected by most of his profession since. Parts of the present chapter are adapted from *Housing and Government* (Sydney, 1974) by permission of its publishers, the Australian Broadcasting Commission.

22 It is a mistake to think that a majority of European apartment-dwellers prefer to live that way. There as elsewhere, those who prefer apartments are usually minorities, often either young or in possession of country retreats. Given options at equal prices Europeans – especially the majorities who live in other-than-capital cities, with no imperative shortage of land or accessibility – are as prone as anyone else to choose private houses on the ground. When they emigrate to Australia they appear to be more ambitious for more suburban land than the native Australians are. (Survey by Ian Halkett, Australian National University, 1973–4.)

23 Economists find various ways of living with these absurdities. Some are aware of them, and support policies which in effect treat allocations to housing like allocations to investment in public goods. Some forget them and work in practical ways on practical housing programs. Some cultivate a specialism called 'economics of housing' which has nothing to do with the economic functions of housing – it chiefly tries to model the behavior of housing markets. Some think the national accounts are satisfactory because they impute rents to owner-occupied houses – as if rents indicated work done and output produced, any more than factory rents do in the commercial economy. Some general economists take their general theory seriously enough to warn that investment in houses tends to reduce economic growth. Others, perhaps uneasily conscious of the size of this largest of all the gaping holes in neoclassical theory, avoid the subject altogether. In the 838 pages of my (sixth) edition of Samuelson's *Economics*, housing – a third of all fixed capital – isn't mentioned.

The best critics of these aberrations are often institutional economists of undeveloped societies. Theories which only notice exchange value are obviously absurd when applied to subsistence-farming economies. (Orthodox development economists have nevertheless applied them often enough, with some ill effects on aid programs and the policies of poor countries.) But there have always been institutional economists who understood the realities of part-exchange, part-subsistence economic systems. See, for example, some of the papers collected in Paul Streeten, *The Frontiers of Development Studies* (London, 1972). Their work makes it less excusable that their colleagues should fail to see that rich countries also have part-exchange, part-domestic productive systems. All studies of family life and uses of time confirm that the richer people become, the more they tend to make and do for themselves, as long as they have the space and opportunity to do it. So orthodox theories are likely to grow *more* deceptive as they are applied to richer systems.

24 The pricing of hitherto-free evils won't usually balance the effects of pricing hitherto-free goods. Taxes collected on pollutant emissions are not distributed to compensate the people who suffer from the pollution. There would often be violent objections if they were – if for example parents could make a living by exposing themselves and their children to dangers. The rich might often be able to make 'offers you can't refuse' to low-paid or under-employed poor, just as they once did in dangerous mines or factories. Would it have been better to tax dangerous machinery out of the early factories instead of banning or regulating it? Or to tax substandard ships until shipowners calculated that it was no longer 'optimal' to drown sailors for the insurance? The same principles apply to a good deal of industrial pollution now. But they still won't apply in a very progressive way until the effects of more expensive production (especially of necessaries) are offset by genuinely progressive tax and transfer policies.

25 Of course some uses change and some neighborhoods change hands, but rarely in ways that improve equalities. When commerce and industry want more urban land they usually take it from poor rather than rich residents. Rich residents sometimes hand over housing (especially if it is landless, as in Harlem) to be overcrowded by poor; and the rich sometimes return to reclaim inner areas of generously proportioned housing designed for them in the first place (like Islington in London, Paddington in Sydney). In poor neighborhoods, comprehensive clearances and redevelopments sometimes create more public open spaces, but they are often fairly arid spaces, and the poor pay heavily for those redevelopments in other ways.

26 This paragraph is drawn from a longer discussion of relations between the size of cities and the inequalities of their citizens, in H. Stretton, *Ideas for Australian Cities* (1970), and is used by permission of its publishers, Georgian House, Melbourne.

27 Because so many bad experts have in the past gulled so many good people on

320

this subject, it may be worth summarizing the objections to what was until lately an orthodox view of the matter. Dense redevelopments are said to be justified because they will not only economize public services in a general way; they will make efficient use of *existing* road, power, sewerage and transport installations, thus avoiding the need to extend those services at suburban outskirts where low residential densities will make less economical use of them (besides eating up good farmland). The outstanding objection to this reasoning (argued in the previous chapter) is that it does not compare the service economies with any domestic diseconomies they may cause. Honest accounting would compare the improved productivity of the transport and sewers with the lost productivity of the housing in which the investment is much heavier. But the service economies themselves are often doubtful. What honest research there is is mostly inconclusive – the public economies depend on which direct and indirect costs you choose to count. There is certainly no knock-down case for very high densities. Moreover, such redevelopments rarely succeed in increasing overall inner-urban densities. Where they increase local density they often force reconstructions of the infrastructure they are supposed to econ-omize; rebuilding main sewers in built-up areas without interrupting the flow of sewage can cost more than it would cost to duplicate them under new land. Where there are genuine savings in pipes and wires they are often more than offset by the inner-urban land cost of providing new schools, recreation space and car parking for the increased population. In most cases those new schools and spaces are simply not provided – the 'economies of dense redevelopment' arise from overloading and degrading poor people's local resources in ways which would not be lawful or politically tolerable in new suburban develop-ment. The most conscientious efforts to accompany dense redevelopment with good local services and public spaces have been made (on any large scale) in the east end of London. Even there a lot of the housing is unsatisfactory; a lot of the open spaces are arid; a good deal of personal and social suffering was caused by the clearances; and population densities have *fallen* throughout. Elsewhere in the world, most believers in the theory are cruel hypocrites when they put it into practice. They scarcely ever choose to clear and redevelop commercial or industrial or rich house-and-garden land where substantial increases in population density are actually available. Instead they bulldoze neighborhoods full of poor who don't want to move – areas where existing density is highest, so gains in density will be least, and will intensify instead of redressing inherited inequalities in the city-wide distribution of private and public space.

These inconsistencies have been most tellingly exposed, for decades past, by Peter Harrison, late director of planning for Canberra. He was one of the earliest to understand that a city's efficiencies depend more on its shape, systems and detailed relations of land uses to communications than on its overall density. If planners nevertheless want higher density, why pick on the residential land? And if on that, why only on the living space of the poor? They should operate first on the public land which is more than a third of most cities, economizing road layouts and widths, ground-level car parking, utility reservations, the little-used landscapes around many public and institutional buildings, etc.; next on wasteful uses of industrial and commercial land; next on the oversupply of public and private land to affluent suburbs; and last (if at all) on the local land of the poorest residents, who usually travel least (except to work) and depend most on strictly local resources. But in practice most density-men do the opposite. Whatever they think they're doing, they are best understood as a faction of the extreme Right which works to increase existing inequalities by reducing the already miserable share of urban land and privacy available to lower-class residents.

Canberra suffers from various effects of bureaucratic planning and uninspired design. But it looks after some equities. It rations land to everyone. There are lower limits to the size of poor men's allotments, upper limits to rich men's allotments, and the two are not nearly as far apart as their incomes often are. The poorest housing is in cottage form with private land – landless apartments are chiefly for richer people, and volunteers. Some Scandinavian cities limit the private land the rich can have, but they mostly give their poor none at all.

28 To give the occupiers the real benefits of ownership, in houses or on land they couldn't afford at open-market prices, but to avoid giving them capital gifts or allowing them to re-sell the houses out of low-income ownership, public agencies can act as follows: They sell the house to the occupier for whatever he can afford. If that is 75% of the market price, they sell him a 75% equity. When he or his heirs re-sell the house, the public agency has an option to buy it back at 75% of its then market value; or (if it doesn't want the house back) it takes 25% of whatever the seller gets for it.

29 Area improvement programs are too blunt as instruments for improving personal equalities. Not all people in poor districts are poor, and plenty of poor people are not in poor districts. So area programs can't replace general measures against poverty, or welfare services which go to people according to individual need and entitlement. But there need be nothing wrong with programs to supply public and communal goods and services and new private investment to areas which lack them.

30 This argument was once orthodox, and something like it is still official policy in the Netherlands. But too many European governments now proceed on opposite principles, building severe constrictions for future generations. For an example, readers are invited to follow the history of municipal housing in Frankfurt/Main by taking a forty-minute walk through its north-western suburbs, from Romerstadt through Westhausen to Nordweststadt. The attractive and dignified row housing begun by Bauhaus architects in the 1920s has generous private gardens, and is lovingly cared for and 'individualized' by its occupiers. The row housing of the 1930s is duller but still decent. The work

of the 1950s is denser; very few occupiers get private land; but at least there is visually interesting composition of diverse housing and building forms, around beautifully designed and useable public open spaces. In the 1960s a banal brutality set in, and it reigns still. Nothing but very large and monotonous apartment blocks stand on uninteresting open land studded with notices which prohibit most of the few things children could do with such land. I wept to see it, and to reflect on the degradation of the professions responsible for it, and the party responsible for it – the oldest and strongest social-democratic party of all.

To restore some faith in the capacities of *good* government, tourists can visit some British new towns, or better still, the public housing and schools of Buckinghamshire. There the chief county architect Fred Pooley was a much-derided conservative through those post-war decades of pervasive techno-cracy. So his tenants have dignified, comfortable houses and gardens, and their children go to individually designed cottage-styled schools whose gardens and playgrounds attract such respect that they need no DON'T notices at all. They are more capacious than their mass-designed meccano-set equivalents; they are well-loved by their users; *and they cost the same or less to build*. Great care needs to be taken, chiefly by politicians, to protect public development from the mass-production mentality, whose work is often expensive as well as degrading to its users, however innovative and technically exciting (and profitable) to its designers and suppliers.

31 If this drives money away from those institutions, it may need to be done with greater care. But if it is merely accused (usually by Right economists) of 'distorting' capital allocations, politicians should remember that economists of that persuasion assume that an 'undistorted' capital structure will be the one that serves people in exact proportion to their spending power. In fact there need be nothing at all inefficient in directing productive capital to poor households whose incomes don't equip them to bid competitively for it.

32 Most construction will probably continue to be done most efficiently by competitive private building contractors. References to public and private building are to the investors, not the building contractors.

33 Jones might even agree with it. His book argues for the shortest cut to the quickest possible arrest of inflation. It recommends permanent *machinery* rather than long-term *policies* of redistribution, and it is conceivable that the recommended machinery might in time revise the principles of distribution. (Unless it did so, I don't believe it would make much progress against inflation.) But the book does not recommend any great reduction of inequalities of income; it makes no serious suggestions at all about the distribution of capital wealth; and its strain to take the control of profits, prices and incomes 'out of politics' makes sense only as a way of freezing their present relativities and curing inflation with the least possible alteration of anything else. Yet the book is still understandable as a short-term or initial program based on its

author's distinguished experience as an arbiter of British prices and incomes, and it may be unfair to suggest that he personally wants to perpetuate present inequalities. Criticism of his program is not meant to impugn its motives – only to forecast that it must either be radicalized, or fail.

34 In a technical rather than a bloodthirsty sense of 'terror'. It stands for various ways of getting people to behave themselves by diffuse rather than precise rules and threats. It is not necessarily as unconstitutional as it may sound. We do it already – 'disorderly conduct', 'nuisance', 'dangerous driving', 'conduct unbecoming an officer' and other dragnet clauses and concepts of care and negligence make plenty of opportunities to define offences after they have been committed, and by broad social judgment rather than precise rule. It is an outstanding bias of capitalist law that it exempts most private business behavior from that sort of discipline, and allows proprietors to get away with anything not precisely predictable and precisely forbidden. There need be nothing unfair or tyrannical in extending principles which already apply to drivers, drunks, vagrants, pedestrians, husbands, street musicians and dozens of others, to include concepts of dangerous, disorderly or excessive pricing, unreasonable income, and deceptive advertising and marketing. There are already some good-behavior clauses in rules about company prospectuses, stock-exchange trading, etc. Such clauses could well be extended to business generally; and there is no reason why penalties for corporate misbehavior should not include public acquisition on terms (anywhere from full compensation to full confiscation) adapted to the gravity of the offence. This wouldn't offend the principle of limited liability, and shareholders would have an interest in ensuring that their directors complied with the spirit as well as the letter of democratic laws. Corporate offenders should suffer confiscation (where milder penalties fail) much as personal offenders suffer imprisonment.

35 Nobody denies that the inequalities are gross but there is argument about their trends. As with incomes, it depends what you count. If income-earning capital is lumped together with other rights to income (e.g. rights to state pensions, notionally capitalized) and with durable goods (houses, furniture, equipment, cars) then distributions of wealth show one sort of improvement. Most of any improvement since 1950 represents the spread of house ownership (in Europe, often from about a quarter to a half of all households) multiplied by the increase of real estate prices against other prices. Even this method of counting reveals improvement of equality among the richer half of the population only; and it hasn't much to do with the capital inequalities which help to unequalize money incomes. Nevertheless commentators persistently muddle the houses and television sets with the stocks and shares, in order to suggest that ownership of profitable working capital is becoming more equal. Once again it depends on what your values prompt you to count. If two men have respectively $1,000 and $100 one year, and $2,000 and $201 the next, almost all economists will say that capital equalities have improved, though the

324

advantage of one over the other has nearly doubled. It also matters whether you think that relativities between (say) the top 1% or 10% and the rest matter more than relativities between the bottom quarter or half and those above them. On almost any of those assumptions, as long as they deal in even divisions of the whole population, the ownership of income-bearing productive capital is unequalizing further every year in most rich countries. It *has* to be unequalizing – there is a steady increase of productive capital per head, and the poorer half of the population continue to own none of it. But you would never know it from the newspapers. As one example of very many, the London *Observer* of 20 January 1974 announces the rapid decline of inequalities of wealth in the United Kingdom. One thousandth of the population who owned 43% of the national wealth in 1954 own only 23% of it now, or if (as the *Observer's* feature-writer advises) you count everyman's furniture and old age pension as 'capital' the figure slips to 19% or 14%. And similar levellings are afflicting all groups within the richest 20% of population. But down in the tables, unremarked up in the text, it appears that the one-in-a-thousand at the top are 34,000 people each with an average £300,000 of which 85% is income-earning capital. The 10% of people whose wealth is between the tenth and twentieth percentile (i.e. the second richest one among every ten Englishmen) average £10,000 of which only 15% is income-earning capital. So where the text describes the top group as each having thirty times as much wealth as people in the second decile, the top people really have each one hundred and seventy times as much 'capitalist' capital. The unearned-income difference is five or six times greater than the wealth difference. And all these relativities are within the top 20%; the remaining 80% of the British people own negligible amounts of productive capital and what they do own scarcely produces unearned income – most of it is working premises and tools of trade for the self-employed. Most of the growth of capitalist capital accrues to the already-rich and increases their absolute and relative distance from the rest; in that conventional sense, i.e. on Right as well as Left assumptions, capital inequalities are increasing nearly everywhere. Nevertheless if 80% of Englishmen manage to double their ownership of kitchen hardware, plumbers' tools and national savings certificates while the richest 34,000 of their countrymen move from a third to half a million pounds' worth each of stocks and shares and city office buildings, all good statists and Financial Editors will announce a further dramatic levelling of British wealth. No other democratic country has quite such extreme capital inequalities as Britain, but they all have financial pages which conceal their distributions on similar statistical principles.

36 Individual assessment invites one sort of trouble and family or household assessment invites others. Individual limits – giving advantage to big families – might be the least bad solution; but there still have to be variations for the ownership of houses, and there is no way to deal with perfect equality between single-person households and others. Similar problems arise in assessing those

entitled to gain from transfers. There would have to be plenty of very rough justice and injustice, with evasive transfers of ownership within both losing and gaining families; but no excessive wealth and no absolutely propertyless poverty need survive.

37 Any calculations must be rough because few countries have reliable or detailed registers of capital ownership. The following is one rough calculation based on data for the United Kingdom in 1970, corrected in some respects to 1974, as referred to in note 18 above. Set £10,000 (at 1974 values) as the limit of productive capital permissible for any United Kingdom owner. Let everyone with less keep what he has, and everyone with more keep £10,000. Confiscate holdings above that limit and distribute them to each eligible man, woman and child in the kingdom in whatever shares are necessary to bring each (allowing for his income and any capital he has already) up to an equal 'floor' of annual net worth. It would not be too inflationary to provide (e.g. from capital taxation or the capital growth of industries in public ownership) for a similar basic ration for children born after the transfer date. In 1974 the mathematical effect of the suggested transfer, if it were to level up capital rather than net worth, would have been to give people at the 'floor' about £750 of capital each. For the four members of an average family that would add up to one year of the national average income after tax for such a family. A 5% dividend on it would give that average family a 5% rise in annual income. It would give rises up to 10% and beyond to many low-income families, and intermediate rises to pensioners. The operation as a whole would confiscate capital from less than 5% of the population and give it to 60 or 70%. Each giver would give to twelve or fifteen receivers. At least half of the givers would give less than half of their capital. Those who lost more than half of their capital would be 2% or less of the population. Together with the loss of unearned income by the givers, this would amount to an equalization worth having. It would be better if based on net worth (but there is no present information on which the effect of a 'net worth' basis of transfer could be calculated). In either case it would be better than the figures indicate, because it would do away with many opportunities for untaxed and unrecorded gains by the rich. And in practice it would no doubt be better still, because any society which had the will to do it would also be acting on other fronts to reduce salary, wage, pension, housing and service differentials.

38 Taxing bachelors may encourage too much wedlock; taxing couples as one income may encourage too little; public policy should probably avoid encouraging either. It can be nearly neutral if it taxes earners singly and pays substantial allowances for children and dependants who cannot work. For example a 15% tax on earnings might finance dependants' allowances at 20–25% of the average adult wage. A more radical and better approach is proposed by Patricia Apps in *Child Care Policy in the Production–Consumption Economy* (Melbourne, 1975) which appeared too late to improve the argument of this present book. Apps

offers new theory and analysis of current mechanisms of appropriation and transfer, and suggests why and how the commercial economy should pay for the production of its labor by paying to the domestic economy the labor costs of child care and development. The analysis is better than mine. The proposed policies might work better. It might be harder to get them accepted. They might however pick up support from parents regardless of class.

39 *R. H. Tawney's Commonplace Book*, ed. J. M. Winter and D. M. Joslin (Cambridge, 1972); R. H. Tawney, *Equality*, 4th edition (London, 1952) p. 118.

40 These paragraphs include some plagiarism from McKay, Boyd, Stretton and Mant, *Living and Partly Living* (Nelson, Melbourne, 1971).

41 In the old Swedish model and in most capitalist democracies to some degree, the original division of responsibility between central government and its business trusts tended to insulate *both* from the grassroots kind of democratic answerability. The trusts had been designed with two aims in mind – to make public business more businesslike than a traditional public-service bureau could make it, and to make it non-capitalist, i.e. to get big business done without enriching private proprietors. But the independent strength which had been given to the trusts for those purposes was too often used to entrench single-purpose or technocratic policies, to give the public what was good for them rather than what they asked for, and to trample (with full statutory power) over all sorts of local social and environmental interests. The Swedish 'lurch to the Left' of the late 1970s was about equally concerned to reduce the capital wealth of the rich, and the arrogance of the public trusts. As one New-Left activist complained, 'Neither listens to us; neither does what the people want with the people's resources; neither is governing by and with our democratic consent or participation.' In the short run neither the political nor the public-service leaders of central government could do much about that. So in the long run they made the drastic changes to institutional structure described in this chapter, and introduced the conditions of executive service to be described later in it. They did not assume any more direct or detailed power over the trusts; instead they forced them to be more sensitive to local democracy by making their senior executives personally sensitive to the requirements of central government. Understandably the upper ranks of the public services didn't encourage these changes; the first of them (until the new patterns became orthodox) had to be forced by continuous electoral pressure organized chiefly by the younger activists of the Left parties.

42 Academic readers will remember Max Weber's anxieties about the human and social costs – but at the same time, the unavoidable necessity – of bureaucratic organization; Roberto Michels' 'iron law of oligarchy'; and similar pessimism in works of Mosca, Pareto, Burnham and others. A more recent forecast of universal grey-faced bureaucracy came at the end of William O'Neill's remarkable history *The Rise of the West* (Chicago, 1963). There is a short general analysis of the problem in Graeme Duncan, *Marx and Mill* (1973), pp. 195–207.

43 It is for the children of successful people that these societies allow some of their biggest concessions to inequality. Superannuation benefits survive for widows and for children until they reach twenty-one. One or two countries even allow benefits to be bequeathed to grandchildren – thus successful parents bless their own grown-up children by endowing the children *they* love best. Most Left critics object to this 'revival of entail' but it doesn't matter much because the benefits are not far above ordinary pensions and children's allowances, and the children concerned would mostly do well anyway, for reasons of nature or nurture. All such differences matter less, now that the inequalities are narrower. But these policies have some historical ironies. When the old Left gave up hope of equalizing wealth or income, they thought they might at least prevent wealth passing to heirs. The new Left regimes took plenty of wealth and income from present owners, but returned a little of it to their heirs. As it turned out, the biggest single aid to inducing fair numbers of the rich to accept capital-transfer losses and stay at work was the provision made for their retirements, widows and children. Similar concessions on more modest scale now help to reconcile able people to the new insecurities of life at the top.

44 It may be objected that the sample doesn't include the creative minority, the vital few on whose motivation we depend for the efficiency of business and government. So I add three occasional visitors to the street – tycoons whose enterprises happen at the moment to be loosely related to each other. One is the chief executive of a multi-national consortium formed to build a billion-dollar petrochemical plant some way up the coast. He's well paid, though his fringe capital gains, as a pampered executive, may be less than those of my hard-slaving blue-collared neighbor (who puts his money into blocks of flats rather than yachts). The second is the public dealer and developer who has kept our land and housing cheap all these years. With some of the millions he gets and spends each week he has to build a town for the petrochemical population. That doesn't pay so well – he makes less than most of the building contractors who work for him. The third is the head of government who hands the consortium its natural resources and the developer his financial resources. When he's in office he gets less than the petrochemist. When he's out he gets less than the developer. If he ever has to retreat to a back bench he'll get less than a couple of people in our street. None of the three would have chosen different work, or worked less hard at it, if the rates for engineering, politics, public service and private building were more equal. They all go for the top, *wherever that is*. As long as nobody is getting ahead of them or short-changing them (which would be disrespectful), money interests them less than it interests their poorer employees or their richer shareholders. Not all affluent people in affluent societies are indifferent to money, or willing to work for narrower margins than hold at present. But a number of the most inventive and productive and powerful people are like that.

Index

academic disciplines, 139, 143–9
alienation, 161, 183–6, 200–4
Allende, President, 127
America, United States of, 42–4, 56–7,
    58–61, 72, 82–3, 94, 99–100, 106–7,
    110, 113, 126, 164–5, 170, 173, 175,
    177–81, 198, 221, 253, 282, 315–16
Apps, Patricia, 236, 326–7
area improvement, 230, 322
aristocracy, 17–18, 27–37, 126
art, 176–7
Attlee, Clement, 317
Australia, 43, 57, 73, 91–2, 110, 115,
    177, 198, 221, 237, 317

bargaining power, 1, 136, 243–56,
    259–65, 312–13
Britain, 41–2, 57, 63–5, 80, 109, 115,
    126, 129–30, 132–3, 170–1, 178, 180,
    198–9, 221, 237, 315, 316, 325–6
Bronfenbrenner, Martin, 317, 319
bureaucracy, 26, 76–7, 121–4, 277,
    299–302, 305–8, 327–8
Burnham, James, 327

Canada, 57, 110, 115, 237
Canberra, 322
capital markets, 86, 196–9, 236–7, 323
capital wealth and redistribution, 47–8,
    84–8, 265–78, 307, 316, 324–6, 328
cars, 21–2, 43, 170–1, 218, 288–91
children, 25–6, 61, 89, 161, 166, 185–6,
    192, 195–6, 199, 208, 214, 256, 275,
    305, 309–12, 328
Chinese revolution, 158, 306
cities, 21–2, 32, 55, 66–9, 74, 78, 88–93,
    118–20, 186, 191–2, 217–9, 221–31,
    287–91
Clark, Colin, 319
class and class conflict, 5–6, 17–8, 23–4,
    34–9, 55–7, 94, 104–5, 114, 180, 203,
    221, 222, 247–51, 309–10

class and conservation, 10, 11, 16–18,
    34–7, 42–52, 72–81, 114, 177
coal miners, 73, 133, 170, 261, 287
cold, 22–3, 171
Commoner, Barry, 285
commons, 31, 38
conservation, 3–14, 16–38, 40, 44–52,
    72–81, 118–20, 150–1, 220–1, 314
conservatism and change, 150–1
consultant and professional services,
    302–4
corruption, 28, 43–4, 57–61, 81–8, 109,
    172, 315–16
cost–benefit analysis, 51
Czechoslovakia, 182, 283

death of the poor, 7, 39, 285
debt under inflation, 235–6
decentralization, urban, 32–3, 66, 119,
    223–6
density, urban and residential, 66–9,
    191, 198–9, 222–3, 227, 289–90, 320–2
distribution between generations, 7–13,
    17–18, 180, 286
distribution of environmental costs and
    benefits, 3, 10–14, 27–36, 41–52, 58,
    62, 69–81, 95, 120, 123, 214–16, 222
distribution of housing and land, 11, 12,
    57–8, 64, 67–9, 78, 88–93, 131, 170,
    178, 182, 187–96, 200–6, 216–42,
    310–11, 324
distribution of income, 34, 47–8, 54–7,
    63–4, 69–71, 88–94, 121–33, 137–8,
    144–6, 165–82, 193, 210–11, 216,
    243–56, 259–65, 318, 324–5
distribution of wealth, 38, 47–8, 54–7,
    84–8, 88–93, 121–33, 144–6, 151,
    165–82, 184, 187–96, 211, 216, 217,
    265–78, 324–5, 326
domestic economy, 21–2, 25, 68,
    183–206, 236, 282, 322
domestic full employment, 195

329

mediocrity and excellence, 175–7
men, 22, 38, 166, 195, 208
Michels, Roberto, 327
migrant labor, 62
Mill, John Stuart, 159
Miller, S. M., 319
Mills, C. Wright, 318
Mosca, Gaetano, 327
multinational corporations, 83, 116, 129–30, 175
Myrdal, Gunnar, 315–16

neighborhood resources, 189–96, 222–31, 321–2
Neutze, G. Max, 237, 317
New Life Settlements, 33–4
New Zealand, 43, 57, 91–2, 109, 115, 178, 198
newspapers, 295
Norway, 42, 73, 91–2, 153, 175, 178–80, 187, 198–9, 221, 265

objectivity and value-freedom in social science, 138–43, 165–8
Observer, London, 325
offshore tax-evasion, 84–8
O'Neill, William, 327

Pareto, Vilfredo, 327
Paris, 191
participation in planning and government, 72–81, 292–3, 301, 311–12, 327
paternalism, 164, 210
Pearce, Ivor, 319
pedestrians, 120, 218, 289–90
people, production of, 183, 185–6, 191–2, 201
persuasion, modes of, 2, 36–7, 75–7, 154–6
Polanyi, George, 319
police, 34–7, 60
pollution, 9, 16, 18–19, 58, 79, 112, 118–20, 214–16, 285, 320
Pooley, Fred, 323
population, 6, 13, 16, 25–6, 32–4, 59
price control, 257–9, 317
private enterprise, *see* public and private ownership
productivity, 54, 95, 173–5, 183, 185–7, 192–9, 282–313
public administration, 46–8, 63, 141, 291–4, 299–301, 305–8, 327

public and private ownership, 103, 115–16, 120–4, 155, 161–2, 175, 183–206, 215–16, 218–21, 231–4, 254–5, 277, 294–300
public servants, 50–1, 67–9, 109, 139, 291–4, 299–301, 305–8
public transport, 21, 66–9, 119, 171, 198–9, 289
public trusts and corporations, 298–301, 308, 327
publishers, 295–6
puritanism, 164, 316

Ramsay, A. M., vi
rationing, 7, 21–32, 41, 115, 119–20, 231
Rawls, John, 165, 170
recreation, 31–2, 89, 152–3, 191
Rein, Martin, 319
research, 17, 38, 41, 42–3, 58, 118, 137–8, 141–3, 171–2, 211, 284–5, 287, 302
Riesman, David, 316
Right environmental policies, 11–12, 16–39, 44–52, 58, 110–13, 204–5
Right government, 18–38, 48–9, 58–61, 94–5, 110–13, 204–5, 249–54
Rolfe, Sydney E., 316
Russia, 57, 103, 158, 177, 204, 258, 282

Samuelson, Paul, 319
scandals, 81–8
Scandinavia, 42, 91–2, 109, 176–8
scarcity, deliberate, 8, 16–39, 80, 118–19, 286
scenarios, uses of, 15
segregation, 32–4, 119, 222, 228–31
shopping, 218–19
social scientists and theorists, 34, 37, 51–2, 66–9, 72, 90, 93, 98–108, 121, 137–57, 164–5, 171–2, 183–4, 197–9, 315–16
South African lessons, 33–7
sovereign government, 62, 84–8, 109–10, 117, 129, 312–13
Spain, 126, 129–30
Streeten, Paul, vi, 146, 314, 315, 320
Stretton, Hugh, 317, 319, 320, 327
Sweden, 41, 94, 99–100, 115, 173, 175, 178, 198–9, 204, 237, 265, 282, 300, 327
Sydney, 73
Szalai, A., 319